AMERICAN–SOVIET RELATIONS

Based on the most recent scholarship, this book is a study of American policy towards the Soviet Union from 1917 to the fall of Communism. From the perspective of the end of the Cold War, it looks at the ideological conflict throughout the period focusing on such issues as the American intervention during the Russian Civil War, the origins of the Cold War, the Cuban Missile crisis, détente in the Nixon–Kissinger era and relations between Reagan and Gorbachev. The book is both an attempt to understand what precisely were the roots of the Cold War and an analysis of the contemporary relationship in the light of its historical evolution since the Russian Revolution.

Peter Boyle's thesis is that American policy has been shaped not only by the external threat from the Soviet Union but also by internal forces within American society, especially domestic politics, economic interests, emotional and psychological attitudes and images of the Soviet Union. The author develops this thesis chronologically, looking in the final chapter at the lessons which the history of the period provide for post-Cold War relations.

'Peter Boyle has written an informed, fair-minded and sensible account of US–USSR relations that general readers will find both readable and edifying.' Edward Pessen, Davidson Professor of the Humanities, Florida International University.

Peter G. Boyle is Lecturer in American History at the University of Nottingham. He took his doctorate at UCLA and has taught as a visiting professor at several American universities. He has written widely on American history and on US–Soviet relations.

AMERICAN–SOVIET RELATIONS

From the Russian Revolution to the fall of Communism

Peter G. Boyle

London and New York

First published in 1993
by Routledge
11 New Fetter Lane, London EC4P 4EE

Simultaneously published in the USA and Canada
by Routledge
29 West 35th Street, New York, NY 10001

© 1993 Peter G. Boyle

Typeset in Baskerville by
NWL Editorial Services, Langport, Somerset

Printed and bound in Great Britain by
Mackays of Chatham PLC, Chatham, Kent

British Library Cataloguing in Publication Data
A catalogue reference for this book is available from the British Library.

ISBN 0–415–02020–4
0–415–09327–9 (pbk)

Library of Congress Cataloging in Publication Data
has been applied for.

ISBN 0–415–02020–4
0–415–09327–9 (pbk)

CONTENTS

Preface		vii
Acknowledgements		xi
List of abbreviations		xiii
1	THE RUSSIAN REVOLUTION AND AMERICAN INTERVENTION, 1917–20	1
2	THE ERA OF NON-RECOGNITION, 1921–33	17
3	FROM RECOGNITION TO WORLD WAR, 1933–41	29
4	WARTIME ALLIANCE, 1941–5	40
5	THE ORIGINS OF THE COLD WAR, 1945–50	54
6	THE UNITED STATES, THE SOVIET UNION AND CHINA	71
7	THE KOREAN WAR, 1950–3	84
8	THE RED SCARE AND McCARTHYISM	101
9	THE EISENHOWER ERA, 1953–61	116
10	KENNEDY AND KHRUSHCHEV, 1961–3	135
11	JOHNSON, VIETNAM AND CZECHOSLOVAKIA, 1963–9	152
12	NIXON, KISSINGER AND DETENTE, 1969–74	163
13	THE DEMISE OF DETENTE, 1974–80	182
14	REAGAN AND THE NEW COLD WAR, 1981–5	199
15	REAGAN AND GORBACHEV, 1985–9	215
16	THE BUSH ERA	227
17	THE LESSONS OF HISTORY	249
	Notes	282
	Bibliographical essay	298
	Index	310

PREFACE

'The Cold War is now behind us'. [1] In these words in a speech at
Stanford University, California, on 4 June 1990, President
Mikhail Gorbachev declared that the Cold War had come to an
end. Historians and political commentators were reluctant to
tempt fate by stating so unreservedly that the Cold War had
passed into history. But the failed coup in Moscow in August
1991 and the collapse of the Soviet Union at the end of 1991
made it seem safe to sound the death knell of the Cold War. The
time seems appropriate, therefore, to raise the basic question of
what the conflict had been all about. This book is an attempt to
deal with this question from the perspective of America's policy
towards the Soviets since the Russian Revolution in 1917.

The bulk of the book deals with the various episodes in
US–Soviet relations since 1917, such as American intervention in
Russia between 1918 and 1920, diplomatic recognition of the
Soviet Union in 1933, the Second World War, the origins of the
Cold War and the succession of crises and thaws throughout the
Cold War such as the Cuban Missile crisis, the détente of the
Nixon–Kissinger era, the new Cold War of the early 1980s, the
collapse of Communism in the Gorbachev era. In examining
these episodes, the book develops the theme that American
policy towards the Soviet Union has been shaped partly by a
rational calculation of the perceived threat to the United States
and partly by a wide variety of internal forces within the United
States, such as political considerations, economic interests and
emotional factors, which, often in a somewhat irrational fashion,
have been a constant part of the process which has determined
US policy towards the Soviet Union. American policy towards the
Soviet Union, it might be suggested, has to some extent been an

expression of American political culture as much as a concern with US national security considerations. Such characteristics are in some ways inherent in the foreign policy of any democracy, but they are present to a much greater degree in the case of the United States. Given the size of the country, the ethnic diversity of its population and the relative brevity of its history, ideology is a gelling force within American society to a much greater extent than in other Western democracies. Nationalism and ideology are bound together in the United States in a manner which existed in only one other country – the Soviet Union. In both nations, ideology has been, as it were, the civic religion. Hence, the ideological conflict of the twentieth century bears resemblance in many ways to the religious conflicts of earlier times.

This book deals with the ideological conflict arising from the Bolshevik Revolution in 1917. It should be borne in mind, however, that an ideological clash between America and Russia predated the Bolshevik Revolution. Throughout the eighteenth and nineteenth centuries American foreign policy was conducted in a fairly pragmatic fashion, despite America's strong sense of ideological commitment. From approximately the 1890s, however, there occurred, as John Lewis Gaddis has observed, 'a shift from the view that Americans could coexist with states of differing social systems to the conviction that this might no longer be possible'.[2] This led to attempts by the United States to influence the internal policies of tsarist Russia – with regard to Jews, for example – and brought about a deterioration in Russian–American relations in the early twentieth century, compared to the generally good Russian–American relations up to the end of the nineteenth century. It is necessary, therefore, to keep in mind the pre-1917 history of Russian–American relations in order to put into proper historical perspective the subject of this book, namely, relations during the Soviet period from 1917 to 1991.

This book, then, focuses upon American policy. It is not an attempt to analyse bilateral relations, with an examination of Soviet policy in the same depth as American policy. The sources on the Soviet side do not in any event permit such a study. Also, even if in the course of time Soviet sources are opened, it must always be kept in mind that the information which these sources may reveal in the future was not known to American policy-makers in the past, whose decisions were shaped by their perceptions of Soviet policy based on the information available at that time and by other influences within American society which helped to determine the course of action which they pursued.

The sources on which the book are based are discussed in the bibliographical essay at the end. In a book of such a wide scope, references in notes have been kept to a minimum, since the citation of the authority for almost any statement could necessitate so many references as to overwhelm the book with the trappings of scholarship. Aside from direct quotations, therefore, references are not normally cited. The book is intended for students and general readers, and specialist scholars are referred to the sources in the bibliographical essay.

The examination of American foreign policy by a British author may produce a perspective which would not be present in the work of an American author. The Norwegian historian of US foreign policy, Geir Lundestad, has exhorted that specialists on the United States who are not themselves American should try 'to find out exactly what if anything was so special about Washington's actions and attitudes'. [3] Since, however, the sources and intellectual influences upon which the present book is based are predominantly American, the author would be hesitant to claim a vision from the European side of the Atlantic which provides clearer insights into the truth than an American author might put forward. Nevertheless, given the author's British background and his previous research in British sources on US–Soviet relations, perhaps a transatlantic viewpoint may provide to some degree a different perspective which will add to the usefulness of the present work. [4]

ACKNOWLEDGEMENTS

The main thanks in a book of such wide scope are due to the authors of the large number of monographs on particular topics, the authors of articles in journals and newspapers and the editors of collections of documents. Particular thanks are extended to the British Academy for research grants in 1988 and 1990. Appreciation is acknowledged to the Hoover Institution, Stanford University, for the opportunity to spend four summers as a Visiting Scholar from 1988 to 1991 and to utilize the splendid resources in the Hoover Institution Library and Stanford University Library, while benefiting from the diverse intellectual standpoints of Hoover Institution Fellows and Stanford University faculty. Appreciation is expressed to Mesa State College, Grand Junction, Colorado, for the invitation to serve in the spring of 1989 as the Wayne S. Aspinall Lecturer, which provided an opportunity to present an outline of the ideas for this book in a course of lectures. Appreciation is also acknowledged to the students who have taken my course on US–Soviet relations at the University of Nottingham and contributed perceptive observations on the subject. I am very grateful to Robert Dallek and John Thompson who read and made comments upon the last chapter of the book and to George Breslauer, Robert Frazier, Walter LaFeber and Edward Pessen for their comments upon the entire manuscript. For assistance on particular points I am grateful to Angela Chandler, Gerald Chandler, Rosemary Kerr, Bill Lomax, Janet McKellar and Derek Spring. Appreciation is acknowledged to Jill Cleaver for her skill in word processing the manuscript and to Freda Duckitt for secretarial assistance.

Assistance from these many quarters has saved me from many errors of fact and of judgement. For those which remain I of course accept responsibility.

LIST OF ABBREVIATIONS

ABM	Anti-ballistic missile
ARA	American Relief Administration
CFE	Conventional forces in Europe
CFM	Confidence-building measures
CND	Campaign for Nuclear Disarmament
COCOM	Co-ordinating Committee of the Paris Consultative Group of Nations
CREEP	Campaign to Re-elect the President
CSCE	Conference on Security and Co-operation in Europe
EDC	European Defence Community
EXCOM	Executive Committee of the National Security Council
FNLA	National Front for the Liberation of Angola
GNP	Gross National Product
HUAC	House Un-American Activities Committee
ICBM	Intercontinental ballistic missile
INF	Intermediate-range nuclear forces
IWW	Industrial Workers of the World
MAD	Mutual assured destruction
MBFR	Mutual balanced force reduction
MFN	Most Favored Nation
MIRV	Multiple independently targeted re-entry vehicles
MPLA	Popular movement for the liberation of Angola
NATO	North Atlantic Treaty Organization
NSC	National Security Council
RFE	Radio Free Europe
SACEUR	Supreme Allied Commander in Europe
SALT	Strategic Arms Limitation Talks
SDI	Strategic Defence Initiative
SLBM	Submarine-launched ballistic missile

LIST OF ABBREVIATIONS

START   Strategic Arms Reduction Talks
UNITA   National Union for the Total Independence of Angola
UNO   United Nations Organization
UNRRA   United Nations Relief and Rehabilitation Agency
USIA   United States Information Agency
VOA   Voice of America

1

THE RUSSIAN REVOLUTION AND AMERICAN INTERVENTION, 1917–20

In March and April 1917 two events of enormous historical significance occurred. On 15 March 1917 Tsar Nicolas II of Russia abdicated. On 6 April 1917 America entered the First World War. For the United States the coincidence in time of these two events was not only immensely significant but also very fortuitous.

From 1914 to 1917 the United States had striven to remain neutral and to avoid being drawn into the European conflict. Neutrality, however, gradually became an untenable policy for the United States on account of such factors as economic ties with Britain, sympathy for the Allies rather than the Central Powers, the long-term threat to America's security from a German victory and violations of America's neutral rights culminating in Germany's declaration of unrestricted submarine warfare on 31 January 1917. The sinking of four American ships by German submarines in March 1917 made American entry into the war unavoidable, but President Woodrow Wilson agonized over the decision. He did not wish to take America into war for such mundane issues as defence of America's right to trade with Britain. The sacrifices of war would be justified in Wilson's eyes if the conflict was for a much grander purpose, a crusade for democracy and for peace. Yet if one of America's co-belligerents was tsarist Russia, the war could hardly be seen as a struggle for democracy. When, however, tsarism was overthrown on 15 March 1917 and democracy proclaimed in Russia, Wilson was able to declare his war aim 'to make the world safe for democracy'.[1] The American ambassador in Russia, David Francis, reported that the Russian Revolution was 'the practical realization of that principle of government which we have championed and advocated, I mean, government by consent of the governed'.[2] Even more explicitly, Wilson stated that

> Russia was known by those who knew it best to have been always in fact democratic at heart. . . . The autocracy that crowned the summit of her political structure, long as it had stood and terrible as was the reality of its power, was not in fact Russian in origin, character or purpose; now it has been shaken off and the great, generous Russian people have been added in all their naïve majesty and might to the forces that are fighting for freedom.[3]

Wilson's statement revealed a characteristic feature of American foreign policy which runs through the history of US–Soviet relations – namely, self-deceptive wishful thinking that the aspirations of other people, such as the Russians, coincide with American aspirations. Woodrow Wilson was a distinguished historian, a Princeton University professor for many years and the author of many excellent historical studies. But it is significant that Wilson's academic work was entirely in the field of American history. He knew almost nothing of the history of Russia. Wilson's preconceptions regarding Russia provides the first of many examples of the manner in which US policy towards Russia was created by the American images of Russia rather than the historical reality.

The reality of Russia in 1917 was a nation with very shallow democratic roots and a deep weariness of the war which had been waged so unsuccessfully since 1914. The Provisional Government which was established after the tsar's fall was led by liberals such as Prince Lvov and Paul Miliukov who urged the Russian people to fight more vigorously against the Central Powers. But through the summer of 1917 the desertion rate from the Russian armies rose steadily and the Russian people were attracted to the appealing programme of 'Peace, Land and Bread' offered by the Bolsheviks. In April 1917 Vladimir Ilyich Ulianov, the Bolshevik leader known to the world as Lenin, returned to Russia from exile in Switzerland in a sealed train provided by the Germans. In the Russian capital, Petrograd (formerly St Petersburg and later renamed Leningrad, with the name St Petersburg restored in 1991), the disintegration of the Provisional Government became apparent as its authority was challenged by the Petrograd Soviet, which was increasingly dominated by the Bolsheviks. In August 1917 Alexander Kerensky, the War Minister and most effective figure in the Provisional Government, became prime minister. But this did not improve the situation, as Kerensky urged more vigorous prosecution of the war while the people wanted peace. The United States extended aid to the Provisional Government, appropriating $450 million and expending $183 million by November 1917, but, as at later times in US–Soviet relations, American economic aid made little impact on internal developments within Russia. In September 1917 a military coup was attempted by General Lavr Kornilov, which led the Provisional Government to turn for assistance to the Bolsheviks, relaxing previous prohibitions against their acquisition of weapons. As the American diplomat and historian George F. Kennan has put it, 'To accept the armed aid of the Bolsheviki was, under the circumstances, to entrust oneself to the protection of a boa constrictor'.[4] The Kornilov revolt was suppressed, but the Provisional Government's position continued to weaken while the power of the Petrograd Soviet, which by this time had a Bolshevik majority, increasingly grew. This led Lenin to conclude that the time to strike was ripe. On 7 November 1917 the Bolsheviks seized power while Kerensky departed into exile in a car provided by the American ambassador.

The Bolshevik Revolution confronted the United States with an entirely different situation from the first Russian Revolution in March. No longer was Russia ruled by a government proclaiming democracy and fighting in alliance with the United States in a war to make the world safe for democracy. Instead, Russia was ruled by an undemocratic minority who had seized power by violence and who intended to make peace with Germany and to withdraw from the war. On 15 December 1917 an armistice was declared between Russia and the Central Powers, and negotiation of a peace treaty commenced at Brest-Litovsk. Lenin, far from regarding the war as a struggle for democracy, denounced the war as the inevitable result of capitalism, and he called on working people of all nations to lay down their arms in the conflict with one another and to engage in arms in the conflict with their true enemy, the capitalist class. Wilson believed passionately in democracy as the best hope for mankind not only for liberty and prosperity but also for peace. Peoples, Wilson argued, did not want war. Wars were brought about in Wilson's view by undemocratic governments over whom the people had no control, such as kings and emperors who were prepared to go to war, with peoples left to fight such wars. Once peoples controlled governments universally, Wilson believed, there would be no more war. But Lenin rejected the fundamentals of Wilson's assumptions. The cause of war, Lenin argued, lay in capitalism. Liberalism was a snare and a delusion which gave democratic forms within which capitalists held ultimate power and pursued a course which inevitably led to war, with peoples left to fight such wars. Hence, the Bolshevik Revolution confronted Wilson with a Russian government which put forward a fundamental ideological challenge and which, more immediately, jeopardized the cause of the Allies by withdrawing from the war against Germany. Wilson felt that the Bolshevik Revolution was a betrayal of the Russian Revolution which had aspired, he believed, to the same democratic ideals which the American people cherished.

The Wilson administration did not grant diplomatic recognition to the Bolshevik government. On 24 November 1917 Secretary of State Robert Lansing informed the ambassador of the Provisional Government, Boris Bakhmetev, that the United States continued to regard him as the official representative of the Russian government in Washington. There was a widespread feeling in US government circles that the Bolshevik regime was likely to be temporary and that it would prejudice good relations with the succeeding Russian government to open relations prematurely with the Bolsheviks. The State Department ruled that the Bolshevik regime did not meet US criteria for diplomatic recognition, since the Bolsheviks were not fully in control of the country, refused to honour the debts and obligations of preceding Russian governments and disseminated propaganda to incite the populations of other countries to overthrow their rulers. More fundamentally, Wilson did not accept that the Bolsheviks were representatives of the Russian people, especially when the Bolsheviks gained less than a third of the votes in the elections for the Constituent Assembly on 25 November 1917 and then proceeded to use force to prevent the meeting of the Assembly in January 1918. In 1913 Wilson set a precedent in the case of Mexico of non-recognition of a government which he regarded as an immoral regime which had seized power by violent means and which did not represent the goals of the revolution. Wilson applied a similar policy towards the Bolsheviks.

As a counter to the ideological challenge put forward by Lenin, Wilson delivered a major speech, the Fourteen Points address,

4

on 8 January 1918. Wilson proclaimed his ideals of national self-determination and a new structure of peace under the League of Nations. In pressing for self-determination for such nations as Poland and Czechoslovakia, Wilson was consistent in arguing for self-determination for Russia. Point Six of the Fourteen Points called for

> the evacuation of all Russian territory and such settlement of all questions affecting Russia as will secure the best and freest co-operation of other nations in obtaining for her an unhampered and unembarrassed opportunity for the independent determination of her own political development and national policy. . . . The treatment accorded to Russia by her sister nations in the months to come will be the acid test of their goodwill, of their comprehension of her needs as distinguished from their own interests.[5]

The first issue on which Wilson faced this 'acid test' was Russian withdrawal from the war. The Bolsheviks who, like Wilson, had been prone to self-deceptive wishful thinking, were brought back to hard reality by the Germans in the negotiations at Brest-Litovsk from December 1917 to March 1918. The German terms for peace were harsh – German control over the formerly Russian part of Poland and over Latvia, Lithuania and Estonia, with independence for the Ukraine. Leon Trotsky, Commissar for Foreign Affairs, who headed the Russian delegation at the negotiations, balked at such terms, and the Bolsheviks considered re-entry into the war against Germany on the Allied side. The British government was aware of developments, the British ambassador reporting from Petrograd on 18 February 1918, for example, that 'Trotsky has returned exasperated to the last degree against Germans and it may be possible to take advantage of his feelings'.[6] The American ambassador, David Francis – a 76-year-old St Louis businessman who was out of his depth in revolutionary Russia – sought a greater degree of safety by moving to the provincial town of Vologda, 250 miles from Moscow, while the Bolsheviks moved the capital from Petrograd to Moscow. Francis therefore provided inadequate information on developments within Russia. The consul-general in Moscow, Madden Summers, was staunchly conservative and reported only the worst features of the Bolshevik regime to Washington.

One American source of information, however, which offered

a different point of view came from Raymond Robins, head of the American Red Cross in Russia. Robins, a dynamic character who was politically a progressive Republican, was no Bolshevik sympathizer. But Robins advocated a pragmatic policy of accepting the reality of the Bolshevik regime and thereby producing a modification of Bolshevik policy and above all the possibility of Russian re-entry into the war. Robins met Lenin and Trotsky on several occasions, and when Robins left Moscow on 5 March 1918 Trotsky came to the railway station to see him off and to give him a number of questions to pass on to President Wilson regarding the possibility of American aid if Russia refused to ratify the Treaty of Brest-Litovsk, which Trotsky had signed on 2 March 1918 but which required ratification by the Congress of Soviets. Delay in the transmittal of Robins's message through Francis and the vague, non-committal nature of Wilson's response resulted in ratification of the Treaty of Brest-Litovsk on 15 March 1918. Robins felt that a great opportunity had been lost. In fact, given the short time for Wilson to respond and the poor communications and general chaos in Russia, it is unlikely that there was such a favourable opportunity as Robins suggested. The incident was an illustration, however, of a general line of approach towards the Soviet Union which would mark US policy towards Communist regimes thereafter, namely, reluctance to accept and to come to terms with such regimes but instead a resort to attempts to undermine and overthrow them.

While Wilson pronounced the theoretical principle of self-determination for Russia, he was surrounded by voices which advocated greater emphasis on more immediate interests. Secretary of State Robert Lansing, who took a much more *realpolitik* approach than Wilson, stressed the high casualties which would be suffered in a long war against Germany if the Bolsheviks remained in power and kept Russia out of the war. Even more so, the Allies had few scruples over violation of the general concept of non-interference in the internal affairs of another country. Not only did the Allies wish to see the removal of radical fanatics in Russia but above all they were aghast at the prospect of the German forces on the Eastern front being transferred to the Western front. Consequently, the Allies exerted relentless pressure on Wilson to change his views on Russia and to agree to intervention, so that at the very least some degree of military activity would take place on the Eastern front and some German forces would be kept from the Western front.

Through the winter of 1917–18 Wilson refused to support intervention in Russia, but he was gradually persuaded to change his mind in July 1918 and to send American troops to Russia. The main single question with regard to American policy towards Russia between 1917 and 1920 is whether Wilson was justified in this change of policy.

A variety of factors influenced Wilson's decision. One matter concerned Allied stores in the ports of Murmansk and Archangel in north Russia. These stores had been transported by sea by the British around Norway, while a railway line was constructed from Murmansk to the main Moscow-Petrograd trunk line. The British wished to recover these stores for use in the war effort and even more so to ensure that they did not fall into German hands. Indeed, on 1 March 1918 Trotsky instructed the Murmansk Soviet to accept British aid to defend the Murmansk railway against the Germans. The British readily accepted the invitation to send forces to north Russia, but they were eager to have American troops sent with them in order to give greater legitimacy to the expedition, which the British realized might develop into an intervention for broader purposes than simply guarding Allied stores and the railway line against the Germans.

A second factor related to escaped German and Austrian prisoners of war. With the breakdown of order following the Bolshevik Revolution large numbers of these prisoners escaped from Russian prisoner-of-war camps. There was fear in Allied quarters that in the chaotic situation in Russia these escaped prisoners might aid pro-German elements within Russia or even seize control in Russia. This apprehension tied in with a general Allied fear of the government in Russia falling under the control of the Germans. There were widely expressed suggestions that the Bolsheviks were in fact German agents, a view which was supported by Ambassador Francis. Lenin, after all, had been assisted by the Germans to return from Switzerland. In May 1918 Edgar Sisson, a representative in Russia of the US Committee on Public Information, returned to the United States with documents which allegedly proved that the Bolsheviks were German agents. The documents were later proved to be forgeries, but a contemporary panel of experts declared the documents to be authentic.

A third factor related to developments in Siberia. There were Allied stores in Vladivostok of potential value on the Western front and which might fall into enemy hands. Even more important, Wilson was very suspicious of Japanese intentions in Siberia and felt that a joint American–Japanese intervention could act as a restraint on Japanese expansionist aims, while also guarding Allied stores in Vladivostok. In contrast to his enlightened views on national self-determination in Europe, Wilson was very illiberal on racial matters and strongly anti-Japanese.

The final element concerned the so-called Czech legion, a force of 70,000 Czechs who had fought alongside the Russians since 1914 with a view to defeating the Central Powers and winning independence for Czechoslovakia, which was part of the Austro-Hungarian Empire. Following the Bolshevik Revolution the Czech legion wished to move to France and to fight alongside the Allies on the Western front. However, as they made their way across the trans-Siberian railway to Vladivostok for trans-shipment from there to Europe, their progress was blocked by the Bolsheviks. Wilson was therefore urged to send an American force to Siberia which, in addition to acting as a check on the Japanese, could clear the trans-Siberian railway and enable the Czech legion to reach Vladivostok and to depart for Europe.

The issue of the Czech legion was in fact rather more complex. The Bolsheviks initially allowed the Czechs to travel across Siberia but later felt that the Czechs were involving themselves in internal affairs in Russia on the side of the Whites. Some Americans, such as E.L. Harris, consul-general in Irkutsk, felt that the Czech legion should not be withdrawn to Europe but should be encouraged to remain in Russia to help to defeat the Bolsheviks. To add further to an already chaotic situation, some of the Czechs were left-wing and began to fight on the Bolshevik side, especially against the Austrian prisoners of war. Moreover, trans-shipment from Vladivostok to Europe was impossible since the necessary transport ships were not available. Wilson, however, felt deeply for the Czechs. He was an admirer of Thomas Masaryk, the Czech patriot and intellectual who became the first president of Czechoslovakia. Moreover, the Czechs appeared to be a potentially valuable contingent for deployment on the Western front. Hence, the issue of the rescue of the Czech legion weighed heavily in Wilson's thinking on the decision to intervene in Russia.

In the autumn of 1917 Wilson held firmly to a position of non-interference in Russia. But he was under constant pressure from the Allies and from many of his advisers to take more positive action. Wilson was torn between his deep feeling for the Russian masses and his unwillingness to compromise his principles with regard to the sovereignty of nations. As the British ambassador in Washington noted, Wilson and other Americans 'cherish the hope that the United States has an exceptional position amongst the Russian masses and that this capital should be husbanded as much as possible.'[7] In December 1917 Wilson compromised to the extent of approving clandestine aid to General Alexei Kaledin, the leader of the anti-Bolshevik Cossacks in the Don region in south Russia. Figures such as Consul-General Summers pressed Wilson 'to lend moral support to the better elements in Russia'.[8] Above all, the Allies pressed the argument relentlessly that, with a desperate situation on the Western front in the spring of 1918, action was needed to keep the Germans occupied to some extent on the Eastern front. Reluctantly, surreptitiously and somewhat ambiguously, Wilson yielded to these pressures and in July 1918 agreed to the dispatch of 5,700 American troops to north Russia and 8,000 to Siberia. But in an *aide-memoire* to Allied governments on 17 July 1918, which Wilson carefully composed himself on his own typewriter, he insisted that these troops were being sent only for the limited purpose of assisting the Czech legion to withdraw and to protect the Allied stores in Murmansk and Archangel in the north and in Vladivostok in the Far East. Wilson warned the Allies that the United States would

> feel obliged to withdraw those forces, in order to add them to the forces at the western front, if the plans in whose execution it is now intended that they should co-operate should develop into others inconsistent with the policy to which the Government of the United States feels constrained to restrict itself.[9]

The American troops who were dispatched to north Russia were, however, employed for much broader purposes than merely to guard Allied stores. On their arrival in Archangel on 4 September 1918 they were placed under British command. The British commander, General Frederick C. Poole, had engineered the overthrow of the local Bolshevik regime in Archangel, and Poole's ambition was to use his forces to expand non-Bolshevik control in north Russia and ultimately in Moscow. American forces were ordered to advance as far as 300 miles from Archangel in furtherance of this expansion of non-Bolshevik control and suffered severe casualties in engagements with Bolshevik forces. Poole hoped that the Russian people would rise up to welcome the Allies as liberators. The American commander, General George Stewart, largely agreed with Poole's strategy, while the American ambassador, David Francis, who had moved from Vologda to Archangel for safety reasons, supported American military intervention in Russia. Wilson's stated purposes in sending American troops to north Russia were therefore ignored, but the president took no action to implement his threat to withdraw the American troops if they were used for purposes other than the limited objectives which he had specified. In the closing stages of the First World War, from September to November 1918, Wilson was preoccupied with issues other than American troops in Russia and was in no position to alienate the Allies by pulling American troops out of Russia when the British set aside Wilson's restrictions and used American troops for Britain's wider objectives in Russia.

With the end of the war against Germany on 11 November 1918 the continuation of fighting in north Russia was even more obviously not for purposes relating to the war against Germany but was part of an Allied effort to overthrow the Bolsheviks. Figures such as Winston Churchill, British Minister for War, made very plain their aim of crushing Bolshevism at its birth. Opposition arose within the United States, however, to the deployment of American forces for hostile engagements in Russia without Congressional authorization and contrary to the president's stated purpose for their deployment. Senator William E. Borah, a progressive Republican from Idaho, stated on 9 January 1919 that 'The Russian people have the same right to establish a Socialist state as we have to establish a republic'.[10] Senator Hiram Johnson of California, another progressive Republican, on 29 January 1919 denounced the 'fantastic theories' of the Bolsheviks but he vigorously objected to the assumption of responsibility by the United States for the suppression of Bolshevism. Johnson proclaimed that he 'would not give one American life for all the Bolsheviks spawned by centuries of tyranny and mad with lust of ruthless ephemeral power'.[11] A Senate resolution demanding withdrawal of American troops from Russia was defeated on 14 February 1919 only by the casting vote of the vice-president in his capacity as chairman of the Senate.

To some extent Wilson came to justify to himself the American involvement in Russia on the grounds that true self-determination in Russia would be possible only if tyrannous usurpers of power were removed and a regime installed which would permit free elections. To a greater extent, however, Wilson's tardiness in withdrawing American troops from Russia was due largely to the same influences which led to his initial decision to intervene, namely, the need to co-operate with the Allies. With the opening of the Versailles Conference in January 1919 Wilson's proposal for a just and lasting peace based on the Fourteen Points received a cool reception from the Allies – especially the French, who pressed for much more severe terms against Germany. As for Russia, which was not represented at Versailles, the French commander Marshal Ferdinand Foch proposed in January 1919 a full-scale Allied expedition into Russia to support the Whites and to destroy Bolshevism. While Foch's extreme position was not endorsed by the Allies, a precipitous withdrawal of American forces from Russia would have further strained Wilson's relations with the Allies, whose co-operation was essential for the achievement of his goals at Versailles.

In February 1919 Wilson proposed a meeting with representatives of all factions in Russia at Prinkipo Island, off the coast of Turkey, on condition that the Bolsheviks agreed to an armistice in the civil war and to repayment of Russia's debts. The Bolsheviks were willing to attend such a meeting on condition that the Allies withdrew from Russia and ended aid to the Whites. Such conditions were unacceptable to the Whites, so that the Prinkipo meeting did not take place. Instead, Wilson decided to send William Bullitt, a member of the American delegation at Versailles, on a fact-finding mission to Russia. Bullitt, an energetic enthusiast in the mould of Raymond Robins, came to a similar conclusion to Robins, namely, that the United States should accept the Bolshevik regime and 'guide the revolution into peaceful and constructive channels'.[12] Bullitt's zeal, however, led him to exceed his instructions in his meetings with Bolshevik leaders. Wilson consequently distanced himself from Bullitt, ceased to reply to his communications and ignored his advice regarding overtures to the Bolshevik government. In disillusionment Bullitt resigned from the peace delegation in May 1919.

In June 1919 the American troops were finally withdrawn from north Russia. But a total of 222 Americans had been killed in north Russia in 1918–19, while hundreds of Russians had died in engagements in which the Americans had participated. In Siberia the American troops were not involved in hostile engagements, but they came to be props in support of the White leader in Siberia, Admiral Alexander Kolchak. Following Kolchak's capture and execution in January 1920 the American presence in Siberia became increasingly pointless and dangerous, resulting in their withdrawal in August 1920.

Like other Western powers, the United States had initially calculated that Bolshevik rule would be short-lived. By 1920 this miscalculation was apparent. Hence, the United States faced a regime in Russia which was not only ideologically antagonistic but which had been acutely alienated by American participation in the foreign intervention in Russia. In 1920 the United States reaffirmed its decision to withhold diplomatic recognition from Russia, and although export licences began to be granted in July 1920 after the end of the Allied blockade, the United States retained many trading restrictions, such as a prohibition of long-term credits and refusal to accept gold in payment for purchases. With the failure of military intervention, then, the United States resorted to a policy of ostracism.

As post-war disillusionment set in, American attention turned from Reds in Russia to Reds in America. In March 1919 the Comintern was established in Moscow to disseminate Communist propaganda world-wide, calling on the proletariat to seize power. In the United States 5 million copies of Lenin's letter 'To the American Worker' were distributed, and in May 1919 the Comintern's official organ, *Communist International*, began to be distributed in the United States. A Congressional committee, the Overman Committee, was set up in March 1919 to hold hearings on Communist propaganda in the United States, and witnesses gave lurid details of the Red Terror in Russia and the programme which Communists would impose if they were to seize power in the United States, including, for example, the nationalization of women. Meantime, in August 1919 left-wing elements in the Socialist Party formed the Communist Labor Party, including such figures as John Reed, Benjamin Gitlow and William Lloyd. At the same time other radicals who were mainly foreign-born formed the Communist Party.

By the summer of 1919 the frenzy of the first Red Scare developed. Attorney-General A. Mitchell Palmer, who had ambitions to exploit the issue as a means to gain the Democratic nomination for president in 1920, established the General

Intelligence Division within the Justice Department, headed by J. Edgar Hoover. Intelligence was gathered on 60,000 radicals, most of whom were foreign-born non-citizens. Palmer concluded that deportation of foreign radicals was an easier course than conviction of American citizens. In November 1919 Palmer ordered a nation-wide raid on members of the Union of Russian Workers. Hundreds were arrested, many were imprisoned for several months without a hearing, and 249 were deported on 21 December 1919 from New Haven, Connecticut, to Hango, Finland, from where they were left to make their own way to Russia. Palmer then focused his attention on the Communist Party and the Communist Labor Party. On 2 January 1920 there were 4,000 arrests, many without warrants. Some Communists were imprisoned in deplorable conditions, suffering ill-health and in some instances death. In June 1920 a total of 591 aliens were deported, though in small numbers, unlike the mass deportation on 21 December 1919.

Palmer's activities at the national level encouraged similar repressive measures at the state level. Many states passed criminal anarchy laws, Red Flag laws and other such measures which enabled the arrest and imprisonment of radicals. The Supreme Court ruled in 1919, in a judgement written by Justice Oliver Wendell Holmes, that the government had a right to limit freedom of speech when exercise of that right constituted 'a clear and present danger'.[13] The popular mood of intolerance, however, led to the suppression of freedom of speech and other basic rights which went well beyond the limitations carefully set in Holmes's ruling. Socialists, for example, were regarded in the same category as Communists and were frequently subjected to harassment. Victor Berger, who had served in the US House of Representatives as a Socialist since 1910, won re-election in November 1918, but the House of Representatives refused to allow him to take his seat, even after he was again elected in a special election in December 1919. The New York state assembly barred five Socialists from taking their seats, even when, as in Berger's case, they were again elected in a special election in September 1920.

The Red Scare of 1919–20 illustrated fundamental contradictions in American attitudes towards Communism which run through the history of US–Soviet relations. On the one hand, it was logical and reasonable for the United States to be concerned by the threat of the world-wide expansion of Communism and by

Communist subversion within the United States. On the other hand, it was illogical and irrational to meet this threat by measures which violated the democratic rights of duly elected Socialists or the civil rights of alleged radicals. American attitudes to Communism arose from emotional responses which ran deep in American life as much as from rational concerns over the actual threat which Communism posed. From the late nineteenth century, fear had grown in America of anarchism, syndicalism or any form of radicalism. Incidents such as the Haymarket riot in 1886 and the Pullman strike in 1894, which were sensationally reported in the American press, added to popular antipathy to left-wing movements. Further fear was added at the turn of the century with the formation of the Industrial Workers of the World (IWW) who, under the leadership of the somewhat wild figure of Big Bill Haywood, sought much more than workers' rights but the destruction of the whole capitalist system. As Michael Heale has put it, 'The IWW was well placed to be perceived as that enemy within that Americans had long been schooled to look for'.[14]

Nevertheless, up to the First World War the Socialist Party and the trade union movement won a moderate degree of acceptance. By 1914 3.5 million American workers were organized in unions within the American Federation of Labor, the politically moderate confederation led by Samuel Gompers. In 1914 there were thirty Socialist members of state legislatures in twelve states and one Socialist member of Congress, while the Socialist candidate for president, Eugene Debs, won almost a million votes in 1912. The First World War and the Russian Revolution, however, created a mood of anti-foreign and anti-radical intolerance which culminated in the hysteria of the Red Scare in 1919–20. The war produced a spirit of chauvinistic super-patriotism which led to the equation of legitimate criticism with disloyalty. Above all, any hint of pacifism was denounced as pro-German. Thus, when the Socialist Party in April 1917 urged opposition by all means to the war among 'predatory capitalists', suspicion grew that Socialists were spies or pro-German.[15] Raids were conducted on Socialist Party and IWW offices, and Eugene Debs, Victor Berger and Bill Haywood were indicted under the Espionage Act.

With the end of the war there were serious problems of post-war reconstruction as well as disillusionment over the peace settlement, which added to anti-foreign prejudices, illustrated by the introduction of immigration restrictions. The general sense

14

of anxiety in 1919 was heightened by a series of strikes, particularly a general strike in Seattle in February, a police strike in Boston in October, a steel strike in October and a coal strike in December. Even more frightening were a series of bombing incidents. On 23 April 1919 a letter bomb was sent to Mayor Ole Hanson of Seattle, and the Post Office disclosed that thirty-six similar letter bombs had been intercepted addressed to such figures as John D. Rockefeller, due to arrive on 1 May. On 2 June 1919 there were eight bombing incidents involving, for example, the mayor of Pittsburg, a manufacturer in Patterson, New Jersey, and, most spectacularly, Attorney-General Palmer, whose home was approached by a sinister figure clutching a bomb who tripped on the steps and blew himself up. None of the intended victims were harmed in these incidents, and Communists and Socialists denied responsibility for this terrorist activity, but the scene was set for the subsequent Red Scare.

By mid-1920 the anti-Red hysteria abated. Palmer's ambition to win the Democratic nomination for president met with failure. The Democratic Party was in serious political difficulty following the defeat of the ratification of the Treaty of Versailles in the US Senate. Wilson doggedly held on to power, though a stroke which he suffered in September 1919 left him seriously incapacitated. The nation became tired of political wrangling and crusades to reform the world and lost interest in Reds at home or abroad. Instead, the country looked to the Republican candidate for president, Warren Harding, and the 'normalcy' which he promised, which took the form of the jazz age at home and isolationism in foreign policy.

In the context of the First World War and Wilson's need to co-operate with the Allies in the war and at the peace settlement, American agreement to join in the intervention in Russia is perhaps understandable. Nevertheless, Wilson had failed the 'acid test' which he had set in Point Six of the Fourteen Points by compromising his principles on self-determination and sending American troops into Russia. As Hiram Johnson put it,

> Why did we enter Russia? I answer, for no very good reason. . . . We have engaged in a miserable misadventure, stultifying our professions and setting at naught our promises. . . . We have sacrificed our own blood to no purpose and into American homes have brought sorrow and anguish and suffering.[16]

The foreign intervention was on too small a scale to make a decisive impact on the outcome of the civil war. On the other hand, foreign support of the Whites enabled the Reds to garner patriotic sentiment behind them among non-Bolsheviks in Russia. Foreign intervention seriously backfired, ultimately strengthening instead of weakening Bolshevik rule in Russia. American intervention, however hesitant and half-hearted, injected poison into US–Soviet relations at their outset, which remained in the system thereafter. Moreover, the reaction to Communism within the United States in 1919–20 brought to the surface a diversity of fears, prejudices and irrational attitudes which, along with other quite rational concerns, influenced the shaping of American policy with regard to Communism at home and abroad in succeeding decades.

2

THE ERA OF
NON-RECOGNITION, 1921–33

In contrast to the 1917–20 period when the United States and the Soviet Union engaged in direct confrontation, after 1920 both countries retreated to the sidelines of world affairs. The course of world events in the 1920s and 1930s was determined by the major European powers, Britain, France, Germany and Italy, while the United States and the Soviet Union reacted to the trend of events rather than determining its course. Although the United States after 1920 was not wholly isolationist but took important initiatives on such matters as the Washington Conference on disarmament in 1921–2 and the Dawes Plan in 1924 and the Young Plan in 1929 on international debts, in the 1920s the United States largely turned inward and concentrated on internal developments, while the Wall Street Crash in 1929 and the ensuing depression made America even more inward-looking in the 1930s. For their part the Bolshevik leaders realized by the early 1920s that world-wide revolution was not imminent and that the immediate need was internal development in the Soviet Union. As a result of the revolution and civil war some parts of the former tsarist empire were lost, such as the Baltic states of Latvia, Lithuania and Estonia, which became independent. The United States had no desire to encourage the disintegration of Russia and, in contrast to strong American commitment to the independence of the Baltic republics in later years, the United States did not grant diplomatic recognition to the new Baltic states until 1922. In other parts of the former Russian empire such as the Ukraine and Azerbaijan the Bolsheviks consolidated their control, and in 1922 the Union of Soviet Socialist Republics was formed. Lenin turned away from promotion of world revolution to internal economic development, with the New Economic Policy (NEP) which was introduced in 1921 allowing a measure of capitalism and free enterprise. Lenin's death in 1924 was followed by a period of collective leadership dominated first by the triumvirate of Joseph Stalin, Lev Kamenev and Grigori Zinoviev and then by Stalin and Nikolai Bukharin until the defeat of the latter's so-called 'Right opposition' in 1929 and the achievement of Stalin's dominance. Trotsky was exiled in 1929 and finally murdered in 1940, while Kamenev, Zinoviev and Bukharin were executed in the purges of the 1930s. Stalin's victory in this struggle for power resulted in less emphasis on the attempt to spread Communism abroad and more emphasis on the building of Socialism at home. Under the slogan 'Socialism in One Country', Stalin introduced the first Five Year Plan in 1928, to collectivize agriculture and to build up Soviet industry. Thus, Stalin's attention, like contemporary American leaders, was focused largely on internal economic development. The ideological rivalry nevertheless remained strong, with firm American assertion of ideological superiority. As Julius H. Barnes, president of the US Chamber of Commerce put it in 1925:

> America's hundred million people and their achievement is the open record to inspire the effort of sixteen hundred million other humans in the world. Fast or slow, other peoples – seeing what in America the average man may aspire to and accomplish and own – will follow.[1]

With the installation of the Republican administration of Warren Harding in March 1921 the Soviets sought an improvement in relations with the United States and, if possible, diplomatic recognition. Commissar for Foreign Affairs George Chicherin sent a note to the State Department referring to the hostility of the Wilson administration and expressing a wish for better relations. Chicherin held out the bait of increased trade, which he hoped would appeal to a Republican administration. The new Secretary of State, Charles Evans Hughes, however, took a legalistic approach to the matter and ruled that diplomatic recognition was impossible while the Soviets refused to honour the debts and obligations of previous governments and disseminated propaganda designed to destabilize other governments. Hughes, as State Department Soviet expert Loy Henderson put it, 'looked upon Russia as an ally which, while weakened by war, had fallen victim to a gang of well-organized, cruel conspirators'.[2] In 1922 the embassy of the Provisional Government in

Washington was closed and Ambassador Boris Bakhmetev sought exile in the United States, but the Harding administration rebuffed Soviet advances to establish diplomatic relations with the Bolsheviks. How justified was the American policy of withholding diplomatic recognition from the Soviet Union until 1933? And did Franklin Roosevelt make a wise decision to end non-recognition and to establish diplomatic relations with the Soviet Union in 1933? These are perhaps the main questions relating to American policy in the 1920s and early 1930s.

The most significant contact between the United States and the Soviet Union in the Harding years was through American famine relief. With widespread famine in the Soviet Union at the end of the civil war, the Bolshevik government, untypically compared to later years, asked for foreign assistance. The American Relief Administration (ARA) was established in response to this request, headed by Herbert Hoover, US Secretary for Commerce, who had worked in Russia in his earlier career as an engineer and who had wide experience in relief administration in Belgium and Germany during and after the First World War. Congress appropriated $20 million, to which further sums were added by private American charities. Half a million tons of food and medical supplies were distributed, reaching 10 million Soviet citizens from 1921 to 1923. The Soviet government made no official recognition of the aid and while they were generally co-operative in dealing with ARA they felt humiliated by the need to request aid and were on occasion obstructive and displayed suspicion of American purposes. American motives behind ARA were mixed. Straightforward humanitarian concern played its part, especially since the financial cost was not great and the food sent to the Soviet Union consisted largely of American agricultural surpluses. At the same time, however, figures such as Hoover were keen to maintain contacts with the Soviet people as opposed to the Soviet government in order to foster anti-Bolshevik sentiment. Hoover, like Wilson and many other leading Americans in the years immediately following the Russian Revolution, expected the Bolshevik regime to be short-lived. But if Hoover had subversive aims behind ARA, they were unfulfilled. While the humanitarian goals were fully accomplished and the United States gained a benefit in the release of American prisoners held since Allied intervention in 1918–20, aid through ARA was of vastly greater benefit to the Soviet regime. By mitigating the impact of the famine, American aid helped to save the Soviet government from a more serious crisis.

Through the 1920s economic contacts comprised the most significant aspect of US–Soviet relations. Despite the restrictions on trade with the Soviet Union which the United States left in place following the lifting of the Allied blockade in 1920, some American businesses were prepared to take the risk of engaging in trade and investment in the Soviet Union, attracted by the allure of an undeveloped country with vast natural resources and, in a number of instances, attracted also by the possibility of improving political relations by commercial contacts. In 1921 Armand Hammer won the first concession in the Soviet Union which was granted to an American, for an asbestos mine. Hammer had more success with a subsequent concession to manufacture pencils, and for the next seven decades Hammer not only continued to engage in profitable business enterprises in the Soviet Union but also established good personal relations with every Soviet leader from Lenin to Gorbachev. W. Averell Harriman won a concession for a manganese mine in Georgia, General Electric built the Dneipostroy dam, while Ford gave invaluable assistance in technical training to build up the Soviet auto and truck industry. The vast majority of American businessmen, however, were uninterested in the Soviet Union and sceptical of the prospect of profits. Such scepticism proved to be justified, since dealings with the Soviet trade monopoly were extremely frustrating. Even Harriman, who gained a reputation as a Soviet expert from his involvement in his manganese mine in Georgia from 1924 to 1928, lost money on the enterprise. Moreover, in contrast to the liberal views of a minority of American businessmen and the exceptional standpoint of Armand Hammer, the majority of American businessmen were antagonistic towards the Soviet regime and opposed diplomatic recognition by the United States.

Calvin Coolidge, who succeeded Harding as president on the latter's death in 1923, was not inclined to make a significant change in policy towards the Soviet Union. A note from Chicherin in 1923 expressing a wish to open negotiations came to nothing, nor did US policy change when in the mid-1920s Britain, France and most other countries recognized the Soviet Union. There were significant elements within the United States who pressed the Coolidge administration to grant diplomatic recognition to the Soviet government, especially some sections of business, progressive Republicans and left-wing groups. In 1923 William E. Borah, chairman of the Senate Committee on Foreign Relations, introduced a resolution in the US Senate favouring recognition of the Soviet government, and hearings were held before the Foreign Relations Committee in January 1924. Borah, along with other progressive Republicans such as Hiram Johnson, Robert La Follette and George Norris, argued that recognition would bring trade advantages to the United States, while ostracism drove the Soviet Union into closer trading connections and political association with Germany, illustrated by the Treaty of Rapallo between the two outcast nations, Germany and the Soviet Union, in 1922. The State Department, however, emphasized credits rather than diplomatic recognition as the key issue if substantial expansion of trade with the Soviet Union was to take place, and Soviet conduct regarding debts and expropriation of property, the State Department suggested, made the Soviet Union lack credit-worthiness. Nevertheless, despite the continuation of trading restrictions on the part of the US government, and the lack of interest on the part of most American businessmen, US exports to the Soviet Union rose to $68 million by 1925, more than any other nation. This added weight to the argument of progressive Republicans and the minority of the business community who were interested in trade with the Soviet Union that, with diplomatic recognition, there was potential for a considerable expansion of trade.

While some interests, then, pressed for diplomatic recognition, other powerful interests were strongly opposed, including right-wing Republicans, patriotic organizations, many business organizations, leading officials in the State and Commerce departments, the American Federation of Labor and the Catholic Church. Following the lead of Pope Benedict XIII and Pope Pius XII, the Catholic Church in America fiercely denounced godless Communism, especially after the execution by the Bolsheviks of many bishops and priests, including Monseigneur Constantine Buchavich, the vicar-general of the Catholic Church in Russia. Within American unions, the skilled workers in unions within the American Federation of Labor were staunchly anti-Communist, while right-wing Republicans, such as Representative Hamilton Fish of New York, and patriotic organizations, such as the Daughters of the American Revolution and the American Legion, were predictably fiercely anti-Communist. Secretary of Commerce Herbert Hoover, as John Lewis Gaddis has pointed out, 'nursed a deep ideological aversion to the Soviet government that precluded normal diplomatic relations.'[3] Hence, given the indifference of the vast majority of the American people towards most issues of world affairs in the 1920s and the vociferous opposition to recognition of the Soviet Union on the part of these powerful interest groups, Coolidge took the line of least resistance and left matters undisturbed.

The United States meantime established a listening post for Soviet affairs in Riga, the capital of Latvia. Within the State Department a Division of East European Affairs was established, which was kept informed of developments within the Soviet Union from the American embassy in Riga. The Riga perspective tended to bias American officials against the Soviet government, and the leading figures within the East European Division, such as Robert F. Kelley, took a firmly anti-Soviet position. Hence, throughout the 1920s, while the American public and most figures within the administration were uninterested in issues relating to the Soviet Union, the State Department experts portrayed a most unfavourable view of the Soviet Union in their reports to Washington. Loy Henderson later wrote:

> As a result of my studies and experiences in the Division I became convinced that the rulers in Moscow, although perhaps differing at times among themselves regarding the methods to be employed, were united in their determination to continue to promote chaos and revolution in the non-communist world with headquarters in Moscow. Even at that time it was fashionable among so-called 'intellectuals' to scoff at convictions of this kind, to intimate that those holding them were actively paying attention to slogans and exhortations rather than to actions. Nevertheless, I did not see how anyone after having gone through all the material I had examined while on that tour in the Department and observing what communists throughout the world were doing under Moscow's directions could come to any other conclusion.[4]

Herbert Hoover's election to the presidency in 1928 brought to the White House a figure who was familiar with Russia but staunchly anti-Communist. Hoover's rags to riches career, from orphan Iowa farm boy to wealthy engineer, left him with a deeply ingrained faith in individual initiative within a capitalist system and a fierce repugnance against any form of collectivist political system such as Communism. However, during Hoover's presidency (1929–33) two developments led the United States to reconsider its policy of non-recognition of the Soviet Union, namely, the Wall Street Crash and the growing threat from Japan.

As the Depression deepened and unemployment rose between 1929 and 1933, greater strength was added to the argument that diplomatic recognition would facilitate trade with the Soviet Union and thereby create employment opportunities for Americans. Even business leaders who had previously been opposed to dealings with the Soviet Union on ideological grounds accepted that in the crisis of the Depression the United States should, as one businessman put it, 'sell the misguided fanatics all they are willing to pay for'.[5] Exports to the Soviet Union, which had declined somewhat in the late 1920s, when Germany overtook the United States as the main trading partner of the Soviet Union, rose by 1930 to $114 million, 3 per cent of total US foreign trade and 25 per cent of Soviet imports. The first Five-Year Plan, introduced in 1928, opened up new economic opportunities for American business. By 1931 over a thousand American engineers were working in the Soviet Union, a number of whom were very impressed by Soviet planning compared to the uncertain volatility of American capitalism. On the other hand, there remained much scepticism in many quarters within business circles in the United States over the potential economic opportunities in the Soviet Union. Balanced against the possibilities of increased exports to the Soviet Union, for example, was the prospect of cheap Soviet imports, which would damage employment prospects in America. Hence, although the number of American businessmen who favoured diplomatic recognition of the Soviet Union increased from 1929 to 1933, that number remained a minority of the American business community. Significantly, it tended to be political figures, especially progressive Republicans, who were the main advocates of diplomatic recognition as a means to expand trade and create employment. As Hiram Johnson put it in April 1932, 'There are billions of dollars worth of future orders in Russia for American workers to fill, and in these times it is simply idiocy for America by its policies to preclude Americans from trade and commerce which could be obtained'.[6]

The United States was also growing increasingly concerned over Japanese expansion in the Far East. Since the turn of the century US relations with Japan had been generally strained, owing to American desire to preserve the Open Door in China and to defend America's colony, the Philippines, while the Japanese felt insulted by US racial and immigration policies, especially the Immigration Act of 1924, which eliminated any quota for Japanese immigrants. When the growing dominance of the militarists over the moderates within the Japanese government culminated in the Japanese invasion of Manchuria in 1931, the United States took the lead in condemning Japan's aggression and in refusing to recognize the puppet government of Manchukuo. The Soviet Union was equally afraid of Japanese expansion. The large Japanese force sent to Siberia in 1918 had aroused grave concern in Moscow, and although the Japanese had finally withdrawn from Siberia in 1922, there were deep fears on the part of the Soviet government of Japanese intentions in the Far East, especially Japanese desire to annex part of Siberia. Thus, the common objective of a wish to contain Japanese expansion suggested that it was in the mutual interest of the United States and the Soviet Union to establish diplomatic relations.

In November 1932 the election of Franklin Roosevelt brought to the White House a statesman of pragmatic bent. The matter of US recognition of the Soviet Union was not a major issue in the 1932 campaign – it was not even mentioned in the Democratic Party platform. But Roosevelt felt that it was unrealistic for the United States to have no relations with a large country of such considerable importance. Moreover, Roosevelt was appreciative of the support in the election of 1932 of progressive Republicans such as Hiram Johnson and George Norris, who did not vote for the Republican ticket and whose support in Congress was important to Roosevelt for the passage of New Deal legislation. Roosevelt willingly accepted the viewpoint of such progressive Republicans that recognition of the Soviet Union could provide economic opportunities in the Soviet Union for American business and thereby create jobs in the United States. Even more significantly, Roosevelt was influenced by strategic consider-ations, not only relating to Japan but also relating to Germany, following Adolph Hitler's accession to the chancellorship of Germany in January 1933.

After his inauguration as president in March 1933 Roosevelt appointed a Special Assistant Secretary of State with responsibility for Soviet affairs. The appointment was made of

William Bullitt, who had exhibited enthusiasm for reaching an accommodation with the Bolsheviks in Wilson's time and whose continuing connections with the Soviet Union through the 1920s included his marriage, until divorce in 1930, to Louise Bryant, the widow of John Reed, the romantic American Marxist who was buried in the Kremlin Wall. British Foreign Office officials, who favoured US diplomatic recognition of the Soviet Union but were wary of the manner in which Roosevelt conducted negotiations, regarded Bullitt's appointment as ominous. Laurence Collier, head of the Northern Department in the Foreign Office, noted that

> Roosevelt appears to be much under the influence of people like Mr. William C. Bullitt, who is both enthusiastic and unscrupulous and who is notoriously pro-Soviet (having married the widow of a well-known Communist) and who may persuade him to leap before he looks.[7]

Bullitt contacted Boris Shevirsky, the head of the Soviet Information Bureau in Washington and was assured of a favourable reception of a request for negotiations for recognition. In October 1933 Roosevelt wrote to Mikhail Kalinin, who was Soviet president and nominal head of state, though his power was insignificant, suggesting that a high Soviet official come to the United States for talks on opening diplomatic relations. The Soviets sent Maxim Litvinov, Soviet Commissar for Foreign Affairs, who had a pro-Western reputation and whose replacement of Chicherin in 1930 had been interpreted as a signal of Soviet desire to establish better relations with the Western democracies, particularly the United States.

The familiar obstacles to the establishment of diplomatic relations remained, namely, settlement of debts and Comintern propaganda. To these was added a further issue, the right of foreign nationals to practise their religion in the Soviet Union. This was a matter of importance, in order to meet the objections to recognition from the Catholic Church at a time when the Catholic vote was of growing importance in the Democratic Party coalition. These various issues were covered in a series of talks between Roosevelt and Litvinov in November and December 1933, in which Roosevelt demonstrated his characteristic preference for personal diplomacy and for dealing with broad issues rather than adherence to the bureaucratic procedures of the State Department and painstaking attention to detail. Hence, the Roosevelt–Litvinov Agreements, signed in December 1933, resolved the major issues partly by ambiguous phraseology and by glossing over certain matters. This made possible the establishment of diplomatic relations between the two countries but produced the result that the establishment of diplomatic relations did not lead to an improvement in political relations but instead added to the American sense of Soviet deceitfulness and untrustworthiness.

The matter of the right of foreign nationals to practise religion in the Soviet Union was satisfactorily resolved. Litvinov appreciated that this was a matter of considerable importance for Roosevelt's political position at home and of minor significance to the Soviet government. Hence, the right of Americans to practise their religion in the Soviet Union was fully conceded in the Roosevelt–Litvinov Agreements. The agreements on Comintern propaganda and debt settlement, however, were much less satisfactory.

Throughout the 1920s and early 1930s propaganda was distributed by the Comintern through the American Communist Party. From the early 1920s the American Communist Party was controlled by Moscow. As a recent historian has put it, 'A group of genuine American revolutionaries in 1919 proceeded to undermine their own movement's independence by accepting Soviet guidance'.[8] The statements of the Comintern seemed alarming, but support for Communism within the United States was so slight that the issue of Communist propaganda was more a matter of irritation to the US government than a serious threat to American security. The Comintern stated in 1922 that

> Every honest Communist will fight against bourgeois society to his last breath, in word and in deed and if necessary with arms in hand. Yes, the propaganda of the Communist International will be pernicious for you, the imperialists. It is the historical mission of the Communist International to be the grave digger of bourgeois society.[9]

But such rhetoric seemed empty bombast in the United States, given the weak support for the Communist Party. In 1923 the Communist Labor Party and the Communist Party amalgamated to form the Communist Party, with a membership throughout the 1920s of at most 10,000 and with a considerable turnover in membership as disillusioned members left the party. The Wall Street Crash and the Great Depression alienated many intellectuals from capitalism and provided Communism with its most favourable opportunity. Yet in the 1932 election the Communist candidate for president won only 103,000 votes, party membership remained small and turnover in membership remained high. As the historian Arthur Schlesinger, Jr, put it:

> In 1930 the party claimed only six thousand members; by 1932 after two years of furious agitation in the midst of economic collapse, only a meagre twelve thousand. Many more signed membership cards in these years; but most passed through the party as through a revolving door, finding the discipline unbearable, the dialectic meaningless and the vocabulary incomprehensible. Some left the party for the same reason they entered it – because they cared deeply about democracy and freedom. The Communist vision had been enticing; but the facts, even after three years of capitalist decay, remained dull – a clique of dreary fanatics and seedy functionaries, talking to themselves in an unintelligible idiom, ignored by the working class, dedicating their main efforts to witch hunts against liberals and Socialists. The party was sodden, contentious, bureaucratic and feeble.[10]

Nevertheless, the US government not unreasonably wished to ensure that the establishment of a Soviet embassy in Washington would not present the Comintern with a channel through which to disseminate propaganda throughout the United States. After negotiation on the matter, the Soviets appeared to concede on this point, accepting the stipulation in the Roosevelt–Litvinov Agreements that no propaganda would be disseminated which was 'aimed at disturbing the tranquillity of the United States'.[11]

On debt settlement the Roosevelt–Litvinov Agreements were, however, much less precise. Other countries such as Britain and France warned that very clear agreement should be reached on the terms of the settlement of debts and compensation for expropriation of property before the United States granted diplomatic recognition. The US government claimed that $187 million had been lent to the Provisional Government by the US government, American bond-holders held $106 million in Russian bonds and property to the value of $336 million had been confiscated. The Soviets counterclaimed that the cost of damage in the American military intervention in Russia 1918–20 came to a total of approximately the same amount. No agreement

27

was reached in 1933 on the precise terms of debt settlement and compensation for confiscated property. Litvinov stated that the Soviet government might be willing to pay somewhere between $75 million and $150 million, while Roosevelt agreed to a loan to the Soviets to enable them to make more purchases in the United States, which could help them to pay their debt. Hence, a vague agreement on principle was reached, with the details to be worked out later.

Roosevelt's diplomacy in the negotiation of diplomatic recognition has come in for much criticism. Yet Roosevelt was justified in his view that insistence on a satisfactory settlement of the details of the debts and expropriation issues would have held up the establishment of diplomatic relations indefinitely. Larger American interests were gained, in Roosevelt's view, by the establishment of US–Soviet relations than were lost by concessions through ambiguous language on the debts and expropriation issues. The United States had with eagerness been the first nation to recognize the new Russian government in March 1917. In 1933 the United States was the last nation of any significance to recognize the Bolsheviks. The implications of non-recognition – a denial of moral authority and an implied hope that the Bolshevik government would not endure – left a permanent mark on the course of US–Soviet relations. In 1933 Roosevelt justifiably concluded that the policy of non-recognition was increasingly self-defeating and that a new administration should grasp the nettle and establish diplomatic relations. A more valid criticism of Roosevelt, however, was that he allowed the impression to be created that the establishment of diplomatic relations opened a new dawn in US–Soviet relations, raising expectations which were bound to be deflated.

3

FROM RECOGNITION TO WORLD WAR, 1933–41

In 1933 the United States had high hopes that the establishment of diplomatic relations would lead to a steady improvement in US–Soviet relations. Instead, diplomatic recognition of the Soviet Union produced deep disillusionment in the United States and increasing distrust of the Soviet Union. The period 1933–41 was characterized by a lengthening list of serious grievances on the part of the United States towards the Soviet government. These issues might well have led to a break in diplomatic relations, except for growing American concern over the policies of Nazi Germany and imperial Japan, which led the Roosevelt administration to avoid a breach in relations with the Soviet Union in order to use the Soviet Union as a counter-weight against Germany and Japan. This trend of events culminated in 1941 with the paradox that after a decade of deepening distrust and hostility throughout the 1930s, the United States and the Soviet Union became allies in the Second World War. The most important question which arises regarding US policy towards the Soviet Union in the 1930s is whether Franklin Roosevelt's policy was a failure, achieving virtually none of the goals sought in establishing diplomatic relations and producing a steadily worsening relationship, or whether Roosevelt shrewdly and successfully refused to allow setbacks on relatively lesser matters to distract attention from the larger objective of utilizing the Soviet Union as a counter-weight to Germany and Japan.

In early 1934 William Bullitt arrived in Moscow as America's first ambassador to the Soviet Union. At a cordial welcome by Stalin, Bullitt was offered a site for a new American embassy which would overlook the Moscow River and where Bullitt planned to construct an embassy based on the design of Monticello, Thomas Jefferson's home in Virginia. Bullitt also received permission to bring an aeroplane to the Soviet Union, to be flown by the US air attaché. The euphoria of the opening of diplomatic relations was short-lived. An official in the British embassy in Moscow noted in April 1934 that 'The American–Soviet honeymoon is not going at all smoothly'.[1] Obstacles were placed in the way of the construction of the proposed new embassy, which did not materialize. In January 1935 the air attaché was withdrawn as part of protests by the United States against Soviet policies on debt repayment, and the aeroplane was damaged in an accident and permission refused for a replacement. Life was very difficult for Bullitt and American diplomats in Moscow, such as George Kennan, Charles Bohlen and Loy Henderson. Henderson commented that 'We frequently likened ourselves to the passengers from a ship which had been wrecked on a desert island surrounded by a shark-infested sea'.[2] The purchase of everyday commodities was made difficult by the unrealistic and quite artificial exchange rate between the dollar and the ruble. Soviet Foreign Minister Litvinov failed to keep his promise to resolve this matter, instead making only the concession that Soviet authorities would turn a blind eye if the American embassy purchased rubles abroad at black-market rates and brought them into the Soviet Union by diplomatic bag. The embassy accepted Litvinov's proposal, yet this solution involved the embassy in illegal conduct and left it in a condition of dependency on the Soviet authorities. Recruitment of domestic staff was difficult, as Soviet employees of the embassy were not infrequently imprisoned or even executed, or they simply disappeared. Other employees were secret police agents. In 1937 a microphone was discovered in the ambassador's office, and such eavesdropping was commonplace. The Soviet Foreign Ministry did not provide information on the arrests of American citizens in the Soviet Union, which the embassy often learned of from other sources, and consular visits were then obtained only after procrastination, obstruction and bureaucratic frustrations.

The first substantial issue which Bullitt took up with the Soviet government was the settlement of debts. Negotiations took place from March 1934 to January 1935 without a satisfactory outcome. The vague phraseology of the Roosevelt–Litvinov Agreements on the matter of debts was exploited by the Soviet negotiators, and the United States soon realized that the Soviet government had no intention of paying its debts. The protracted negotiations on debt settlement brought about the disillusionment of Ambassador Bullitt. In January 1935 Bullitt passed on a stinging message of rebuke to the Soviet government, and the United States closed its consulate-general in Moscow and reduced the embassy staff in protest over Soviet intransigence over debt settlement. Roosevelt's firm stand on the issue was influenced by domestic political considerations. As Edward Bennett has argued, Roosevelt calculated that Soviet lack of good faith on the debt issue had the result that 'the president would lay himself open to attack for not having observed the danger signs when the Russians went back on their word. . . . Public opinion and political expediency were never out of FDR's mind'.[3]

The matter of the dissemination of Communist propaganda proved to be equally contentious in negotiation. The Soviet ambassador in Washington, Alexander Troyanovsky, gave an assurance that no propaganda of any sort was distributed by the Soviet government. Propaganda could, however, be distributed by the Comintern, which, it was claimed, was an independent agency not under the control of the Soviet government. Such cynical casuistry incensed the American government and American public opinion. It added powerfully to the feeling in America that the Soviets would lie, cheat, steal and engage in any activity, however reprehensible, to further their goals.

Propaganda was distributed through the American Communist Party. In the course of the 1930s, party membership grew from 12,000 in 1932 to 80,000 by 1939. The expansion of the federal bureaucracy in the New Deal years enabled Communists to gain positions in government as well as in other institutions such as trade unions and schools. Communist cells were formed to organize penetration of government, such as the Harold Ware group, which included Alger Hiss, who from 1933 to 1937 allegedly supplied State Department documents to contacts who passed them over to the Soviet government. American Communists followed the party line set down at the Seventh All-World Congress of the Communist International in Moscow in 1935, namely, a popular-front approach of co-operation with other left-wing groups and an attempt to infiltrate government in the manner, as one delegate to the Congress put it, of the Trojan horse. Earl Browder, William Z. Foster and Thomas Green, leading American Communists, were elected to the executive committee of the Comintern. American Communists pledged allegiance to the red flag and denounced all other flags as flags of the capitalist class. Among liberal intellectuals, large numbers sympathized with Communist aspirations and were prepared to overlook the shortcomings of Soviet practices at home and abroad. As one writer put it, 'By 1934 exaggerated faith in the Soviet experiment had become the intellectual fashion'.[4] Many liberals scathingly denounced the failure of Western capitalism, feared the rise of Hitler and praised the Soviet Union as the only resolute bulwark against Fascism. As one liberal intellectual, Malcolm Cowley, later expressed it, 'All through the 1930s, the Soviet Union . . . was not so much a nation, in the eyes of Western radicals, as it was an ideal, a faith and an international hope of salvation'.[5]

The United States resented Soviet exploitation of domestic discontent in the time of the Great Depression to undermine the institutions of American life and to distribute propaganda which advocated the violent overthrow of capitalism in general and of the US government in particular. Congressional committees under Representative Hamilton Fish and Representative Martin Dies were formed to investigate Communism in America, and J. Edgar Hoover and the FBI kept Communists under surveillance. Paradoxically, there was less hysteria over Communism in America in the 1930s when Communist Party membership was at its height and Communist penetration of government at its most extensive than at a later time in the Red Scare of the late 1940s and early 1950s when Communist influence was much less. Fish, Dies and Hoover were as concerned with Nazis as much as with Communists. Nevertheless, the sense of treachery on the part of the Soviet Union was added to greatly by Soviet apparent agreement in 1933 to end Communist propaganda within the United States and the blatant continuation of such propaganda in order to exploit America's domestic difficulties through Communist Party fifth columnists. The stiff US note of protest of 27 August 1935 with regard to Soviet failure to adhere to promises concerning non-interference in domestic affairs marked William Bullitt's final disillusionment with the Soviet Union. Bullitt reported to the State Department that ample reason existed for the United States to break off diplomatic relations, but he argued that the interests of the United States were better served by the maintenance of a listening post in Moscow.

A further disappointment to the United States concerned trade with the Soviet Union following diplomatic recognition. In July 1935 a trade agreement was signed, by which the Soviet

Union was granted Most Favored Nation status and the Soviets promised to purchase 30 million dollars worth of American goods within the next year. The expected surge in trade, with consequent employment opportunities for American factories, did not materialize. As State Department experts had advised, credits were more significant in increasing trade than diplomatic recognition. Yet, with the Soviet record on debt resettlement, Soviet credit-worthiness was non-existent. Moreover, the Johnson Act of 1934 barred the extension of loans and credits to any country which had defaulted on its debt repayments to the United States. A number of American companies continued business in the Soviet Union, such as Ford and International Harvester, and as in the 1920s they played a useful role in training Soviet personnel in manufacturing and engineering. But the difficulties of dealing with the Soviet authorities on trade produced the result that after 1935 there was even less trade than in the 1920s. At the same time, tourist travel in the Soviet Union sharply declined. Unlike the 1920s and early 1930s, when 10,000 Americans per annum had travelled in the Soviet Union and travel was relatively unrestricted, from the mid-1930s until the 1960s tourist travel by Americans in the Soviet Union almost disappeared. The diminution of contacts through trade and tourism played its part in accentuating the image in America of the Soviet Union as a remote, barbaric, threatening power. This image was given substance by the purges and show trials of the mid-1930s.

In 1934 Sergei Kirov, the popular Communist leader in Leningrad, was assassinated. The assassination was probably on Stalin's orders, in order to eliminate a potential rival, but the evidence is not definitive. The evidence is not in dispute, however, that Stalin used the incident to eliminate all possible rivals on the charge that they were plotting against him and against the state. In the first show trial, in 1936, Lev Kamenev, Grigori Zinoviev and other leading figures of the Bolshevik Revolution were put on trial for treason, confessed their guilt and were shot. In 1937 Karl Radek and other leading figures were found guilty of plotting against the state. In 1938 Nikolai Bukharin was executed and Stalin's chief assistant in the selection of victims for the first two show trials, Genrikh Yagoda, was himself put on trial, confessed and was shot. After the elimination of political rivals Stalin then proceeded to a purge of military leaders. The purges reinforced in the American mind the association of Bolshevism with Red Terror, horrific brutality and ruthless totalitarianism. Americans had been only vaguely aware of Stalin's savage policies of the early 1930s, in which countless millions died in the forced collectivization of agriculture, but the purges of the mid-1930s, with the bizarre drama of public confessions followed by instant executions, were widely reported in America and created a deep impact. A number of left-wing liberals accepted the defendants' admissions of guilt at their face value or condoned the purges as an acceptable price for the higher goal of the creation of a superior form of society which the Soviet experiment was achieving. For the vast majority of Americans, however, the purges added significantly to their feeling of repugnance and revulsion towards the Soviet Union.

The Roosevelt administration was even more concerned by Stalin's foreign policy in the later 1930s than by his domestic policy. The suspicion grew that Stalin wished to lead the Western powers into war with Germany and Japan, leaving the Soviet Union to pick up the pieces and to expand Communism and world revolution. As the *New York Herald Tribune* noted, 'The one strongest Soviet interest in the whole situation is . . . to see the axis and democracies kill each other off . . . and that makes Stalin a more dubious ally than ever'.[6] The *Omaha Morning World-Herald* wrote that 'Safe in his lair, Stalin may behold the soul-warming spectacle of his enemies destroying each other, then . . . he may emerge in safety to glut his appetite, vulture-like, on the carcass of what was once European civilization'.[7] As Hitler expanded into the Rhineland, Austria and Czechoslovakia, the United States continued to pursue a policy of isolationism, while Britain and France appeased Hitler. Western policy was interpreted by the Soviet Union as an attempt to direct Hitler to the East. Strenuous efforts by Stalin and Litvinov to align Britain and France with the Soviets in a collective front against Hitler made no progress, while Roosevelt, given the strongly isolationist mood of American public opinion, was unable to convince the Soviets that alignment with the Western powers was the most hopeful means of deterring Nazi aggression. The replacement of Litvinov by V.I. Molotov as Commissar for Foreign Affairs in May 1939 was the first indication that the Soviets planned to come to terms with Hitler. The US government was well-informed on Soviet plans in this regard owing to a remarkable contact between Charles Bohlen and a Second Secretary at the German embassy in Moscow, Hans Heinrich Herwarth von Bittenfeld, who kept

Bohlen fully informed about Nazi–Soviet relations from May 1939. Prior secret information, however, only slightly softened American outrage at Soviet treachery in signing the Nazi–Soviet pact in August 1939. Hitler was enabled to attack Poland on 1 September 1939 in the knowledge that if Britain and France declared war, which they did on 3 September 1939, Germany would not face war also with the Soviet Union.

The Soviet share of the spoils of the Nazi–Soviet pact amounted to eastern Poland, Bessarabia and northern Bukovina. Moreover, in a secret protocol of the pact, the Soviet Union was given a free hand in the Baltic states of Latvia, Lithuania and Estonia. The US government knew the terms of the secret protocol, from Bohlen's contacts with Herwarth. In order to protect this source it was not possible for the United States to inform the governments of the Baltic states of the secret protocol. The American government watched helplessly and with disgust as the Soviets forced the Baltic states to sign mutual security treaties in October 1939 and be subjected to an increasing degree of control until they were absorbed into the Soviet Union in July 1940. The United States continued to recognize the previous governments of Latvia, Lithuania and Estonia and froze their assets in America.

The United States was more forthright in its condemnation of Soviet policy towards Finland. In October 1939 the Soviet government made territorial demands on Finland, which the Soviets claimed were for reasons of military security but which the Finns rejected as a threat to their independence. Faced with adamant Finnish refusal to come to terms, Soviet forces invaded Finland on 30 November 1939. The American government and public opinion was overwhelmingly sympathetic to Finland. There was great admiration for the gallantry and skill of the Finnish troops in the so-called 'Winter War' of 1939–40, as they made their way through the snow and forest in silence on skis and outmanoeuvred the vastly numerically superior Soviet troops. Moreover, Americans did not forget that while all other nations defaulted on their the First World War debts, Finland alone repaid its debts. As a British diplomat noted, America regarded Finland as 'the one honest-debtor and the blue-eyed boy among all foreign nations'.[8] On 2 December 1939 the United States declared a moral embargo, recommending American manu-facturers of aircraft to reconsider entering contracts with countries which used bombing as a means of terrorizing neighbouring countries – the Soviets had bombed Finland. The United States gave $100 million in non-military aid to Finland and allowed Finland to purchase forty-six aeroplanes which the US War Department declared to be surplus. Furthermore, the United States co-operated with other nations in diplomatic moves which led to the expulsion of the Soviet Union from the League of Nations in December 1939.

After the initial successes, the Finnish troops were eventually overwhelmed by superior Soviet manpower and forced to come to terms in March 1940. Finland agreed to the new border with the Soviet Union, which demolished the Mannerheim Line, Finland's line of defence, leaving Finland dependent on Stalin's tender mercies. The State Department expected that Finland would in due course suffer the same fate as the Baltic states. American public opinion had been provided with yet a further piece of evidence of Soviet treachery and villainy.

US–Soviet relations in the years after 1933, therefore, sharply deteriorated, with a long list of grievances on the part of the United States against the Soviet Union – debt resettlement, Comintern propaganda, trade, the purges, Soviet duplicity in foreign policy, the Nazi–Soviet pact, the take-over of the Baltic states, the Winter War against Finland. In some quarters within Congress, the press and public opinion, there were demands to break off diplomatic relations. The Roosevelt administration was, however, increasingly afraid of the threat from Germany and Japan, and although US–Soviet collaboration against Japan became less likely in the late 1930s, the United States was eager to attain the co-operation of any potential opponent of Nazi Germany.

When Bullitt resigned as ambassador in 1936, Roosevelt replaced him by Joseph Davies, who took an extraordinarily pro-Soviet line. Davies was a wealthy businessman who in 1936 married Marjorie Meriwether Post, heiress to the Post cereal fortune and owner of *Sea Cloud*, the most luxurious yacht in the world, which sailed to Leningrad in 1937 and on which Davies entertained guests on weekend cruises. Davies's reports from Moscow gave Stalin and the Soviet government the benefit of every doubt. The apologies for Soviet behaviour from such an arch-capitalist seem quite extraordinary. But Davies was useful to keep in Moscow in order to help to smooth over US–Soviet differences as far as possible. In 1939 Davies was replaced by Laurence Steinhardt, whose reports were more objective and were very critical of Soviet policy. Nevertheless, although the United States spoke out over such policies as the annexation of the Baltic states and the invasion of Finland, criticisms were sufficiently tempered to avoid an open breach with the Soviet Union. Even after the Nazi–Soviet pact, as Robert Dallek has shown, Roosevelt 'wished to avoid anything that might encourage Moscow to fight Britain and France'.[9]

From intelligence sources the United States was convinced that, despite the Nazi–Soviet pact, the Nazis and the Soviets would soon fall out and that Germany would attack the Soviet Union. From the summer of 1940, the United States passed on to Moscow intelligence reports of Hitler's designs to invade the Soviet Union. Stalin refused to believe this, and the United States was unable to cite its sources of information in order to convince Stalin. But the US administration was certain that the Nazi–Soviet pact would be broken by Hitler, and the United States planned accordingly. With the fall of France in June 1940 Roosevelt aimed to aid Britain as far as possible, and he hoped that Britain would soon benefit from Soviet involvement in war with Germany. Hence, in January 1941, Roosevelt lifted the moral embargo. In March, when the Lend-Lease Act was passed, which greatly increased aid to Britain, Roosevelt ensured the defeat of Congressional amendments which could have excluded the Soviet Union as a possible future recipient of Lend-Lease aid.

When Hitler finally launched his attack on the Soviet Union on 22 June 1941, some Americans felt that the United States should remain on the sidelines and allow the Nazis and the Communists to destroy one another. Senator Harry Truman said that 'If we see that Germany is winning the war we ought to help Russia, and if Russia is winning we ought to help Germany, and in that way let them kill as many as possible'.[10] This was not, however, the view of the Roosevelt administration. The United States was afraid that the Germans would win the war swiftly and gain access to the resources of the Soviet Union, making Nazi Germany a formidable foe in the succeeding conflict in the West against Britain and ultimately against the United States. Hence, Roosevelt wished to aid the Soviet Union at least to slow down German progress in the war on the Eastern front and to help Britain to build up its strength. Roosevelt, like Winston Churchill, regarded Nazi Germany as the main threat and he was therefore willing to give aid to any opponent of Hitler, even Stalin. Churchill said that 'If Hell declared war on Hitler, I would at least make a favourable reference to the Devil in the House of Commons'.[11] Roosevelt basically agreed with this viewpoint.

From the summer of 1941, Roosevelt decided that the United States should enter the Second World War, but he needed an incident which would unify public opinion behind a decision to intervene. In the autumn of 1941, therefore, as German armies advanced into the Soviet Union, Roosevelt was eager to aid the Soviet effort as this would assist the United States when America entered the war. Roosevelt needed to proceed cautiously, however, in order not to alienate Congressional and public opinion. Isolationists, especially right-wing Republicans, were strongly opposed to the extension of Lend-Lease aid to the Soviet Union. Hamilton Fish, a right-wing Republican Congressman from New York, attacked 'the attempt to turn the Lend-Lease Bill into the Lenin-lease bill'.[12] In July 1941 Roosevelt sent Averell Harriman and Harry Hopkins to Moscow to assure Stalin of American support. Stalin was not wholly reassured and American aid was slow to arrive, but the commitment of the United States to support the Soviet Union had been made clear. On the Soviet side, the appointment of the allegedly pro-Western Maxim Litvinov as ambassador to the United States in November 1941 was interpreted as a signal of a desire for better relations.

On 7 December 1941 the Japanese attack on Pearl Harbour brought America into the war with a united public opinion. Three days later Hitler declared war on the United States. After a decade and a half of non-recognition from 1917 to 1933 and a period of poisonous relations from 1933 to 1941, Hitler and the Japanese had produced a paradoxical outcome, an alliance between the United States and the Soviet Union. Roosevelt's critics argue that the United States was persistently outfoxed by Stalin throughout the 1930s and that only Hitler's folly in attacking the Soviet Union saved Roosevelt from a record of persistent failure in relations with the Soviet Union throughout the 1930s. Roosevelt has also come under criticism for devoting too much attention to sources of information which portrayed the Soviet Union in an overly favourable light, especially Joseph Davies, Eleanor Roosevelt and some left-wing New Dealers, and paying too little attention to the hard-headed analyses of the State Department Soviet experts. Yet, though in his relations with the Soviet Union Roosevelt was, as in all matters, probing in different directions and sounding out varying sources of opinion, his overall policy was in fact fairly consistent. Isolationist pressures within the United States and appeasement on the part of Britain and France ruled out the creation of an anti-Nazi deterrent force of Britain, France, the United States and the Soviet Union. Moreover, Soviet weakness meant that the Soviet Union could not be used as a counter against Japan as well as Germany. In these circumstances Roosevelt's policy was to recognize Nazi Germany as the main threat and to maintain channels of communication with the Soviet government. In this crucial respect Roosevelt's policy was successful. Moreover, Roosevelt hoped that in the course of time the Soviet Union could also be brought into the war against Japan. Even more so, Roosevelt hoped that co-operation in war might lead on to a new relationship of co-operation in the post-war era. How far the short-term set-backs in American policy towards the Soviet Union in the 1930s were outweighed by benefits in the longer term, remains to be examined in the discussion of US–Soviet relations in the Second World War and its aftermath.

4

WARTIME ALLIANCE, 1941–5

One view of the US–Soviet alliance during the Second World War is that it was purely a wartime alliance of convenience which was bound to evaporate once the common enemy was gone, bringing underlying US–Soviet hostility to the surface again and producing the confrontation of the Cold War. As Linda Killen has put it, during the Second World War 'the facade of allied unity was just that, a false front'.[1] The opposing view is that, however much the formation of the alliance was due to basic mutual security needs, the co-operation and increased contacts during the war made a continuation of such co-operation in the post-war era not impossible, but the prospect of peaceful co-existence was destroyed and a Cold War brought about by policies pursued in the years immediately after the war. The question of whether the Second World War relationship was anything more than a wartime alliance of convenience can be answered by an examination of the major issues of that period, especially the second front, American economic and military aid, Eastern Europe and the atomic bomb.

The United States was brought into the war by an attack by Japan, and there was support in many quarters in the United States for a concentration of the American war effort in the Far East. Roosevelt's first strategic decision of the war, however, was to designate Germany as the main enemy against whom the major effort should be made. The Soviet Union remained neutral in the war against Japan, which was acceptable to the United States in 1941, although in the course of time America was eager for the Soviet Union to enter the war against Japan when the war in Europe was over. Roosevelt's decision to concentrate the American effort against Germany was pleasing to

Churchill, who came to see Roosevelt in late December 1941. The decision was equally pleasing to Stalin, who faced a desperate plight in the face of the German invasion of the Soviet Union.

Less pleasing to Stalin, however, was the slow speed of effective American military involvement in the war in Europe which might draw German divisions away from the Eastern front. Stalin's main wish was the early opening of a second front in France by Britain and the United States. When Soviet Foreign Minister Molotov came to the United States in May 1942 to press the Soviet case for opening a second front in 1942, he won strong support from General George Marshall, chairman of the US Joint Chiefs of Staff. Churchill, however, was strongly opposed to an early opening of a second front. Churchill had vivid memories of British losses in France in the First World War and the recent memory of the narrow escape of the British army from Dunkirk in 1940. Churchill therefore felt that it would be foolhardy to engage in a frontal assault against the strongly defended French coast before Germany had been weakened by aerial bombing and by engagements in other areas such as North Africa. Roosevelt therefore agreed to postpone the opening of a second front and instead to send American forces under General Eisenhower to Algeria to liberate French North Africa and then to join with the British effort to drive Rommel's army from North Africa. Stalin, however, was left with the suspicion that the Americans and British were willing to allow the Soviet Union to bear the brunt of the fighting against Germany and only when the Nazis and the Soviets had gravely weakened one another would Anglo-American forces arrive to pick up the spoils of victory.

The American government and public opinion felt great sympathy for the Soviet Union in 1942 and were conscious that the United States were making a relatively minor military contribution to the war in Europe while the Red Army bore the brunt of the battle against Germany. As Charles Bohlen put it, 'The fact that the Russians were carrying so heavy a load led to a guilt complex in our relations'.[2] Roosevelt attempted to atone for the delay in opening a second front by assisting the Soviets in other ways as much as possible. Lend-Lease aid was shipped to Murmansk in north Russia around Norway, despite the hazards of U-boats based in the Norwegian fjords. In diplomatic moves Roosevelt attempted to appease the Soviets by, for example, the transfer of Loy Henderson, a hardline critic of Soviet policy, from the East European desk at the State Department after Litvinov had commented that 'the Soviet Union would never have good relations while Henderson held that position'.[3] In January 1943 the decision by Roosevelt and Churchill at Casablanca to declare a policy of unconditional surrender towards Germany was motivated in part to reassure Stalin of their unreserved commitment to fight Hitler to the finish.

Soviet suspicions persisted, however, so long as the United States delayed the opening of a second front in France. Hence, a major crisis in the alliance developed when the second front was again postponed in 1943. Churchill persuaded Roosevelt that for logistical and strategic reasons the best step after the defeat of Rommel in North Africa was to send Anglo-American forces across the Mediterranean to Sicily and Italy, in order to knock Mussolini's Italy out of the war and to attack Germany from the south. Stalin was appalled by this decision. The Soviets had held back the German offensive in the winter of 1942–3, holding out in the seige of Leningrad, repulsing the Germans in the battle of Moscow and above all encircling and defeating the German forces at Stalingrad. Yet the Red Army was to be left to continue a lonely battle in 1943 while Anglo-American armies engaged in what Stalin regarded as peripheral engagements in Sicily and Italy. Churchill tried to mollify Stalin, telling the Soviet leader that, using the analogy of an attack on a crocodile, the most effective approach was to strike at the 'soft belly' of the Axis in Italy while preparing to hit later at the hard snout of the Normandy coast.[4] But Stalin was not impressed by Churchill's floral expressions and remained suspicious that the Anglo-American purpose was to allow the Soviets to be bled white by the Nazis before the British and American armies arrived.

Relations between the Western powers and the Soviet Union greatly improved following the decision in November 1943 at Tehran, the first of the Big Three wartime conferences, to open a second front in France in 1944. Moreover, Roosevelt had great faith in personal diplomacy, and as a result of his conversations with Stalin over four days at Tehran he felt confident that agreement could be reached to ensure post-war co-operation despite ideological differences. In January 1944 Eisenhower arrived in London to make preparations for the invasion of France. The Soviets agreed to undertake an offensive in early June to prevent the withdrawal of German troops to the West after the Allied landing in Normandy on 6 June 1944. When the

Soviets duly kept their agreement on this matter, Eisenhower was impressed and concluded that the Soviets could be relied upon to keep their word, at least in military matters.

The American image of the Soviet Union altered profoundly during the Second World War. The American media, especially cinema newsreels, gave wide coverage to 'Our gallant Soviet ally' and heaped praise on the courage and resourcefulness of the Soviet people. *Life* magazine, published by the inveterate anti-Communist Henry Luce, produced vivid photographs to illustrate its stories of the resilience of the Soviet army and people. In a *Life* special issue on the Soviet Union in May 1943, Lenin was proclaimed as 'perhaps the greatest man of modern times', the NKVD was referred to as 'a national police similar to the FBI' and the Russians were described as 'one hell of a people . . . [who] to a remarkable degree . . . look like Americans, dress like Americans and think like Americans'.[5] The Red Army's performance against the Germans made memories of the purge of the armed forces in the 1930s and Soviet military ineptitude in the Winter War against Finland fade into the background. Hollywood documentary films commissioned by the US government portrayed the heroism of the Soviet people and the Red Army, while feature films such as *Mission to Moscow* which was based on former ambassador Joseph Davies's best-selling book, presented the Soviet Union in a very sympathetic light. The degree of personal contact between Americans and Soviets was limited, but where there was contact there was goodwill. Americans were, moreover, appreciative of Soviet gestures of goodwill such as the abolition of the Comintern in 1943, while the American Communist Party took a very patriotic posture during the war, with the American flag flying alongside the red flag.

By 1944, after three years of pro-Soviet propaganda the American people became attuned to the idea that, when Hitler and the Japanese militarists had been defeated, a new world order of peace and friendship could come into being, a vital part of which would be continuing Soviet–American co-operation in the post-war era. Wendell Willkie, the defeated Republican candidate for president in 1940, summed up these aspirations in his concept of One World, which he publicized widely. Franklin Roosevelt sought similar objectives by the formation of the United Nations Organization, which Roosevelt hoped would succeed where the League of Nations had failed and would provide a world forum within which US–Soviet differences could be reconciled and a post-war new world order of peace and tolerance could be created.

Roosevelt sought to use the instrument of American economic aid to ameliorate US–Soviet differences in the war years and as a means of building on wartime co-operation for a new era of post-war co-operation. Roosevelt's primary goal in extending Lend-Lease aid to the Soviet Union was to stave off a Soviet collapse in the early war years and thereby to engage German forces on the Eastern front. But Roosevelt also sought to use aid as a means to mollify Stalin until the second front was opened and as an expression of American goodwill to the Soviet Union. Consequently, whereas Churchill was more willing to suspend convoys to north Russia in 1942 and 1943 when losses became heavy from U-boat attacks, Roosevelt sought to avoid interruptions in the flow of supplies to the Soviet Union. In the time of critical peril for the Soviet Union in 1942–3, Lend-Lease aid was of insufficient quantity to make a significant impact on the military outcome, but American sacrifices in naval losses suffered in the hazardous delivery of goods to north Russia constituted substantial evidence of American goodwill. By 1944–5, with the opening of new routes in the south through Iran, American aid was delivered in considerable quantity and significantly assisted the Soviet military machine as it drove the Germans back across Europe. Roosevelt hoped that American wartime aid, along with the promise of post-war reconstruction aid, would be a significant sweetener in US–Soviet relations.

Yet, while American public opinion and many elements within the Roosevelt administration grew more optimistic with regard to closer US–Soviet relations in the war years, hard-headed diplomats such as George Kennan and Charles Bohlen were much more wary of the prospects of US–Soviet reconciliation continuing into peacetime. Kennan, who became counsellor in the US embassy in 1944, argued that gestures of goodwill were of no value in dealing with the Soviets. Indeed, he warned that they could be counter-productive and be interpreted as signs of weakness to be exploited to Soviet advantage. With regard to economic and military assistance, for example, the Soviet government did not reveal the source of Lend-Lease aid to the Soviet people until June 1944. By 1944–5 two further issues of immense importance developed which suggested even further that the euphoria of the wartime spirit of co-operation concealed deep-seated differences between the two sides, namely, Eastern Europe and the atomic bomb.

When the Red Army in January 1944 pushed beyond the Soviet border and began to liberate Eastern Europe from the Nazis, major problems arose between the Soviets and the Western allies. In Poland the government established in the wake of the Red Army in the city of Lublin appeared to be manifestly a Communist puppet government which would make Poland a satellite of the Soviet Union. Furthermore, various incidents seemed to reveal a cynical Soviet aim of eliminating non-Communist opposition in Poland. In April 1943 the bodies of thousands of Polish army officers who had been executed in 1941 were discovered in the Katyn Forest, and whereas it had earlier been thought that the destruction of this elite of the Polish army had been the work of the Germans, strong suspicion arose that the massacre had in fact been perpetrated by the Soviets. In August 1944 when the Red Army approached Warsaw it halted its advance when the Polish resistance rose up against the Nazis and only when the Germans had annihilated the Polish resistance did the Red Army resume its advance into Warsaw. Although Stalin offered a not implausible case on military grounds for the halt of the Red Army before Warsaw and claimed that the Polish resistance had not co-ordinated plans with Soviet forces, the US government and American public opinion suspected a more sinister purpose behind Stalin's action. The assumption in the United States was that Stalin wished the Germans to eliminate the Polish resistance, who were strongly anti-Communist, so that a Soviet puppet government could be more easily installed in Poland. In Poland, as in Rumania, Hungary and elsewhere in Eastern Europe, Stalin appeared to be pursing the policy which he later enunciated to the Yugoslav leader, Marshal Tito, 'Whoever occupies a territory imposes on it his own social system. . . . It cannot be otherwise'.[6] At the same time the Soviet Union pressed ahead with the rearrangement of Poland's borders, pushing Poland's eastern frontier to the west with Soviet annexation of the intervening territory, while Poland was compensated by the acquisition of German territory with the extension of Poland's western frontier to the Oder–Neisse line.

Some Americans, such as George Kennan, argued that the United States should accept its impotence in Eastern Europe and write off the region as a Soviet sphere of influence, while preventing Soviet expansion elsewhere. Kennan, however, was a calculating professional diplomat with no political constituency and with disdain for the passions of democratic politics. Roosevelt, on the other hand, was a consummate politician who faced re-election in November 1944 and was under severe pressure from Polish-Americans in particular and from the American public in general to express moral repugnance over Soviet policy in Eastern Europe. Roosevelt refused, therefore, to endorse a *realpolitik* settlement which Churchill made with Stalin in October 1944, whereby percentages of influence in different countries were assigned, such as 90 per cent British influence in Greece, 75 per cent Soviet influence in Rumania.

Roosevelt assessed, however, that Soviet policy in Eastern Europe was motivated partly by ideological ambition to expand Communism but also by security considerations, given the devastation caused by the German invasion of the Soviet Union and the Soviet need to ensure that the Germans could not again march unimpeded through Eastern Europe in an assault against the Soviet Union. Roosevelt therefore concluded that a major task of American statesmanship was to allay Soviet security concerns while preventing the imposition of Soviet puppet regimes on the East European countries. Roosevelt set out to achieve this objective by his usual approach of pragmatism and obfustication, which he hoped would succeed as a result of personal diplomacy with Stalin. Arrangements were therefore made for a summit meeting at Yalta in the Crimea in February 1945 between Roosevelt, Churchill and Stalin. Pessimists in US government circles, however, despaired that the equation of satisfaction of Soviet security requirements and preservation of democratic rights in Eastern Europe was in any circumstances attainable and that, moreover, Soviet purposes went beyond security concerns to an unremitting drive for unlimited Communist expansion. Churchill came to share this gloomy prognosis, writing to Roosevelt on the eve of Yalta, 'This may well be a fateful conference. . . . The end of this war may well prove to be more disappointing than was the last'.[7]

The name Yalta has become synonymous with betrayal and stab in the back. In fact, the terms of the Yalta Agreement on Eastern Europe, particularly on Poland, were quite satisfactory. It was not the terms of Yalta, but Stalin's failure to abide by the terms, which created difficulties. Stalin agreed that the Lublin government should be broadened to include representatives of the Polish government-in-exile in London as well as other non-Communist elements from within Poland. Moreover, this was to be merely an interim government and there should shortly be 'free and unfettered elections' in Poland.[8] When Roosevelt asked how long it might be before elections took place, Stalin, as Diane Clemens has written, 'guessed only a month, accepting Roosevelt's hint that the arguments over the composition of an interim government were unimportant since the future would be decided by free elections'.[9] Furthermore, although it was a statement of generalizations, the Declaration on Liberated Europe stipulated that all liberated countries should enjoy democracy when freed from Nazi occupation.

With regard to the terms of Yalta relating to the Far East, Roosevelt's major concern was to win a Soviet commitment to enter the war against Japan after the end of the war in Europe. Stalin agreed that the Soviet Union would enter the war against Japan three months after the end of the war against Germany. Roosevelt was prepared to pay a price for Stalin's commitment, namely, agreement that the Chinese, on whose behalf Roosevelt spoke without informing the Chinese leader Chiang Kai-shek, would grant to the Soviet Union the lease of Dairen and accept joint Soviet-Chinese use of Port Arthur and of the Chinese Eastern and Southern Manchurian Railway. Roosevelt resented Soviet *realpolitik* which led him to make these concessions behind China's back. But this was more than compensated for, in Roosevelt's view, by Soviet commitment to enter the war in the Far East, which it was calculated – at a time when reliance could not be placed on the atomic bomb – would shorten the war against Japan and save a great number of American lives.

Roosevelt's other major interest at Yalta was to secure Soviet agreement to join the United Nations Organization. Roosevelt, as Adam Ulam has put it, appeared to have a 'strange infatuation' with the United Nations.[10] Churchill, by comparison, viewed the United Nations as an embodiment of pious hopes. Roosevelt, however, was far from a naïve moralist, but a shrewd politician with an ear close to the grassroots of American public opinion. Roosevelt appreciated that the United Nations not only helped to ensure against a post-war relapse into isolationism, which Roosevelt feared, but also filled American psychological needs in making the post-war settlement seem not simply a division of the spoils by the victorious powers but the establishment of a new world order of peace, a vital element of which was the continuation of good relations with the Soviet Union.

Personal relations at Yalta between Roosevelt, Churchill and Stalin were good, and after the conference Roosevelt expressed the view that the United States could expect to get along very well with Stalin and with the Soviet people. Within days after the end of the Yalta conference, however, it became clear that Stalin was not adhering to the terms of the agreement. Harriman, who had been appointed US ambassador to the Soviet Union, sent gloomy reports from Moscow in March and April 1945 that the Soviet interpretation of democracy was widely at variance with the accepted Western view of the term. In the last month of Roosevelt's life he sent several messages to Stalin regarding violations of the Yalta agreements on Eastern Europe.

With Roosevelt's death on 12 April 1945, the succession of President Harry Truman, some commentators suggest, marked a sharp break in American policy towards the Soviet Union. Roosevelt, it is suggested, was sensitive to Soviet needs and, while objecting to undemocratic policies in Eastern Europe, sought a compromise acceptable to Stalin. Truman, on the other hand, the argument runs, was guided by hardline anti-Soviet advisers such as his aide Admiral William Leahy, thereby bringing on a sudden deterioration in relations. Denna F. Fleming goes so far as to suggest that 'It is altogether probable that if Roosevelt had been able to finish his fourth term in the White House there would have been no Cold War'.[11]

The evidence suggests, however, that Truman essentially continued Roosevelt's policies of protesting on the one hand over the denial of democratic freedom in Eastern Europe but attempting on the other hand to maintain a basis of agreement with the Soviet Union. Truman demonstrated the first side of this policy – namely, blunt protest over Soviet policies in Eastern Europe – in a celebrated meeting with Molotov on 23 April 1945. Truman gave the Soviet Foreign Minister a dressing down, prompting Molotov to state that he had never been talked to in that manner in his life. 'Carry out your agreements and you won't get talked to like that' was Truman's curt reply.[12] 'How I enjoyed translating those words', wrote Charles Bohlen, who was interpreter at the meeting.[13] Bohlen, Truman and other writers of memoirs as well as later historians have galvanized Truman's straight talking at this meeting which more than any other single incident created the image of Truman as a resolute, unequivocating leader who, unlike Roosevelt, was willing to express blunt truths in plain, straightforward language. In fact, however,

Truman's curt decisiveness has been exaggerated in accounts by Truman himself and by other writers. After the opening encounter with Molotov, Truman's policy towards the Soviet Union was equivocating, exploratory and hesitant, differing little from Roosevelt's. He sought advice not only from hardliners but also, for example, from Joseph Davies, a fellow Missourian with whom he had frequently played poker over the years. Davies told Truman that he feared a 'Soviet Napoleon' who might 'overthrow and destroy the present altruistic, ideological purpose of peace and brotherhood which the present government avows'.[14] In May 1945 Truman sent Harry Hopkins, who was closely identified with Roosevelt, to Moscow to smooth over differences. Truman told Hopkins that 'he could use diplomatic language or he could use a baseball bat if he thought that was the proper approach to Mr Stalin'.[15] When Hopkins predictably chose the former, Truman gave his support and in July 1945 granted diplomatic recognition to the new Polish government, which had been broadened from the Lublin government but only to the extent of one-third representation of non-Lublin Poles and with many reservations made with regard to free elections in the future.

Truman also continued Roosevelt's policy regarding adherence to the zones of military occupation which had been agreed with the Soviets in 1943. By early 1945 Churchill concluded that Britain and the United States should gain as much territory as possible. On 1 April 1945 Churchill wrote to Roosevelt advocating that 'we should march as far east into Germany as possible and that should Berlin be in our grasp we should certainly take it'.[16] Roosevelt disagreed with Churchill on political grounds, since this would be a blatant breach of faith which would destroy all possibility of post-war co-operation with the Soviets, while Eisenhower, on military grounds, felt that to take Berlin would distract from the major military objective of destroying Germany's armies. After Roosevelt's death, Churchill tried to persuade Truman of the wisdom of gaining and holding as much territory as possible, irrespective of earlier agreements. On 4 June 1945 Churchill wrote to Truman, deploring the withdrawal of Allied troops to the agreed lines, 'thus bringing Soviet power into the heart of Western Europe and the descent of an iron curtain between us and everything to the eastward'.[17] But Truman was adamant that the zones of occupation should remain as agreed earlier.

When American and Soviet troops met, relations between them were very warm. The first meeting took place on 25 April 1945 when Lieutenant William Robertson crossed a bridge over the Elbe to meet Major Alexei Gorlinsky. Twenty miles to the south at Torgau Lieutenant Albert Kotzebue and Private Joseph Polowsky met Colonel Alexander Olshansky. Gorlinsky greeted Robertson with the words, 'You are a capitalist, I am a communist', and they laughed, embraced, took out bottles and had drinks.[18] The meeting at Torgau was in similar spirits. Ideological differences, it seemed, were no obstacle to good relations when face-to-face contact was established and there was soldierly comradeship. At the highest level Eisenhower and the Soviet commander, Marshal Georgi Zhukov, developed a very good relationship while working together in Berlin after the German surrender in May 1945. In early August 1945 Eisenhower flew to Moscow and at a soccer match in Moscow Dynamo stadium Eisenhower and Zhukov were introduced to the crowd at the half-time interval with arms around one another's shoulders and were greeted with wild applause.

Following the end of the war in Europe, the third and last of the Big Three wartime conferences was held on the outskirts of Berlin at Potsdam between 17 July and 2 August 1945. Agreement was reached on the occupation zones in Germany and on the level of reparations to be extracted from Germany. A more dramatic issue, however, surfaced at Potsdam – news of the successful test of the atomic bomb at Los Alamos in New Mexico.

At the outbreak of the Second World War the British were furthest advanced in nuclear physics, but they feared that the Germans might overtake them in this field and develop an atomic bomb. Consequently, Churchill approached Roosevelt in 1941 and proposed that the nuclear project be transferred to the United States, where British and American scientists would collaborate, along with some exiled French nuclear physicists and with the assistance of the Canadians, who could supply uranium. Although the United States in 1941 was still neutral, Roosevelt agreed to Churchill's proposal and the Manhattan Project was begun. The matter was a secret unknown to all but a tiny handful in the United States and Britain. It was not revealed, for example, to the vice-president of the United States or to the deputy prime minister of Britain. Very significantly, it was not revealed to the Soviet Union. Among American scientists who worked on the project some felt that the Soviet Union should be informed. Robert Oppenheimer, for example, felt that if it proved possible to manufacture an atomic bomb, it was all the more vital to ensure post-war Soviet–American friendship, since hostility could result in nuclear war. Post-war friendship could not be achieved, Oppenheimer felt, if the West concealed from their wartime ally a matter of such momentous potential importance. Physicist Niels Bohr argued that in any event the Soviets were liable to find out from their intelligence sources about the atomic project, and it was therefore preferable that the United States should officially inform the Soviet government, even if specific details were not revealed.

Roosevelt decided, however, that no information on the nuclear project should be disclosed to the Soviet Union. At a meeting at Hyde Park between Churchill and Roosevelt on 18 September 1944 agreement was confirmed by the two Western leaders to withhold knowledge of the existence of the nuclear project from the Soviet Union. Did Roosevelt commit a serious error in withholding information on the atomic bomb from the Soviets, losing an opportunity to add substantially to Soviet–American trust and co-operation? A good case can be made for an affirmative answer to this question. Martin Sherwin concludes that 'In relation to the complex problem of the origins of the Cold War, the Hyde Park meeting . . . is far more important than historians have generally recognized'.[19] On the other hand, if Roosevelt had given information in general terms regarding the bomb this would inevitably have led to a Soviet request for more specific information, and disclosure of details on nuclear matters to the Soviet Union was so liable to produce a later political backlash within the United States that it was out of the question.

When Truman became president on 12 April 1945 he had no knowledge of the Manhattan Project, and he required a lengthy briefing on the atomic bomb on 13 April by Secretary of War Henry Stimson. The date of the Potsdam conference was fixed to coincide with the test of the bomb at Los Alamos, so that Truman was at Potsdam when the code message was delivered to him, 'The baby is born', that is, the test had been successful. Truman decided that he would inform Stalin. After the formal negotiating session on 24 July 1945 Truman stayed behind to talk to Stalin and told him, in somewhat general terms, about the atomic bomb and the successful test. Charles Bohlen, who acted as interpreter, records in his memoirs that Stalin was stoney-faced and showed no particular reaction. Bohlen concluded that either Stalin did not fully understand or that he already knew about the matter from intelligence sources. The latter was the correct interpretation. Among other sources, Klaus Fuchs, a Communist, German-born naturalized British nuclear physicist, had worked at Harwell and Los Alamos and supplied information to the Communist cell headed by Julius and Ethel Rosenberg, who passed on information to Soviet contacts.

On 26 July 1945 the Potsdam Proclamation was issued, calling on Japan to surrender. When Japan did not, an atomic bomb was dropped on Hiroshima on 6 August 1945, and a second atomic bomb dropped on Nagasaki on 9 August 1945. Some historians, such as Gar Alperovitz, have argued that the primary reason for the use of the atomic bomb on Hiroshima and Nagasaki was to intimidate the Soviet Union rather than to defeat Japan. Such historians suggest that Japan was on the point of surrender and had sent out peace feelers to the Soviet Union, so that the use of the atomic bomb was unnecessary in order to end the war against Japan. Its use in a wartime situation, it is argued, was intended to make a dramatic impact on the Soviet Union by sending an implied warning of the possible consequences if the Soviets alienated the United States. Truman, however, asserted that his purpose in using the atomic bomb was simply to end the war swiftly and to save American lives. Truman argued that the peace feelers to the Soviet Union were not sufficiently substantial and that only the shock of the atomic bomb would persuade the Japanese emperor to surrender, which he did on 14 August 1945. As Truman and his apologists recognize, however, an incidental consequence of the dropping of the atomic bomb on Japan was to cause grave anxiety to the Soviet Union. Heated controversy has continued on the question, as Barton Bernstein cogently expressed it:

> whether anti-Soviet purposes constituted the *primary* reason for using the bomb . . . or a *secondary but necessary reason* . . . or a *confirming but not essential* . . . reason is the general range of the ongoing dispute about why the bombs were used.[20]

But, as J. Samuel Walker concluded in a survey of the historiographical literature on the subject, 'The consensus of the mid-1970s, which held that the bomb was used primarily for military reasons and secondarily for diplomatic reasons, continues to prevail'.[21]

On 8 August 1945 the Soviet Union entered the war against

Japan, adhering precisely to the agreement to enter the Far Eastern war three months after the end of the war in Europe. Hiroshima, however, had changed the situation entirely, so that whereas a major goal of American diplomacy throughout the war had been to bring about Soviet entry into the war against Japan, the dropping of the atomic bomb on 6 August 1945 made the United States wish to keep the Soviet Union out of the Far Eastern war, since this would enable the Soviets to seek concessions and to exert influence in China and Japan. It was suggested that Soviet entry into the war against Japan might act as the shock needed to bring about Japanese surrender, without the need for the use of the atomic bomb. Truman asserted that the atomic bomb was a weapon like any other weapon, though vastly more powerful, and when ready for use it should be used. It is clear, however, that Truman much preferred a victory over Japan achieved by the United States by means of the atomic bomb than a victory brought about by Soviet entry into the war against Japan.

The issue of the atomic bomb, therefore, illustrated very clearly the fundamental lack of trust between the United States and the Soviet Union during the Second World War. This distrust had also been demonstrated with regard to other issues such as the second front, suspicion of Soviet intensions in Eastern Europe or the bitter Soviet accusation in February 1945 that the rapid advance of the Allied armies was due to a secret agreement negotiated with the Nazis. On the other hand, trust was not the heart of the matter. Neither Roosevelt nor Truman was so naïve as to trust Stalin. The heart of the matter was to achieve an accommodation based on mutual self-interest which would permit a post-war settlement of peaceful co-existence between two nations of different ideologies. That the US–Soviet alliance of the Second World War was in many respects a wartime alliance of convenience is self-evidently obvious. But it is too simplistic to characterize the developing relationship in those years as no more than an alliance of convenience for short-term purposes which was bound to disintegrate when the common enemy was defeated. Given the exhaustion of the Soviet Union at the end of the war, the desire in the United States for demobilization, the residue of goodwill towards America's gallant Soviet ally and the American faith that the United Nations might symbolize and embody universal aspirations for a new world order of peace, an accommodation between the two superpowers in 1945 seemed not impossible.

5

THE ORIGINS OF THE COLD WAR, 1945–50

The hope that wartime US–Soviet co-operation could be sustained in the post-war years turned to ashes in the late 1940s. Instead of the dream of One World and reconciliation between nations with different social systems, a relationship of deeply bitter hostility developed between the United States and the Soviet Union, bringing on the Cold War and the arms race. Why did the wartime alliance break down and the Cold War ensue? Broadly, two answers have been given – namely, the traditional and the revisionist interpretations of the origins of the Cold War. According to the traditional interpretation, which was advanced in the memoirs of participants such as Harry Truman and Dean Acheson and by the majority of contemporary commentators and by historians until the 1960s, the onset of the Cold War was due quite simply to Soviet failure to adhere to wartime agreements and to Soviet ambition to expand Communism as far as possible and the American need to prevent such expansion. The revisionist view, which was put forward by some contemporary dissidents such as Henry Wallace and by a number of historians writing in the 1960s, holds that the causes of the Cold War are by no means so black and white and that the United States was as responsible for the Cold War as the Soviet Union. Revisionists argue that Soviet objectives were largely defensive and were misinterpreted by American policy-makers. American objectives were not so innocent and idealistic as simply the defence of freedom and democracy . . . but, revisionists suggest, included also the goal of global economic imperialism. How convincing is the traditional or the revisionist interpretation? An assessment can be made by an examination in some detail of each in turn.

Traditionalists argue that the Soviet goal of world-wide expansion of Communism had not altered since 1917. There had been changes of tactics, it is suggested, to adjust to Soviet weakness in the inter-war years and to the Second World War threat from Hitler, but underlying objectives did not change. With the Nazi defeat and the build-up of the Red Army, Stalin exploited the opportunity at the end of the war to expand Communism into Eastern Europe and was bent on the expansion of Communism into Western Europe, the Middle East and elsewhere. The Cold War was brought on by the resistance to Soviet ambitions on the part of the Western powers, especially by the only Western nation with sufficient strength to hold back the Communist tide, namely the United States. As Arthur Schlesinger, Jr, put it, the Cold War was 'the brave and essential response of free men to Communist aggression'.[1]

In Eastern Europe, traditionalists suggest that the pattern of events in Poland, Czechoslovakia, Hungary, Romania and the other countries of East Europe illustrate a cynical manipulation of events in order to produce the Soviet goal of a Communist puppet government in each of these countries. In Poland, for example, the government which the United States recognized in July 1945, which was a coalition of Communists and non-Communists, was steadily taken over by Polish Communists with Soviet assistance. From late 1945 to early 1947 non-Communists were systematically eliminated from the government by means of intimidation, terror and manipulation, leading to the imprisonment, exile or death of any figures who attempted to resist Communist pressure, such as Stanislaus Mikolajczyk, the former leader of the Polish government-in-exile in London, who was forced out of his position of deputy premier and driven into exile. Only when the Communists were fully in control of the government was an election held in Poland in January 1947, which was blatantly rigged and illustrated the ruthless methods of Communist take-over.

In Hungary, relatively free elections in November 1945 produced a coalition of Communists and non-Communists such as the Smallholders Party. Hungarian Communists, however, with Soviet support, gradually removed non-Communists from power, so that by the end of 1946 Hungary was a Soviet satellite with a puppet Communist government in full control. In Rumania, King Michael was forced into exile and non-Communists were driven out of government, leading to complete Communist control by early 1947. A similar pattern developed in other East European countries, while British and American requests to send in observers to Bulgaria, Rumania and Hungary, as permitted under Allied Control Commission agreements, were curtly refused.

In Yugoslavia, Communists under Tito had come to power in 1945 independently of Moscow, but when Tito refused to accept Stalin's orders, Stalin broke with Tito in 1948 and attempted to exert pressure within Yugoslavia for his overthrow and replacement by a more compliant Communist leader. Meantime in 1947 the Cominform was established, which the West viewed as a revival of the old Comintern, designed to use Communist parties world-wide as agents of destabilization and as tools of Soviet foreign policy.

The clearest example of Soviet Communist imperialism in Eastern Europe, traditionalists argue, was Czechoslovakia. The Czechs had a tradition of friendship with the Russians, their fellow Slavs to whom they looked for protection against their common enemy, the Germans. Pre-war Czechoslovakia had been a democratic state which was quite well-disposed towards the Soviet Union, unlike other East European countries which had right-wing, anti-Soviet regimes in the inter-war years. After the Second World War Czechoslovakia resumed its democratic tradition, with an election in 1946 in which the Communists won 38 per cent of the vote and formed part of the governing coalition. Hence, traditionalists argue, Czechoslovakia was a model of the type of country which revisionists allege that the Soviet Union wished to have on its borders, namely, a government which was progressive rather than reactionary in domestic policy and friendly to the Soviet Union in foreign policy. But the same pattern of events developed in Czechoslovakia as in other East European countries. Czechoslovak Communists used their positions in office, especially in the Labour and Interior departments, to destabilize the government, encouraging violent strikes which the police did not control, and on 25 February 1948 the Communists seized power. Two weeks later on 10 March 1948 Jan Masaryk, the most prominent non-Communist in the Czech government, fell from a top-floor window of the Foreign Ministry and though the Communists claimed that his mysterious defenestration was suicide, there was strong suspicion that he had in fact been pushed. The Communist coup in Czechoslovakia was the clearest evidence to contemporary American statesmen and to later traditionalist historians that Soviet designs were far from merely defensive, seeking friendly governments in countries which bordered on the Soviet Union, but were manifestly aggressive, seeking every opportunity to accomplish the goal which they had held since the Bolshevik Revolution of expanding Communism world-wide by means of violent revolution.

Soviet policy in Germany, traditionalists argue, provided further evidence of the dangerous trend of Soviet expansionism. At Potsdam Germany was divided into four occupation zones, with four-power occupation of Berlin, which lay within the Soviet zone, and it was agreed that Germany should be treated as an economic unit. To allay Soviet fears of a revived military threat from Germany, the United States offered in 1946 to sign a twenty-year mutual security treaty stipulating that an attack by Germany on any of the signatories would be regarded as an attack on all. Britain and France were willing to sign such a treaty, but the Soviet Union rejected the offer. The Soviets received reparations from the western zones of Germany and they took reparations from the eastern zone in the form of tearing apart German factories and taking the parts back to the Soviet Union, illustrating the fate which would befall Western nations, traditionalists suggest, if marauding Soviet conquerors gained control. The Soviets set up a puppet regime in the eastern zone of Germany headed by the Communist Walter Ulbricht. But Soviet objectives with regard to Germany went beyond control of the eastern zone. As Herbert Feis, a State department official and later historian, put it:

> Almost certainly Stalin and his Bolshevik company had hoped that the beaten and disillusioned masses in *all* of Germany, not merely in the eastern zone, might, in the chaos and distress, turn to Russia. Would the revolutionary veterans in Moscow have forgotten that call to revolution – of which Stalin had been one of the co-signers – sent to the leaders of the militant section of the German Social Democratic Party in 1918, or the affirmation of Lenin's Farewell Letter to the Swiss workers written before he entrained for Russia: 'The revolution will not stop at Russia. The German proletariat is the most faithful and reliable ally of the Russian and world-wide revolution'.[2]

In the Middle East the Soviets aimed to expand, in the traditionalist view, into Iran and Turkey and from there throughout the entire Middle East. During the war Iran was occupied by the British in the south and by the Soviets in the north, in order to prevent German occupation. An agreement was made that British and Soviet forces would withdraw six months after the end of the war. In September 1945 a withdrawal date of 2 March 1946 was agreed upon. In late 1945, however, it became clear that the Soviets were adding to their troop levels in Iran and using the Iranian Communist party, the Tudeh Party, to encourage a separatist movement in the Iranian province of Azerbaijan in order to incorporate it into the Soviet republic of Azerbaijan across the border. Soviet forces blocked roads to prevent the Shah's troops from moving into Azerbaijan, and despite Iranian protests to the United Nations Soviet forces remained in northern Iran beyond the withdrawal date of 2 March 1946. Meanwhile, Turkey came under pressure to cede to the Soviet Union the provinces of Kars and Ardahan in northern Turkey, to allow Soviet ships the right of transit through the Straits and to grant a base in the Straits to the Soviet navy. The Soviet aim, traditionalists argue, was to expand into Turkey and Iran and thereby into the Middle East, in the same manner as they expanded into Eastern Europe, fulfilling the twin objectives of achieving traditional Russian foreign policy goals and expanding Communist ideology. As Dean Acheson later wrote, 'In picking the Straits and Iran as points of pressure, they followed the route of barbarians against classical Greece and Rome and later of the czars to warm water'.[3]

Further Soviet malevolence was shown, traditionalists suggest, by Soviet policy over the atomic bomb. In the United States intense and lengthy discussions took place within government circles in late 1945 and early 1946 over the implications of the development of atomic weapons. The outcome was the Baruch Plan, presented to the United Nations in June 1946 by Bernard Baruch, US Special Representative on the UN Atomic Energy Commission. The Baruch Plan proposed that all atomic energy development should be under the control of the United Nations, which would promote atomic energy development for peaceful purposes and ensure against atomic energy development for military purposes. To make effective the prohibition against military development, the United Nations would have wide powers of inspection and the right to impose severe sanctions on violators. Moreover, to make certain that no violator could escape detection and the imposition of sanctions, the permanent members of the Security Council would not have a veto on this issue, as they did on all other matters. When the plan came into operation and the machinery for its enforcement was in place, the United States would destroy its stockpile of atomic bombs. The United States felt that this proposal for international control of atomic energy was a very imaginative and generous approach to the matter. As James Byrnes, US Secretary of State from 1945 to 1946, later wrote, 'I do not believe in all history there is a record of a more unselfish offer than this willingness to surrender our monopoly of this terrible weapon, nor stronger evidence of our desire for peace'.[4]

The Soviet Union, however, rebuffed the Baruch Plan. Instead, the Soviets proposed that all nuclear weapons should be destroyed and a ban imposed on their manufacture in future. No provision was made on verification, however, as the Soviets rejected any proposals regarding inspection as attempts to gain opportunities for spying. Moreover, the Soviets refused to give up their Security Council veto on the issue. In the traditional view, the Soviets aborted the American proposal and submitted a manifestly unacceptable counter-proposal because the Soviet government had already begun work on an atomic bomb, aided by information from Western spies and captured German scientists, and they aimed to deploy atomic weapons as soon as possible in order to enable them to exert political blackmail.

In the traditional interpretation, the United States made every effort in the years 1945–7 to show goodwill to the Soviet Union but was persistently rebuffed. The United States demobilized very rapidly, reducing its manpower in the armed forces from 12 million in mid-1945 to 1.5 million by the end of 1946, so that the conventional forces of the United States were clearly no threat to any other power. In diplomatic negotiations, the US Secretary of State met every three months at meetings of the Council of Foreign Ministers, which had been established at Potsdam for quarterly meetings of the foreign ministers of the United States, the Soviet Union, Britain and France. Secretary of State Byrnes tried to appreciate the Soviet point of view, to such an extent that Truman told him in January 1946 that he was 'tired of babying the Soviets'.[5] But Soviet Foreign Minister Molotov was so negative and obstructive that meetings of the Council of Foreign Ministers were suspended after December 1947. Meantime, the United States became concerned over a speech by Stalin in February 1946 which seemed to suggest a return to ideological denunciation of the warlike attitudes of the capitalist states. In response to a State Department request to the US embassy in Moscow for an interpretative analysis of this speech, George Kennan, counsellor in the embassy, sent back a long telegram in which he enunciated the concept of containment, which became the cornerstone of US policy towards the Soviet Union.

Kennan argued that Soviet policy was expansionist but at the same time cautious. Kennan did not feel that Stalin had abandoned the proselytizing aims of the Bolsheviks but that Stalin on the other hand was not willing to take risks, especially the risk of war, in order to expand Communism. Kennan therefore recommended a policy of containment, holding back the forward march of Soviet expansionism, not in a manner to provoke war but in order to produce a stalemate until the time would come when the Soviet Union would reform from within. In an article in *Foreign Affairs* in July 1947 in which Kennan, under the pseudonym of X, published his ideas on containment, he wrote that 'the main element of any United States policy toward the Soviet Union must be that of a long-term, patient but firm and vigilant containment of Russian expansionist tendencies'.[6]

The first application of containment occurred with the Truman Doctrine in 1947 with regard to Greece and Turkey. In February 1947 Britain informed the United States that financial difficulties necessitated a cut-back of overseas commitments, which would involve the withdrawal of British troops who were sustaining the Greek Royalist government against Communist insurgents in the Greek civil war. Truman asked Congress in March 1947 for $400 million in military and economic aid for Greece and for Turkey. In his message to Congress Truman went beyond a specific request for aid for Greece and Turkey but pronounced the Truman Doctrine in universalist terms, stating that 'It must be the policy of the United States to support free peoples who are resisting attempted subjugation by armed minorities or by outside pressures'.[7]

By 1947 economic chaos in Western Europe appeared to present an excellent opportunity for Communism to expand into Western Europe, especially in countries with a large Communist party such as France and Italy. Despite piecemeal aid since 1945 through UNRRA (United Nations Relief and Rehabilitation Agency) the economies of Western European countries had failed to make a significant start to recovery from the war, and the unusually severe winter of 1946–7 left most of Western Europe in economic crisis by early 1947. In response to the crisis, the United States devised the Marshall Plan, whereby the United States supplied the Western European countries with dollar aid to enable them to purchase food, fuel, machinery and other necessities in order to avoid collapse and to achieve a level of self-sustaining economic growth. The Marshall Plan was so successful that, although initially intended to be a four-year programme from 1948 to 1952, aid ceased to most countries after December 1950. The Marshall Plan was enlightened self-interest on the part of the United States. It was a generous, humanitarian programme which saved vast numbers of Europeans from hunger and devastation, while at the same time it built up Western Europe as a prosperous trading partner of the United States and reduced the prospect of a Communist assumption of power in any nation of Western Europe.

Economic recovery was of limited value, however, while Western Europe felt vulnerable to a military threat from the Soviet Union. In June 1948 the Soviets appeared to probe at Western Europe's most vulnerable point, West Berlin, closing off access by rail and road from the western zones of Germany to West Berlin, in violation of wartime four-power agreements. Truman's measured response of the airlift to Berlin avoided either war or surrender and resulted in triumph for the West with the reopening of the overland access routes in May 1949. The Berlin crisis, however, together with such episodes as the Czech coup in February 1948 and Soviet threats to Norway in March 1948, led to negotiations between the Western European countries and the United States to devise a security arrangement which would deter the Soviet Union from an attack on Western Europe. The negotiations culminated in the North Atlantic Treaty of 4 April 1949 and the formation of NATO. In September 1949 the shock of a successful Soviet atomic test acted as a spur to closer co-ordination between the United States and her NATO allies, while America's arsenal of atomic bombs, grew from two in 1945 to thirteen in 1947 to 250 in 1949.

The traditional interpretation concludes that the establishment of this collective security system in resistance to Soviet threats was necessary and successful. It defended the interests of the West in deterring the Soviet Union, preventing the expansion of Communism and keeping peace. Post-war American leaders, like their contemporaries in Europe, felt that they must learn from the mistakes of the 1930s. Isolationism, appeasement and military weakness, it was concluded, had tempted Hitler to aggressive expansion. The post-war generation of Truman, Marshall, Acheson and such figures felt that they constructed unity and strength which contained the new threat from Stalin, as their predecessors had failed to contain Hitler. In the traditional view of the origins of the Cold War, therefore, it was regrettable that it proved necessary to devote vast resources to military expenditure rather than to peaceful purposes, but the responsibility for this state of affairs lay squarely with the Soviet Union. Moreover, given the formidable threat from the Soviet Union, the West, under the leadership of the United States, could take pride in its accomplishment of keeping peace, deterring Communist expansion and building a prosperous, non-Communist Western Europe.

Revisionists, however, challenge many of the basic assumptions upon which the traditionalist interpretation rests. With regard to Eastern Europe, revisionists emphasize Soviet security requirements, which Hitler's invasion of the Soviet Union had made abundantly clear. With the loss of over 20 million people – the most recent Soviet figures place the number as high as 27 million – and the devastation of a third of its territory in the Second World War the Soviets deemed it vital for Soviet security that the countries which bordered on the Soviet Union should not have anti-Soviet governments which would either support or be unable to prevent another invasion of the Soviet Union. The Soviet Union did not set up Communist puppet governments in the wake of the Red Army as nations of Eastern Europe were liberated. In 1945–6 each country in Eastern Europe had a coalition of Communists and non-Communists. Revisionists argue that the Soviet Union was prepared to accept such coalition governments. The Truman administration, however, showed intransigence and inflexibility and in its criticism of the imperfections of the new democracies in Eastern Europe appeared to press for changes which were likely to result in the accession to power of staunchly anti-Soviet governments in Eastern European countries. In response to Western inflexibility, the Soviet government became less flexible in the years 1945–7 and concluded that only complete control of neighbouring countries by means of a Communist satellite government could ensure Soviet security, and the Soviets therefore eliminated non-Communists from the governments of East European nations. 'Had their security requirements been met', Gar Alperovitz writes, 'there is evidence that their domination of Eastern Europe

THE ORIGINS OF THE COLD WAR

might have been different from what it turned out to be'.[8] In Finland, a nation with which the Soviet Union had been at war in 1939–40 and which sided with the Nazis in 1941–5, the Soviet Union accepted a non-Communist government which was progressive in domestic policy and pro-Soviet in its foreign policy. Revisionists argue that the Soviet Union was prepared to accept the Finnish model for the whole of Eastern Europe, but US intransigence made it seem that the Soviet Union needed to choose between pro-Western, anti-Soviet regimes or Communist satellite governments. Faced with such a choice, the Soviets had to choose the latter, which was then misinterpreted in the West as a drive towards world-wide expansion of Communism rather than as a limited defensive measure to protect Soviet security by ensuring friendly governments in bordering countries.

Furthermore, revisionists argue, Soviet policies in Eastern Europe were little different from British and American policies in Western European countries such as Italy and Greece. The Soviet Union did not aid the Greek Communists, though aid was sent by Yugoslav, Albanian and Bulgarian Communists. Thus, Stalin abided by the October 1944 percentages agreement with regard to Greece, and it was reasonable, therefore, revisionists argue, that the Soviet Union should have its terms of the percentages agreement in Eastern Europe. Similarly, in Italy the United States refused any Soviet participation in the occupation of Italy, as the Soviets refused Allied participation in the Balkan countries, and while the United States professed adherence to the solemn principles of freedom and democracy the CIA secretly worked to support the Christian Democrats in Italian elections and to discredit the Italian Communists. As Henry Wallace argued,

> We should recognize that we have no more business in the political affairs of Eastern Europe than Russia has in the political affairs of Latin America, Western Europe or the United States. . . . Whether we like it or not, the Russians will try to socialize their sphere of influence just as we try to democratize our sphere of influence.[9]

With regard to Germany, revisionists argue that the United States was very insensitive to legitimate Soviet fears of a revised German threat. The levels of industry agreement of Potsdam, which were designed to ensure against a more rapid economic recovery by Germany than by other nations, were soon abandoned by the United States. The United States was more interested in German economic recovery as the key to Western European economic recovery and was prepared to turn a blind eye to prominent ex-Nazis in important positions in industry in the western zones of Germany. Byrnes's offer of a four-power mutual security treaty as a guarantee against attack by Germany is dismissed by revisionists as an unreliable paper promise in which the Soviets could not be expected to place their trust for their security. The Soviets consequently aimed to reduce the German threat by the imposition of a loyal Communist regime in the sector of Germany which they controlled. With regard to reparations, the United States was in a financial position to regard reparations as unimportant, but the devastation of the Soviet economy as the result of the German invasion meant that the Soviet Union vitally required German reparations from the eastern zone, yet General Lucius Clay in 1946 ordered the end of reparations from the western zones of Germany to the Soviet Union, in violation of the Potsdam agreement.

In Iran, revisionists argue, the Soviet Union had no intention of attempting to spread Communism through Iran into the Middle East. Given the long border between Iran and the Soviet Union, the Soviet government wished to ensure order in northern Iran before Soviet forces withdrew, especially with possible danger to Soviet oil refineries in Baku if there was instability across the border in Iran. Western protests in the United Nations against the Soviet Union were therefore quite unjustified. The Soviet forces had not withdrawn by the agreed date of 2 March 1946, but they withdrew in May 1946, where-upon an agreement by Iran to cede oil concessions to the Soviet Union was repudiated by the Majlis, the Iranian parliament, and instead Iranian oil continued to be controlled by the British until they were gradually replaced by the Americans. As for Turkey, the provinces of Kars and Ardahan had been part of the tsarist Russian empire which were lost to Turkey in the turmoil of the Bolshevik Revolution and Civil War. As for the Straits, Soviet desire for access to the Mediterranean was perfectly reasonable and legitimate, as even Churchill conceded to Stalin, and her request for a base in the Straits was to ensure the safe passage of Soviet ships through the Straits which only American paranoia could interpret, as Acheson did, as a demand that Turkey 'allow the USSR to participate in what it called the defense of the straits but which meant the occupation of Turkey'.[10]

As for atomic weapons, revisionists argue that the Baruch Plan was not so generous and altruistic as traditionalists assert. 'Let us not say that we made Russia a generous offer when we proposed the Baruch plan for international control of atomic energy', wrote atomic scientist Leo Szilard in 1949. 'We would not fool anyone else, but we might fool ourselves.'[11] Revisionist historians agree with Szilard's assessment. Denna F. Fleming writes that 'No Great Power could be put through a long catechism to prove that it could be trusted to receive and handle atomic energy under rigid regulation and control'.[12] Even a traditionalist historian, Herbert Feis, concedes that 'because of the craving for absolute certainty that the agreement could not be evaded, in retrospect it seems to have been almost overbearing'.[13] Moreover, a crucial disadvantage to the Soviet Union in the Baruch Plan was that, if implemented, the United States would retain the knowledge of how to manufacture an atomic bomb, while the Soviet Union would be barred, under threat of severe sanctions, from ever acquiring that knowledge. In late 1945 Secretary of War Henry Stimson warned that 'If we negotiate with them, having this weapon rather ostentatiously on our hip, their suspicions and distrust of our purposes will increase'.[14] Revisionists suggest that the United States did not take effective action to allay Soviet suspicions, so that the Soviet government took the reasonable counter-action of engaging in a crash programme to build its own atomic bomb. Rather than wishing to make use of possession of the atomic bomb for purposes of political blackmail, revisionists suggest that the Soviet Union was adopting a defensive position to protect itself from the political blackmail exerted by the United States during the period of the American monopoly of the atomic bomb from 1945 to 1949.

Finally, with respect to economic issues, revisionists argue that Roosevelt planned to grant economic aid to the Soviet Union for post-war economic rehabilitation, hoping that this would help to maintain good relations. Truman, however, abruptly terminated Lend-Lease at the end of the war and did not reply for over six months in 1945–6 to a Soviet note requesting $6 billion in post-war aid, the delay due, it was alleged, to an administrative error. When the reply was finally sent, it was a negative response. The Soviets were invited to participate in the Marshall Plan in 1947, but, as the US administration was well aware, the terms of the Marshall Plan were bound to be unacceptable to the Soviet Union, since strings were attached which even the Western powers found irksome and which the Soviet Union was certain to reject. The US post-war goal, which had been clear during the war, was to remake the economic world order with a system which the United States was bound to dominate. The British resented American pressure to impose this new economic order by elimination of imperial preferences, bilateral trading agreements and other trading restrictions. To the Soviet Union the American designs were wholly unacceptable, so that the Soviet Union prevented their implementation at least in the area under its control, namely Eastern Europe. The American condemnation of Soviet policy in Eastern Europe, revisionists contend, was not simply due to the denial of democracy in these countries – most of which, such as Bulgaria, had no tradition of democracy whatever – but because it blocked opportunities for American exports to these areas and the import of inexpensive raw materials from these countries.

Hence, revisionists argue that the causes of the Cold War were by no means so straightforward as a Soviet attempt to expand Communism which was blocked by American resistance in the defence of freedom and democracy. Revisionists suggest that in the critical immediate post-war years 1945–7 there was a possible basis for US–Soviet agreement and peaceful co-existence. Truman's policies, however, on such matters as Eastern Europe, Germany, atomic weapons and economic issues destroyed this possibility and brought on an unnecessary Cold War.

Since the early 1970s a 'post-revisionist' synthesis on the origins of the Cold War has developed. The historical debate progressed, as John L. Gaddis put it, 'from truculent orthodoxy through militant revisionism to . . . postrevisionism'.[15] A number of the revisionist arguments have been widely accepted. As James V. Compton writes:

> An increasing number of writers have offered the proposition that in three areas – guarantees against German rearmament and aggression, non-political economic assist-ance to Russia and international nuclear control – the United States might well have used greater imagination and flexibility in exploring various options.[16]

On the other hand, the broader thesis of the revisionist interpretation, especially with regard to the assessment of the defensive and relatively benign nature of Soviet intensions, has failed to convince. European scholars of the Cold War, for example, have viewed the revisionist viewpoint with scepticism. The Norwegian historian Geir Lundestad concludes that

> Most European Cold War historians clearly continued to think that the Soviets were primarily to blame and probably saw revisionism as just another example of American moralistic self-flagellation or another swing of the pendulum so characteristic both of American foreign policy and American scholarship.[17]

Since the early 1970s a mass of new documentary evidence for the late 1940s has been opened, especially State Department, White House and British government papers. From the massive documentation in these newly opened sources, two major conclusions can perhaps be suggested. First, US policy towards the Soviet Union in the early Cold War years was much more hesitant and much less self-assured than either the traditionalists or revisionists suggested. Second, contacts between the United States and the Soviet Union on the level of such matters as trade, tourism, educational, cultural and scientific exchanges were virtually non-existent in the late 1940s and increasingly the image of the Soviet Union in the United States changed from the wartime image of Our Gallant Soviet Ally to a demonic image of the red peril.

In Dean Acheson's traditional interpretation *Present at the Creation* the United States is portrayed as the defender of the West creating the structures of peace and security which enabled the West to defend its civilization without war against the threat from totalitarian forces. In Lloyd Gardner's revisionist account *Architects of Illusion* the United States is portrayed as the defender of capitalism creating the structures of economic imperialism which enabled the United States to dominate the post-war world politically, economically and militarily. Evidence from new sources suggests that each of these views requires considerable modification. Second World War propaganda regarding the Soviet Union, combined with the euphoria at the end of the war, left the United States in 1945 disinclined to lead a crusade against Soviet imperialism and very willing to clutch at straws which held out hope of continuing US–Soviet co-operation. Averell Harriman commented that most Americans after the Second World War wanted to 'go to the movies and drink Coke'.[18] When in March 1946 Winston Churchill delivered his celebrated Iron Curtain speech at Fulton, Missouri, the reaction in America was, as Martin

Gilbert writes, 'almost universally hostile'.[19] British diplomats were scathing in their criticisms of a lack of realism in the American view of the Soviet Union. The British ambassador to the United States, Lord Halifax, expressed his concern in November 1945 over 'this wishful attitude about American–Soviet relations' and reported that 'America is behaving like a lumbering young giant, racked by indecision, troubled by a guilty conscience, and uncertain about how long his strength will endure'.[20] The swings of mood in the United States worried British diplomats. 'From gloom about Soviet–American relations', Bernard Gage, head of the North American Department in the Foreign Office, observed in late 1945, 'opinion is now in the usual mercurial way swinging to renewed hope'.[21] In a pessimistic mood, there was fear of American resort to war. As Geoffrey Harrison reported from the British embassy in Moscow in 1947, 'Any immediate danger to world peace lies in the possible itch of the American trigger finger'.[22] Yet in an optimistic mood, there was fear of unrealistic American moves for détente. Despite his fierce denunciation of Soviet foreign policy, Truman stated in June 1948 with regard to Stalin that 'I like old Joe'.[23] A British Foreign Office official, Peter Pares, noted in January 1949 that Truman hoped for détente and 'rather naïvely is apt to delude himself from time to time that it can be achieved by some overnight miracle'.[24]

With regard to economic issues, a number of Americans, especially in the State and Treasury departments, had clear ideas on using America's dominant position to reform the world economic system, break down economic nationalism and create a more open world of free trade with an abolition of cartels, quantitative agreements, non-convertible currencies and other such trading restrictions. But the majority of Americans were not confident capitalists. There was great fear of a return to the Depression conditions of the 1930s once wartime spending ended. Yet the solution to a depression of military Keynesianism – that is, priming the economic pump by means of defence expenditure – which the Second World War had brought about and which was pursued from 1950 onwards, was not supported in the late 1940s. Instead, the dominant mood was timidity and a desire to cut taxes and to reduce government expenditure. The defence budget fell from $81 billion in 1945 to $13 billion in 1947 and remained below $15 billion until 1950. Opposition to the Marshall Plan in Congress was considerable, with the view commonly expressed that American tax-payers' money was being thrown down a 'rat hole', while reluctance to undertake the commitment to the entangling alliance of NATO was widespread. British influence was an important factor in persuading the United States to undertake the Marshall Plan and to join NATO. Thus, rather than a domineering United States coercing the European nations to join with America in an economic and military block to deter the Soviet Union, the evidence suggests that the United States moved hesitantly, with two steps forward and one step back, and often requiring the encouragement of Western European nations to accept the commitments of international involvement.

Gradually, however, between 1945 and 1950 the changing American image of the Soviet Union made an increasingly deep impact on American policy. Contacts between American and Soviet soldiers in Germany, Czechoslovakia and elsewhere in 1945 were shortlived. Personal contacts between American and Soviet citizens at any level virtually ceased. Trade was almost nil. No cultural, educational and scientific exchanges were developed after the war. Tourist travel was impossible. A request by Ambassador Walter Bedell Smith that *Pravda* and *Izvestia* might publish the times and wavelengths of Voice of America was ignored, and in 1949 Voice of America began to be jammed. Diplomats in Moscow were allowed to travel only a short distance from Moscow. The Soviet Union became an increasingly closed society, with an emphasis on cultural nationalism and the introduction in 1947 of a law on criminal association with foreigners. Furthermore, a terrifying new element had been added to America's image of an alien threat, namely the atomic bomb. As Paul Boyer has written, 'The bomb had transformed not only military strategy and international relations, but the fundamental ground of culture and consciousness'.[25]

The United States came to view the Soviet Union as the new red peril, the successor to the Nazis. Americans were resolved not to repeat the mistakes of the 1930s but to deter the new peril by international involvement at an early stage. Isolationism became a tainted doctrine, with connotations of folly and treachery. By 1950 the mood of America had swung firmly from hope of accommodation with the Soviets to crusading fervour against the red menace. The new mood was expressed in April 1950 in NSC-68, a National Security Council document which expressed the conflict with the Soviets in Manichaean terms of good against evil, of civilization against barbarism, and called for a massive increase in US defence expenditure. The catalyst which brought about American acceptance both of greatly increased defence spending and of the NSC-68 portrayal of the Communist threat came with the outbreak of the Korean War in June 1950. American attitudes towards Communism and the Soviet Union were shaped not only by developments in Europe and the Middle East but increasingly also by developments in the Far East, especially with the ominous turn of events in the late 1940s in China.

6

THE UNITED STATES, THE SOVIET UNION AND CHINA

Before the Second World War Communism held sway in only one relatively remote and weak power, the Soviet Union. Communist expansion did not therefore pose a serious immediate threat to the United States. By the late 1940s, however, the Soviet Union had developed an immensely strong army, gained control of Eastern Europe and acquired atomic weapons. Then, on 1 October 1949, Mao Zedong declared victory for the Communists in the civil war in China and proclaimed the establishment of the People's Republic of China. The threat of the world-wide expansion of Communism had taken on perilous new dimensions for the United States.

Two central questions arise with regard to America's policy towards China and China's relationship with the Soviet Union in the events which culminated in Communist victory in China in 1949 and the Sino-Soviet Treaty of 1950. How far was Communist victory in China due to deficiencies in American policy towards China? How far did American policy drive China into alliance with the Soviet Union instead of encouraging the development of a nationalistic brand of Communism in China which would be independent of the Soviet Union?

In response to the first question, a dispassionate analysis demonstrates very clearly that Communist victory in the Chinese civil war was due to inefficiency and corruption on the part of the Nationalists under Chiang Kai-shek and to superior organization and greater popularity on the Communist side, with the American role of secondary importance in a situation in which American power was necessarily very limited. Dispassion, however, was notably lacking in the American response to events in China, so that wide support was given to the conspiratorial interpretation which explained Communist victory in China in

71

terms of American statesmen selling China down the river, especially at Yalta, and of a State Department infiltrated by Communists who plotted Chiang's downfall within the US government. No serious scholar gives any validity to the latter interpretation, which was based upon ignorance and fear rather than upon rational analysis. In the emotional atmosphere of 1949, however, with the shocks of Communist successes and American impotence in Eastern Europe, the development of the Soviet atomic bomb and Communist triumph in China, there was widespread willingness in America to accept a simplistic interpretation rather than a complex analysis. The conspiratorial explanation of the so-called 'loss of China' had, therefore, immense political impact which profoundly influenced the shaping of American policy towards China.

The proclamation of a Communist regime in China was particularly traumatic to the United States on account of America's historical tradition of an assumed special relationship between the United States and China. America, it was felt, was the special friend and protector of China, compared to the imperialist despoilers of China such as Britain, France, Germany, Russia and Japan. From the early nineteenth century, American missionaries had gone to China and built schools, hospitals and universities as well as churches. American philanthropy brought Chinese students to the United States for their education. In trade with China the United States insisted upon the Open Door, unlike the imperialist powers who sought to acquire exclusive spheres of influence. In the twentieth century America took China's side against Japanese encroachments on China, which was a major factor in bringing the United States into confrontation with Japan, culminating in Pearl Harbor. During the Second World War the United States gave military and economic aid to China, and in Roosevelt's vision of the post-war world a democratic, progressive China would be America's closest ally in the Far East.

With the resumption of civil war in China after the Japanese surrender, Truman sent George Marshall to China in December 1945 to try to bring about a truce and the formation of a coalition government in which all political factions would be represented. Marshall succeeded in bringing about a truce for a time in early 1946, but when the warring factions resumed conflict by the middle of the year, the United States gave aid to the Nationalists while endeavouring to persuade Chiang to reform. With corruption and nepotism rife in the Nationalist regime, however, with inflation out of control and indiscipline in the army, the United States was powerless to prevent the steady deterioration of the Nationalist position, while Communist efficiency and good government in the areas under their control produced growing popular support for the Communists. American aid to the Nationalists frequently fell into Communist hands, as Nationalist troops deserted to the other side or abandoned their weapons, which the Communists acquired. American threats to withhold aid from Chiang unless effective reforms were introduced were of no avail. Hence, by summer 1949 the United States realized that Chiang's cause was doomed and that the Communists would come to power. A State Department White Paper, which was published in August 1949 to explain the Nationalist failures and Communist strengths, sought to demonstrate that, as Secretary of State Dean Acheson wrote in the Foreword:

> The ominous result of the civil war in China was beyond the control of the government of the United States. Nothing that this country did or could have done within the reasonable limits of its capabilities could have changed that result; nothing that was left undone by this country has contributed to it.[1]

The reception given to the White Paper, however, illustrated that cold logic was unlikely to convince the majority of Americans on the emotive subject of China. A memorandum by four right-wing senators, Styles Bridges, Joseph Knowland, Kenneth Wherry and Pat McCarran, denounced the White Paper as a '1,054 page whitewash of a wishful, do-nothing policy which has succeeded only in placing Asia in danger of Soviet conquest'.[2] Rather than wishing to analyse the perplexing realities of the Chinese situation, American public opinion was receptive to simplistic explanations of treason in high places as the reason for the 'loss of China'. Such figures as the publisher Henry Luce, historian William H. Chamberlin and politicians such as Knowland, McCarran and Congressman Walter Judd, made various points in support of the stab-in-the-back theory. In particular, these figures charged that China's loss to Communism was the result of a sell-out at Yalta, insufficient aid to China and the treachery of Communists in the US State Department.

It was pointed out that at Yalta in February 1945 Roosevelt agreed with Stalin to certain terms regarding China behind

Chiang's back, with no Chinese representation at Yalta. Roosevelt made concessions at China's expense in order to bring the Soviet Union into the war against Japan. Yet as a result of the atomic bomb Soviet entry into the war proved to be unnecessary, but it enabled the Soviets to invade Manchuria in August 1945 and to provide assistance to the Chinese Communists against the Nationalists. It was alleged that left-wingers in the American delegation at Yalta, such as Alger Hiss, persuaded Roosevelt to accede to these terms, which were the first steps towards Chiang's downfall.

While it is true, however, that the terms of Yalta regarding China were made without Chiang's agreement and that Roosevelt was very eager to win Soviet commitment to enter the war against Japan, the relationship between the Yalta agreement and Communist victory in the Chinese civil war is very tenuous. By the terms of Yalta the port of Dairen in Manchuria was internationalized, with pre-eminent Soviet interests recognized; the lease of Port Arthur to the Soviet Union as a naval base was restored; and joint Chinese–Soviet operation of major Manchurian railroads was accepted, with pre-eminent Soviet interests safeguarded. While these terms, which were similar to spheres of interest agreements with imperialist powers in the nineteenth century, were galling to the Chinese, they bore little relationship to Nationalist defeat at the hands of the Chinese Communists. Soviet entry into the war against Japan brought Soviet troops into Manchuria, who hampered Nationalist troop movements and allowed the Chinese Communists to gain possession of captured Japanese weapons. This was, however, the only significant assistance rendered by the Soviet Union to the Chinese Communists in the civil war in the 1940s. The evidence suggests that Stalin preferred a weak, non-Communist China to a strong, unified China under Mao, who, even if an ideological ally, was not a Soviet puppet. On 14 August 1945 Stalin signed a Treaty of Friendship and Alliance with Chiang, whereby Chiang agreed to the territorial concessions of Yalta, but Stalin promised to support a unified China under Chiang. By the end of 1945 Stalin was very helpful in facilitating Nationalist entry into Manchuria, and Chiang even asked Stalin to keep Soviet troops in occupation of the area. In 1944 Stalin described Mao as a 'margarine Communist', and in 1945 Soviet Foreign Minister Molotov told Patrick Hurley, US ambassador to China, that the Chinese Communists were not true Marxists.[3] The lack of evidence on the Soviet side does not permit an informed analysis of the Soviet assessment of the Chinese situation. The most plausible interpretation would seem to be that, whatever doubts Stalin had with regard to Mao's ideological purity, of greater significance was Stalin's dislike of a strong Chinese government which he could not control, whether Communist or not. In any event, Soviet aid to the Chinese Communists as a result of the Yalta agreement or in the course of the later 1940s was minimal and was an inconsequential factor in determining the outcome of the Chinese civil war.

A second point in the theory that China was sold out, is that American aid to China in the 1940s was insufficient. When Marshall sought support for aid to Greece and Turkey in 1947, National Security Adviser William Leahy expressed inability 'to understand why Marshall is willing to get involved in order to save the Greek and Turkish regimes, but resigned to letting the Nationalist Government of China go down the drain'.[4] However, as Marshall had seen on his mission to China in 1945–6, the vast quantities of aid to China were of little benefit without political reform in China. In the autumn of 1945 the United States had airlifted half a million Nationalist troops to northern and eastern China and dispatched 50,000 American troops to reinforce 60,000 American marines in Beijing, Tienstin and nearby mines and railways, pending the arrival of Nationalist troops. American forces were withdrawn from China in early 1946, but massive quantities of American economic and military aid were delivered to Chiang up to 1949. Marshall's efforts to bring about a coalition government of Nationalists and Communists perhaps seem unrealistic from a later perspective. As one historian has put it, 'As well expect Thaddeus Stevens and Jefferson Davis in the same government, with the Confederate Army still intact and aggressive'.[5] But the attempt to bring about political re-organization and an end to civil strife was an option worth exploring before resorting to the unpromising alternative of aiding Chiang while attempting to persuade him to reform. Another alternative, direct American military intervention, was not advocated even by Chiang's most ardent American supporters, while the Joint Chiefs of Staff were totally opposed to such an idea, fearing the diversion of America's scant military resources to China and leaving Western Europe more vulnerable to a Soviet attack.

Yet aid to Chiang in the form of economic assistance and

military supplies was ineffective. Lord Inverchapel, Halifax's successor as British ambassador, reported from Washington that 'Majority opinion believes that the United States should not pour money into a Nanking sieve'.[6] Even moderate critics of Truman's China policy, such as Senator Arthur Vanderberg, realized that much American aid fell into Chinese Communist hands and that Chiang could exasperate the US government with impunity by ignoring threats of American reduction or termination of aid in the confident knowledge that for domestic political reasons the Truman administration would not dare to cut off aid to China. Hence, in addition to the aid extended in 1945–8, increased aid of $125 million was granted to China in 1948 under the Foreign Assistance Act, which was the price demanded by Chiang's supporters in Congress for support of the Marshall Plan for Europe. Yet, as Inverchapel noted, 'The administration has little confidence in its own China Relief Programme. . . . A number of well-informed critics regard aid to the present government of China as certain to prove the "Operation Rat Hole" of all time'.[7] Chiang's demise, then, was the result of the corruption and ineptness of his regime, not the insufficiency of American aid.

The third point in the stab-in-the-back explanation of Chiang's downfall, namely Communist influence in the State Department, is equally unconvincing. China specialists in the US Foreign Service such as John Patton Davies, O. Edmund Clubb, John Stewart Service and John Carter Vincent provided sophisticated and well-informed analyses of the China situation. They reported that the Communists were likely to win the civil war and that the United States should prepare to deal with a Communist government. Like Marshall, these Foreign Service officers were favourably impressed in many ways by the Chinese Communists and very unimpressed by many aspects of Chiang's regime. They met the Communist leaders in the Communist headquarters in Yenan and they reported extensively on developments within the Communist ranks as well as within the Nationalist government. Most of these Foreign Service officers held liberal, progressive political views, but none of them were Communists. They did not welcome a Communist victory in China, but their reports simply presented the realistic assessment that the Communists were likely to win the Chinese civil war and that the US government should come to terms with this reality. They suggested that the US government could arrive at a *modus vivendi* with a Communist Chinese government, provided that such a government was not driven into close alliance with the Soviet Union. But this relatively sophisticated view of developments in China left these Foreign Service officers open to demagogic attacks by a figure such as Senator Joseph McCarthy who charged that 'It was not Chinese democracy under Mao that conquered China. . . . Soviet Russia conquered China and an important ally of the conquerors was this small left-wing element in our Department of State'.[8]

From 1945 to 1949 the United States pursued a pragmatic policy towards China, accepting the limits of American power and appreciating that, unless the Nationalists joined with the Communists in a coalition or the Nationalists become efficient and defeated the Communists, the United States was unable to alter the course of events in China and prevent a Communist victory. The actuality of Communist accession to power in October 1949, however, lit the fuse of the simmering emotional undercurrent in America which began to explode by early 1950 and which shifted American policy towards a much less pragmatic policy. This was reflected in US policy with respect to three matters in particular, namely US diplomatic recognition of China, admission of Communist China into the United Nations and policy regarding Formosa.

Following Mao's proclamation of the People's Republic of China on 1 October 1950 the Soviet Union gave immediate diplomatic recognition on 2 October 1950. Over the next few months many other nations, such as Britain and India, gave diplomatic recognition to the Communist Chinese government. At a press conference on 12 October 1950 Acheson gave three conditions for diplomatic recognition, namely that the government had effective control of the country, accepted the debts and obligations of its predecessors and had the acquiescence of the people. In the autumn of 1949 the consensus within the State Department was that the new Chinese government broadly met these conditions and that it should be granted diplomatic recognition. Acheson had expressed his views on the general issue of the diplomatic recognition of governments on 11 September 1949, stating that 'We maintain diplomatic relations with other countries primarily because we are all on the same planet and must do business with each other. We do not establish an embassy or legation in a country to show approval of its government'.[9] In late 1949 the US government was not opposed to the establishment of diplomatic relations with the new

Communist regime in China, but matters were delayed by various incidents involving insulting treatment of American personnel in China, culminating in the seizure of US government property in Beijing on 14 January 1950. As a result, all US diplomatic personnel were withdrawn from China and the issue of diplomatic recognition was put on ice, though in principle it was assumed that the United States would in due course recognize the Communist Chinese government.

Similarly, it was assumed in late 1949 and early 1950 that Communist China would be admitted to the United Nations. On 10 January 1950 the Soviet Union proposed the expulsion of the Nationalist Chinese representative to the United Nations and the admission of the representative of Communist China. The motion was defeated, but on procedural and technical points rather than on the general principle of Communist China's admission to the United Nations, which had wide support and which even the United States accepted, however grudgingly. The Soviet response to the defeat of its motion was the somewhat extreme reaction of a walk-out from the United Nations and a Soviet boycott of the United Nations for the next eight months. Thus, Communist China's principal advocate was not present in the United Nations to press the case for reconsideration of Communist China's admission. Hence, the matter of Communist China's admission to the United Nations was, like the issue of US diplomatic recognition of Communist China, put on ice, with reluctant American acceptance in principle. Even a figure such as John Foster Dulles said in April 1950 that 'If the Communist government of China in fact proves its ability to govern China without serious domestic resistance, then it, too, should be admitted to the United Nations'.[10]

Moreover, with regard to Formosa the US government in late 1949 and early 1950 accepted that Formosa was part of China and ruled out the use of American forces to prevent the anticipated invasion of Formosa by the Chinese Communists. This position continued to be adhered to in spite of growing pressure from such senators as Joseph Knowland and Robert Taft and former president Herbert Hoover, who urged that, although the United States could not save the Nationalist regime in mainland China, the US navy could protect Chiang in Formosa, an island ninety miles from the Chinese coast to which Chiang withdrew in December 1949. The Joint Chiefs of Staff made clear their view that US military action to defend Formosa was not justifiable. On 29 December 1949 the National Security Council endorsed the policy of non-interference in Formosa. On 5 January 1950 Truman issued a statement that 'The United States has no predatory designs on Formosa or any other Chinese territory. . . . The United States government will not pursue a course which will lead to an involvement in the civil conflict in China'.[11] In the spring of 1950 US intelligence reports indicated that the Chinese Communists were making preparations to invade Formosa in the summer, but although the Pentagon was under increasing pressure from supporters of Knowland, Taft and Hoover to reconsider the wisdom of allowing Formosa to fall to the Communists, no public change took place in the US government position with regard to non-intervention in Formosa.

The growing swell of McCarthyism in early 1950 and the outbreak of the Korean War on 25 June 1950 brought about a change of American policy on diplomatic recognition of China, admission of Communist China into the United Nations and on Formosa. With the United States involved in war in Korea, and particularly after Chinese intervention in the Korean War in October 1950, any suggestion of diplomatic recognition of Red China or admission of Red China into the United Nations was regarded as tantamount to disloyalty to the United States and a betrayal of American boys who had died in the war against the Communists in Korea. Policy on Formosa was reversed on 27 June 1950 with an order to the US Seventh Fleet to patrol the Formosa Straits and to prevent the Communists from attacking Formosa or the Nationalists from attacking mainland China. With the outbreak of the Korean War, Formosa had greater strategic importance, but of much greater significance was Formosa's political symbolism. It had become politically un-acceptable for the Truman administration, which had come under increasing fire from the McCarthyists for being 'soft on Communism', to stand by and allow the Chinese Communists to take over Formosa while the United States was engaged in war against the Communists in Korea.

These changes in American policy towards China not only alienated the Chinese from the United States in general but in particular drove the Chinese Communist government into closer liaison with the Soviet Union. Commentators and historians have reached different conclusions on the question of whether there was a 'lost chance' in China, that is, whether the Chinese Communist government moved closer to the Soviet Union as a result of American policies towards China or whether China was inevitably bound to seek close alliance with her ideological neighbour whatever policies the United States pursued.

In favour of the 'lost chance' interpretation, Mao had good reason to be wary of the Kremlin. China had territorial disputes with Russia from the time of Russian acquisition of territory north of the Amur River in the nineteenth century to the territorial concessions at Yalta. Moreover, Stalin had given little encouragement and little aid to the Chinese Communists. Ideologically, Mao's brand of Marxism was more peasant based than the industrial worker basis of Soviet Communism. Indeed, some American commentators questioned whether the Chinese Communists were really Communists at all. The *New York Times* reported in November 1944 that the Chinese Communists 'are in fact peasant agrarians'.[12] State Department expert John Patton Davies, in a memo entitled 'How Red are the Chinese Communists?' concluded that 'The Chinese Communists are backsliders. . . . Like the other eminent backslider Ramsey MacDonald, they have come to accept the inevitability of gradualness. . . . Yenan is no Marxist New Jerusalem'.[13] John Stewart Service reported that

> The Communists, from what little we know of them, are friendly towards America, believe that democracy must be the next step in China, and take the view that economic collaboration with the United States is the only hope for speedy rehabilitation and development. It is vital that we do not lose this good will and influence.[14]

Other American specialists were more ambivalent regarding Communist China's attitude towards Moscow and towards Washington. George Kennan, as Acheson recorded:

> stated frankly that he did not know what the relationship between Yenan and Moscow was. Quite prepared to believe that the Chinese Communist party, like others, was subservient to Moscow, he still hesitated to accept it as established truth. Moscow–Yenan relations were subtle and obscure.[15]

The British were more definite in their view. Sir John Balfour, minister in the embassy in Washington, wrote in 1947 that 'China was probably the one country in which the leaders of the local Communists could not be regarded as mere instruments of Kremlin policy'.[16]

In January 1945 Mao Zedong and Zhou Enlai transmitted a request to American army officers that they come to Washington to talk to Roosevelt about establishing a 'working relationship' with the United States. Their offer received no response from the White House. Marshall made contact with the Communist leaders in 1945–6, developing a good relationship with Zhou Enlai in particular, but after the breakdown of the truce in 1946 he took the Nationalist side, despite his bitter criticisms of Chiang Kai-shek, and he did not develop further his contacts with the Communists. In 1948 Tito's break with Stalin illustrated the possibility of a Communist regime which was independent of Moscow and which was therefore not seriously detrimental to American interests. The British were aware of the possibilities of Titoism in China. The British Cabinet Russia Committee noted in 1949 that 'The Russians were extremely worried about the situation in Yugoslavia and China. Both these countries had achieved and were achieving Communist independence without Soviet aid, and the Russians were inclined to think of Mao Tse-tung as a potential Tito'.[17]

Acheson made many statements emphasizing China's disputes with the Kremlin and urged that the United States exploit these in order to keep the Chinese Communists and the Soviets apart. Acheson stressed the territorial disputes regarding four provinces, namely Outer Mongolia, Inner Mongolia, Sinkiang and Manchuria, into which the Soviets had penetrated in various ways. In a speech to the National Press Club on 12 January 1950 Acheson stated that 'The fact that the Soviet Union is taking the four northern provinces of China is the single most significant, most important fact in the relations of any foreign power in Asia'.[18] Acheson therefore stressed in 1949 and early 1950 that American intervention in Formosa would be very ill-advised, since it would raise the spectre of an American-created irredentist issue just at the time the United States sought to exploit Soviet-created irredentist issues. Acheson argued that 'We must not undertake to deflect from the Russians to ourselves the righteous anger and the wrath and the hatred of the Chinese people which must develop'.[19]

Within the State Department many officials advocated a policy of wooing the Chinese Communists away from the Kremlin by impressing upon them the incompatibility of Soviet and Chinese interests and the value to China of Western economic contacts. Roger Lapham, head of the US economic aid mission in China, suggested in March 1949 that economic aid should be given to the Communists to win their favour. John Cabot, who had recently served in Yugoslavia, pointed out ways in which Titoism could be encouraged in China. W. Walton Butterworth, Assistant Secretary of State for Eastern Affairs, wrote to Acheson in February 1949 that the ultimate Soviet objective in China was 'the imposition of the alien Lenin-Stalin dogmas' which would 'eventually conflict with aroused Chinese nationalism'.[20]

On the Chinese Communist side, feelers seemed to be put forward in early 1949, especially by Zhou Enlai and by Huang Hua, head of the Communist Alien Affairs Bureau in Nanking, through American missionaries and businessmen, suggesting a conciliatory approach to the United States and appreciation of the values of economic contacts with the United States. It seemed clear that divisions existed in the Communist side between pragmatists such as Zhou Enlai who favoured a *modus vivendi* with the United States and ideological purists who wished no dealings with capitalist imperialism.

On 16 December 1949 Mao arrived in Moscow for the negotiation of a military alliance and a trade agreement with the Soviet Union. It was Mao's first trip outside of China in his life, and negotiations continued until a treaty was signed on 4 March 1950. The length of the negotiations and the consequent length of time spent by Mao outside of China suggest that negotiations were difficult. But if Mao was weighing up the advantages of keeping open channels to the West rather than allying himself to the Soviet Union, American policy did not show him many advantages in the former course. During the Moscow negotiations the United States blocked Communist Chinese admission to the United Nations, and the United States reacted very vigorously to the Communist seizure of American property in Beijing. Communist overtures since Mao's letter to Roosevelt in 1945 had met almost entirely with rebuff. And while many American diplomats floated suggestions with regard to the encouragement of independent nationalistic Communism in China, the tactic of encouraging Titoism in China was not pursued diligently and consistently by the US government. Acheson was preoccupied with the European theatre; he was wary of McCarthyist charges of being 'soft on communism'; and he was basically rather contemptuous of Asian people and willing to allow them to stew in their own mess rather than to pursue carefully calculated policies which astutely explored available opportunities for constructive relations with the Communists. Hence, some argue, there was a lost opportunity to prevent the development of the Sino-Soviet bloc which menaced the United States through the 1950s.

Others argue, however, that there was no such 'lost chance' in China. Mao Zedong was a committed Communist, it is argued, who made tentative overtures to the United States from time to time for temporary tactical purposes, but who, especially in his vulnerable position when he first came to power, was bound to form an alliance with the only nation from whom he could seek protection, namely the Soviet Union. The Chinese Communists faithfully followed the zigzags of Soviet foreign policy, defending, for example, the Nazi–Soviet pact in 1939. Truman wrote that

> Neither Marshall nor I was ever taken in by the talk about the Chinese being just 'agrarian reformers'. The General knew he was dealing with Communists, and he knew what their aims were. . . . Marshall's messages from China show, also, that he fully assumed that the Chinese Communists would, in the end, be able to count on Russian support.[21]

On 1 July 1949 Mao issued a declaration, 'On People's Democratic Dictatorship', in which he stated that in the choice between imperialism and socialism the United States was the 'one great imperialist power' which sought 'to enslave the world' and that China must 'lean to one side' and ally itself 'with the Soviet Union, with every New Democratic country and with the proletariat and broad masses in other countries'.[22]

In conclusion, American policies failed to make adequate attempts to strengthen the position of those among the Chinese Communists who were inclined towards a practical reconciliation with America and to minimize the influence of anti-Western ideological purists. It is debatable, however, whether a more subtle and calculated American wooing of Mao would have kept him out of the Soviet embrace in the early years of Communist rule in China, given Mao's vulnerability and need for Soviet protection. In any event, the Chinese–Soviet–US triangular relationship, like many other significant aspects of US–Soviet relations, was soon to be profoundly affected by the outbreak of the Korean War.

7

THE KOREAN WAR, 1950–3

On 25 June 1950 North Korean troops swept across the 38th Parallel into South Korea in massive numbers in a surprise attack. The United States assumed that the invasion had been ordered by the Kremlin as a probe at a weak spot in America's defence. Truman therefore responded with the dispatch of American forces to South Korea, who drove the North Koreans back to the 38th Parallel by September 1950. In October 1950 American and South Korean forces invaded North Korea, which brought about Chinese intervention on the North Korean side and led to a prolonged conflict until an armistice was signed in July 1953. At the same time, the United States responded to the Korean War with a vast increase in defence expenditure, while the British engaged in a huge rearmament programme and discussions on West German rearmament began. From a later perspective, historians have raised questions regarding American policy in the Korean War which have deep implications. Was American policy based on a false assumption that the North Korean attack was on the order of Moscow rather than the outcome of a local North Korean initiative in a Korean civil war? Did the United States commit a serious error in crossing into North Korea in October 1950? Did the United States overreact to the Korean War with massive increases in defence expenditure which escalated the arms race and created the military-industrial complex in America and aroused Soviet fears of NATO's intensions? These are perhaps the main questions to be considered in examining the impact of the Korean War on US–Soviet relations.

Until 1950 Korea was a distant Asian peninsula of little concern to the United States. At the Cairo conference between

Roosevelt, Churchill and Chiang Kai-shek in 1943 it was resolved vaguely that 'in due course' Korea, a Japanese colony since 1910, should become independent.[1] The timing and procedure for Korea's attainment of independence was left undecided, however, since Korea was a minor issue. At Yalta in February 1945 Roosevelt suggested that Korea should be governed for twenty to thirty years by a joint US–Soviet–Chinese trusteeship to prepare Korea for independence, to which Stalin responded that he would prefer a shorter period of trusteeship. No agreement on Korea was included in the final Yalta documents. In August 1945, with the sudden end of the Far Eastern war, it was decided that Japanese troops should surrender to Soviet forces in Korea north of the 38th Parallel and to American forces south of the 38th Parallel. The hastily created military demarcation line of the 38th Parallel was fated to become a long-standing political boundary.

In December 1945, at the meeting of the Council of Foreign Ministers in Moscow, Byrnes and Molotov agreed that a two-power Soviet–American Commission should rule Korea until Korea was ready for independence. The first meeting of the Commission in January 1946 degenerated into acrimony, and further meetings were equally unproductive. Meantime, the military authorities in North and South Korea supervised the establishment of regimes suitable to the Soviet Union in the north and to the United States in the south – namely a government under the Korean Communist Kim Il Sung in North Korea and a pro-American regime in South Korea under Syngman Rhee, who returned to Korea in 1945 after forty years in exile in the United States. With lack of progress in the Soviet–American Commission meetings, the United States decided to take the matter of Korea to the United Nations, and in November 1947 the UN General Assembly voted in favour of the creation of the United Nations Temporary Commission in Korea, which was authorized to supervise elections by 31 March 1948, after which Soviet and American forces should withdraw. The Soviet military authorities in North Korea refused to co-operate with the UN Temporary Commission, which decided to hold elections in South Korea in May 1948, resulting in a comfortable victory for Syngman Rhee's party in the Assembly and the election of Rhee as president. The Communists denounced the election as a fraud and in August 1948 elections were held in North Korea for a Supreme People's Assembly, resulting in an overwhelming

Communist triumph. Both North Korea and South Korea claimed that their respective assemblies were the legislatures for the whole of Korea, and both sides sought unification on their own terms. In December 1948 Soviet forces withdrew from Korea, but Moscow had built up the North Korean army as a powerful force and Soviet troops were close on hand across the border in Siberia. In June 1949 American forces withdrew from South Korea.

In 1949–50 the impression was given by the United States that Korea was such a low priority that America would not be prepared to defend South Korea against an attack. On 12 January 1950 Acheson defined America's defence perimeter as a line running through offshore islands from the Aleutians to Japan, thereby omitting Korea. In March 1949 General Douglas MacArthur had referred to the same defence perimeter. In June 1950 Senator Tom Connally, chairman of the Senate Committee on Foreign Relations, expressed the view that South Korea was likely to be overrun and would have to be abandoned. American actions reinforced the impression of these words, especially Joint Chiefs of Staff support for the withdrawal of American troops from South Korea and the rejection by the House of Representatives of aid for South Korea in January 1950. American policy-makers had their attention focused upon Europe and China and took little notice of developments in Korea.

Against this background of relative American inattention towards Korea, the North Korean invasion of 25 June 1950 came as a great shock to the US government. Border skirmishes had been sporadic for years, and American intelligence did not attach particular significance to the build-up of North Korean troops in the spring of 1950. Truman had gone home for the weekend to Independence, Missouri, which indicated that no crisis was expected. When he received the news of the North Korean attack Truman reflected, as he flew back to Washington, that 'Communism was acting in Korea just as Hitler, Mussolini and the Japanese acted ten, fifteen and twenty years earlier. . . . If this were allowed to go unchallenged, it would mean a Third World War, just as similar incidents had brought on the Second World War'.[2] There was unanimity in US government circles that North Korea's action should be viewed as a Soviet manoeuvre and that it should be resisted. In a series of intense meetings during the week of 25–30 June vital decisions were taken on the means of resistance. On 25 June it was decided that the issue should be taken to the UN Security Council, where, with the Soviet delegate absent in the continuing Soviet boycott of the United Nations in protest over Communist China's exclusion, support for American proposals was forthcoming. At an emergency meeting of the Security Council on 25 June, North Korea's aggression was condemned and an immediate end to hostilities was demanded. On 26 June, with the North Koreans ignoring the UN resolution, the United States decided to send arms and equipment to South Korea from Japan. On 27 June MacArthur was instructed to use air and naval forces to assist South Korea; a change of policy regarding Formosa was announced, namely to interpose the US Seventh Fleet between Formosa and the Chinese mainland; aid was granted to the Philippines government in its struggle against Communist insurgents; and aid to the French in Indo-China, which had begun in May 1950, was stepped up in order to strengthen the French in their war with the Vietminh. On 28 June the North Koreans captured Seoul, capital of South Korea, in their relentless drive forward, and American air and naval power proved to be ineffective. On 29 June Truman decided to send American ground troops to Korea.

Truman's resolute action in Korea was supported by America's allies, especially the British, who immediately sent naval forces to Korea and in July 1950 sent in a contingent of ground forces. The British had no doubt that the Kremlin was behind the North Korean invasion. A Foreign Office memo of 26 June 1950 stated that it was 'virtually certain that the Soviet Government had connived at if they had not instigated the aggression by the Communists of North Korea'.[3] British Foreign Secretary Ernest Bevin, however, was eager to pursue diplomatic initiatives in Moscow in order to persuade Stalin to desist from his rash action and to call off the North Koreans. The Americans were sceptical that such diplomatic moves could produce effective results unless the military situation in Korea was turned around. Moreover, the Americans felt that, as Acheson noted to the British ambassador in Washington, Oliver Franks, concessions under duress 'would whet Communist appetites and bring on other aggressions elsewhere'.[4] In reply to a US note of 27 June asking assurance 'that the USSR disavows responsibility for the unprovoked and unwarranted attack', the Soviet Union denied complicity and asserted that the South Koreans had begun the war with attacks on North Korea to which North Korea had responded in self-defence, without Soviet knowledge or involvement. This view, which the American government angrily dismissed as absurd and typical of Soviet mendacity, was put forward during the Korean War by the left-wing journalist, I.F. Stone, who argued that Rhee's political position had become increasingly weak as he ruled tyrannically and imprisoned opposition leaders and that he calculated that his only opportunity to retain power and to unite Korea was to provoke war with the North, which would bring in the Americans in an anti-Communist crusade. Although Stone's credibility was steadily enhanced in later years when his apparently far-fetched views on many issues, especially relating to the war in Vietnam, proved to be quite plausible, his interpretation of South Korean instigation of the Korean War has not been sustained by later writers.

Much wider support, however, has been given to the view that the origins of the Korean War lay not simply in the manipulations of outside powers but in developments deep within Korean society. Fundamentally, the conflict was, as Bruce Cumings has argued, 'a civil and revolutionary war to unify and transform the country'.[5] In particular, much support has been offered for the view that, at least in its timing, the Korean War was not initiated on the orders of the Kremlin but resulted from an independent North Korean decision. The lack of evidence on relations between North Korea and the Soviet Union rules out a firm conclusion. It is puzzling, however, that, if Moscow planned the attack, the Soviet delegate continued to boycott the United Nations when, as was the case when the Soviets returned to the UN in August 1950, the opportunities for obstruction were considerable. Khrushchev recounts in his memoirs that Kim Il Sung went to Moscow in 1949 and in 1950 and received only grudging, vague acceptance by Stalin of a decision to invade South Korea, so that Stalin was taken by surprise by the attack in June 1950. Many recent historians, such as Burton Kaufmann and Peter Lowe, have been inclined to accept this interpretation. Moreover, Kaufmann and William Stueck both argue that in retrospect it may have been in America's longer term interests to allow the unification of Korea under a Communist regime, which could have proved a troublesome satellite inclined to Titoism. These historians, however, as other writers on the Korean War, accept that in the context of the time in 1950 Korea had such symbolic significance, as a test of American resolve not to pursue appeasement and to prevent the United Nations from suffering the fate of the League of Nations, that American intervention was essential. As Acheson put it:

> Plainly, this attack . . . was an open, undisguised challenge to our internationally accepted position as the protector of Korea. . . . To back away from this challenge . . . would be highly destructive of the power and prestige of the United States. By prestige I mean the shadow cast by power, which is of great deterrent importance.[6]

While the British strongly endorsed the American policy of intervention in Korea in June 1950, policy regarding Formosa was another matter. The British were not convinced of Formosa's strategic importance and questioned the argument that, in order to keep the war limited to Korea, Formosa should not be allowed to fall to the Chinese Communists at that time. The evidence supports the British view that the interposition of the US Seventh Fleet in the Formosa Straits would incense the Chinese Communists and drive them more firmly into the Soviet camp. On 28 June 1950 Mao Zedong declared that

> Although Truman announced last 5 January that the United States would not intervene in Taiwan he himself has just proven the hypocrisy of that statement and at the same time has broken every international agreement by the United States that it would not interfere in the internal political affairs of China.[7]

On 28 June 1950 Zhou Enlai stated that the actions of the US navy 'constitute armed aggression against the territory of China and total violation of the United Nations Charter. The Chinese people will surely be victorious in driving off American aggressors and in recovering Taiwan'.[8] As historian Gordon Chang has put it, 'The United States had reinjected itself into the Chinese civil war'.[9]

Of even greater significance than Formosa, however, was the decision whether the UN forces should cross the 38th Parallel into North Korea. From late June to early September 1950 the North Koreans overran all of South Korea except the Pusan perimeter in the south-east, an area of fifty by eighty miles around the port of Pusan which was defended with great tenacity by forces under General Walton Walker, enabling supplies and reinforcements to arrive via Pusan. On 15 September 1950 MacArthur directed a brilliant amphibious landing at Inchon on the west coast of Korea and cut North Korean supply lines, leaving the North Korean invaders at the mercy of Walker's forces as they broke out of the Pusan perimeter and linked up with MacArthur. By late September the course of the war had been dramatically reversed, and the question arose whether the United States should adhere to the limited goal of restoration of the status quo or whether the more ambitious goal should be attempted of the invasion of North Korea in order to destroy the North Korean army, overthrow the Communist regime and unite Korea under a non-Communist government.

Debate had taken place in US government circles on this question since the outbreak of the war in June 1950. Two aspects of the question have arisen, namely whether invasion of North Korea should be undertaken for military reasons, to prevent the North Koreans from regrouping in a safe sanctuary, and whether invasion should be undertaken for political reasons, to bring about the unification of Korea under a pro-Western regime. The evidence which is now open in US archives makes it clear that a prolonged debate took place within the US government over the summer of 1950 which concentrated upon the second aspect – the political issues involved in crossing the 38th Parallel. Many figures urged caution. Alan Kirk, US ambassador in Moscow, warned that crossing the 38th Parallel might provoke the Soviet Union to enter the conflict. Paul Nitze, head of the State Department Policy Planning Staff, warned of the dangers of Soviet or Chinese intervention if the 38th Parallel was crossed. George Kennan, who had supported intervention in June 1950, writing that 'The aggression must be defeated and discredited', sent a memo to Acheson that 'It was not essential to us or within our capabilities to establish an anti-Soviet regime in all of Korea'.[10] The Joint Chiefs of Staff did not wish an extended war in Korea, lest the United States be exposed if new acts of aggression were committed in other areas of greater strategic importance.

The majority opinion within the government, however, favoured a more hawkish approach. John Allison, director of the State Department Office of North-East Asian Affairs, argued that if UN forces stopped at the 38th Parallel, 'The real aggressor, the Soviet Union, would presumably go unpunished in any way whatsoever. The aggressor would be informed that all he had to fear from aggression was being compelled to start over again'.[11] Warren Austin, US ambassador to the United Nations, emphasized that from the legal point of view UN resolutions in 1947 and 1948 in favour of a free, united Korea justified UN action to implement these resolutions by force when the opportunity presented itself in 1950. 'Korea's prospects would be dark indeed', said Austin on 10 August, 'if any action of the United Nations were to condemn it to exist as "half slave and half free" '.[12] There were, moreover, political pressures to pursue the bolder course of crossing the 38th Parallel. The Democratic administration was reeling from charges of being 'soft on Communism', with Acheson's position particularly vulnerable, especially as a result of his 12 January speech which omitted Korea from America's defence perimeter, thereby, it was alleged, sending North Korea an invitation to attack. A spectacular victory in the Korean War which not only repelled Communist aggression but which ended in the liberation of Communist North Korea would provide a firm rebuttal to the Democrats' critics. Furthermore, Representative Hugh Scott, a former chairman of the Republican Party, accused the State Department of planning 'to subvert our military victory by calling a halt at the 38th Parallel'.[13]

With Congressional elections due in November 1950 the Democrats did not wish to lay themselves open to Republican charges in the campaign that a timid policy of settling for the status quo had cost America the fruits of victory in Korea. Above all, many Americans in influential positions in government were allured by the heady prospect that a successful invasion of North Korea and reunification under a non-Communist government would be the climactic turning point in the Cold War. The North Korean people, it was felt, would welcome liberation; a united Korea would serve as a model of economic prosperity and democratic freedom; and Communism would lose its appeal world-wide. MacArthur's success at Inchon made the attainment of a swift victory in North Korea seem all the more feasible. Support therefore became overwhelming for the more adventurous policy of crossing into North Korea and attaining a wider victory which could have a deep impact on the course of the Cold War.

On 1 September 1950 the National Security Council (NSC) recommended that MacArthur should extend his operations north of the 38th Parallel and make plans for the occupation of North Korea. If the Chinese intervened, MacArthur could continue operations for as long as he believed that his forces were capable of successful engagement against them. In the event of Soviet intervention, MacArthur was to go on the defensive and consult Washington immediately. Truman approved this NSC recommendation and on 15 September a directive was sent to MacArthur on the basis of this decision. A resolution, sponsored by eight nations, was introduced in the General Assembly, expressing support for United Nations action to establish a 'united, independent and democratic government in the sovereign state of Korea'.[14] On 7 October this resolution was passed by the General Assembly, and on 8 October American forces crossed the 38th Parallel into North Korea.

In deciding to cross the 38th Parallel the United States made the calculation that this action would not lead to intervention in Korea by China or the Soviet Union. In the initial stages of the Korean War the Chinese focused upon the Formosa issue rather than upon Korea itself, though a result of America's 27 June 1950 decision to send the Seventh Fleet to the Formosa Straits was the withdrawal of Chinese forces from southern China, across from Formosa, to Manchuria, across the border from North Korea. Beijing made relatively little reference to the Korean War over the summer of 1950, except for vituperative condemnations of America's Formosa policy, and on 20 September Loy Henderson, US ambassador to India, reported that Zhou Enlai had told K.M. Panikkar, Indian ambassador to China, that China had no intention of intervening in Korea, short of a world war. As the threat loomed larger, however, of MacArthur's forces sweeping through North Korea up to the Chinese border, the Chinese began to issue warnings to the United States not to invade North Korea. On 25 September the acting chief of staff of the People's Liberation Army, General Nieh Jung Chen, told Panikkar that the Chinese did not intend to sit back and allow the Americans to come to their border. On 30 September Zhou Enlai said in a speech that the Chinese would not 'supinely tolerate seeing their neighbours being savagely invaded'.[15] Most dramatically, on 3 October Zhou summoned Panikkar to the Chinese Foreign Ministry in the early hours of the morning and issued a blunt warning that if American forces crossed the 38th Parallel, China would intervene.

The United States dismissed these warnings as a bluff, probably intended to influence the UN vote on the eight-nation resolution. In later testimony before Congress Acheson stated that the United States did not believe that the Chinese would intervene because China would fear that her forces would be utterly defeated by MacArthur's army and that the Chinese Communist leaders, who had been in power only since October 1949, would fear that military defeat would weaken their position at home and lead to their downfall. Most contemporary observers agreed with this assessment. James Reston, the influential *New York Times* columnist, wrote on 1 October 1950 that 'Mao Zedong will hesitate to commit suicide'.[16]

There was little opposition to the decision to cross the 38th Parallel within America or from America's allies. A Gallup Poll on 13 October found 64 per cent in favour of crossing the 38th Parallel and 27 per cent opposed. The British and the Canadians, allies who were always on guard to check extremes in American actions, quietly went along with the decision.

On 16 October the first Chinese 'volunteers' crossed into Korea and on 25 October the UN forces encountered Chinese in the enemy ranks. On 6 November, however, the Chinese disengaged, which was interpreted either as a sign of Chinese weakness or as a signal that the Chinese were firing a warning shot indicating that unless the Americans withdrew they would intervene in force. MacArthur, who did not fear Chinese intervention and whose wish was to extend the war into China, pressed northward with all speed. MacArthur was instructed to proceed with caution, to establish a firm line at the narrow neck of Korea, which was a strong defensive position at the 40th Parallel, and to use only South Korean troops in the northern-most provinces which bordered on China. But George Marshall, who had been appointed Secretary of Defense in September 1950, had given leeway to MacArthur with the instruction of 29 September 1950 that 'We want you to feel unhampered tactically and strategically to proceed north of the 38th Parallel'.[17] MacArthur used the discretion given to him as commander to press northward precipitously, using American troops all the way up to the Chinese border. On 24 November MacArthur announced the commencement of his final 'Home by Christmas' offensive. On 28 November the Chinese intervened in massive numbers, cut off the UN forces in the east from those in the west, necessitating a hurried evacuation by sea and a disorderly retreat. The Chinese and North Koreans advanced swiftly through North Korea, crossed the 38th Parallel and captured Seoul on Christmas Day 1950.

The debacle produced bitter recriminations. The British, who had been concerned by MacArthur's advance to the Chinese border and who had proposed a buffer zone between China and North Korea, were greatly alarmed by the massive Chinese intervention and advocated the offer of a settlement, with favourable terms to the Chinese regarding Formosa and admission of Communist China into the United Nations. The Americans angrily rejected such proposals, arguing that concessions under duress would encourage further aggression. A careless remark by Truman on 30 November with regard to the possible use of the atomic bomb in Korea brought the British prime minister, Clement Attlee, flying across the Atlantic to seek reassurances regarding American policy. While Attlee concluded from his talks with Truman that the United States would not use atomic bombs, the British succumbed to strong American pressure to accept an uncompromising policy towards China, particularly the UN resolution of 1 February 1951 condemning China as an aggressor nation, which the British regarded as an unhelpful gesture which would make a negotiated settlement more difficult. The United States also imposed an embargo on trade with China on 3 December 1950, which, given the virtually non-existent trade between China and the United States, was intended as a symbolic gesture and an act of pressure on other countries, especially Britain, to cut off trade with China.

The US administration laid much of the blame for the disaster in Korea on MacArthur. Yet, while MacArthur's outrageous insubordination fully justified his dismissal by Truman on 11 April 1951, the MacArthur controversy blurred issues and enabled the administration to use MacArthur as the scapegoat for the reversals which had resulted from the decision taken by the Truman administration to cross the 38th Parallel in the calculation that the Chinese would not intervene. MacArthur's precipitous drive northward, dividing his forces in east and west North Korea and without consolidating his position at the narrow neck, left UN forces dangerously exposed. Even more so, MacArthur's dismissal was undoubtedly the proper response to his frequent public criticisms of administration policy, especially his advocacy of policies which were liable to extend the war into China. It was not MacArthur's excesses, however, but the basic decision of the administration to take a gamble in crossing the 38th Parallel which led to the calamity which followed Chinese intervention. The situation was stabilized with considerable difficulty by General Matthew Ridgeway's Eighth Army, which halted the Chinese and North Korean advance and drove the invaders back to a line close to the 38th Parallel by April 1951.

While Chinese intervention created extremely serious difficulties, the United States did not encounter the more greatly feared possibility of Soviet intervention. Paucity of evidence makes assessments of Sino-Soviet relations in this period speculative. It seems clear, however, that American intervention in Korea in June 1950, together with the American naval presence in the Formosa Straits, aid to French Indo-China and the Philippines and the American occupation of Japan, made China feel more encircled and look for protection to the Soviet Union. In October and November the United States assumed that the Chinese had consulted with the Kremlin before intervening, and the Joint Chiefs of Staff and CIA feared that Chinese intervention might be a precursor to Soviet intervention and the outbreak of general war. In December the United States strongly considered attacks on China as retaliation for Chinese intervention in Korea, but Acheson warned that this could bring the Sino-Soviet treaty into operation. The Soviets in fact seemed quite restrained in Korea and willing to allow the Chinese to do the fighting on their behalf. Nevertheless, fears persisted in the United States that the Soviet Union might enter the war and, along with the Chinese, drive the Americans out of Korea and threaten Japan.

The Korean War ended any lingering hopes that Communist China and the Soviet Union would not necessarily be close allies and that significant differences existed between varieties of Communism which could be turned to the advantage of the United States. Truman recorded that when Attlee visited Washington, 'Attlee observed that opinions differed on the extent to which the Chinese Communists were Kremlin satellites. I said that in my opinion the Chinese are Russian satellites'.[18] Dean Rusk described the Chinese Communist government as 'a colonial Russian government – a Slavic Manchukuo'.[19] Fierce anti-Chinese sentiment on the part of the United States blinded America from differences between China and the Soviet Union which grew during the Korean War, especially a growing Chinese self-confidence as a result of their triumph in North Korea which made them feel less reliant on Soviet protection and more of an equal with the Soviet Union.

The United States also felt that the Korean War placed the Soviet Union in a strong position in Europe, diverting American forces to the Far East and leaving Europe exposed. This enabled the Soviet Union not only to pose a graver military threat to Western Europe but to advance tempting proposals, such as a settlement on Germany, which might divide the Allies. The United States was determined to increase the military strength of NATO and to hold the Allies together in resistance to the seductive Soviet peace offensive.

In June 1950 the greatest fear of America and her allies was that Korea was a feint to distract American troops which would be followed by an attack in Europe. But even if such an extreme threat did not materialize, the Korean War brought the United States to the conclusion that Western defences in Europe were woefully inadequate. Hence, the Korean War acted as the catalyst for acceptance of the analysis of the world situation and recommendations for increased defence spending of NSC-68. Following the North Korean attack, US military expenditure swelled, not only to meet military needs in Korea but to construct a position of military containment. Defence expenditure was increased to $50 billion in December 1950, and as a percentage of Gross National Product (GNP) it rose from 5 per cent in June 1950 to 14 per cent by 1953. Between June 1950 and the spring of 1951, America's military establishment grew from 1.4 million to 2.5 million, with growth in the Air Force from forty-eight to seventy air groups, a 50 per cent increase in the number of combat ships and an increase of 1.1 million in the army. The stockpile of atomic bombs grew from fifty in 1948 to 1,000 by 1953, while Truman overrode the scruples of Robert Oppenheimer and other scientific advisers to press ahead with the development of the hydrogen bomb, which was tested in 1953 and deployed in 1955. NATO was transformed from a paper organization to a military establishment, with 300,000 additional American troops sent to Europe in 1950 and Eisenhower appointed the first Supreme Allied Commander in Europe (SACEUR). Treaties were also negotiated with many non-NATO countries to establish new American bases in such countries as Spain and Morocco. As Charles Bohlen put it, 'It was the Korean War, not the Second World War, which made the United States a world military-industrial power'.[20]

The United States also greatly increased military assistance to her allies. The evolution of containment from its economic to its military form was illustrated by the end of Marshall aid in December 1950 and the increase in the Military Assistance

Program. Britain, the only military power of consequence in Europe, engaged in a massive rearmament effort at a cost of £3.6 billion in September 1950, increased to £4.7 billion in January 1951, which, with less American military assistance forthcoming than Britain had expected, overstretched the British economy and was an important factor in Britain's post-war economic decline. Most controversially, the Americans insisted on West German rearmament. At the Lisbon meeting of the North Atlantic Council in Lisbon in September 1950 Acheson made West German rearmament a condition for American commitment of troops to Europe. A compromise was reached in the form of the European Defence Community (EDC), a scheme whereby German battalions would be part of a European army under a European Defence Minister instead of an independent West German army. But the principle of West German rearmament was accepted, in spite of vigorous denunciations and accusations by the Soviet Union. Stalin's proposal in 1952 of German unification and neutralization was summarily rejected, and when the French legislature ultimately voted against ratification of the EDC treaty in 1954, West Germany was instead admitted into NATO in 1955.

To a figure such as Acheson the defence increases of the Korean War period made containment a reality which deterred Soviet aggression and led to a generation of peace. Others have criticized America's military build-up as an overreaction to Korea, provocative to the Soviet Union and responsible for the creation of the military-industrial complex in America. The father of containment, George Kennan, was extremely critical of West German rearmament, to which he felt that the Soviets were bound to be extremely sensitive. Charles Bohlen concluded that

> Acheson, influenced, I think, by those in the State Department who did not know Soviet Russia, felt that the Korean War represented a new Soviet foreign policy of military expansion and that all of the areas contiguous to the free nations in Europe were threatened by attack. As a result of this erroneous judgement, the United States overinterpreted the Korean War and overextended our commitments.[21]

Burton Kaufman agrees, arguing that on the basis of the unique situation in Korea, America developed 'a warped perception of a world-wide Communist threat'.[22]

American opinion of the Soviet Union was, moreover, increasingly geared towards an image of a demonic society which was repellent to the United States. On the Soviet side, in the last years of Stalin the Soviet Union was growing even more reclusive. When Kennan was appointed ambassador to the Soviet Union in 1952, he became so frustrated by the isolation of the diplomatic community which was enforced by the Soviet authorities that he commented in September 1952 that he had been interned in Germany in the Second World War and that 'the treatment we receive in Moscow is just about like the treatment we internees received then'.[23] Kennan's remarks led to his declaration as *persona non grata* by Moscow, reducing US–Soviet contacts even further.

The United States wished also to restrict trading contacts with the Soviet Union as much as possible. In 1949 the Co-ordinating Committee of the Paris Consultative Group of Nations (COCOM) was formed to establish regulations for trade with the Soviet Union by the United States, Western Europe and Japan. All nations agreed on a prohibition of the export of items of obvious military value, but with regard to the grey areas of items with dual military and civilian use, the United States pressed for the most narrow interpretation. The Battle Act, sponsored by Representative Hugh Battle, banned American military assistance to any nation which exported to the Soviet Union items on a stipulated list, which included anything of conceivable potential military value. Cold War attitudes had developed to their fullest extent, as Americans viewed Soviet Communism in abstract terms of a mysterious evil power which the United States must hold at bay.

With a stalemate in the fighting in Korea following the re-establishment of a UN defensive line approximately along the 38th Parallel in April 1951, the United States was eager to initiate peace negotiations. On 31 May and 5 June Kennan met Jacob Malik, the Soviet ambassador to the United Nations, who suggested that the United States should make an approach to the Chinese and North Koreans. In response to these Soviet promptings General Matthew Ridgeway broadcast on 30 June to the commander of the Communist forces that he was prepared to send representatives to cease-fire talks, to which the Communists replied favourably. On 10 July armistice negotiations began at Kaesong, moving a month later to Panmunjon, where for two years talks went on between the Americans and South Koreans on one side and the Chinese and North Koreans on the other side. The most difficult issue was exchange of prisoners of war, while in the background Syngman Rhee was a difficult ally, eager to continue the war to successful reunification and even willing to disrupt the peace process by the unilateral release on 25 June 1952 of 25,000 North Korean prisoners, many of whom wished to remain in South Korea. With 12,000 of the 33,000 American fatalities in the Korean War occurring in the period when the peace talks were conducted, pressure grew in the 1952 presidential election campaign for decisive action to end the war.

In Eisenhower's campaign for president in 1952, he pledged that if elected he would go to Korea between his election and inauguration, which was interpreted as a pledge that he would end the war. Following his visit to Korea from 2 to 5 December 1952 and his inauguration in January 1953, Eisenhower took various diplomatic and military measures in an attempt to gain Soviet, Chinese and North Korean agreement to an armistice. He authorized the bombing of the Suilo hydroelectric plants on the Yalu River, and veiled threats were signalled to the Chinese of the possible use of atomic bombs. It is not clear, however, whether the Chinese leaders understood the American nuclear threats, so that, as Roger Dingman has put it, 'nuclear weapons were not easily usable tools of statecraft that produced predictable results'.[24] Meantime, Stalin's death on 5 March 1953 brought to power a new Soviet leadership which seemed to wish a reduction in East–West tensions. American leaders, such as Vice-President Richard Nixon, attached important significance to the Soviet role in bringing about a Korean settlement. The evidence does not allow a clear answer to the question of how far Soviet pressure, Chinese fear of Eisenhower's threats or Chinese and North Korean exhaustion led to the end of the war, but after an agreement was reached on an exchange of prisoners of war through India, an armistice was signed on 23 July 1953.

From a later perspective, American intervention in June 1950 to prevent the success of the North Korean invasion seems justified. Even if Soviet instigation of the attack was less clear-cut than was assumed at the time, American inaction and Communist triumph would have been interpreted world-wide as a major Soviet victory, which would have undermined America's credibility and created dangerous instability in international relations. The decision to cross the 38th Parallel, on the other hand, seems most unwise, as the Truman administration succumbed to the temptation to use force in a policy of liberation which its Republican successors proclaimed with a fanfare of oratory but shrunk from pursuing in practice. The disasters which followed the crossing of the 38th Parallel provided a salutary warning against a policy of liberation from Communism by means of American military force. The defence increases in response to Korea seem justified to an extent, to give NATO credibility in military terms, but they were carried to excess. At the same time, the reduction in the few remaining human contacts between Americans and Soviets and the increasingly demonic image of the Soviet Union in the United States were worrying portents. These latter unhealthy trends were partly caused by and partly reflected in the development within the United States of the Red Scare and McCarthyism.

8

THE RED SCARE AND McCARTHYISM

On 9 February 1950 Senator Joseph McCarthy said in a speech in Wheeling, West Virginia, that

> While I cannot take the time to name all the men in the State Department who have been named as members of the Communist party and members of a spy ring, I have here in my hand a list of 205 that were known to the Secretary of State as being members of the Communist party and who, nevertheless, are still working and shaping policy in the State Department.[1]

McCarthy's astounding charge triggered off four years of national hysteria which had been building up since 1945 and which reached its climax in the phenomenon of McCarthyism from 1950 until McCarthy's condemnation by the Senate in December 1954.

The Red Scare arose partly from rational concerns over Soviet expansionist ambitions and possible infiltration into the US government of American Communists whose ideological allegiance to the Soviet Union was stronger than their national loyalty to the United States. To a much greater extent, however, McCarthyism arose from irrational and emotional factors within American society in the late 1940s and early 1950s. McCarthy's charge that there were 205 members of the Communist Party employed by the State Department in 1950 provided a vivid example of the irrationality of McCarthyism. McCarthy's accusation, when considered in a literal sense, was staggering. Its absurdity in a literal sense was easily demonstrable, but this missed the deeper significance of McCarthy's accusations. McCarthy had hit a responsive chord in the fears, anxieties, suspicions, frustrations and other such emotional concerns of

Americans of the time. An analysis of these emotional responses of the American people during the Red Scare reveals significant aspects of American attitudes towards Communism which played an important role in shaping American policy towards the Soviet Union.

The irrational features of the Red Scare can perhaps be demonstrated with respect to four developments: increasing anxiety over Communists in government at a time when new security procedures had greatly reduced the dangers of Communist penetration; the accusations of 'soft on Communism' against firm anti-Communists such as Dean Acheson and George Marshall; the ludicrous nature of the 'Reds under the bed' search for Communists in every walk of American life; and the embodiment of the crusade against godless Communism in so unsuitable a champion as Joseph McCarthy, a thoroughly reprehensible charlatan.

Communist infiltration into American government peaked in the 1930s and during the Second World War. With the expansion of the federal bureaucracy during the New Deal and the Second World War, opportunities for penetration into government by Communists presented themselves, at a time when Communist strategy in the Popular Front era in the later 1930s and during the Second World War encouraged Communists to take positions within the US government. The number and importance of Communists in government is impossible to ascertain precisely, by the very nature of the evidence, or lack of evidence in the case of successful infiltrators and spies. From FBI surveillance, however, and especially from the testimony of former Communists who recanted, such as Whittaker Chambers, Elizabeth Bentley and Louis Budenz, it would appear that, as Earl Latham writes, 'members of the Communist Party and their supporters occupied numerous positions in the Federal service. . . . The evidence does not seem to warrant the conclusion that the influence of these functionaries was very substantial'.[2]

If Communist penetration was of only minor importance at its height, it diminished considerably in the course of the late 1940s. Allan Matusow writes that 'Between 1945 and 1949 steadily mounting resistance would eradicate all the former achievements of the party and leave the movement in a shambles'.[3] Liberals, who until the mid-1930s were sympathetic to Communism, became staunchly anti-Communist in the late 1940s, with prominent liberals in Americans for Democratic Action such as Arthur Schlesinger, Jr, in the forefront of the condemnation of Communist tactics at home and abroad. Labour, which had been content to accept Communists in leadership positions in unions when effective organizers were needed in the 1930s, became fiercely nationalistic and anti-Communist as figures such as Walter Reuther, who defeated a Communist candidate in the election for president of the United Auto Workers in 1946, rose to prominence in the labour movement. Meantime, loyalty investigations were conducted within the government. In 1946 Truman appointed a Temporary Committee on Employment Loyalty and on the basis of its report issued an executive order in March 1947 establishing a new loyalty programme for the Federal government. Under the programme, the FBI checked against its files the names of all government employees in influential or sensitive positions and reported to the appropriate department suspicious information about any employee, who was then summoned to a hearing before a loyalty board within the department.

At the same time, investigations were carried out by Congress. In 1947–8 the 80th Congress, which had a Republican majority, held hearings on Communists in government before four committees, who all covered much of the same ground. The chairman of the House of Representatives Foreign Affairs Committee, at the end of his committee's hearings stated that 'There is one department in which the known or reasonably suspected subversives, Communists, fellow-travellers, sympath- izers and persons whose services are not in the best interests of the United States have been swept out. That is the Department of State'.[4] The *Chicago Sun-Times* commented on 12 March 1950 that 'Anybody who stops to think, anybody who listens to reason, must realize that the State Department and other agencies of government have been loyalty-tested to death'.[5]

In 1950 Congress passed the McCarran Act, which required Communist organizations to register with the Attorney-General and furnish membership lists, withheld passports from Communists and denied entry into America of aliens who belonged to Communist organizations. In the courts, eleven leading Communists, who were indicted by the Justice Department on the grounds of violating the Smith Act of 1940, which made it illegal to advocate the overthrow of the government, were found guilty and imprisoned for five years.

The Supreme Court upheld the conviction in 1951, ruling that freedom of speech could be curtailed when exercise of freedom of speech might create a 'clear and present danger'.[6] Many further prosecutions of Communist Party members followed, while at the state level un-American Activities committees were established to investigate Communist activity in individual states.

From this vast web of investigations and prosecutions, two significant cases of Communist infiltration into government emerged, which became *causes célèbres*: Alger Hiss and the Rosenbergs. At a hearing of the House Un-American Activities Committee (HUAC) in 1948, the former Communist Whittaker Chambers testified that Alger Hiss had been a Communist Party member in the 1930s and had passed State Department documents to a Soviet contact. Liberal supporters of Hiss argued that he was no Communist but a liberal New Dealer from an east coast Establishment background, Yale-educated, a Roosevelt adviser at Yalta, and that his case was an attempt to smear all figures from such backgrounds with association with Communism. The evidence suggests, however, that Hiss had indeed been a Communist and passed on State Department documents to the Soviet Union between 1933 and 1937 and that his conviction, which was vigorously pursued by Congressman Richard Nixon, was justified. Likewise, in the case of Julius and Ethel Rosenberg, their supporters alleged an anti-Semitic persecution of two Jews, at a time when many liberal intellectuals were Jewish. Yet, although the behaviour of the judge in their trial suggested prejudice against them, there was nevertheless strong evidence that the Rosenbergs had organized a spy ring which received information about the atomic bomb from figures including the British physicist Klaus Fuchs and passed on this information to Soviet agents. The sentence of execution on the Rosenbergs, who went to the electric chair in 1953, was harsh but not irrational.

All other cases of Communist penetration into the US government in the 1940s were of a minor nature. Judith Coplon, an official in the Foreign Agents Registration Division in the Department of Justice, was caught red-handed passing documents to a Soviet intelligence contact and escaped conviction only on a technicality. John Stewart Service was indiscrete in giving documents which were classified to *Amerasia*, a journal on America and Asia, but the documents, although classified, were of an innocuous character. Julian Wadleigh, a minor State Department official, passed documents to a Soviet agent, but the documents were unimportant. Investigations of other obscure minor officials produced only trivial matters, such as the State Department official who was said to have sung the Internationale in Russian from the steps of the Lincoln Memorial. The FBI checks and subsequent loyalty board hearings between 1947 and 1949 led to sixty-one dismissals of federal employees – in no case for espionage but on the grounds of alcoholism, homosexuality or some such matter which led the employee to be considered a security risk. Communist Party members who were prosecuted and imprisoned were not government employees but were convicted for inciting the overthrow of government.

Civil libertarians protested vigorously that the administration, Congress, the states and the courts were engaging in gross violations of the constitutional rights of the individual in these investigations and prosecutions. In loyalty board hearings, for example, the accused did not have the right to confront the accuser and subject the accuser to cross-examination; the McCarran Act had sweeping provisions on the government's right to internment without trial; and the 'clear and present danger' restriction on freedom of speech was overturned by the Supreme Court in 1957. The evidence is indisputable that the government ran roughshod over individual rights in its determination to eliminate the threat to security from Com- munists who held positions in the US government. The British were critical of American overzealousness in this regard. A Foreign Office official noted that in the United States there was a belief that 'Communism is an almost occult menace, the defence against which is not necessarily to be found with the exercise of the full freedom of Western democracy'.[7] But British laxity in rooting out Communists in government had appalling consequences. Donald MacLean, First Secretary in the British embassy in Washington from 1945 to 1949, was a Communist and regularly reported to the Soviets on top-secret matters, as did Guy Burgess, another British Communist who served in various posts in the Foreign Office. Kim Philby, likewise a secret Communist, who warned Burgess and MacLean of their impending arrest and thereby enabled them to escape to the Soviet Union in May 1951, served as British intelligence liaison with the CIA from 1949 to 1951 and faithfully reported information to Moscow, which led to the arrest and execution of many Western intelligence contacts. Anthony Blunt was a fourth British Communist in the Foreign Office, and there may have been others.

American fears regarding Communist infiltration into government were therefore very rational. It was, moreover, a matter of reasonable debate whether some sacrifices of civil liberties were justified in order to attain a more effective internal security system. In the Cold War, as in America's previous wars such as the Civil War, the First World War and the Second World War, civil liberties were clearly compromised to some extent in the name of national security. Civil libertarians have a very reasonable case in arguing that the United States was acting in a contradictory manner in abrogating the rights of individuals in a free society in the name of defending the United States against the perils of totalitarian Communism. The McCarthyist case, however, was totally unreasonable in the suggestion that after several years of extensive investigations of Communists by somewhat unconstitutional procedures there were still large numbers of Communists within the US government, such as 205 in the State Department. Yet the McCarthyist case won wide support among the American people. The roots of that support lay in emotion rather than logic.

Equally irrational were the charges that such figures as Dean Acheson or George Marshall were 'soft on Communism'. Acheson has been criticized by revisionist historians of the Cold War as a hardline Cold Warrior who failed to explore diplomatic opportunities to reach negotiated settlements on issues with the Soviet Union and China but instead took pride in the creation of a militarized form of containment, including a rearmed West Germany. McCarthy, however, paid little attention to the details of foreign policy, and his record in fact included votes against the Marshall Plan and NATO. McCarthy's allegations were based on smear and innuendo. He referred to Acheson as 'this pompous diplomat in striped pants with a phoney British accent'.[8] Acheson made himself vulnerable by his appearance as a character witness for Alger Hiss and by his statement after Hiss's conviction that he would not turn his back on Hiss and recommended a rereading of the passage in the New Testament on Christian charity. In McCarthy's distortion of these remarks, Acheson 'proclaimed to the American people that Christ on the Mount endorsed communism, high treason and betrayal of a sacred trust' and 'the blasphemy was so great that it awakened the dormant indignation of the American people'.[9] George Marshall seemed an even less plausible candidate for allegations of Communist sympathy. The architect of American victory in the Second

World War as chairman of the Joint Chiefs of Staff, the good soldier *par excellence* with a legendary devotion to duty and unimpeachable integrity, it was surely bizarre to suggest disloyalty on his part. But Marshall's mission to China in 1945–6 led McCarthyists to attack him. Senator William Jenner said that 'Marshall has been an unsuspecting, well-intentioned stooge, or an actual co-conspirator with the most treasonable array of political cut-throats ever turned loose in the executive branch of our government'.[10] The British were somewhat astonished that such wild accusations were not dismissed out of hand. The British embassy in Washington noted that 'Such excesses . . . do not arouse as much revulsion as they would among a less volatile and more restrained people'.[11] In British society a charge of soft on Communism against, for example, Foreign Secretary Anthony Eden, who in background, attitude and even physical appearance was very like Acheson, would have been regarded as sheer lunacy. Yet there were forces within American society which caused McCarthyist insinuations to damage Acheson's tenure of office as Secretary of State very severely and to destroy Marshall's effectiveness as a unifying influence in the Korean War when Truman appointed him Secretary of Defense in September 1950.

Aside from alleged Communists in government the search for Reds in every area of American life was carried to ludicrous lengths. In films and in education, for example, there was some logic in theory in the fear of the dissemination of Communist propaganda through Communist teachers and film directors. Yet, while there were certainly a number of Communists and left-wingers in the film industry, in practice Hollywood of the 1940s, controlled by arch-capitalists such as Joseph Kennedy and producing innocuously entertaining films, was an unlikely hotbed of Communist revolutionaries. As Stephen Whitfield notes, 'The work of writers and directors was subject to decisions of studios. Not even the House Un-American Activities Committee (HUAC) could find much of an ideological virus infecting American films'.[12] Hollywood was singled out for investigation partly due to overreaction to the Second World War pro-Soviet films such as *North Star* and *Mission to Moscow*, partly in response to extremely conservative studio owners such as Jack Warner, Louis Mayer and Walt Disney who attributed union trouble to Communist agitation, and partly to the desire of HUAC and its chairman, J. Parnell Thomas, to gain the glamour and publicity of calling star witnesses such as Gary Cooper and Robert Montgomery. The blacklist of writers and directors with suspected left-wing leanings was an outrageous violation of individual rights, but even more so the hounding of alleged Communists in the improbable setting of the tinsel town of Hollywood, barring, for example Charlie Chaplin from re-entry into the United States on the grounds of alleged Communist associations, produced an unsettling and ridiculous aura of a witchhunt out of control.

Similarly in education, there was a logical argument that Communist teachers might propagandize children, but the measures taken to deal with this matter were ludicrous. The suspension and dismissal of teachers and professors who refused to take loyalty oaths was a serious breach of civil liberties, but even more so obsessive fear of Communism in schools left America open to ridicule. Mrs Thomas J. White, a member of the Indiana school textbook committee, stated in 1953 that 'There is a Communist directive in education now to stress the story of Robin Hood. They want to stress it because he robbed the rich and gave to the poor. That's the Communist line. It's just a smearing of law and order.' A letter was sent to the Sheriff of Nottingham in England for advice on the matter. Sheriff William Cox sent a reassuring reply, 'Why, Robin Hood was no Communist'.[13]

The ultimate irrationality of McCarthyism lay in Senator McCarthy himself. Joseph McCarthy was a lawyer from an Irish-American background in Appelton, Wisconsin. In his election campaign for circuit court judge in 1939 McCarthy demonstrated the economy with the truth which was one of his notably persistent characteristics throughout his career. McCarthy stated frequently that his opponent, who was 66, was 73, and on one occasion he referred to his opponent as an 89-year-old man. Following his success in the election, McCarthy's record as a judge was undistinguished, causing the *Milwaukee Journal* to comment in 1946 that 'Judge McCarthy, whose burning ambition for political advancement is accompanied by astonishing disregard for things ethical and traditional, is doing serious injury to the judiciary of this state'.[14] In 1943 McCarthy took a leave of absence from the bench to serve in the armed forces. As an intelligence officer in the Far East he flew on a number of reconnaissance missions, usually, as was the practice of intelligence officers on missions where no enemy aeroplanes were expected, occupying the empty tail-gunner's seat. McCarthy referred to these flights in his later political career as '14 dive-bombing missions over Japanese positions' in a 1944 election campaign, '17 official missions in the South Pacific' in the 1948 Congressional Directory and '30 dive-bombing missions' in 1951.[15] A 1946 campaign leaflet brazenly stated that

> Joe McCarthy was a Tail Gunner in the Second World War. . . . He fought on land and in the air all through the Pacific. He and millions of other guys kept you from talking Japanese. Today, Joe McCarthy is home. He wants to serve America in the Senate. Yes, folks, Congress needs a tail-gunner.[16]

Elected to the Senate in 1946 McCarthy gained an unsavoury reputation as a senator whose main interest was in cards and drink and who solved his problems of gambling debts by receipt of dubious loans from lobbyists, such as an unsecured loan from the Pepsi-Cola Company, which earned him the name in Wisconsin of the Pepsi-Cola Kid. But McCarthy had intuitive political skills of a high order. When his 9 February 1950 speech brought him national attention, he exploited this to the full. He was unable to substantiate his charges before the Senate committee headed by Senator Millard Tydings which was drawn up to investigate the matter. In particular, McCarthy could not produce names of alleged Communists, and the few names which he gave lacked credibility. On 21 March 1950 he promised to name 'the top USSR espionage agent in the United States', and on 27 March he gave the name of Owen Lattimore – an academic specialist on China who held sympathetic views with regard to the Communists in China but who had no espionage connections whatever with the Soviet Union. The Tydings committee reported on 20 July 1950 that

> We are constrained fearlessly and frankly to call the charges, and the methods employed to give them ostensible validity, what they truly are: a fraud and a hoax perpetrated on the Senate of the United States and the American people. . . . For the first time in our history we have seen the totalitarian technique of the 'big lie' employed on a sustained basis.[17]

McCarthy skilfully deflected this condemnation, asserting that the Tydings report was a

> signal to the traitors, Communists and fellow travellers in our

government that they need have no fear of exposure from this administration. . . . The most loyal stooges of the Kremlin could not have done a better job of giving a clean bill of health to Stalin's Fifth Column in this country.[18]

Tydings came up for re-election in November 1950, and McCarthy worked for his Republican opponent, who defeated Tydings. McCarthy denounced Tydings as a Communist sympathizer, though Tydings was a right-wing Democrat whom Roosevelt had unsuccessfully attempted to replace by a liberal Democrat in 1938. McCarthy aides drew up a pamphlet on Tydings's alleged Communist associations, showing, for example, a composite photograph, which was taken from two separate photographs joined together, of Tydings with Earl Browder, the General Secretary of the American Communist Party. Tydings's defeat in the 1950 election, like the defeat of Senator Scott Lucas in Illinois against whom McCarthy also campaigned, was due to a wide variety of factors aside from McCarthy's intervention, but McCarthy acquired a reputation as a formidable political foe who could not be challenged with impunity. In 1951 Senator Thomas Benton lodged a complaint regarding McCarthy's tactics in the Tydings election campaign and called for a Senate inquiry. McCarthy refused to co-operate with the inquiry, stating that 'the Benton type of attack can be found in the *Daily Worker* almost any day of the week and will continue to flow from the mouths and pens of the camp-followers as long as I continue my fight against Communists in government'.[19] When Benton came up for re-election in Connecticut in 1952, McCarthy campaigned against him, and Benton lost. Even Eisenhower, who despised McCarthy, especially on account of McCarthy's attacks on Marshall, came to fear McCarthy. Eisenhower planned to repudiate McCarthy in a speech in Wisconsin in October 1952, but under pressure from McCarthy aides the passage which criticized McCarthy was deleted.

With Republican victory in the Congressional elections of 1952 McCarthy became chairman of the Committee on Government Operations, with its Permanent Sub-committee on Investigations. In 1953–4 McCarthy conducted three investigations, into the Voice of America, the International Information Agency and the Department of the Army. The investigations were noisy and disorganized and did not result in orderly reports or proposals for legislation. As part of the International

Information Agency hearings, two young McCarthy aides, Roy Cohn and G. David Schine, undertook a tour of International Information Agency libraries in American embassies in Europe to search for Communist books, which led frightened officials to remove from the shelves the books of such suspect authors as Theodore Dreiser, Arthur Schlesinger, Jr, and W.H. Auden, and on occasion a number of books were burned.

Refusal to give preferential treatment to G. David Schine when he was drafted into the army was one of the reasons which led McCarthy to investigate the Department of the Army. McCarthy discovered that at Camp Kilmer, New Jersey, Major Irving Peress had left-wing affiliations and refused to sign a loyalty certificate, yet he had nevertheless been given promotion when regularly due and received an honourable discharge when his term in the army came to an end. It was beside the point to McCarthy that Peress's political affiliations hardly constituted a security risk, since Peress was an army dentist. Senator Ralph Flanders said on 9 March 1954 that McCarthy 'dons his warpaint. He emits his warhoops. He goes forth to battle and proudly returns with the scalp of a pink dentist. We may assume that this represents the depth and seriousness of Communist penetration at this time'.[20]

Criticisms of McCarthy became more forthcoming, especially Edward Murrow's *See It Now* television programme on 11 March 1954. McCarthy's downfall then came about with the televised Army–McCarthy Hearings in April and May 1954. McCarthy was seen as an uncouth boor with no substance to his accusations. By the end of 1954 fear of McCarthyism had declined and the Senate had sufficient courage to condemn him on two counts of misconduct. By 1955 his influence had declined so much that the Post-Master General even rejected his nomination of a candidate for postmaster of his home town of Appelton, Wisconsin. In 1957 McCarthy died at the age of 48 of cirrhosis of the liver, brought on by long-term overindulgence in alcohol.

There are many rational points of explanation for McCarthy's rise to prominence. He was a skilful and ruthless political manipulator with a natural flair for self-publicity. It is understandable, if not admirable, that few dared to stand up to him. Nevertheless, his 50 per cent approval rating in a Gallup Poll in January 1954, with only 29 per cent disapproval, revealed the unhealthy nature of attitudes towards Communism within American public opinion. For Americans to allow the cause of the defence of decent, democratic Christian values against totalitarian Communism to be championed by such a manifestly flawed and worthless character as Joseph McCarthy constitutes irrefutable evidence that American opposition to Communism was not wholly rational.

The roots of the Red Scare and McCarthyism lay in anxieties with regard to aspects of American foreign policy but also in various trends in social and political developments at home. With regard to foreign policy, the experiences of the United States in the late 1940s and early 1950s was quite different from earlier American foreign-policy encounters. Historically, America had remained aloof from world affairs and when drawn into wars such as the First World War and the Second World War American intervention had brought about swift and complete victories. By the late 1940s, however, America was drawn into world affairs on a long-standing basis with, instead of rapid victories, stalemates and frustrations in Eastern Europe, China and Korea. Explanations of the complexities of the international situation and the limitations of American power were confusing and dissatisfying. The Truman administration resorted to some oversimplification of the issues, whipping up anti-Soviet fears in order to win Congressional support for appropriations for aid to Greece and Turkey and for the Marshall Plan by warning, as Acheson wrote, that 'The Soviet Union was now a superpower, unabashedly hostile to us, operating all over the world through fifth columns of national Communist parties'.[21] But the more blatantly simplified McCarthyist explanation had much wider appeal, namely that American inability to win swift victories as in previous times was due to treachery within the US government. American engagement in fighting in Korea brought amorphous Cold War anxieties to a head, and the rapturous popular welcome to MacArthur when he returned to the United States after his dismissal for insubordination revealed the widely-held latent desire for an old-style, clear-cut quick victory.

Frustrations over foreign policy were intermingled, however, with powerful forces which arose from anxieties over trends in domestic political and social developments since the New Deal. In the 1920s the business class had been dominant in American life, with government in the era of Coolidge and Hoover very clearly the spokesman of business. American businessmen and their allies in government confidently proclaimed business enterprise and free-enterprise capitalism as the wave of the future, which would eliminate poverty and social ills in the course of time. Little interest or fear was directed towards the opposing ideology of Communism in the backward, poverty-stricken Soviet Union.

The 1929 crash, however, and Hoover's failure to cope with the Depression led to the fall from dominance of American business and, with Roosevelt's election and the New Deal, the rise to predominance of government and the bureaucracy. Business, humiliated and scorned, became growingly resentful and frustrated, denouncing the New Deal as the first steps to Socialism. With so domineering a figure as Roosevelt in office, business was able only to fume on the sidelines, establishing organizations such as the Liberty League and damning 'that man in the White House'. With Roosevelt's death in 1945 and Truman, a less dominating figure, as president, business was determined to regain the status and power which it had lost during the Roosevelt years. With the spy scares and fears over Communists in government, hatred of the New Deal found an outlet in attacks on Communists in government, in a sub-conscious as much as in a cynically manipulative manner. Senator Homer Capehart, for instance, asked in early 1949, 'How much more are we going to have to take? Fuchs and Acheson and Hiss and hydrogen bombs threatening outside and New Dealism eating away at the vitals of the nation. In the name of heaven, is this the best America can do?'[22] The reference to Acheson was significant, since Acheson was not a New Dealer but a conservative Democrat who had resigned as Acting Secretary of the Treasury in 1934 in protest against Roosevelt's monetary policies. Yet, as Senator Hugh Butler said of Acheson,

> I look at that fellow. I watch the smart-alec manner and his British clothes and that New Dealism, everlasting New Dealism in everything he says and does, and I want to shout, Get Out, Get Out, you stand for everything that has been wrong with the United States for years.[23]

Related to the frustrations of American business were the frustrations of the Republican Party, especially after its unexpected defeat in the presidential and Congressional elections in 1948. After Democratic control of Congress since 1930, the Republican Party assailed the Truman administration's record on post-war economic reconstruction and with rising inflation and bitter labour disputes the Republicans were victorious in the 1946 Congressional elections. The Republican

Party looked forward to regaining the presidency in 1948, which seemed certain with Truman's low prestige and low ratings in opinion polls, splits in the Democratic Party with Strom Thurmond running as a Dixiecrat and Henry Wallace as a Progressive, and a very strong Republican ticket of two successful, moderate Republican governors of the two largest states, Thomas Dewey of New York and Earl Warren of California. But in the most surprising upset in American political history, Truman won re-election as president and the Democrats regained control of Congress. The political atmosphere after the Republican defeat became increasingly bitter. The bipartisanship which had characterized foreign policy up to 1948 faded away, as a disgruntled Arthur Vandenberg relinquished the chairmanship of the Senate Foreign Relations Committee to the Democrat, Tom Connally. The Republicans were in the mood to use any issue with which to attack the Democrats, so that when the issue of Communists in government proved to be effective, they were prepared to exploit it. Senator Robert Taft, a respectable conservative Republican who disapproved of McCarthy, nevertheless urged McCarthy 'to keep talking and if one case doesn't work he should proceed to another'.[24] Senator J. William Fulbright later wrote that

> In retrospect the surprise Democratic victory in the election of 1948 was probably a misfortune for the country. Frustrated and enraged by their fifth successive defeat, the Republicans became desperate in their search for a winning issue. They found their issue in the threat of communism at home and abroad and they seized upon it with uncommon ferocity.[25]

McCarthyism, however, cannot be explained simply in terms of the frustrations of the right-wing in America. Its basis of support was much broader. Sociological analyses of the roots of McCarthyism have varied in their conclusions, but it would seem that McCarthyism provided an outlet not only for pent-up tensions of businessmen against the New Deal but more broadly for the alienation of the forgotten small man in American society in an age of complex problems. Education and age, for example, were important factors in explaining support for McCarthy, with older people and people of lower education more likely to support McCarthy.

A final element in explaining McCarthyism lies in the press. McCarthy associated closely with newspapermen, with whom he played cards regularly. McCarthy provided sensational stories for reporters in time for their deadlines, and such stories boosted newspaper circulation. Dean Acheson bitterly complained that McCarthy was a creation of the press, who published news that was not fit to print. Yet it is clear that the press did not create McCarthyism but reflected in exaggerated form the concerns and preoccupations of large numbers of Americans. The press did, however, play an important role in reinforcing this phenomenon.

George Kennan later wrote that

> What the phenomenon of McCarthyism did ... was to implant in my consciousness a lasting doubt as to the adequacy of our political system. . . . A political system and a public opinion, it seemed to me, that could be so easily disoriented by this sort of challenge in one epoch would be no less vulnerable to similar ones in another.[26]

Kennan's dismay needs to be kept in perspective. McCarthyism was not a unique aberration but the most extreme manifestation of forces which have been present throughout the entire history of the United States. The foreign policy of any country is shaped to some degree by fears, prejudices, political pressures and other such factors within the country as much as by dispassionate analysis of the country's interests and objectives. This is the case to an even greater extent in the very open democracy of the United States. Throughout American history, political opponents have been smeared with disloyalty, from the association of Jeffersonian Republicans with Jacobism by the Federalists in the 1790s to the exploitation of the pledge of allegiance issue by George Bush in the presidential election campaign in 1988. As a nation in which nationalism is closely bound up with ideology, as a nation of immigrants whose loyalty to America was required to be demonstrated, and as a nation which, along with its loudly proclaimed commitment to liberty, has always, paradoxically, at the same time had strong pressures towards conformity, America has been particulary vulnerable to the abuse of emotional appeals to national loyalty. McCarthy disappeared from the political scene after his condemnation of the Senate in 1954, but the irrational attitudes which he represented persisted, though in a less virulent form, and formed a vital part of the pressures which helped to shape American foreign policy, especially policy towards the Soviet Union.

9

THE EISENHOWER ERA, 1953–61

Eisenhower's inauguration as president in January 1953 was followed shortly thereafter by Stalin's death in March 1953 and the Korean armistice in July 1953. The first thaw appeared in the Cold War, which had gone through its most intense period from 1947 to 1952. Eisenhower's presidency was marked by a succession of thaws and freezes in the Cold War, yet by 1961, as Eisenhower noted in his Farewell Address, the US–Soviet relationship of suspicion and hostility was basically unaltered and the arms race had escalated dangerously. In one sense, Eisenhower's record was successful, since he ended the Korean War and, in a time of great peril, defended America's interests and kept the peace at an affordable cost. In another sense, however, was Eisenhower overly cautious in his relations with the Soviet Union, with the result that opportunities for détente and disarmament were missed? This is perhaps the major question which needs to be examined with respect to US–Soviet relations in the Eisenhower era.

As a war hero with a very appealing public personality, Eisenhower had powerful assets to enable him to pursue bold initiatives. On the other hand, to an even greater extent than most presidents Eisenhower was under severe political constraints, while at the same time he was not personally inclined to take any gambles on Soviet goodwill, which he believed to be virtually non-existent. Eisenhower won the presidential election in 1952 by a wide margin, but the Republicans gained control of the Senate only by the casting vote of the vice-president and held a slim majority of eight in the House of Representatives. Moreover, a serious political division existed within the Republican Party between the conservatives and moderates. Eisenhower, a moderate Republican, needed to heal the breach

116

with conservative Republicans which had opened up with Eisenhower's victory for the Republican nomination over the conservative Robert Taft, who became Senate Majority Leader in 1953. Moreover, McCarthy's power was at its peak and, although Eisenhower despised McCarthy personally, he needed to avoid a confrontation with the McCarthyists, which could split the Republican Party. Against such a political background, an opening to improve relations with the Soviet Union would have been difficult even if Eisenhower had been inclined to attempt it, which essentially he was not.

As well as domestic political forces, there were strong economic and international pressures which militated against initiating an opening to the Soviet Union. The American economy had been sustained in the late 1940s by the expenditure of savings accumulated in the Second World War. With this short-term bonus exhausted by 1950, the continuing health of the American economy and the avoidance of the greatly feared post-war depression became dependent on military Keynesianism, namely high levels of defence expenditure to provide the boost of public expenditure which had been lacking during the Depression days of the 1930s. Hence, as Eisenhower perceptively observed in his Farewell Address, a 'military-industrial complex' was created of arms manufacturers, sub-contractors, trade unions, universities and a whole web of interests whose prosperity was open to jeopardy by détente and disarmament and who were therefore inclined to impute the worst intentions to Soviet moves and to insist that a continuing build-up of arms was the only realistic policy towards the Soviet Union. Moreover, internationally, the United States had with great difficulty created a degree of consensus within NATO in 1949–52 in favour of rearmament, including acceptance of West German rearmament. The United States was afraid of Soviet peace offensives designed to destroy Western unity by means of siren calls for international brotherhood instead of the burden of rearmament and for German reunification and neutralization instead of West German alignment with the West. In the State Department and in the British Foreign Office there was strong feeling that calls for a summit meeting and other such measures which raised the hopes of public opinion did serious damage to the NATO consensus, which the remote possibility of the achievement of meaningful détente did not justify.

Eisenhower's stock among historians has risen considerably.

The image portrayed by contemporary intellectuals of a weak, ill-informed chief executive who spent his time on the golf links while the government was run by powerful subordinates such as John Foster Dulles, has been shown to be quite false. Recent historians have demonstrated that Eisenhower self-consciously developed a style which camouflaged the subtle, premeditated manoeuvres of his administration by a guise of amateurish, bumbling avuncularity. As Richard Nixon observed, 'He was a far more complex and devious man than most people realized, and in the best sense of both words'.[1]

American foreign policy in the 1950s was controlled by Eisenhower rather than by Dulles. Eisenhower's choice of Dulles as Secretary of State was partly to appease the Republican right-wing with the appointment of a successor to Dean Acheson of a manifestly outspoken and uncompromising anti-Communist. To a greater extent, however, Eisenhower selected Dulles as a seasoned professional with experience as a foreign-policy adviser to Thomas Dewey as well as a consultant to the Truman administration and negotiator of the Japanese Peace Treaty in 1951. A grandson of John W. Foster, Secretary of State from 1889 to 1893, John Foster Dulles seemed almost to have been preparing for the office of Secretary of State throughout his life. Moreover, Eisenhower fundamentally agreed with Dulles's views on Communism, though he tempered the extremes of Dulles's position. Eisenhower's hatred of Communism grew in the late 1940s. Eisenhower enjoyed good relations with his Soviet military counterparts in the Second World War, and he found that on military matters the Soviets were reliable partners who kept their promises. In 1945–7 Eisenhower was sure that the war-ravaged Soviet Union had only peaceful, defensive objectives. Incidents in the late 1940s, however, such as the Berlin Blockade, led to disillusionment on Eisenhower's part towards the Soviet Union, which grew into bitter hostility which he maintained thereafter with only minor modification.

With regard to Communism at home, Eisenhower loathed McCarthy, but he was not unduly concerned by violations of civil liberties in the investigations into Communists in government. He told news publisher C.L. Sulzberger that 'It was silly to think that the liberties of the United States were being endangered merely because we were trying to squash communism'.[2] Eisenhower has been widely criticized, even by his sympathetic biographer, Stephen Ambrose, for failing to speak out against

McCarthy. Eisenhower argued that he should leave McCarthy sufficient rope with which to hang himself, which in due course McCarthy did, though not until after two years of further damage in 1953 and 1954. Yet Eisenhower's motives for not confronting McCarthy were more subtle. Eisenhower wished to avoid a public dispute within the Republican Party, but also he exploited the McCarthyist mood to replace large numbers of New Deal Democrats in the Federal bureaucracy with Republican loyalists. In a memo to Dulles in March 1953 Eisenhower wrote of the dominance within the federal bureaucracy of those who believed 'in the philosophy of the preceding administration', so that among higher officials there was 'a studied effort to hang on to those believing in the New Deal philosophy and to eliminate those who show any respect for the ideals of independence and self-reliance'.[3]

A new loyalty programme was introduced in 1953 which led to 5,000 resignations and 3,000 dismissals by the end of 1954. No cases of espionage were involved, and in the exaggeration of the figures by the end of 1954 a number of dismissals included personnel appointed by the Republican administration in 1953. But by the time of the Congressional elections in 1954 Richard Nixon could claim that 'We've been kicking the Communists and fellow travellers out of government not by the hundreds but by the thousands'.[4] Within the State Department China experts John Carter Vincent and John Patton Davies were dismissed, while George Kennan was left without an appointment and thereby compelled to retire. In January 1953 Dulles met State Department employees and informed them that 'positive loyalty' needed to be demonstrated.[5] F. Scott McLeod, a former aide to Senator Styles Bridges, was appointed head of the State Department Bureau of Security. When Charles Bohlen was nominated as ambassador to the Soviet Union, with strong support from Eisenhower, his confirmation hearings produced controversy since Bohlen had served as Roosevelt's interpreter at Yalta, with the result that eleven right-wing senators vociferously opposed and voted against the nomination.

Eisenhower had used a two-edged sword against McCarthyism. He not only bowed to but utilized the forces of McCarthyism to avoid a break with his party's right wing and to serve his own purposes in replacing New Dealers in the bureaucracy. But the most pernicious consequence of these developments was a timidity within government, especially in the State Department, to analyse issues other than in the relatively simplistic anti-Communist terms which, it was assumed, the new administration wished to hear.

The Republican campaign in 1952 proposed 'liberation' in place of the allegedly failed Democratic policy of containment. The Republican platform included a plank that 'We shall make liberty into a beacon light that will penetrate the dark places. It will mark the end of the negative, futile and immoral policy of "containment" which abandons countless human beings to a despotism and godless terrorism'.[6] Support for liberation in place of containment came from James Burnham, Sidney Hook and many other such intellectuals who had swung from Marxism in the 1930s to right-wing conservatism in the 1950s. Burnham wrote that 'Containment has no goal. . . . Its inner law is: let history do it'.[7] Walter Lippmann, a centrist thinker and influential newspaper columnist, supported this view, arguing that with a policy of containment, 'Moscow, not Washington, would define the issues, would make the challenges, would select the ground where the conflict was to be waged and would choose the weapon'.[8] There was a respectable intellectual case for the argument that containment consisted of 'treadmill policies', as Dulles put it, 'which, at best, might perhaps keep us in the same place until we drop exhausted'.[9] Kennan, however, probably had the better of the argument in his view that Western democracy had much firmer roots than Soviet Communism, which was an unnatural, alien imposition upon Russia and had within it the seeds of its own decay, so that time was on the West's side if Soviet expansion was contained.

Much more significantly, however, the argument was essentially not intellectual but emotional and political. As John Spanier has put it, containment was 'psychologically and emotionally in contradiction with American values and experience in foreign affairs'.[10] Moreover, in narrow political terms, Republican proclamation of liberation won support from ethnic minorities such as Polish-Americans, most of whom normally voted Democratic. Advocacy of liberation, therefore, arose from mixed motives of conviction, emotion and partisan advantage. Both Eisenhower and Dulles were careful to qualify statements in support of freedom for the peoples of Eastern Europe. In the 1952 campaign Eisenhower said that 'The American conscience can never know peace until the millions in Soviet satellites are restored again to be masters of their own fate', but, he added, this should come about by 'peaceful liberation'.[11] Similarly, Dulles in 1953 said that liberation 'must and can be a peaceful process'.[12] In February 1953 Congress passed the Captive People's Resolution which affirmed America's support for freedom in Eastern Europe and which, said Dulles, would 'register dramatically the desire and hope of the American people that the captive peoples shall be liberated'.[13]

As the American response to the East German revolt in 1953 and to the Hungarian Revolution in 1956 made clear, however, American policy towards Eastern Europe was in practice cautious. The Eisenhower administration was not prepared to risk war with the Soviet Union for the sake of the liberation of Eastern Europe. The Republicans talked of liberation but pursued in practice the same policy of containment as their Democratic predecessors. The call for liberation was largely rhetorical for domestic political purposes. It cannot be ascertained, however, how far this was appreciated in Moscow, where Dulles's rhetoric may well have been regarded as threatening and provocative and thus reduced even further any dim prospects of an improvement in relations.

On 5 March 1953 Stalin died, leading to a period of uncertainty and fluidity within Soviet leadership and in US–Soviet relations. Stalin was succeeded by a collective leadership of Georgi Malenkov, Chairman of the Council of Ministers; Nikita Khrushchev, First Secretary of the Communist Party; Nikolai Bulganin, Minister of Defence; Vyacheslav Molotov, Foreign Minister; and Lavrenti Beria, Minister of Internal Affairs and State Security. In June 1953 Beria was arrested for alleged treason and was executed in December 1953. Malenkov appeared to be the effective new Soviet leader, although Khrushchev's power steadily grew. In February 1955 Malenkov was demoted and replaced as Chairman of the Council of Ministers by Bulganin, who ruled jointly with Khrushchev for the next three years. In March 1958 Khrushchev took over Bulganin's post as Chairman of the Council of Ministers while he continued also to be First Secretary of the Communist Party, signifying Khrushchev's unquestioned supremacy, which he maintained until his fall from power in 1964.

In the spring of 1953 the new Soviet leadership sent tentative conciliatory signals to the West. On 15 March 1953 Malenkov said that 'There is no litigious or unsolved question which could not be settled by peaceful means or on the basis of mutual agreement with the countries involved. This concerns our relations with all states, including the United States of America'.[14] Over the next few months the Soviet government made concessions on a number of minor matters such as fishing rights and permission to some Soviet wives of foreigners to emigrate. These Soviet moves were variously interpreted in Western foreign ministries as either a ruse to divide the West and to give the new Soviet leadership time to consolidate itself or as an opportunity to initiate détente. Winston Churchill, who had returned to office as Britain's prime minister following the Conservative victory in the 1951 election, was very eager to explore the possibility of improving relations with the new Soviet government, especially by means of a summit conference. In one of the earliest letters in the personal correspondence in which Churchill and Eisenhower engaged during the period when they were both in office, from Eisenhower's inauguration in January 1953 to Churchill's retirement in April 1955, Churchill wrote to Eisenhower on 11 March 1953 that

> I have the feeling that we might both of us together or separately be called to account if no attempt were made to turn over a new leaf so that a new page would be started with something more coherent on it than a series of casual and dangerous incidents at many points of contact between the two divisions of the world.[15]

Eisenhower was not convinced and replied that

> I tend to doubt the wisdom of a formal multilateral meeting since this would give our opponent the same kind of opportunity he has so often had to use such a meeting simultaneously to balk every reasonable effort and to make of the whole occurrence another propaganda mill for the Soviets.[16]

Eisenhower felt that the Soviet government must demonstrate solid evidence of good will before a summit meeting should be considered, such as a settlement in Korea, an Austrian peace treaty or perhaps even an agreement on Germany.

Eisenhower decided on an alternative approach of a major speech deploring the arms race. While Eisenhower was dubious and hesitant with regard to improvements in US–Soviet relations by means of meetings and diplomatic exchanges, he had very strong feelings on the diversion of resources from civilian purposes to military spending. Paradoxically, the former general engaged in endless disagreements with the Pentagon throughout his presidency over the level of defence expenditure. Eisenhower feared that excessive defence spending would not only lead to an unbalanced budget and inflation but also would make America into a garrison state and endanger liberty. Eisenhower spent countless hours in debates on the 'great equation' of how far the defence budget could be pruned without jeopardy to national security. With enthusiasm, therefore, Eisenhower sought to convince the new Soviet leaders of the economic benefits of mutual restraint in arms expenditure. On 16 April 1953 Eisenhower delivered one of the most eloquent speeches in the post-war era on the waste of resources on armaments, stating that

> Every gun that is made, every warship launched, every rocket fired, signifies – in a final sense – a theft from those who hunger and are not fed, those who are cold and are not clothed. . . . The cost of one modern heavy bomber is this: a modern brick school in more than thirty cities. It is: two electric power plants, each serving a town of 60,000 population. It is: two fine, fully equipped hospitals. It is some fifty miles of concrete pavement. We pay for a single fighter plane with a half billion bushels of wheat. We pay for a single destroyer with new homes that could have housed more than 8,000 people. . . . This is not a way of life at all, in any true sense. Under the cloud of threatening war, it is humanity hanging from a cross of iron.[17]

Eisenhower's 16 April speech was very warmly received in the West and published in full in *Pravda*. Churchill wrote to Eisenhower that public opinion would now press for a summit meeting. 'How do you stand about this?', Churchill asked. 'In my opinion the best would be that the three victorious powers who separated at Potsdam, should come together again.'[18] Eisenhower poured cold water on the summit proposal. 'We should not rush things', he replied to Churchill. 'We would risk raising false hopes of progress toward an accommodation which would be unjustified'.[19] An arrangement was made instead for a preliminary meeting between the United States, Britain and France to discuss a possible summit with the Soviets. The meeting was postponed owing to a stroke suffered by Churchill in June 1953, and when the three-power meeting finally convened at Bermuda in December 1953, Churchill found himself alone in his eagerness for bold initiatives to reach out to the Soviet government. The British Foreign Office, as much as Dulles and the State Department, were very sceptical of Soviet intensions. Evelyn Shuckburgh, Principal Private Secretary to Anthony Eden, expressed disapproval of Churchill 'fostering the sentimental illusion that peace can be obtained if only the "top men" get together. It seems an example of the hubris which afflicts old men who have power'.[20] Britain's ambassador in Moscow, William Hayter, warned that 'in Western Europe the appearance of the faintest gesture on the part of the Soviet immediately arouses disproportionate hopes'.[21] Eisenhower stated his views on Soviet intensions in blunt terms at the Bermuda conference. With regard to signs of changes in Soviet policy, Eisenhower stated that 'Russia was a woman of the streets and whether her dress was new, or just the old one patched, it was certainly the same whore underneath. America intended to drive her off her present "beat" into the back streets'.[22]

Eisenhower felt that indications of Soviet goodwill on specific issues were required. The Soviets were assumed to have played an important role in one of Eisenhower's tests of good faith, namely the Korean armistice, but Eisenhower now asked for Soviet co-operation on the peaceful development of atomic energy. On 8 December 1953 Eisenhower advanced proposals on 'Atoms for Peace' in a speech at the United Nations. This rather complex plan for nuclear co-operation for peaceful purposes did not lead to constructive developments, while the Foreign Ministers conference in Berlin in early 1954 on Germany and Austria bogged down in disagreements. Churchill was distressed that relations with the Soviet Union were being conducted on the level of acrimonious exchanges between officials at the lower level, where 'little men are tied to their texts', rather than bold, imaginative moves at a meeting at the top level.[23] He wrote to Eisenhower that

> It will seem astonishing to future generations that with all that is at stake no attempt was made by personal parley between the heads of Government to create a union of consenting minds on broad and simple issues. . . . Fancy that you and Malenkov should never have met, or that he should never have been outside Russia, when all the time in both countries appalling preparations are being made for measureless mutual destruction. . . . *Now* I believe, is the

moment for parley at the summit. The whole world deserves it'.[24]

Eisenhower was not prepared to hold a summit until, among other matters, the issue of West German rearmament was resolved. The European Defence Community (EDC) treaty remained unratified by many countries and in August 1954 it was rejected by the French legislature. This, however, spurred the rapid negotiation of the entry of West Germany into NATO in March 1955. Also, the Soviet Union agreed to an Austrian peace treaty, signed on 15 May 1955, thereby fulfilling another important requirement of a test of Soviet goodwill. As a result, ironically shortly after Churchill's retirement, the summit which he had so desired took place, at Geneva in July 1955. In terms of cordial personal relations the summit was a success, and a so-called 'spirit of Geneva' developed. Agreements were reached on cultural and educational exchanges, but no progress was made on substantial political issues. Eisenhower's proposal of Open Skies – namely reconnaissance by American and Soviet aeroplanes in one another's air space – was dismissed by Khrushchev as a propaganda ploy.

Similarly, elaborate Soviet proposals for major arms reductions, which had been discussed in negotiations in the United Nations Subcommittee on Disarmament since 1952 and presented by the Soviets with a fanfare on 11 May 1955 and repeated at Geneva, were rejected by the United States as inadequate with regard to verification procedures and as essentially propaganda. The Foreign Ministers conference in November 1955, which was a follow-up to Geneva, degenerated into unproductive wrangling. The Geneva summit, therefore, was a useful step in the process of humanizing the US–Soviet relationship and moving away from the darkest days of the Cold War of Stalin's last years. But it achieved almost nothing by way of resolving the basic differences between the two sides.

Eisenhower, then, had little faith in the prospects of improving US–Soviet relations or achieving disarmament by the process of diplomacy and summit meetings, while at the same time he feared the effects of high levels of defence spending on the American economy and on American society. The solution to which he therefore reverted was emphasis on the nuclear deterrent as a less expensive but very effective means of containment and by the use of the CIA in covert operations.

Eisenhower cut back on conventional defence spending and placed priority on the development of nuclear weapons. The stockpile of atomic bombs was built up at an accelerated rate. The hydrogen bomb, which had been successfully tested in 1952, was miniaturized sufficiently to fit the bomb bay of the B-47, the principal US aeroplane designed to deliver nuclear bombs, while the B-52 was developed to succeed the B-47. Disquiet over atomic tests, especially following an incident in 1954 when twenty-three Japanese fishermen died from radiation following the Bravo test in the South Pacific, was brushed aside and pushed into the background. Research and development of missiles was given top priority, both ground-launched missiles and the most futuristic technology of the 1950s, submarine-launched missiles. Short-range missiles and nuclear artillery shells were deployed in Europe in 1954.

The strategic implications of this so-called New Look in defence policy were spelled out most dramatically in Dulles's statements on brinkmanship, namely willingness to go to the brink of war in order to deter an adversary. The policy of brinkmanship was not so rigid and inflexible as Dulles's critics suggested. The Eisenhower administration did not threaten the use of strategic nuclear weapons in any crisis of any level of gravity, however serious or slight. The essence of the policy lay in the uncertainty aroused in the other side by the threat that the possibility existed that the United States might respond with nuclear weapons of any magnitude in any situation, and this fear and uncertainty supposedly made deterrence effective.

Eisenhower was ruthlessly calculating in his use of CIA covert operations as a means to contain Communist expansion. In Iran, a left-wing government under Mohammed Mossadeq had come to power in 1951 and nationalized the Anglo-Iranian Oil Company. The British had been eager to try to overthrow Mossadeq, but Truman and Acheson feared a backlash against blatant foreign aggression which might strengthen the Communists. Eisenhower supported CIA plans to stir up a mob in Tehran to bring down Mossadeq and replace him with the exiled Shah in August 1953. In 1954 the CIA aided Guatemalan exiles in Honduras under Colonel Carlos Costillo Armas to overthrow the left-wing government of President Jacobo Arbenz Guzman, who had nationalized American companies and received arms from the Soviet Union.

Eisenhower's emphasis on covert military measures and

strong nuclear defence rather than diplomatic negotiations with the Soviet Union was influenced also by his views on Communism in the Far East. Eisenhower regarded China as essentially part of a unit, the Sino-Soviet bloc, which conspired to bring about a world of Marxist-Leninist states. Furthermore, the strength of the China lobby and the emotional undercurrent in US public opinion regarding China brought strong political pressure to bear on the Eisenhower administration with regard to Far Eastern policy. Consequently, Eisenhower pursued bolder and more aggressive policies in the Far East than towards the Soviet Union in Europe. On 2 February 1953 Eisenhower made a change of order to the Seventh Fleet in the Formosa Straits from Truman's order of 27 June 1950. The US fleet was now instructed to continue to protect Formosa from invasion from the Chinese mainland but to discontinue the prevention of attacks from Formosa against the mainland. The change in order was largely theoretical, since Chiang Kai-shek's forces were in no way capable of mounting an invasion of China, while minor raids on the mainland of a nuisance value had regularly taken place, with the US fleet unwilling or unable to prevent them. But the order to 'unleash Chiang' was warmly received in right-wing Republican circles and strongly criticized by the British, who regarded the move as a needless provocation.

In Indo-China Eisenhower stepped up aid to the French in their war against the Vietminh, until by 1954 80 per cent of French costs were borne by the United States. The French position nevertheless continued to deteriorate, culminating in the crisis when a French army was encircled at Dien Bien Phu. In a dramatic debate within US government circles the question of direct American military intervention was considered. Air Force Chief of Staff Nathan Twining advocated an air strike with tactical nuclear weapons which would 'clean those Commies out of there and the band would play the Marseillaise and the French would come marching out of Dien Bien Phu in fine shape'.[25] Eisenhower wished to bring together an *ad hoc* coalition of a number of nations, the formation of which would deter the Communists and enable the French to succeed. Churchill, however, rejected this so-called 'united action' proposal, so that the French were left to negotiate peace in Geneva in a weak position following their surrender at Dien Bien Phu.

The United States was not a signatory of the Geneva agreement in 1954, but with American support Ngo Ding Diem, in breach of the Geneva agreement, established the republic of South Vietnam. Eisenhower frankly admitted in his memoirs that at the end of the war with the French 'possibly 80 per cent of the population would have voted for the Communist Ho Chi Minh'.[26] Yet, with American encouragement Diem refused to allow elections in Vietnam in 1956 as stipulated by the Geneva agreement. Thus, whereas the Geneva agreement had drawn a temporary demarcation line at the 17th Parallel, Diem established, on very dubious legal grounds, a new state of South Vietnam, to whose defence the United States became increasingly committed. The Eisenhower administration gave economic aid and military equipment to South Vietnam throughout the 1950s and enabled Diem to consolidate his position. Eisenhower drew the line of containment in the Far East at the 17th Parallel in Vietnam, stating that Vietnam was like the first in a row of dominoes, and if the first domino fell, others, such as Japan, would inevitably follow as Communism advanced.

The most acute Far Eastern crisis arose in early 1955 over the islands of Quemoy and Matsu off the coast of China. Since 1949 the Nationalists had controlled and garrisoned not only Formosa and the large group of islands close by, the Pescadores, but also a number of small islands close to the coast, Quemoy, Matsu and the Tachens. In late 1954 the Chinese Communists began to shell these off-shore islands, and the Nationalists evacuated the Tachens, but they were determined to defend Quemoy and Matsu. Eisenhower supported the Nationalists in their stand on Quemoy and Matsu and threatened nuclear retaliation if the Chinese Communists invaded the islands. The British were greatly alarmed and Churchill wrote to Eisenhower arguing in very strong terms that, while defence of Formosa and the Pescadores, which were nearly 100 miles from the mainland, was feasible and desirable, it made no sense not to evacuate Quemoy and Matsu, which were less than ten miles from the Chinese coast. The threat of nuclear retaliation, Churchill warned, could lead to world war involving the Soviet Union as well as China. Eisenhower replied that evacuation under threat would be dangerous appeasement and that American insistence on evacuation would create demoralization among the Nationalists, who were likely to oppose it, and a confusing situation was liable to follow ending with the loss of Formosa to the Communists. By the summer of 1955 the crisis passed, with the off-shore islands remaining in Nationalist hands. Although Quemoy and Matsu were subjected to intermittent Communist shelling throughout the 1950s, Eisenhower felt that a resolute stand had produced greater stability and raised the prospects of peace. The British felt that an unwarranted risk of great magnitude had been taken unjustifiably. A recent historian concludes that 'Newly available documentary evidence ... shows that Eisenhower actually brought the country to the "nuclear brink", far closer to war than a distraught public feared in 1955 ... and closer than most historians even suspected'.[27]

Meanwhile in Europe the first slight thaw in the Cold War continued from 1953 to 1956. American rhetoric regarding liberation died down after the 1952 election campaign. Instead, the State Department worked quietly for a policy of gradual change in Eastern Europe, with the most hopeful approach seen as the encouragement of Titoism and national Communism in Eastern Europe. The Soviet Union appeared to condone such developments, seeking reconciliation with Tito with visits by Khrushchev to Yugoslavia in 1955 and by Tito to Moscow in 1956, and, following a series of protests in Poland, the acceptance in October 1956 as General Secretary of the Polish Communist Party of Wladyslaw Gomulka, who had been deposed as a Titoist in 1949. Along with Khrushchev's remarkable speech denouncing Stalin at the Twentieth Party Congress in Moscow in February 1956, these developments towards gradual evolutionary change seemed promising.

Hopes that the first buds of spring were appearing in the Cold War, however, were cruelly dashed with the brutal Soviet suppression of the Hungarian Revolution in November 1956. The Hungarians, encouraged by Khrushchev's denunciation of Stalin and by reforms in Poland, replaced their Stalinist leader, Matyas Rakosi, by Erno Gero in July 1956. But momentum grew for more sweeping changes, which resulted in student demonstrations on 23 October and the reconstitution of the government under Imre Nagy, a reform Communist whom Rakosi had expelled from the party. Events developed rapidly in the last week of October, with Nagy agreeing to an election with a multi-party system. The Soviet government appeared to accept these developments, asserting on 30 October 'the principles of complete equality, of respect for territorial integrity, state independence and sovereignty, and of non-interference in one another's internal affairs'.[28] When Hungary declared a policy of neutralism, however, announcing withdrawal from the Warsaw

Pact on 31 October, the Soviet ambassador, Yuri Andropov, demanded a renunciation of this measure.

The situation was complicated by the Suez crisis in the Middle East, which occurred at the same time, with an attack on Egypt on 29 October by Israel, in collusion with Britain and France, thereby distracting world attention from Hungary to some extent. Lack of authoritative Soviet sources makes it impossible to ascertain whether the Soviets had initially merely stalled to give themselves time to prepare an attack on Hungary, or whether they were initially prepared to accept the Hungarian reforms but came to feel that the reforms went too far or whether the Soviets were initially afraid to launch an attack but the contemporaneous Suez crisis gave them the opportunity which emboldened them to invade. In any event, on 4 November Soviet forces attacked in large numbers, and Nagy was deposed and later executed, being replaced by Janos Kadar, who requested the Soviet army 'to help our nation in smashing the sinister forces of reaction'.[29] Some 5,000 Hungarians were killed in the courageous but useless resistance to Soviet armed forces, which put down the revolt within ten days. Thousands of Hungarian reformers were arrested, while others fled to the West as refugees. The United States watched impotently from the sidelines. Broadcasts by Radio Free Europe, which was theoretically independent but which was in fact financed by the CIA, had, like the speeches of Eisenhower and Dulles on liberation, not specifically advocated violent revolution, but they had given the impression that in the event of revolution the United States would provide assistance. The Eisenhower administration fully realized, however, that intervention was likely to lead to war, and the United States was not willing to go to war with the Soviet Union to liberate Eastern Europe. The pathetic, unanswered pleas for help from Hungarian revolutionaries left Americans with emotions of guilt, betrayal, frustration and, above all, rage over vicious Soviet perfidy. The Cold War reverted to a condition of deep freeze.

At the time when the violent suppression of the Hungarian Revolution made America look more towards its defences against the Soviet threat, further shocks befell the United States in 1957 when the Soviet Union successfully tested an intercontinental ballistic missile (ICBM) and, even more dramatically, placed in orbit a satellite, Sputnik. In fact, within months of the Soviet tests the United States successfully tested an ICBM and a satellite and was better placed to deploy both in large numbers at an earlier date than the Soviet Union. The United States was also far ahead of the Soviet Union in submarine technology, which became clear with the deployment of Polaris submarines in 1959. The 'bomber gap' which was alleged by Congressional critics of Eisenhower's defence cuts, such as Senator Stuart Symington, was a myth created by Soviet deception over the number of its aeroplanes. The United States was well-informed on the realities of the military balance from a new source of intelligence, the U-2, a spy aeroplane which from 1956 flew on photo-reconnaissance missions at high altitude over the Soviet Union, despite protests from the Soviets, who were aware of U-2 flights but were unable to shoot down an aeroplane at such an altitude. In reality, Sputnik illustrated what had been evident since the surprisingly swift development of a Soviet atomic bomb in 1949, namely that the Soviet Union was able, by concentrating its scarce scientific resources into the military area, to compete closely with the United States in the technological advances of the arms race. In the popular mind in the United States, however, Sputnik aroused fears that the United States had fallen behind the Soviet Union militarily, technologically and even in basic education. A sense of panic grew in the United States, with the introduction of crash educational improvement programmes, nuclear war air raid drills and the construction of nuclear bomb shelters.

In 1958 a further crisis arose with the Soviet Union over the perennial Cold War tension point, Berlin. In November 1958 Khrushchev announced that within six months he would sign a peace treaty with East Germany, which would transfer control over the air, road and rail routes from Western Germany to Berlin from the four-power authorities, as stipulated in previous agreements, to the East Germans. Eisenhower vigorously protested and warned Khrushchev of serious consequences if he took unilateral action. Additional American troops were sent to Germany, and the situation seemed ominous. The six-month deadline date passed without Soviet action on Berlin, however, and the crisis passed. By early 1959 signs of an easing of tensions appeared, leading to the second thaw in the Cold War. With growing concern over radiation effects of nuclear tests in the atmosphere, a moratorium on tests was agreed after a series of Soviet and American tests in late 1958. In January 1959 Harold Macmillan, who had succeeded Eden in 1957 as British prime minister after the Suez debacle and who was a close Second

World War associate of Eisenhower, made a successful visit to Moscow, the first Western leader to visit the Soviet Union since the Second World War. In 1958 Vice President Nixon visited Moscow and, after exchanging banter with Khrushchev in a celebrated 'kitchen debate' at an American Trade Fair in Moscow, issued an invitation to Khrushchev to visit the United States. Khrushchev's visit in May 1959 led American public opinion to view more favourably this coarse but jolly peasant figure, as he was portrayed, and the 'spirit of Camp David' emerged from Eisenhower's talks with Khrushchev at the president's retreat at Camp David. Arrangements were made for a four-power summit in Paris in May 1960 and a visit by Eisenhower to the Soviet Union later in 1960.

The growing mood of détente ended abruptly on 1 May 1960 when a U-2 was shot down over the Soviet Union. Eisenhower initially issued an implausible cover story that the flight had been a weather aeroplane which had strayed off course. The Soviets easily and gloatingly demonstrated the falsity of this account when they produced not only the wreckage of the aeroplane but also the CIA pilot, Gary Powers, who had not taken his own life to avoid capture but who had bailed out and fallen into Soviet hands. Khrushchev chose to exploit the incident to the full for propaganda purposes, berating Eisenhower in harsh, insulting terms, storming out of the Paris summit and cancelling Eisenhower's visit to the Soviet Union. In September 1960 Khrushchev returned to the United States to attend the meeting of the UN General Assembly, at which he denounced the West and, in an extraordinary episode, expressed his displeasure during a speech by Macmillan by taking off his shoe and banging it on a table. Hence, instead of Eisenhower's final years in office producing a mood of international good feelings, his administration ended, as one writer has put it, 'like the final act in a comic opera'.[30]

There was, however, a further issue close to American shores which in any event seriously jeopardized any prospect of détente in Eisenhower's last days, namely Cuba. In January 1959 Fidel Castro overthrew the Cuban dictator Fulgencia Batista and took power in Havana, promising social, economic and political reforms on the Western liberal model. In the spring of 1959 he visited the United States and was enthusiastically welcomed by the American public. By the end of 1959, however, it became apparent that Castro was no liberal but a Communist, as he imprisoned and executed political opponents, nationalized many foreign companies without compensation, established the economic and political structures of a Communist state, received economic aid and military assistance from the Soviet Union and encouraged Cuban-style revolutions in neighbouring countries in the Caribbean and in Central America. The United States felt that, as in Russia in 1917, the Cuban revolution had been betrayed and a revolt to bring American-style democracy had been hijacked by Communist thugs. The solution, in Eisenhower's view, lay in the methods employed in Guatemala in 1954 and Iran in 1953, namely a covert CIA operation. The CIA, headed by Allen Dulles, trained Cuban exiles for an invasion to bring about Castro's overthrow. Preparations were well under way but not advanced to the stage of implementation when Eisenhower's term came to an end and the matter was left as a first item of business for his successor, John F. Kennedy.

As Eisenhower prepared to leave office in January 1961 he delivered a most memorable Farewell Address, in which he warned against the influence of the 'military-industrial complex' and stated that with regard to disarmament there had been no progress and as a result he laid down his office with a heavy heart. Although Eisenhower had held down the costs of conventional defences, defence spending nevertheless diverted vast resources from civilian purposes, as Eisenhower had so eloquently described in his speech on 16 April 1953. The US–Soviet relationship in the Eisenhower era was marked by thaws and freezes in the Cold War, with the relationship in 1961 very little different from that in 1953. Did Eisenhower fail to explore sufficiently the possibility of détente in the 1950s and thereby abort any prospects of disarmament? In the early to mid-1950s, with an insecure Soviet leadership, with strong economic, political and international pressures opposed to détente and with Eisenhower himself very suspicious of Soviet purposes, the conducive conditions required for the onset of détente did not appear to exist. By 1959–60, however, undisputed Soviet leadership had been attained by Khrushchev, who was a mercurial but basically reformist leader, McCarthy was gone and Eisenhower was in a stronger political position after his landslide re-election in 1956. Hence, in his final years, especially after Dulles's death in January 1959, Eisenhower was more inclined, like Churchill in his last years, to strive for a breakthrough in negotiations with the Soviet Union.

Perhaps even in the late 1950s there was no real chance of a lasting détente, given the underlying ideological conflict and the particular issues such as Cuba and Khrushchev's reaction to the U-2 incident, which suggested that Khrushchev needed to protect his political position at home by an aggressive stance. Yet perhaps Eisenhower's plaintive call in his Farewell Address revealed an appreciation that to achieve disarmament there was need for a somewhat less negative approach to the Soviet Union than his administration had for the most part displayed through the 1950s. At Bermuda in 1953 Churchill had said that 'We should not repulse every move for the better. There should not be a question of finding a reason for suspicion for giving evil meaning to every move of the Soviets'.[31] The prospects of a significant improvement in US–Soviet relations throughout the 1950s were fairly remote, but the overly negative attitude of the Eisenhower administration contributed to the entrenchment and institutionalization of the Cold War in the economic and political life of the United States as well as in its foreign policy, which Eisenhower belatedly deplored in his Farewell Address.

10

KENNEDY AND KHRUSHCHEV, 1961–3

In 1961 John F. Kennedy, the youngest man to be elected president of the United States, brought to the presidency the vigour and energy of youth, along with its inexperience and immaturity. In the 1930s Kennedy was a fierce critic of appeasement and isolation, writing his Harvard honours thesis on the subject, which he later published as a book, *Why England Slept*.[1] He fought in the Second World War in the Far East and sustained a back injury which aggravated earlier back trouble and left him in pain throughout his life. From an Irish-American Catholic family, he was a staunch anti-Communist. The combination of virulent anti-Communism and belief in the folly of appeasement was the essence of Kennedy's thinking on foreign policy when he entered the White House. Added to this was a fighting, adversarial frame of mind encouraged by his father and his family, Irish-American Catholic outsiders who needed to battle constantly to succeed. This was reflected in Kennedy's oratory, which was often thrilling in its eloquence but revealed a penchant for the apocalyptic. 'Let every nation know', he said in his Inaugural Address, 'whether it wishes us well or ill, that we shall pay any price, bear any burden, meet any hardship, support any friend, oppose any foe to assure the survival and the success of liberty'.[2] As one historian has said, 'Kennedy's summons to national service reminded some of Henry V's salutation to his forces before Agincourt'.[3] Kennedy's critics argue, in debunking accounts which allege a mythologizing of Kennedy since his assassination, that Kennedy and the arrogant young men around him – such as Theodore Sorensen, McGeorge Bundy, Robert McNamara and Robert Kennedy – took dangerous risks which exacerbated problems in US–Soviet relations, such as Berlin, Cuba and the arms race, and which led to disaster in Vietnam.

Kennedy's admirers argue that he showed cool courage in dangerous Cold War crises and that he matured as a statesman in the course of his presidency, so that by 1963 he had developed from a relatively inexperienced hardline anti-Communist into a statesman with a good appreciation of the complexities and nuances of relations with the Soviet Union. An analysis of the major issues of US–Soviet relations during Kennedy's presidency allows an assessment of how far his critics or his admirers appear to have the stronger case.

During the 1950s, Kennedy criticized Eisenhower's defence cuts and in the 1960 campaign Kennedy made a major issue of the alleged 'missile gap' which, it was said, would enable the Soviet Union to gain a lead over the United States in ICBMs by the early 1960s. Kennedy criticized the rigidity of the concepts of massive retaliation and brinkmanship, and in general Kennedy and his entourage were scathingly critical of the Eisenhower administration as stodgy and unimaginative. Once in office, Kennedy learned from intelligence sources that there was no missile gap. As Frank Costigliola writes, 'The missile gap on which Kennedy had based much of his 1960 campaign turned out to be huge – but in America's favor'.[4] Kennedy was nevertheless determined to increase America's nuclear capability to a position of vast superiority over the Soviets. One thousand Atlas and Minuteman ICBMs were deployed between 1961 and 1963, while 656 submarine-launched ballistic missiles (SLBMs) were added to America's fleet of Polaris submarines, compared to a total Soviet deployment of 300 ICBMs. To control defence costs Kennedy appointed as Secretary of Defense Robert McNamara, president of the Ford Motor Company and the epitome of modern, cost-effective business management methods. Right-wing critics such as Senator Barry Goldwater charged that, especially with regard to the air force, McNamara cut too deeply. Other critics argued that while McNamara was a reasonably successful Secretary of Defense, the almost mystical reverence for his highly publicized, super-efficient cost control methods related more to the public relations image of the dynamic, vigorously intelligent New Frontier than to the mundane realities of the administration of the Pentagon. In essence, Kennedy presided over a massive increase in America's defence capability at every level, which, his critics charge, produced a Soviet build-up in response in due course and a consequent escalation of the arms race which ultimately left neither side any more secure.

Kennedy introduced the concept of flexible response in place of massive retaliation. Instead of the inflexibility of massive retaliation by strategic nuclear forces in response to any assault on the United States or her allies, the theory of flexible response was that the United States would respond step by step, putting pressure on the Warsaw Pact to cease aggression, even after the nuclear threshold had been crossed, making possible a controlled, graduated response which was a more effective policy than a choice between surrender or a full-scale nuclear holocaust. In fact, Kennedy's policy was not so different from Eisenhower's as New Frontier publicity suggested. The deployment of tactical nuclear weapons in Europe in 1954 had been aimed to provide the possibility of graduated flexible response. Moreover, the reasoning behind flexible response rested upon assumptions which in a practical situation were liable to become complicated beyond practical value. Furthermore, one part of flexible response was the creation of various forces units which could be deployed in differing situations, which was in theory commendable but in practice questionable. Kennedy would not deal with the Vietnam situation with the inflexible response of the threat of massive retaliation as in the Quemoy and Matsu crisis in 1955, but with the deployment of special anti-guerrilla troops, the Green Berets. As the Republicans in 1952 tried to differentiate themselves from their Democratic predecessors, the bright young men of the Kennedy administration wished to differentiate themselves from the preceding Eisenhower administration. The Kennedy administration, however, to a greater extent than its Republican predecessor, acted upon its rhetoric, often with unfortunate consequences.

The first critical policy issue facing Kennedy was Cuba. Kennedy received different opinions from his advisers on the wisdom of proceeding with Eisenhower's plan for an invasion of Cuba by Cuban refugee forces organized by the CIA. Doves such as Senator William Fulbright, chairman of the Senate Foreign Relations committee, were opposed. Fulbright said that 'The Castro regime is a thorn in the flesh, but it is not a dagger in the heart'.[5] More surprisingly, the hawkish Dean Acheson, who was brought in as a 'wise old man', described the planned invasion as 'a wild idea'.[6] But other advisers were enthusiastically in favour, such as Allen Dulles, head of the CIA. Castro presented, it was argued, a dangerous bridgehead for Soviet penetration of Central America and Communist expansion throughout Latin

America, and Kennedy would seem weak if it became known that he had abandoned a plan prepared by the Eisenhower administration to eliminate Castro. Moreover, it was felt that the Cuban people would rise up in support of the invading Cuban refugees and overthrow Castro and instigate the democratic revolution which they had sought and which Castro had betrayed. The final outcome would therefore be a major triumph for democracy and a severe set-back for Communism world-wide.

Kennedy accepted the view of his more hawkish advisers, which was more in keeping with the macho image of the new administration and conformed to Kennedy's belief in bold, courageous action against Communism rather than weak appeasement. On 17 April 1961 the invasion force landed at the Bay of Pigs in Cuba. Castro's defences held firm and the invasion force suffered heavy losses on the beaches. A plea was made for the US Air Force to make an air strike against Castro's defensive position, but Kennedy ruled this out. There was no rising of the Cuban people in support of the invasion force. The disastrous episode left Castro in a much more strongly entrenched position, with the forces of Cuban nationalism behind him in repelling the Yankees and their lackeys. American prestige was dealt a severe blow by such a blatant violation of international law in attempting to overthrow by violence the government of a small neighbouring state and by the incompetence in the execution of the invasion by Cuban refugees, who at first implausibly denied their control by the CIA and later confessed it. Kennedy's new aid programme for Latin America, the Alliance for Progress, had been well received as an imaginative plan in the spirit of Franklin Roosevelt's Good Neighbor policies to promote progressive democratic development instead of Communism. The Bay of Pigs portrayed Kennedy in the spirit of Theodore Roosevelt's Big Stick approach to Latin America, though at least the marines in Teddy Roosevelt's day were successful in their interventions. Castro looked more towards the Soviet Union for his defence and Khrushchev was very willing to exploit the incident for propaganda purposes.

Kennedy arranged a meeting with Khrushchev two months later, in Vienna in June 1961. Some State Department advisers felt that an early summit meeting was unwise, as it was liable to produce a confrontation with Khrushchev, who might try to bully his much younger American opposite number. Kennedy was eager, however, to have a face-to-face meeting with Khrushchev and felt that he could handle any pressure which Khrushchev attempted to apply. The outcome of the Vienna meeting suggested that the cautious, staid State Department approach had more to commend it. Kennedy engaged in a fairly heated discussion at Vienna with Khrushchev on ideology, and although Kennedy's quick-witted intelligence enabled him to defend his position reasonably, it was an unwise strategy to have allowed himself to be drawn into a confrontation on a subject where Khrushchev was on very familiar ground, since such matters were debated endlessly in Kremlin circles, and where the discussion was bound to be adversarial. Khrushchev then renewed his threat regarding Berlin, which he had made in 1958 but quietly dropped, that within six months he would sign a peace treaty with East Germany and give control of access routes from West Germany to Berlin to the East German authorities. It is open to question whether Khrushchev would have made this threat in any event or whether it was precipitated by the face to face confrontation with Kennedy. As Khrushchev said to Averell Harriman, Berlin was a 'bunion on your toes, which I can step on at any time'.[7]

Kennedy regarded the threat against Berlin as a test of his resolve on which it was imperative to show no signs of appeasement. Rejecting Khrushchev's right to abrogate unilaterally four-power agreements on Berlin, Kennedy sent a diplomatic signal by calling up the reserves and increasing defence spending substantially. The immediate crisis was resolved, paradoxically, by Khrushchev's decision to construct the Berlin Wall in August 1961. On the one hand, the United States was impotent to deal with the crude means of dividing the city and preventing emigration of East Germans to West Germany. On the other hand, Khrushchev dropped his threat to sign a peace treaty with East Germany, and the Berlin Wall presented the United States with a very potent propaganda issue which Kennedy and his successors used to advantage. As Kennedy put it, 'It's not a nice solution, but a wall is a hell of a lot better than a war'.[8]

With regard to the Far East, Kennedy had denounced the Communist Chinese in virulent terms in the late 1940s and early 1950s, and he had been critical of the Truman administration for weakness in allowing China to fall to the Communists. Kennedy chose as Secretary of State Dean Rusk, Assistant Secretary of State for Far Eastern Affairs from 1949 to 1952 and an uncompromisingly bitter opponent of the Chinese Communists. Although Kennedy felt that continuing ostracism of China was rather pointless and that evidence of the Sino-Soviet split was very plain by the late 1950s, and although Kennedy intended to control foreign policy himself and use Rusk largely as a bureaucratic figurehead, nevertheless Kennedy's choice of Secretary of State was one of many pieces of evidence that Kennedy planned no moves towards diplomatic recognition of China or attempts to develop better relations with China as a lever against the Soviet Union.

The first immediate issue in the Far East facing Kennedy lay in Laos. Negotiations had begun in 1960 between the three warring factions, the Royalists, the reformers and the Communist Pathet Lao. Kennedy's hawkish advisers recommended support of the Royalists to crush the Pathet Lao, but Kennedy backed a negotiated settlement which produced a coalition of all the parties, which appeared to be a reasonably satisfactory solution and produced relative stability in Laos for over a decade. This pragmatic and reasonably enlightened approach taken in the small and obscure nation of 2 million in Laos was not followed, however, in the more important neighbouring country of Vietnam. In 1960 the Viet Cong (National Liberation Front) was formed in South Vietnam, a coalition of Communists and non-Communists who opposed President Diem's oppressive rule, with support for the Viet Cong coming from Ho Chi Minh, who bitterly resented the failure of Diem and the Americans to permit elections in 1956 and the unification of Vietnam. With growing violence in South Vietnam, especially assassinations by the Viet Cong of village chiefs loyal to Diem, Diem wrote to Kennedy in December 1961 in terms which Diem knew, from his experience of forty years in exile in the United States, would appeal to Kennedy. Diem wrote that South Vietnam was a small nation on the edge of the free world holding back the tide of international communism. To Kennedy's way of thinking, this tied in also with Khrushchev's boast on 6 January 1961 and repeated to Kennedy at Vienna in June 1961 that wars of national liberation were the wave of the future and would be the path to the universal triumph of Communism. Hence, Vietnam seemed to be the testing ground for the success or defeat of Communism's global aims.

Kennedy made the fateful decision to send in American

troops, small in number and disguised by the euphemism of 'advisers', but destined to escalate relentlessly. One thousand troops were sent to South Vietnam in December 1961, and on 22 December 1961 the first American soldier was killed in Vietnam. By the time of Kennedy's death in November 1963, the number of American troops in Vietnam had risen to 17,000 and seventy-three had been killed. Kennedy received warnings from various figures against intervention in Vietnam. Charles de Gaulle, president of France, suggested that the United States might learn from the experience of the French in Indo-China in 1946–54, warning Kennedy in Paris in 1962 that the United States would sink into an ever-deepening quagmire. But Kennedy disliked de Gaulle, whom he found haughty and exasperating, and Kennedy was somewhat contemptuous of the French, who had cravenly capitulated to the Nazis in 1940 rather than engaging in the Churchillian type of bulldog resistance which Kennedy admired. Kennedy therefore concluded that whereas the inefficient, rather cowardly French had failed in Indo-China, the Americans, under tough-minded leadership and with modern military technology and specially trained anti-guerrilla forces, would succeed. American intervention in South Vietnam not only brought about increased support to Ho Chi Minh from China but also made the North Vietnamese, who had a historical tradition of enmity towards China, look for protection and assistance to the Soviet Union. Kennedy was interested in exploring the development of Titoism in Europe, illustrated by his appointment as ambassador to Yugoslavia of George F. Kennan, who was recalled to the Foreign Service. In Asia, however, Kennedy did not follow the path of seeking a Titoist Vietnam but aimed at victory for Diem and the non-Communists in order to hold the line of containment against the expansion of Communism at the border of South Vietnam.

In the early 1960s Vietnam remained a relatively low-level conflict, while attention was focused on Berlin and, above all, on Cuba, culminating in the Cuban missile crisis in October 1962. Following the Bay of Pigs Castro was afraid of a further American attempt to overthrow him. His fears were well-grounded, as the CIA pursued Operation Mongoose, making a number of attempts to assassinate Castro by such far-fetched means as supplying him with a cigar which would explode in his face. Michael Beschloss calculates that there were 'at least thirty-three different schemes intended to culminate in Castro's removal'.[9]

The Kennedy adminstration was clearly intent not only on containing the greatly feared spread of Castroism to other Latin American countries but of engaging in vigorous efforts to bring down Castro in Cuba. At the same time, the continuing American economic boycott of Cuba made Castro increasingly dependent on Soviet economic aid. Furthermore, in military terms Cuba looked to the Soviet Union for protection against the United States.

Against this background, in June 1962 the Cuban government gladly accepted a Soviet proposal to install offensive nuclear weapons in Cuba. Such a scheme provided Cuba with an extremely powerful defence against the United States, while it served Soviet interests to establish a base for SS-4 and SS-5 missiles, which had a range of approximately 1,000 and 2,500 miles respectively, and whose deployment would enable the Soviet Union to counter the American lead in ICBMs and SLBMs. At a series of conferences attended by participants in the 1962 crisis held in the United States, Moscow and Havana in 1987, 1989 and 1992, significant details were revealed.[10] It is now known that by the time of the crisis in mid-October 1962 the Soviets had deployed twenty-four SS-4 launchers, fully equipped with missiles and nuclear warheads plus a 50 per cent refit (i.e. thirty-six missiles and warheads), while sixteen SS-5 launchers were under construction in Cuba and their missiles and nuclear warheads were in transit on Soviet vessels. At the time, however, although US intelligence revealed the presence of SS-4 launchers and missiles, it was not known whether nuclear warheads had been delivered. 'In October 1962 it was believed they probably were not', Raymond Garthoff concludes, 'but the consensus prudent assumption was nonetheless that they must be assumed to be there'.[11] An even more alarming detail unknown to the US government in 1962 and revealed only at the 1992 Havana conference was that six tactical nuclear launchers with nine tactical rockets and nuclear warheads had been delivered to Cuba for contingent use against an American invasion and that the Soviet commander in Cuba had been given discretionary authority 'to fire the tactical nuclear rockets at a US invasion force if he considered it necessary, without need to seek further authority from Moscow'.[12]

In September 1962 reports began to appear in the *New York Times* that missiles were being sent to Cuba. Political pressure on Kennedy grew, with Congressional elections due in November.

Kenneth Keating, a highly respected Republican senator from New York, stated that his sources revealed Soviet deception to conceal deployment of offensive nuclear missiles in Cuba. Intelligence was more difficult to gather in October, since it was not possible in the hurricane season to have flights over Cuba by U-2s, which had been discontinued over the Soviet Union but which provided vital intelligence from flights over Cuba. On 14 October a break in the weather permitted a U-2 flight, which brought back very clear photographs of missile sites, missiles and Soviet personnel. It seemed plain that the Soviets planned to complete missile construction and missile emplacement while the weather prevented U-2 flights and to present the United States with a *fait accompli*.

Every effort was made by the Soviets to conceal missile deployment in Cuba from the United States. The deception process included barefaced lying on the Soviet part. Soviet ambassador to the United States Anatoly Dobrynin told US ambassador to the United Nations Adlai Stevenson on 7 September that only surface-to-air (SAM) anti-aircraft missiles were being supplied to Cuba, and on 11 September TASS reported that 'the arms and equipment sent to Cuba are designated solely for defensive purposes'.[13] On 16 October Khrushchev assured US ambassador to the Soviet Union Foy Kohler that 'Soviet purposes in Cuba were wholly defensive'.[14] On 18 October Soviet Foreign Minister Andrei Gromyko, who was in the United States for a UN meeting, told Kennedy that the Soviet Union would not introduce 'offensive weapons' into Cuba, and on 22 October Robert Kennedy was told by Soviet counsellor Georgi Bol'shakov, a trusted back channel from Khrushchev personally, that he had just returned from Moscow and been told to convey an assurance that 'no missile capable of reaching the United States would be placed in Cuba'.[15] Such blatant deception, which after 14 October was known by the United States to be false, had as profound an impact on the crisis as the substantial matter of the emplacement of the missiles themselves. As Raymond Garthoff has pointed out, 'The decision to undertake the action in secrecy, rather than publicly announcing it in advance, had a more significant effect on the American reaction and the whole course of events than was appreciated in Moscow'.[16]

Soviet mendacity hit a raw American nerve which affected the American psyche profoundly and added an emotional dimension of considerable significance to the crisis. Garthoff writes that his enquiries to 1962 US policy-makers regarding the American position if the Soviets had made a public announcement of planned missile deployment instead of proceeding by stealth, produced the response that 'All believed it was much less likely that the US government would have sought, or been able to compel, restriction of the Soviet decision'.[17]

On 16 October Kennedy was presented with the photographic evidence of the missiles in Cuba. From that day until 22 October a series of extremely tense meetings were held of the Executive Committee of the National Security Council (EXCOM), while the public was still unaware of the crisis and no approach was yet made to the Soviet government. The members of EXCOM unanimously agreed that appeasement, in the form of acquiescing in the emplacement of the missiles in Cuba, was ruled out. From the military point of view it was accepted that, since Soviet ICBMs had the capability to strike targets in the United States, missiles in Cuba did not introduce a totally new dimension to the strategic balance, although they would strengthen the Soviet nuclear capability very considerably. From the political and psychological point of view, however, American acquiescence in the deployment of missiles in Cuba, it was argued, would embolden the Soviets to attempt further probes elsewhere, creating an instability in international relations which, as in the days of appeasement in the 1930s, could culminate in world war. The argument that in international law Cuba as a sovereign state had the right to receive from an ally any weapons system she should choose in order to secure her defence, was not even entertained. Even doves such as Fulbright argued strongly that the missiles must be removed. The debate in EXCOM was not whether the missiles should be removed but how this should be accomplished.

The Joint Chiefs of Staff favoured an air strike against Cuba or an invasion. There were grave risks, however, that not all the missiles could be destroyed in a surgical air strike, so that the remaining ones could be fired against the United States, armed with conventional or possibly nuclear warheads, since the United States was uncertain whether nuclear warheads had been delivered to Cuba. An invasion would certainly allow time for the missiles to be fired. Moreover, the Soviet government was liable to retaliate against an air strike or invasion with actions which could escalate to firing ICBMs from the Soviet Union. This possibility would become greater if Soviet personnel were killed in an American air strike or invasion (a virtually certain contingency in the light of the number of Soviets in Cuba, which had risen to 40,000, a much larger number than the Americans realized in 1962). Despite overwhelming American nuclear superiority, in an all-out US–Soviet nuclear exchange even a 10 per cent Soviet success strike rate would have resulted in the incineration of thirty American cities. Moreover, Robert Kennedy, the president's closest adviser, felt that an air strike would seem a crude surprise attack, almost like Pearl Harbor, and some preliminary incidents needed to be manufactured to prepare world opinion before such a move could be made. Defense Secretary McNamara suggested a naval blockade. This had the advantage that it prevented any further importation of missiles into Cuba and in a non-violent manner gave the Soviet government time to consider its response slowly. Kennedy took the decision that a blockade was the best course – though the term 'quarantine' was used, as it sounded less aggressive – since an air strike or invasion could still be employed as a next step if a quarantine was ineffective. Also, along with the American imposition of a quarantine to prevent the landing of further missiles a demand would be issued to the Soviet government to ship back to the Soviet Union the missiles which had been delivered to Cuba and to dismantle the missile sites.

With agreement reached in EXCOM on the strategy to be pursued, a further decision was required on whether negotiations should take place secretly or whether the matter should be aired publicly. Adlai Stevenson advocated private negotiations through diplomatic channels, since this would more easily allow a Soviet climb down without loss of face, with a *quid pro quo*, Stevenson suggested, of the removal of American Jupiter missiles from Turkey (which were obsolete and which the United States intended to remove anyway). Kennedy, however, adamantly refused any *quid pro quo* which might appear to reward Soviet aggression. Moreover, Kennedy decided that the issue must be made known to the public, since this would put more pressure on the Soviets and make clear the seriousness of American purposes and also since in a democracy the public had a right to know of a crisis which so greatly endangered American security and world peace. Consequently, on the evening of Monday 22 October Kennedy gave a television address in which he explained the crisis and the action taken by the US government, namely a quarantine enforced by the US navy prohibiting ships from crossing a line 400 miles east of Cuba without being stopped and searched by American ships and a demand that the Soviet missiles which were in Cuba should be sent back to the Soviet Union. The installation of the missiles could not be accepted, said Kennedy, 'if our courage and commitments are ever to be trusted again by either friend or foe'.[18] An hour before the speech was broadcast, the Soviet ambassador was provided with the text.

In the first week of the Cuban missile crisis, then, from the discovery of the missiles on Sunday 14 October, until Kennedy's broadcast on Monday 22 October, the matter was known only to the small group in the US government who attended the EXCOM meetings. In the second week, from Monday 22 October, until the crisis ended on Sunday 28 October, the issue was conducted in full public glare in an atmosphere of high-noon drama. The world held its breath and watched to see which side in the eyeball to eyeball US–Soviet confrontation would blink first. In fact, although Kennedy's stance appeared to be rigid and unyielding, in various ways he showed flexibility and he endeavoured to enable Khrushchev to back down with minimum loss of face. Kennedy, for instance, announced the quarantine in his speech on 22 October, but its imposition was delayed until after the Organization of American States had given its support on 23 October, so that when the quarantine was imposed on 24 October most Soviet ships had already altered course or turned back. Moreover, Kennedy agreed to pull back the quarantine line 200 miles to give the Soviets more time. Yet, although no Soviet ships carrying missiles attempted to cross the quarantine line, work continued on the construction of missile sites and missile deployment on Cuba.

Demands rose from some members of EXCOM for an air strike or invasion of Cuba. On Friday 26 October, however, Khrushchev sent a letter to Kennedy which seemed to contain the basis for a settlement. In this long, rambling, emotional letter, Khrushchev wrote of his fear of nuclear war and its horrors and suggested as a solution to the crisis Soviet agreement to withdraw its missiles from Cuba in exchange for American agreement not to invade Cuba. This was acceptable to the United States, though the United States wished to reserve the right to take action against Cuba if, for example, Cuba was aggressive elsewhere in Central America or committed atrocities against its own people. Before Kennedy had time to reply to Khrushchev's letter, however, a second letter was received from Khrushchev on Saturday 27 October, which was much more threatening and abrasive in tone and made the specific demand of the *quid pro quo* of the removal of American missiles from Turkey in exchange for the removal of Soviet missiles from Cuba. Moreover, on the same day a U-2 was shot down over Cuba and the pilot killed. As tensions rose again, Kennedy concluded that the first letter indicated Khrushchev's true feelings, but that he had been subjected to pressure from hawks in the Kremlin, which had led him to write the second letter. As a means of defusing the crisis, on Robert Kennedy's suggestion, the president replied to the first letter and ignored the second letter. At the same time, Robert Kennedy was sent to meet the Soviet ambassador, Dobrynin, on the evening of 27 October to offer an agreement that in exchange for the withdrawal of Soviet missiles from Cuba the United States would promise not to invade Cuba and would also agree to withdraw its missiles from Turkey, although the withdrawal of missiles from Turkey would not be publicly announced as a *quid pro quo*. Although the American promise not to invade Cuba was not unreserved, Khrushchev accepted the terms offered by Robert Kennedy to Dobrynin as a basis for the resolution of the crisis. The next morning, Sunday 28 October, Sir Frank Roberts, the British ambassador in Moscow, sought Khrushchev with a message from Macmillan. Khrushchev, however, had gone to his *dacha*, and when Roberts told his chauffeur to turn on the car radio, light music was being played rather than sombre, martial music. The Cuban missile crisis was over.

Kennedy's handling of the Cuban missile crisis was for the most part highly praised by his contemporaries within the United States and abroad. Kennedy's performance, it was felt, was a finely orchestrated exercise in crisis management. Arthur Schlesinger, Jr, wrote that it was 'a combination of toughness and restraint, of will, nerve, wisdom, so brilliantly controlled, so meticulously calibrated that it dazzled the world'.[19] Kennedy's critics, however, charged that only Khrushchev's willingness to accept humiliation prevented catastrophe, and Khrushchev paid the price by his fall from power two years later. Moreover, it is suggested that Kennedy conducted the confrontation in public, because of an inclination towards high drama and a desire to reap the political rewards in the form of a good performance by the Democrats in the Congressional elections in November, in which the Democrats gained four seats in the Senate and lost only two in the House of Representatives, the best performance for the party in power in off-year elections since 1934. Kennedy's admirers argue that his unflinching public stand was essential in order to deter Soviet adventurism and to create stability and strengthen the prospects of peace. On the whole, Kennedy's supporters appear to have the stronger case. It should be observed, however, that Kennedy was not unyielding, but made concessions such as pulling back the quarantine line and agreeing to the withdrawal of American missiles from Turkey, although this was not to be made public. Moreover, the one clear American concession, namely agreement not to invade Cuba, even though it was not stated in writing in a watertight agreement, was regarded by the Soviets and Cubans as a more substantial matter than the Americans appreciated, since Cuban and Soviet fears before 1962 of a further American invasion had been considerable. Above all, however, the extremely dangerous encounter in the eyeball-to-eyeball confrontation in the Cuban missile crisis acted as a catharsis in the process of Kennedy's development from a relatively narrow-minded, hardline Cold Warrior into a mature world statesman.

By late 1962 into 1963 Kennedy's energy and enthusiasm was directed less towards a military build-up and more towards a nuclear test ban treaty. From October 1958 the United States, the Soviet Union and Britain had observed a moratorium on nuclear tests in the atmosphere. Scientific evidence was accumulating on the harmful effects of radioactive fall-out, and Kennedy wished to continue the moratorium. When the Soviets began testing again, however, in September 1961, Kennedy accepted the view of his military advisers that the United States must resume testing and a series of American tests was authorized in April 1962. In 1963 further negotiations led to the Test Ban Treaty signed on 5 August 1963. This was a limited accomplishment, since it covered only atmospheric tests and since in order to secure Senate ratification the number of underground tests was increased to exceed the previous combined total of atmospheric and underground tests. Nevertheless, the danger of radioactive fall-out had been dealt with effectively. Moreover, the first disarmament agreement in post-war history had been signed, breaking the psychological deadlock in disarmament talks and improving considerably the overall atmosphere in US–Soviet relations.

Kennedy appeared, moreover, to be rethinking policy in

Vietnam. His disillusionment grew with constant Joint Chiefs of Staff requests for increases in troop numbers in Vietnam, with assurances from the military that one further increase would bring final success. Kennedy said to his aide, Arthur Schlesinger, Jr, of such troop increases, 'It's like taking a drink. The effect wears off, and you have to take another'.[20] He was highly critical of the corrupt and tyrannical rule of Diem and his brother Ngo Dinh Nhu and his imperious wife, Madame Nhu. Kennedy expressed the need for greater effort by the South Vietnamese, saying to Schlesinger that the war 'could be won only so long as it is *their* war. If it were ever converted into a white man's war, we would lose as the French had lost a decade earlier'.[21] In private, Kennedy made some revealing comments which suggested an intention to de-escalate the war and to withdraw from Vietnam. Most significantly, in a conversation with his aide Kenneth O'Donnell and Senator Mike Mansfield in 1963 Kennedy told Mansfield of his growing doubts regarding policy towards Vietnam and he said to O'Donnell that 'If I tried to pull out completely now from Vietnam, we would have another Joe McCarthy red scare on our hands, but I can do it after I'm re-elected. So, we had better make damned sure that I *am* re-elected'.[22] The remark rings true, revealing Kennedy's aggressive political instincts and his appreciation – from his familiarity with the political fall-out from the loss of China – of the political flack likely to follow from Communist victory in Vietnam. There is a good argument, then, in support of the view that Kennedy intended to maintain the Vietnam conflict at its current level through the election of 1964 but thereafter to withdraw American troops and be prepared to accept a Communist victory in South Vietnam.

Kennedy's critics, however, show that there is abundant evidence that Kennedy's course was set not on de-escalation and withdrawal from Vietnam but on victory and that only his assassination saved his reputation from the same fate as his successor, Lyndon Johnson. George Herring, in his judiciously well-balanced history of the Vietnam War, concludes that Kennedy's defenders, 'many of whom would later become outspoken opponents of the war, would later argue that at the time of his death he was planning to extricate the United States from what he had perceived to be a quagmire. The record suggests otherwise'.[23] Throughout his presidency Kennedy constantly reiterated denial of any intention to withdraw from Vietnam. At a press conference on 17 July 1963, for example, he stated that 'For us to withdraw from that effort would mean a collapse not only of South Vietnam but Southeast Asia. So we are going to stay there'.[24] On 9 September 1963, when asked by television newscaster David Brinkley if he had 'any reason to doubt this so-called 'domino theory' that if South Vietnam falls, the rest of Southeast Asia will go behind it', Kennedy firmly replied, 'I believe it'.[25] On 2 October 1963 McNamara and General Maxwell Taylor, two close and trusted advisers, reported after a visit to Vietnam that the war could be won by 1965, with more rapid progress if a more effective government was in place than Diem. On 1 November 1963 Diem and his brother were overthrown and assassinated. The CIA did not organize the coup but knew of the plot and took no steps to warn Diem. Kennedy's critics suggest that Kennedy's moral responsibility for Diem's over-throw and murder illustrated the callous arrogance which took the United States deeper and deeper into the Vietnam quagmire.

The evidence on Kennedy's intentions in Vietnam is therefore mixed. It is clear, however, that Kennedy was increasingly dissatis-fied with America's negative policy towards China. Kennedy felt that Dean Rusk was an unimaginative bureaucrat who was too locked into attitudes of an earlier time and Kennedy intended, according to Arthur Schlesinger, Jr, 'to accept his resignation after the 1964 election and seek a new Secretary', assuming Kennedy's victory in the 1964 election.[26] The weight of evidence on the whole supports the view that Kennedy was moving towards attempts to resolve the Vietnam issue within the overall context of improved relations with China and the Soviet Union, as Richard Nixon would do later, rather than to plunge headlong into massive military escalation in Vietnam, as Lyndon Johnson did.

Kennedy continued to portray himself as a champion of freedom and democracy against totalitarian Communism. With exciting rhetoric he aroused the crowds on his visit to West Berlin on 26 June 1963, proclaiming 'Ich bin ein Berliner'.[27] Yet, through diplomatic channels Kennedy worked patiently for rapproachment with the Soviet Union. A hot line was installed between Washington and Moscow to ensure rapid telegraphic communication in the event of a crisis. On economic issues, Kennedy negotiated the first agreement to sell surplus wheat to the Soviet Union in 1963. He sought slow but steady liberalization in Eastern Europe, encouraging Titoism and national Communism in countries such as Poland, accepting that rapid change was beyond America's power to attain and liable to be counter-productive, as it would seem threatening to the Soviet Union. Above all, in personal correspondence with Khrushchev from the time of the Cuban missile crisis Kennedy sought to explore areas of co-operation with the Soviet Union and means of achieving a *modus vivendi*.

In the years after Kennedy's death, the glamorized image of John F. Kennedy and the Court of Camelot has become badly tarnished. With regard to foreign policy the substantial charges against Kennedy by his debunkers are that he was a shallow, ambitious politician with narrow, arrogant, machoistic views, which led America into serious dangers and into disaster in Vietnam. There is a good case to support this interpretation of Kennedy when he assumed office. His accusations of a missile gap in 1960 were ill-informed and irresponsible and his military build-up in 1961 excessive. The Bay of Pigs was not only a gross violation of international law in the worst traditions of gunboat diplomacy but it was also incompetent bungling, which left Castro as a much closer Soviet ally and a graver threat to the United States. Kennedy's precipitous meeting with Khrushchev in Vienna in 1961 helped to bring on the crisis in Berlin. Yet, in his hour of greatest peril, in the Cuban missile crisis, Kennedy showed cool judgement, rejecting the more extreme military options and displaying flexibility while achieving the essential goal of the defeat of deceptive Soviet adventurism, which, if allowed to succeed, could have destabilized the international situation and imperilled world peace. In Vietnam, Kennedy initially felt that the Green Berets and the dynamic spirit of the New Frontier would bring victory to the anti-Communist cause, but by 1963 he was prepared to contemplate de-escalation and a negotiated settlement, even if this involved acceptance of a Communist Vietnam. On 10 June 1963 Kennedy made a speech on foreign policy at American University in Washington, which illustrated the development of a more mature, sophisticated appreciation of the complexities of world affairs in an age of nuclear rivalry and ideological competition with the Soviet Union. When Kennedy was assassinated on 22 November 1963, Khrushchev came to the American embassy in Moscow to sign the book of condolence, and his grief over Kennedy's death seemed clearly genuine. Just as Kennedy was developing a promising approach in US–Soviet relations, he was cut down. The loss was severe for the prospects of an improvement in US–Soviet relations.

11

JOHNSON, VIETNAM AND CZECHOSLOVAKIA, 1963–9

Kennedy's assassination brought to the Oval office a president with little interest or experience in foreign affairs. Lyndon Johnson's passionate ambitions lay in domestic affairs, especially in the fields of anti-poverty and civil rights. His noble goals in these domestic issues were destroyed by the escalating war in Vietnam. The impact of the Vietnam War on America in all its ramifications was profound and widespread. The question of its impact on the course of US–Soviet relations is the principal issue with regard to US–Soviet relations in the Johnson years, with the escalation in Vietnam occurring at a time of new leadership in the Soviet Union, with the fall of Nikita Khrushchev in October 1964.

With Johnson's accession to the presidency the prospects receded of de-escalation and withdrawal from Vietnam. Johnson retained the principal foreign-policy advisers from the Kennedy administration, especially Dean Rusk at the State Department and Robert McNamara at the Pentagon, but Rusk's influence grew considerably. Rusk, a Georgian, had, like his fellow Southerner Lyndon Johnson, felt excluded from the inner circles of power in Kennedy's presidency and had been derided as ponderous and lacking in vision by the bright young men in the Kennedy entourage. Whereas Kennedy had planned to replace Rusk in a second term, Johnson made him his principal foreign-policy adviser. More than any other figure, Rusk reinforced Johnson's straightforward, simplistic view that Vietnam was like Czechoslovakia or Manchuria in the 1930s and that there must not be a repetition of Munich or Manchuria. As Johnson put it, he was determined to show that he was 'no Chamberlain umbrella man'.[1] As a Representative and Senator from Texas in the 1940s and 1950s Johnson had supported containment in crises such as Berlin, Iran and Korea. As president, Johnson's basic error was the misapplication of containment to Vietnam, an area to which it was not applicable in the way in which it had been applicable to Berlin, Iran and Korea. In the 1930s, Germany and Japan were manifestly responsible for such crises as Czechoslovakia and Manchuria as part of policies of blatant expansion. The Soviet Union clearly orchestrated the Berlin crisis in 1948–9 and the Iranian crisis in 1945–6, and the contemporary American suspicion in 1950 was not unreasonable that the Soviets instigated the North Korean invasion, even if later evidence makes this less certain.

In Vietnam, however, Ho Chi Minh was no tool of Moscow, or of Beijing. The Soviets gave aid to Ho Chi Minh, and Brezhnev insisted on the Soviet right to support struggles for national liberation, following on from Khrushchev's assertion that wars of national liberation would be the wave of the future as the means of Communist expansion. This was a more subtle matter, however, than a crude expansionist drive such as by Hitler into Czechoslovakia or the Japanese into Manchuria or even the invasion of South Korea, which, it was not illogical to conclude in 1950, was Soviet sponsored and Soviet directed. Johnson's attitude towards Vietnam, however, excluded any finer subtleties. He did not consider the possibility of a Titoist Vietnam which would be a puppet of neither the Soviets nor the Chinese. Nor did Johnson consider the possibility that Vietnam need not necessarily be a first domino whose fall to Communism would inevitably be followed by others, but that the spread of Communism to Thailand, Malaysia, India and other such countries was dependent on internal conditions within these countries rather than upon interference by external Communists from Vietnam, China or the Soviet Union.

Johnson was also overly simplistic in his faith in the ability of American military power to determine the outcome of the conflict in Vietnam. Johnson was confident that a display of America's military technology, especially air power, would intimidate the Vietnamese to side with the Americans as the force which, with such formidable military might, was bound to prevail. Johnson was wary, however, from the experience of Korea a decade earlier, of an open attack on North Vietnam which might bring about Chinese or Soviet intervention. He therefore proceeded cautiously in a gradual escalation of the war. Moreover, Johnson had learned from his mentor, Franklin Roosevelt, the arts of deviousness which Roosevelt practised in

1939–41 as he edged an unwilling public opinion into war. Hence, Johnson escalated the war not only gradually but also surreptitiously, which resulted not in an ultimate consensus in favour of American involvement as in the Second World War but in a credibility gap which poisoned the political atmosphere and added to public confusion over American objectives in Vietnam.

On his succession to the presidency in November 1963, Johnson's immediate task was to gain confidence in his overall leadership, which he succeeded in accomplishing admirably. His next concern was his re-election in 1964, which Johnson wished to achieve in as decisive a manner as possible in order to establish himself as president in his own right rather than an accidental inheritor of Kennedy's mantle. Johnson's attention was therefore for the most part focused upon domestic political issues in 1963–4, so that he did not follow up the initial moves towards a potential détente with the Soviet Union which had developed in Kennedy's final months in office. A few days after his inauguration, Johnson met Soviet Deputy Premier Anastas Mikoyan and said that 'I can assure you that not a day will go by that we will not try to reduce the tension in the world'.[2] But although Johnson made a speech in May in 1964 on 'building bridges' with the Soviet Union and tried to expand trading links, US–Soviet relations engaged his energy only intermittently.[3] The foreign-policy issue with which Johnson concerned himself virtually exclusively was Vietnam, and until the 1964 election Johnson pursued policies to maintain the conflict at a relatively low level. His Republican opponent in 1964, Senator Barry Goldwater, appeared to advocate extreme policies of escalation in Vietnam, including hints of possible use of nuclear weapons. Johnson showed willingness to be resolute when necessary, ordering air strikes against North Vietnam, for example, following allegedly unprovoked attacks on American vessels by North Vietnamese gunboats in the Gulf of Tonkin, which led Congress to pass the Tonkin Gulf resolution, giving the president a virtual free hand in the use of American forces in Vietnam. But, compared to Goldwater's extremism, Johnson's policies seemed restrained. For example, in an election campaign speech in Manchester, New Hampshire, in late September 1964, Johnson said that

> I have not thought that we were ready for American boys to
> do the fighting for Asian boys. What I have been trying to do

... was to get the boys in Vietnam to do their own fighting with our advice and our equipment.... We are not going north and drop bombs at this stage of the game.[4]

Once re-elected Johnson embarked upon the fatal escalation of the war which led America to disaster and destroyed his presidency. In February 1965 he began regular air strikes against North Vietnam and in March sent 100,000 additional troops to Vietnam. By 1967 the number of troops had escalated to 500,000 and the number of sorties by American aeroplanes had exceeded 1,000. Yet, as American casualties rose to 30,000 by 1968, the benefits of American involvement in Vietnam were difficult to discern. North Vietnamese industrial targets were few in number, and bridges which were bombed were soon repaired, while the terror impact of bombing stiffened resistance rather than demoralizing the North Vietnamese people. Communist losses, which were reported in weekly 'body counts', were easily replaced by reinforcements from North Vietnam or defections to the Viet Cong of South Vietnamese, who became disenchanted by their American allies. The purpose of saving 'democracy' in South Vietnam seemed very dubious as a succession of inept and corrupt military leaders held office after Diem's overthrow. At the same time, democracy in America suffered severe damage with the lack of candour of the administration in revealing its policies and with disorder in the streets as anti-war protests and demonstrations grew in number and intensity, while Johnson's ambitious domestic programme failed as funds were diverted from the war on poverty to the war in Vietnam.

In October 1964 Khrushchev was removed from power. Leonid Brezhnev and Alexei Kosygin, who succeeded as General Secretary of the Communist Party and Chairman of the Council of Ministers respectively, were the dominant figures in a new collective leadership, with Mikhail Suslov, party secretary for ideology, also an influential figure. Khrushchev's fall was primarily due to internal Soviet matters, especially failures in agriculture, but it was also partly due to Soviet humiliation over the Cuban missile crisis, both the Soviet climb-down in itself and also the inferiority of the Soviet nuclear arsenal which the events of the Cuban missile crisis had clearly illustrated. Brezhnev and Kosygin were determined to remedy this state of affairs and to achieve nuclear parity with the United States, which they essentially achieved by the end of the 1960s. Given this determination by the new Soviet leadership, which had indeed been shared by the Soviet military in Khrushchev's last days, the prospects of any significant improvement in relations with the United States were dim until the Soviet build-up of its nuclear strength had been achieved. But American involvement in Vietnam made certain a deterioration in US–Soviet relations in any event.

The Soviets could not stand by while the Americans pounded into submission a small Communist power, North Vietnam. The Soviets increased aid to North Vietnam as American involvement grew. Soviet wrath over American military actions in Vietnam grew when the US Air Force launched an assault on Hanoi on 7 February 1965, while Kosygin was in Hanoi for talks with Ho Chi Minh. Soviet determination grew to support the Communists in Vietnam not only in their defence of North Vietnam but also in the war of 'liberation' in South Vietnam.

Moreover, the Soviet Union realized the growing competition with China for leadership of the Communist world. It was therefore vital for the Soviets to assert themselves in giving aid to the Communists in Vietnam lest the Vietnamese, who received aid also from China, side with the Chinese in the Sino-Soviet rivalry. The Sino-Soviet split had become open since the early 1960s and, following the outbreak of the Great Cultural Revolution in China in 1966, the Soviet ambassador was withdrawn from Beijing until 1970. The United States continued to maintain a relationship of ostracism and mutual vituperation with the Chinese. Fear of China grew when on 16 October 1964, two days after Khrushchev's downfall, the Chinese announced the successful test of a nuclear device. No attempt was made to exploit the Sino-Soviet dispute during the 1960s. American involvement in Vietnam made it difficult to take advantage of the growing split within the Communist world.

Johnson's attitude towards Communism in the Caribbean and Central America was as rigid and relatively simplistic as his attitude towards Communism in South-East Asia. In the Dominican Republic in 1965 when it seemed that Juan Bosch, a progressive reformer, might come to power, Johnson accepted the view that Communists were taking control of Bosch's movement and sent in US marines. Johnson stated that he would not allow 'a band of Communist conspirators' to take control of 'a popular democratic revolution'.[5] Johnson felt that his action was proved justified when in UN-supervised elections in 1966 the moderate conservative Joaquin Balaguer was elected and stable conditions persisted in the Dominican Republic. Johnson also realized, as a shrewd political analyst, that American public opinion strongly supported decisive action against a perceived threat that Castroism might spread beyond Cuba and that the Soviets might be presented with another bridgehead for the expansion of Communism into Central and Latin America and with a further opportunity to establish a base in the Caribbean. The Latin American nations, however, condemned America's action as unjustifiable interference in the internal affairs of a small neighbouring country, resulting from American association of progressive reform with Castroism and pro-Soviet Communism.

Yet, while Vietnam, the Dominican Republic and the build-up of the Soviet nuclear arsenal mitigated against an improvement in US–Soviet relations in the 1960s, in such areas as trade and cultural exchanges there was steady improvement. The Cultural Agreement of 1958 was renewed and expanded every two years, leading to prominent events such as visits to the United States by the Bolshoi and Kirov Ballet Companies. In 1966 a US–Soviet track meeting was cancelled in protest over Vietnam, but in 1967 US–Soviet track meetings resumed. In February 1965 Johnson appointed a Special Committee on Trade Relations with Eastern European countries and the Soviet Union, which reported that trade could be 'the means of reducing animosities between ourselves and individual Communist countries and can provide a basis for working out mutually acceptable solutions to common problems'. Johnson accepted the report, stating that he saw 'increased trade as a way to begin easing some of the worst tensions and suspicions of the Cold War'.[6] In a speech on 7 October 1966 Johnson declared that 'Our task is to achieve a reconciliation with the East – a shift from the narrow concept of co-existence to the broader vision of peaceful engagement'.[7] A trade bill was introduced in Congress to facilitate East-West trade, but Johnson found that Congressmen 'asked how we could be fighting Communists in Southeast Asia while negotiating and trading with them in Europe'.[8] The trade bill was therefore not passed. As Johnson noted, 'The East–West trade bill became a victim of the war in Vietnam'.[9] In Congressional hearings on Vietnam in 1966 George Kennan testified that a major effect of the war in Vietnam was in distracting America to a peripheral area in a local conflict in a minor South-East Asian country instead of focusing upon the central area of importance in American foreign policy, namely relations with the Soviet Union, where the prospects for improvement were fair.

In 1967 Kosygin came to the United States to attend the UN General Assembly, and a meeting was arranged with Johnson on 23–5 June in Glassboro, New Jersey, half way between New York and Washington, since Kosygin objected to coming to Washington in the midst of the Vietnam War. As William Hyland has observed, 'It was indicative of growing American weakness and Soviet arrogance that Kosygin refused to come to the US capital'.[10] As with previous summits at Geneva in 1955 and Camp David in 1959, the Glassboro summit produced an outburst of goodwill in America and good personal relations between Johnson and Kosygin. An invitation was extended to Johnson to visit the Soviet Union in 1968, which he accepted. The most substantial issue which was raised was arms control. With American appreciation that the Soviets were approaching parity in nuclear weapons, there was a desire to avoid an uncontrolled further spiral upwards of the arms race but to achieve stability in the military balance through the process of arms control. Moreover, the United States was concerned by Soviet development of an anti-ballistic missile system (ABM), which the United States felt that it needed to match or to develop means to overcome. Discussions at Glassboro on these matters of arms control did not produce concrete results. Kosygin was particularly adamant that the Soviets would continue deployment of its ABM, since defence against missiles, he argued, was a morally superior as well as a strategically more effective means of retaliation against nuclear attack than mutual assured destruction (MAD) in the form of a massive counter-strike. Defense Secretary Robert McNamara replied that, while this was theoretically logical, in practice deployment of an ABM system by one side would be matched by the other side as well as by means to overcome the other side's defensive system, so that after vast expenditure on both sides neither side would be any more secure. Agreement was reached that Strategic Arms Limitation Talks (SALT) should begin, combined with discussion of ABM. Moreover, in 1968 substantial progress was made in arms control with the signature of the Nuclear Non-proliferation Treaty by the United States, the Soviet Union and many other nations, to prevent the spread of nuclear weapons to non-nuclear powers.

In Eastern Europe small steps towards liberalization in

economic matters in such countries as Hungary had been accepted by the Soviet Union, while a measure of independence in foreign policy on the part of Romania was tolerated and Albania had *de facto* withdrawn from the Warsaw Pact in 1961 with Soviet acquiescence. The changes in Eastern Europe were not profound, but hopes quietly developed that with growing prosperity a gradual liberalization and greater freedom from Moscow's control might come about. These developments culminated in the Prague Spring in Czechoslovakia in 1968. In January 1968 the Stalinist Communist Party leader Anatol Novotny was replaced by Alexander Dubcek, who promised 'Communism with a human face'. Dubcek made clear that he was a committed Communist, not a social democrat or a liberal, and that he was loyal to the Warsaw Pact in matters of defence and foreign policy. In internal affairs, however, Dubcek introduced reforms which not only permitted greater freedom in economic matters, with less centralized direction of the economy, but also allowed a wide measure of freedom of speech, freedom of the press and cultural liberalization. A wave of euphoria swept through Czechoslovakia, with the feeling that a model was being shown to all of Eastern Europe, including the Soviet Union, of the means of transformation from drab, repressed, economically backward societies to vibrant, progressive, prosperous nations under a Communist system which was not so threatening to the West. The majority of Americans welcomed the Dubcek brand of Communism with a human face, though conservatives felt that reform Communism was Communism nonetheless and was indeed in some ways more dangerous to the United States, since it was liable to have wider appeal to other countries than unreformed Stalinism, while economic reforms could build a stronger base for the military strength of the Warsaw Pact.

The promising, exciting developments in Czechoslovakia, however, remained in the background of American attention as the climactic events of the Vietnam War unfolded. In the spring of 1968 Dubcek's reforms in Prague made little impact on an American public preoccupied with casualties in Vietnam, which had risen to 500 deaths per week. In late 1967 the American commander in Vietnam, General William Westmoreland, reported that the war was being won and requested reinforcements of a further 200,000 troops in order to achieve complete victory. As Westmoreland's request was being considered, the Viet Cong and their North Vietnamese allies mounted a massive assault on 30 January 1968 during Tet, the Vietnamese New Year holiday period, on the American embassy in Saigon and on every provincial capital in South Vietnam. In fierce fighting over the next three days the Tet offensive ended in Communist defeat in a narrow military sense, with the rebuttal of the attacks on every point which was assailed and with very heavy Communist losses. But in psychological terms, the Tet offensive marked the beginning of the end of American involvement in Vietnam. It made clear to the American public that, even with large-scale American reinforcements, victory in Vietnam was either unattainable or achievable only at an unacceptable, prolonged massive cost.

In March 1968 Johnson took the momentous decision to change course in Vietnam, turning down Westmoreland's request for reinforcements and halting American bombing in North Vietnam, except in a zone immediately north of the border with South Vietnam, as a means to try to initiate peace talks. As a token of his sincere intentions and to make clear that his move was not for narrow, electoral motives, Johnson announced that he would not be a candidate for another term as president in 1968. The contests in the Democratic primaries between Eugene McCarthy, Robert Kennedy and Hubert Humphrey brought out the deep divisions in the county over Vietnam, which campus protests and demonstrations had earlier illustrated. Robert Kennedy's assassination after his victory in the California primary on 5 June 1968 added powerfully to a sense of frightening violence in the nation in the midst of the Vietnam War. Along with race riots in 1967 and Martin Luther King's assassination in 1968, Robert Kennedy's assassination left a deepening sense of a nation out of control, which seemed to be vividly illustrated by the violent demonstrations and police brutality at the Democratic National Convention in Chicago in August 1968.

While American attention was riveted with horror on the streets of Chicago, events were taking place in the streets of Prague of profound significance for US–Soviet relations. Brezhnev, who was increasingly emerging as the dominant leader in the Soviet Union, grew disturbed that Dubcek's brand of reform Communism would spread throughout Eastern Europe, weaken Moscow's hold over the satellites and under-mine the authority of the Communist Party within the Soviet Union. Brezhnev had the support of hardline Eastern bloc leaders such as Walter Ulbricht in East Germany, while the other satellite countries at least acquiesced in the decision to crush the reform movement in Czechoslovakia by force. On 20 August 1968 Warsaw Pact forces moved against Czechoslovakia in overwhelming strength. The Czechs realized from the experience of Hungary in 1956 that resistance was hopeless. With relatively little bloodshed, the Czech government was overthrown and Dubcek replaced by a conventional old-style Communist, Gustav Husak, who restored Czechoslovakia to drab, repressive Communist orthodoxy for the next twenty years. Dubcek was not executed, like Nagy after the Hungarian Revolution in 1956, but demoted to a minor post. With a minimum of violence, Brezhnev attained his objective, which he articulated in a speech to a group of high-ranking Czechoslovak party and government officials who served in Dubcek's government and who were arrested in Prague and flown to Moscow:

> Your country lies on territory where the Soviet soldier trod in the Second World War. We bought that territory at the cost of enormous sacrifices, and we shall never leave it. . . . In the name of the dead of the Second World War who laid down their lives for your freedom as well, we are therefore fully justified in sending our soldiers into your country, so that we may feel truly secure within our common borders. . . . That is how it will be, from the Second World War until 'eternity'.[11]

The Brezhnev Doctrine had been proclaimed, namely that the Soviet Union had the right to intervene in any East European country which deviated from the path of orthodox Communism.

In response to the invasion of Czechoslovakia Johnson's visit to the Soviet Union was cancelled. Moreover, all diplomatic contacts with the Soviets were frozen and the SALT talks, which were about to commence, were postponed. The possibility had been destroyed that in the midst of the Vietnam debacle Johnson might keep the overall US–Soviet relationship on a reasonably steady course. The invasion of Czechoslovakia set off alarm bells in Beijing, where there was great fear of a Soviet application of the Brezhnev Doctrine in some form or other towards China. But Johnson was in no position to exploit the deteriorating Sino-Soviet relationship to US advantage.

Johnson ended his presidency with attention, inevitably, focused upon issues relating to Vietnam. In the final days of the presidential election campaign, partly as a boost to the

Democratic candidate, Hubert Humphrey, Johnson ended bombing in all of North Vietnam, and as a result peace talks were arranged, to begin in Paris in January 1969. The boost to Humphrey's campaign, however, was too little and too late, and settlement of the Vietnam War was left to the Republican victor in the 1968 election, Richard Nixon.

12

NIXON, KISSINGER AND
DETENTE, 1969–74

The new president inaugurated in January 1969, Richard Nixon, had made notoriety as a hardline anti-Communist the hallmark of his early career. Yet Nixon initiated and presided over an era of détente. At his side, his National Security Adviser, Henry Kissinger, contributed not only intellectual analysis but also glamour, flair and chic such as the conduct of foreign affairs rarely attracted. What was the substance of détente in the Nixon–Kissinger era? Was there, beneath the high-profile summitry and flurry of activity, a solid foundation for the development of an ongoing improvement in US–Soviet relations? And did the Watergate affair destroy the promising beginnings of a more constructive US–Soviet relationship, or was the structure of détente as created by Nixon and Kissinger inherently unstable? These are perhaps the major questions to be assessed in an examination of the dramatic events in one of the most significant chapters in the history of US–Soviet relations.

Nixon's reputation as a hardline anti-Communist gave him leeway in seeking an accommodation with Communist powers. In 1946 Nixon won election to the House of Representatives by smearing his liberal Democratic opponent, Jerry Voorhis, as a fellow-traveller. In 1948, as a prominent member of the House Un-American Activities Committee, Nixon pressed the case against Alger Hiss, which brought Hiss to trial and won Nixon national publicity. In 1950 Nixon repeated his success of associating a liberal Democrat with Communism, dubbing his Democratic opponent in the Senate election in California, Helen Gahagan Douglas, as 'The Pink Lady'.[1] In 1952 the choice of Nixon as running mate to Eisenhower was of a candidate acceptable to the Republican right wing who could be used as a channel to McCarthy and his associates and who was willing to use McCarthyist tactics against the Democrats. By 1968, however, Nixon had mellowed and grown more self-confident as a wealthy, successful corporation lawyer in the 1960s after his defeat by John F. Kennedy in the presidential election in 1960. Political commentators in 1968 referred to 'the new Nixon', a more mature, self-assured statesman, compared to the low-hitting political infighter of his earlier career.

One sign of Nixon's maturity and self-confidence was his selection as National Security Adviser of Kissinger, an adviser and associate of Nelson Rockefeller, a Nixon rival for the Republican presidential nomination. Nixon had first taken note of Kissinger in 1957 when Kissinger's book *Nuclear Weapons and Foreign Policy* was published, which Nixon read and concluded that 'we were very much alike in our general outlook'.[2] Nixon, an intelligent, reasonably well-read man with a keen interest in foreign affairs, had visited the Soviet Union as vice-president in 1958, when he held his celebrated Kitchen Debate with Khrushchev, and as a private citizen in 1967. Nixon had formulated his ideas on the conduct of foreign policy in general and relations with the Soviet Union in particular, but he sought a National Security Adviser who was of similar thinking to himself and who could conceptualize the issues and present the alternative policy options. His choice was Kissinger, a Jewish refugee from Nazi Germany who had risen to become a Harvard professor and consultant on foreign affairs and whose political association with Rockefeller Nixon was prepared to overlook.

The first order of business facing Nixon was Vietnam. At a later time Nixon said that

> The major mistake I made as president was – this will surprise you – not doing early in 1969 what I did on May 8 of 1972 and on December 15 of 1972, and that was to bomb and mine North Vietnam. . . . If we had done that then, I think we would have ended the war in Vietnam in 1969 rather than 1973.[3]

Détente would thereby have been launched from the pad of victory in Vietnam rather than from a position of weakness as a result of the Vietnam embroilment. Kissinger likewise, as William Hyland noted, 'often wondered whether seeking a military decision would not have been the wisest and the most prudent course'.[4] Yet, as Hyland also observed, 'It would probably have been political suicide, in view of the poisonous atmosphere of those days'.[5] At the other extreme, Senator William Fulbright suggested to Nixon that, like De Gaulle and Algeria in 1958, Nixon should immediately withdraw from Vietnam and in one authoritative stroke lance the boil which was eating away at the vitals of the fabric of American society. Nixon, although an admirer of De Gaulle, did not seriously consider such an idea. Instead, Nixon embarked on the much more complex course of seeking to defuse tensions within America by gradual troop withdrawals, building up the South Vietnamese forces by increased military aid under the Vietnamization programme and endeavouring to play off the Soviet Union and China against one another in order to strengthen the American negotiating position with North Vietnam. In March 1969 Nixon, as he records in his memoirs, 'confidently told the Cabinet that I expected the war to be over in a year'.[6]

The formal peace negotiations which had been arranged in Johnson's last months opened in Paris in January 1969 and continued with weekly meetings for four years. The sessions were, however, little more than fruitless exchanges of propaganda, while the meaningful negotiations were conducted secretly. Meantime, an easing of domestic strains was sought by withdrawal of American troops – 25,000 in June 1969 and announcements of more withdrawals over succeeding months. But Nixon's goal in Vietnamization was to bring about gradual reductions and eventual total withdrawal of American troops while enabling the South Vietnamese to prevent Communist victory. Nixon was not prepared to accept defeat in Vietnam. Some commentators have suggested that Nixon and Kissinger aimed at a settlement which would provide a respectable fig leaf for American withdrawal, allowing a 'decent interval' between American withdrawal and South Vietnamese collapse.[7] But Nixon's objective was undoubtedly a settlement which resulted in American withdrawal and the survival of a non-Communist South Vietnam. The South Vietnamese government stabilized after the election of Nguyan Van Thieu in 1967, and Nixon increased military aid to Thieu.

Moreover, an important element in Nixon's diplomacy was to keep the other side off its guard by showing readiness to employ force in an unpredictable manner. From the experience of the Korean War peace negotiations, Nixon concluded that no movement in negotiating position on the other side would take place unless there existed the element of fear and uncertainty regarding America's actions. Nixon aimed deliberately to create an aura of mystery and unpredictability by his use of force at times in Vietnam, especially the invasion of Cambodia in June 1970, the invasion of Laos in July 1971, the mining of Haiphong in May 1972 and the massive bombing of North Vietnam in December 1972. Such actions were designed to deter the North Vietnamese by instilling fear of the possible consequences if they did not adhere to the terms of the peace agreement. These bold military actions and increased military aid under Vietnamization were also designed to strengthen Kissinger's hand in his secret negotiations with the North Vietnamese. In 1969–70 Kissinger secretly met twelve times with Le Duc Tho, the chief North Vietnamese negotiator. The meetings were revealed at the end of 1970, and Kissinger and Le Duc Tho negotiated in sessions in 1971–2 which were reported, although the details of their discussions were not disclosed. The peace settlement which Nixon had hoped to reach within a year, took four years to conclude, in January 1973.

Nixon and Kissinger felt that a resolution of the Vietnam War was interlinked with the objectives in seeking détente with China and the Soviet Union. A key element lay in the Sino-Soviet dispute which had worsened to the extent that severe casualties were inflicted on both sides in border disputes on the Usurri River in March to September 1969. Nixon took steps to improve US–Chinese relations in order to use China as a lever against the Soviet Union. America's intention, however, was not to take China's side against the Soviet Union. As Kissinger put it, 'The hostility between China and the Soviet Union served our purposes best if we maintained closer relations with each side than they did with each other. The rest could be left to the dynamics of events'.[8]

As Nixon realized, the Chinese, although in the depths of the Cultural Revolution, were so apprehensive over Soviet designs that they were interested in responding to American overtures. The US administration began to send diplomatic signals to the Chinese of a desire to establish communications. In July 1969 the State Department announced that American students and scholars could have their passports validated automatically for travel to China, without the need for special permission. In October 1969 the US ambassador to Poland was instructed to seek out a high-ranking Chinese official at the next diplomatic function and propose the resumption of talks between Chinese and American diplomats in Warsaw, which had taken place since the 1950s sporadically and generally unfruitfully. In January 1970 the American ambassador agreed to meet Chinese diplomats at 'the embassy of the People's Republic of China', the first time the United States had employed the term 'the People's Republic'.[9]

The Chinese began to send signals in return. On 1 October 1970 the American journalist Edgar Snow was invited to stand at the National Day celebrations in Beijing at the side of Mao Zedong, who said to Snow that the Sino-Soviet conflict was irresolvable and spoke of the United States in more sympathetic terms than Snow had heard for years. In April 1971 a very public signal was sent by means of a Chinese invitation to an American table tennis team to play in China, and visas were granted to American journalists to provide wide publicity for this 'ping-pong diplomacy'. Messages were secretly exchanged through Pakistan, culminating in an invitation in April 1971 by the Chinese government to send an American envoy to Beijing. In July 1971 Kissinger made a trip to Pakistan in the course of which, under cover of illness in Pakistan, he made a two-day visit to Beijing as the American envoy and received a Chinese invitation for Nixon to visit China. On Kissinger's return, Nixon made a television announcement of his acceptance of the Chinese invitation to an astonished American public. In October 1971 Communist China was admitted to the United Nations, and, although the United States had wished to retain a General Assembly seat for Taiwan, the replacement of the Nationalist delegation to the UN by the Communist delegation removed a long-standing obstacle in the path of better US–Chinese relations.

In February 1972 Nixon's visit to China was a spectacular success. The one issue of substance which was discussed, the thorny question of Taiwan, was smoothed over by a diplomatic formula whereby the Chinese claim to Taiwan was recognized, while agreement was stated of a desire for a peaceful resolution of the issue. To a much greater extent than any substantial agreements, however, the Nixon visit to China was symbolic. After twenty years of vicious mutual recriminations, the new relationship between the world's most powerful and most populous nations was projected in image by Nixon and Mao exchanging toasts in the Great Hall of the People in Beijing. In 1973 Kissinger returned to Beijing and arranged the establishment of a liaison office, which was an embassy in all but name. US–Chinese relations were set on a course of steady, virtually uninterrupted improvement for the next twenty years. With consummate skill Nixon had changed the course of US–Chinese relations, spiking the guns of the American political right, who would have vociferously condemned such action by a liberal Democratic president. Nixon had played the China card with masterly finesse, but his objective was not to side with China against the Soviet Union but to reap the benefits of his diplomacy with the Chinese in his relationship with the Soviet Union.

In August 1969 Nixon visited Romania, the first American president to visit an East European Communist country. This signalled to Moscow his willingness to make approaches to Communist countries but also indicated a lack of deference to Moscow by selecting a Warsaw Pact country which had begun to assert a measure of independence in foreign policy. Meantime, in October 1969 Willi Brandt and the Social Democrats came to power in West Germany, eager to pursue their brand of détente, *Ostpolitik*. In 1970 Brandt signed a Non-Aggression Pact with the Soviet Union and made a treaty with Poland accepting the Oder–Neisse line as the Polish–German border and in 1972 West Germany and East Germany agreed to mutual recognition. To Nixon, *Ostpolitik* was characterized too much by one-sided concessions and was not the 'hard-headed détente' which he sought. Thus on a further issue of *Ostpolitik* – namely Berlin, on which negotiations involved the four occupying powers as well as the West Germans – Nixon determined to take a firmer stand, linking Berlin to other East–West issues and applying pressure on the Soviets from America's developing relationship with China. In October 1970 Nixon met Gromyko in Washington and tentatively agreed to a summit in 1971, but Moscow held back, seeking a prior agreement on Berlin which would be linked to a summit. Similarly, in SALT I talks, which opened in November 1969, little progress was made during the first year and a half. The announcement of Nixon's visit to China seemed to concentrate Soviet minds and helped to produce a breakthrough in the negotiations on Berlin on terms more acceptable to the West, while there was movement in the SALT talks and agreement was reached on a US–Soviet summit meeting in Moscow in May 1972.

Shortly before the Moscow summit a crisis developed in Vietnam, with a full-scale North Vietnamese assault on 30 March

1972. Nixon was determined not to go to Moscow in a weak, humiliating position. On 8 May 1972 he took the bold measure of bombing and mining Haiphong, where Soviet ships landed supplies for the North Vietnamese, resulting in Soviet casualties. Nixon calculated that the Soviets would not cancel the summit and that he would go to Moscow in a stronger position, better able to win Soviet support to exert pressure on the North Vietnamese to reach a settlement, while the bombing and mining brought the North Vietnamese offensive to a halt and strengthened Kissinger's hand in his talks with Le Duc Tho.

Whereas the Beijing summit was largely symbolic, the Moscow summit covered a wide range of substantial matters, particularly arms control, economic issues, cultural, scientific and educational exchanges, avoidance of incidents at sea and a Basic Principles Agreement. The most significant agreements were on arms control, namely SALT I and the ABM Treaty. Nixon accepted that strategic parity at controlled levels was preferable to an unrestrained arms race in which each side strove for superiority. The attainment of this general objective was, however, immensely complex in practical details, especially with rapid advances in technology and difficulties over verification. The protracted SALT I negotiations since 1969 produced a formula whereby nuclear weapons would be limited on both sides to fixed, agreed levels in a number of categories. The SALT process was intended to be ongoing, with SALT II lowering levels and covering more categories, and with later SALT agreements lowering levels further and beginning a reduction in the arsenals of the two sides, whereas the first step of SALT I set an agreed limit to which both sides could build up. The deadline of the summit acted as a spur to the negotiators to reach compromises and to produce an agreement which, however imperfect on many points of detail, was the first significant arms control agreement in the Cold War and held out the promise of a continuing process of arms control. By the terms of SALT I each side was permitted to build up to a level of 1,400 launchers, that is, missiles and bombers. SALT I covered the number of launchers, not warheads, throw-weight or qualitative differences. The United States had a qualitative superiority in accuracy of missiles and, above all, had made the technological breakthrough of MIRVs (multiple independently targeted re-entry vehicles) whereby one missile carried many independently targeted warheads. American negotiators were unwilling to give up this advantage and felt that Congress would not ratify a treaty which made such a concession. But the exclusion of MIRVs from SALT I resulted in a rapid matching development of MIRVs by the Soviets, leading to an arms race in the most sophisticated aspect of nuclear weaponry of the 1970s and severely affecting the usefulness of SALT I.

Critics on the right argued that SALT I was a failure, precluding the United States from competing in areas of Soviet advantage, especially ICBM throw-weight, while permitting Soviet qualitative improvement in the areas of American advantage, especially MIRVs and missile accuracy. This provided further ammunition for the argument regarding the alleged 'window of vulnerability', which would enable the Soviets, when their very heavy missiles were improved in accuracy, to destroy most American ICBMs in their silos in a surprise attack. This concept was given 'marginal plausibility' in a National Security Council discussion in 1969, but it won growing support from critics of SALT I.[10] Liberal critics charged that the arms limitations of SALT I were so relatively slight that the pace of technology overtook the pace of arms control. Moreover, in order to gain Congressional support for SALT I Defence Secretary Melvin Laird requested in 1971 an accelerated offensive programme, particularly with regard to Trident submarines and the B-1 bomber, which Congress accepted. Thus, SALT I did not result in lower levels of manpower, weaponry and spending. Its main value lay in creating the basis for possible substantial reductions in the future. Also, with the establishment of the Standing Consultative Committee for discussion of suspected treaty infringements, a forum was set up for frank, private discussions of verification procedures.

In addition to SALT I, the ABM treaty was signed at the Moscow summit. In the late 1960s the Soviets had deployed an ABM system around Moscow and around one major ICBM site. In the United States there was much doubt, especially within Congress, of the value of an ABM system, since its deployment was likely only to escalate the arms race, with mutual deployment of ABM systems and of offensive measures to overcome the ABM system of the other side. Shortly after coming into office Nixon concluded that 'Although every instinct motivates me to provide the American people with complete protection against a major nuclear attack, it is not within our power to do so. . . . And it may look to an opponent like the prelude to an offensive strategy threatening the Soviet deterrent'.[11] Robert McNamara argued in 1967 for an ABM system as a defence against a Chinese offensive, that is, against a missile assault of a less sophisticated nature. But when ABM was debated in Congress in 1969 and approval gained by a margin of one vote in the Senate, the key argument was the need for a bargaining chip to make possible a treaty on the matter with the Soviets. Whereas Kosygin had argued strongly at Glassboro in 1967 in favour of an ABM system, by 1970 the Soviet position had changed and they wished to avoid an ABM race with the United States. Agreement was reached, therefore, in the 1972 ABM treaty that each side could deploy an ABM system only around its capital and around one missile site. Hence, the two superpowers agreed that the quest for comprehensive defence which would give absolute security was a mirage and that the attempt of one side to attain this would create instability, arousing fears of the other side of preparation of an impregnable shield from behind which a first strike could be launched. Both sides agreed that they would remain vulnerable to a nuclear attack and would not attempt to build a foolproof defence against it. Indeed, the United States completed only one site, in North Dakota, which was operated briefly and then abandoned, while the site around Washington was never even begun.

With regard to economic issues, whereas Khrushchev had boasted that the Soviet Union would surpass the United States economically by 1970, it was clear by the late 1960s that not only was such a boast nonsensical but that Soviet economic backwardness made urgently necessary the acquisition of technological equipment and of grain from the United States. Nixon avoided the terminology of a crude carrot-and-stick approach, but his objective was clearly to make the Soviet Union so eager to gain the commercial benefits of détente that they would pay a political price. Nixon did not believe that the Soviet desire for economic gain would be so great that they would accept internal political changes within the Soviet Union but that linkage could subtly be made between economic and foreign policy issues, such as Soviet leverage on the North Vietnamese to come to terms. Economic agreements were reached in principle at the Moscow summit which produced a wheat sales agreement in July 1972 and a general economic agreement in October 1972, which included the grant of Most Favored Nation status to the Soviet Union, but this required Congressional approval. A lend-lease settlement was reached at Moscow for repayment of

$740 million over thirty years for civilian goods delivered to the Soviet Union during the Second World War. The economic benefits to the United States of all of these agreements was marginal, except for American farmers and a number of individual American companies. The political significance, however, was deemed to be of great importance, tying the Soviet Union to more normalized contacts with the West which would be mutually beneficial and which the Soviets would be eager not to lose. As Nixon put it, 'This was the first stage of détente: to involve Soviet interests in ways that would increase their stake in international stability and the status quo'.[12]

A wide range of agreements were also signed at Moscow on cultural, educational and scientific agreements. Extensions were made to the agreements for tours of musical companies and artistic exhibitions in one another's countries and for an increase in the number of students exchanged. On scientific matters, there was agreement on joint environmental projects and, most spectacularly, a joint mission in space. Within military circles an area of co-operation for which there was much support was CFM (confidence-building measures), concerning such matters as forewarnings of military manoeuvres. Given the suspicion on both sides over revelations of military information, agreement on such matters proved difficult. A beginning was made, however, with an agreement on avoidance of incidents at sea.Finally, a Basic Principles Agreement was signed, which seemed to imply that, while ideological competition between capitalism and communism would continue, it would be conducted by means of peaceful competition. The United States accepted the principle of peaceful co-existence.

The Moscow summit was, moreover, a personal triumph for Nixon. He was cordially received by his Soviet hosts, and he struck up a good personal relationship with Brezhnev. In a speech on Soviet television, he spoke of US–Soviet co-operation in the Second World War and described the horrors of war with an emotional description of the siege of Leningrad (1942–4) and the story of a Russian child, Tanya, who lost all her relatives one by one and finally perished herself. The speech not only moved his Soviet audience but was so well received in the United States that the excerpt on little Tanya was used as a commercial in Nixon's re-election campaign later in the year.

On his return from Moscow, Nixon gave his assessment of its success in a speech to Congress, stating that 'We will be able to go forward and explore the sweeping possibilities for peace which this season of summits has now opened up for the world'.[13] In 1972 Nixon was in an extremely strong political position, with almost no criticism from the right and with even the liberal left compelled, however grudgingly, to applaud Nixon's foreign-policy accomplishments, so that Nixon was well placed to build upon the achievements of the Moscow summit and to pursue policies which would bring out the tendencies in Soviet policy conducive to détente.

Two weeks after Nixon's trip to Moscow, on the night of 30 May 1972, a burglary took place in the office of the headquarters of the Democratic National Committee in the Watergate complex in Washington. This apparently trivial incident set in motion the course of events which not only destroyed Nixon's presidency and forced his resignation but profoundly affected the process of détente and the course of US–Soviet relations. The immediate impact of the Watergate affair was slight. Relatively little media attention was given to this somewhat odd incident. The focus of attention was on George McGovern's victory in the California primary, which assured McGovern the Democratic nomination and made Nixon's re-election task much easier, running against an opponent who was perceived as an extreme liberal. In a landslide victory in the election on 5 November Nixon won forty-nine of the fifty states.

Media attention was also focused upon the final stages of the negotiation of the Vietnam settlement. On 26 October 1972 Kissinger announced that 'Peace is at hand', which assisted Nixon's re-election.[14] When obstacles then arose in the peace talks, Nixon engaged in the extreme measure of massive bombing of North Vietnam from 15 December to 30 December, which aroused world-wide condemnation. On 23 January 1973, however, an agreement was signed, whereby American troops withdrew from Vietnam, prisoners of war were returned, and a complex arrangement was made regarding the political situation within South Vietnam which, Nixon and Kissinger claimed, provided Thieu and the South Vietnamese non-Communists with the opportunity to sustain themselves in power after American withdrawal. At the very time, however, when the end came to the catastrophe of American involvement in Vietnam, which for a decade had been the single most important impediment to an improvement in US–Soviet relations, the Watergate affair (successfully covered up until the election was safely over and given little attention while the Vietnam negotiations were concluded) began to dominate the news.

In December 1972 two *Washington Post* reporters, Carl Bernstein and Bob Woodward, began to publish stories linking figures in high positions in the Campaign to Re-elect the President (CREEP) to the Watergate affair. In January 1973 the trial took place of the five Watergate burglars, and, under threat from the judge, John Sirica, of very heavy sentences if the burglars did not reveal who were behind them, one of the five, James McCord, revealed their connection with CREEP. In March 1973 the Senate established a committee under Senator Sam Erwin to investigate the Watergate affair. Under all of these pressures details gradually emerged which led to suspicions not only that the planning of the Watergate break-in went as high as John Mitchell, the Attorney General and Nixon's campaign manager, but also that Nixon himself was deeply implicated in the cover-up. Furthermore, it became clear that Watergate was not an isolated incident but part of a pattern of illegality and abuse of power which pervaded the Nixon White House. With almost daily revelations of more and more sensational details throughout the spring and summer of 1973, Nixon's political position plummeted from impregnable strength following his landslide re-election victory to extreme vulnerability, with growing calls for his impeachment.

At the time when the president's authority was being undermined, incidents arose which led to a souring of public enthusiasm for détente. The first such incident arose over wheat sales. Following a poor Soviet harvest in 1972 the Soviets quietly bought up at very favourable prices much larger quantities of American wheat than anticipated, using to the full extent the credits extended in the July 1972 agreement, causing wheat shortages in America and consequent price rises. As Kissinger noted, 'It was painful to realize that we had been out-manoeuvred, even more difficult to admit that the methods which had gained that edge were those of a sharp trader skilfully using our free market system. . . . The Soviets beat us at our own game'.[15] Americans did not enjoy the experience of being made laughingstocks. More fundamentally, inflation had been a growing problem in the United States since the late 1960s, and the American economy, which had enjoyed a long period of boom since the early 1950s, with low unemployment, low inflation, large export surpluses, a close to balanced budget and a steady growth rate, began to run into a multitude of problems, which fundamentally arose from the end of American world economic dominance and the beginning of an era of much stronger competition from Western Europe, Japan and elsewhere. The spurt of inflation in the early 1970s, which Nixon tried to curb with price controls, was the first sign of America's underlying economic difficulties. But there was public awareness that Soviet sleight of hand over the wheat agreement was one factor involved in causing inflation. Soviet ability to operate skilfully in a capitalist market won no admiration. Instead, on an issue which hit the man in the street and the woman in the supermarket, namely higher bread prices, the old slogans appeared to be justified that the Soviets were treacherous and untrustworthy.

Nevertheless, public support for détente still appeared to be strong when Brezhnev visited the United States in June 1973. The Erwin Committee suspended its hearings for the week of Brezhnev's visit to save the president embarrassment, and Nixon was relieved to turn his attention away from Watergate to US–Soviet affairs. A few further agreements were reached, which were mainly refinements of the 1972 agreements. An agreement was signed on the Prevention of Nuclear War, which elaborated upon the Basic Principles agreement of 1972, while agreements were also signed on more mundane matters such as expansion of air passenger services between the two countries, exchanges of information in oceanography, transportation, agriculture and peaceful uses of atomic energy, and an expansion of educational, cultural and scientific exchanges. Above all, Nixon consolidated his personal relationship with Brezhnev and hoped that the custom was becoming institutionalized of annual summit meetings between American and Soviet leaders. The nature of Nixon's personal relationship with Brezhnev was illustrated in the episode of the presentation at Camp David (where Brezhnev stayed over a weekend during the summit) of a gift to Brezhnev of a Lincoln Continental. 'Brezhnev, a collector of luxury cars, did not attempt to conceal his delight', Nixon later wrote. 'He insisted upon trying it out immediately. He got behind the wheel and enthusiastically motioned me into the passenger's seat. The head of the Secret Service detail went pale as I climbed in and we took off down one of the narrow roads'.[16] Brezhnev roared around the perimeter road of Camp David at high speed, with tyres screeching on dangerous curves. A personal relationship which could involve such an escapade of the two leaders behaving together like irresponsible teenagers did not preclude war between the two countries, but it made it less likely.

With Brezhnev back in Moscow, Nixon sunk deeper into the mire of Watergate troubles. The revelation in July 1973 of a taping system in the Oval Office initiated a demand from Congress and the courts for Nixon to hand over the tapes, which he refused to do. From July 1973 to July 1974, when the Supreme Court ruled that the tapes must be handed over, Nixon's presidency was played out against a background of the ticking time bomb of the imminent release of the tapes, while further scandals were revealed and the formal process of impeachment began.

In October 1973 attention switched to foreign affairs, with the outbreak of the Yom Kippur War in the Middle East. Nixon's leadership was steady as the United States braved Arab threats and resupplied Israel with arms, thereby preventing the defeat of America's ally, Israel, and producing the outcome of a stalemate which was not unsatisfactory to the United States. The outcome of the war, however, did not bode well for détente. The Soviet Union had forty-eight hours advance warning from the Arabs of the impending attack, and while the US administration accepted that the Soviets did not encourage the assault and could not be expected to divulge their Arab allies' plans, American public opinion was ready to accept, as Richard Pipes put it, that the Soviets 'connived' with the Arabs to launch a surprise attack.[17] Even more dramatically, in the course of the war, when Nixon rejected Brezhnev's proposal of a joint US–Soviet peacekeeping force, Brezhnev sent a letter to Nixon on 24 October 1973 stating his intention to send in a Soviet force, which caused Nixon to call a world-wide nuclear alert, Defense Condition III, to deter Brezhnev from sending in a unilateral Soviet force. Nixon's extreme action aroused the public's anxieties, while enemies of détente such as Senator Henry Jackson denounced the Brezhnev letter of 24 October as 'brutal' and 'threatening'.[18]

In the aftermath of the war, Kissinger engaged in highly successful shuttle diplomacy in the Middle East, but Kissinger aimed at the exclusion of Soviet influence in the Middle East rather than an attempt to gain Soviet co-operation in achieving a Middle East peace settlement. Détente had in fact helped the United States and the Soviet Union to defuse the crisis of the

Yom Kippur War, while the United States gained unilateral advantage by increasing its influence in the Middle East and reducing Soviet influence. The public perception of the war, however, was that it showed the Basic Principles Agreement to be a worthless piece of paper and that the Soviet Union would seek its own narrow advantage in a situation such as the outbreak of war in the Middle East. American public opinion was influenced above all by the economic consequences of the war, with a six-month Arab oil boycott, for which the Soviets expressed public approval, and a 400 per cent increase in oil prices by the Organization of Petroleum Exporting Countries (OPEC), a cartel of oil-producing nations whose Arab members were emboldened to support sharp oil price increases following the Yom Kippur War. As the American economy ran into acute difficulties of inflation and recession, the American political mood turned sour, which contributed to the impression that the international goodwill of the heyday of détente in 1972 had been an illusion and a manipulation by the Nixon White House. The American public regarded OPEC and the Arabs as the main villains responsible for the economic problems of the mid-1970s, but there was a sense that the Soviets, who supplied arms to such nations as Syria, were very willing to stir up trouble in the volatile Middle East rather than to co-operate for a peaceful settlement in a dangerous area.

Meantime, in Vietnam the North Vietnamese and the Viet Cong flaunted the peace agreement of January 1973 and, with American troops withdrawn, increased pressure on the South Vietnamese. The Soviets showed no inclination to encourage the North Vietnamese to exercise restraint and to abide by the complex arrangements of the peace treaty. Nixon sought to bring pressure on the North Vietnamese by renewed bombing raids on their positions in Laos and Cambodia. But Congress became more assertive, while the president's position grew weaker with the Watergate affair. Congress passed the War Powers Act of 1973 to prevent the executive taking America into war without Congressional approval and passed the Cooper Amendment, which brought bombing in Indo-China to an end in May 1973. Moreover, in its general attitude Congress made clear that, despite the somewhat ambivalent provisions of the 1973 peace treaty regarding renewed American aid to South Vietnam if the North Vietnamese did not abide by the treaty terms, there was no prospect of renewed involvement in Vietnam on the part of the United States. Nixon fumed impotently as a clear signal was given that the North Vietnamese could, with Soviet backing, assault the South Vietnamese without fear of American retribution.

Congress was also emboldened to exert its authority with regard to the economic agreement of 1972. In March 1973 the Jackson–Vanik amendment to the Trade Reform Bill was introduced by Henry Jackson in the Senate and Charles Vanik in the House of Representatives, requiring Soviet agreement to permit larger-scale emigration of Jews from the Soviet Union before Congress would ratify the trade agreement and grant Most Favored Nation status to the Soviet Union. The amendment was drawn up by Jackson's aide, Richard Perle, and skilfully took up an issue which was difficult to oppose in Congress, since it attracted the support of liberals and the Jewish lobby as well as conservatives uneasy over détente. Kissinger, who became Secretary of State as well as National Security Adviser in Nixon's second term, argued strongly that such an amendment would destroy the whole web of interconnected agreements which made up détente. Such was indeed the aim of Jackson and Perle. Kissinger had worked for emigration of Jews from the Soviet Union by means of quiet diplomacy, and the numbers allowed to emigrate had risen to 35,000 in 1973. Gromyko promised in 1974 to increase the number to 45,000, but Jackson demanded an increase to 60,000. Kissinger felt certain that the Soviets would not make concessions on a human rights issue in response to public threats such as the Jackson–Vanik amendment. As Kissinger noted, Jackson 'wanted an issue, not a solution'.[19] Despite Kissinger's pleas, Congress refused to withdraw the Jackson–Vanik amendment, and support for its passage seemed assured.

Moreover, with regard to arms control, negotiations on SALT II became bogged down in technicalities, while Jackson made constant claims that SALT I was to the Soviet advantage. Information and misinformation was leaked which purveyed overestimates of Soviet military advantage. Thus, an accumulation of issues began to militate against détente, such as criticisms of SALT, the Jackson–Vanik amendment, suspicion of Soviet conduct in the Middle East and Soviet exploitation of the wheat agreement, while more generally, as Kissinger put it, 'There was a growing debate over détente, a mounting clamour that in some undefinable way we were being gulled by the Soviets'.[20]

In June 1974 Nixon again visited the Soviet Union. A few agreements of some substance were signed, such as a 150-kiloton limit on underground nuclear tests and a ban on the alteration of environmental conditions for military purposes. But rather than universal respect for the president's achievements as in 1972, the public reaction was mainly anxiety that the embattled and increasingly pathetic president might try to make unwarranted concessions to the Soviets in order to achieve a foreign policy success which might enable him to stay in office. As Nixon fell, détente appeared to be crumbling under him.

Nixon's reputation is well deserved that in his first term of office (1969–72) he achieved the most successful record of any American president with regard to the conduct of US–Soviet relations. Inheriting a very weak position, with calamity in Vietnam and the Soviet Union approaching nuclear parity, Nixon justifiably rejected either extreme in Vietnam of escalation or immediate withdrawal but instead worked for a solution to Vietnam within the framework of exploiting the Sino-Soviet split and seeking détente with both the major Communist powers. By early 1973 there was less danger and fear of a major clash between the superpowers than at any time since the start of the Cold War. The accomplishments of détente were, of course, overstated by Nixon in his inevitable desire to gain maximum political advantage and by Kissinger, whose tendency towards vanity and arrogance led him to over-intellectualize the subtleties of détente. Several other criticisms of détente of this era can validly be made. Its negotiation was excessively secretive, cutting out Secretary of State William Rogers and the normal machinery of government bureaucracy, which created misunderstandings and resentments and undermined détente in the longer term. Also, the United States clearly sought unilateral advantage, such as in the Middle East or, for example, in the use of the CIA to help to overthrow Salvador Allende in Chile in 1973, while the United States was swift to criticize alleged Soviet pursuit of unilateral advantage. Nixon and Kissinger had little interest in Third World countries except as pawns in international power politics. Moreover, the emphasis on triangular US–Soviet–Chinese diplomacy became almost a fixation, leading to neglect of other US interests. India, for example, moved into closer liaison with the Soviet Union, while the United States sided with Pakistan, which aided in contacts with China.

A less legitimate criticism of détente is that it froze the status quo and did not attempt to bring about change in the Soviet Union. Joan Hoff-Wilson, in a scathing denunciation of 'Nixingerism', writes that the potential existed 'not only to substitute for the strategy of containment but also to transcend the procrustean ideological constraints that were at the very heart of the post-World War II conflict'.[21] Nixon's biographer, Roger Morris, wrote in 1989 that 'His mutual propping with Leonid S. Brezhnev's corrupt and sclerotic government may have delayed and obstructed the liberalization we now see unfolding in the Soviet Union, and the savage repression in China shows all too clearly the character of the regime he embraced so expediently in China'.[22] Nixon was on much stronger ground in the counter-argument that in the early 1970s the establishment of détente, whereby tensions were reduced and the Soviets felt less threatened, was not only the more prudent path in the quest for eventual change in Soviet attitudes and Soviet internal structures but also was vital in order to avoid dangerous confrontation in the short term. As Nixon said in 1974:

> Would a slow down or reversal of détente help or hurt the positive evolution of other social systems? . . . We would not welcome the intervention of other countries in our domestic affairs, and we cannot expect them to be co-operative when we seek to intervene directly in their affairs. We cannot gear our foreign policy to the transformation of other societies. In the nuclear age our first responsibility must be the prevention of war that could destroy all societies'.[23]

Nixon, then, prudently sought a policy of co-existence, with a goal of containing Soviet expansion while easing tensions and working for internal Soviet changes in the long term. He rejected the alternative policy of conversion, that is, attempting to coerce the Soviets into major changes by confrontational policies.

Within the United States the pragmatic diplomacy and patient negotiation of agreements between 1969 and 1972, together with public relations skills in Nixon's summitry and Kissinger's flair, produced by 1972 a solid consensus in support of the creation of an increasingly constructive relationship with the Soviet Union. Yet the consensus was fragile. Conservatives were stunned into silence when conciliatory moves towards the Soviet Union were undertaken by such a surprising figure as the old red-baiter, Richard Nixon, but when an opportunity arose, conservative voices of criticism were soon heard. Liberals chafed at the acclaim awarded to their *bête noire* and longed for a chance to attack Richard Nixon and all his works, including détente. Public opinion at large had been raised to fear and to distrust the Soviet Union, so that beneath the unfamiliar new mood of conciliation there lay readiness to denounce Soviet perfidy whenever it raised its head, and indeed to attribute to Soviet malevolence the major ills of the times whether or not there was any degree of Soviet responsibility.

Détente had no natural consistency and was consequently vulnerable to rapid erosion. Given the difficulty of maintaining such a consensus for détente, a strong political position on the part of the president was vital. The disastrous weakening of Nixon's position as a result of Watergate was therefore fatal, undermining the president's authority and his ability to be firm or conciliatory towards the Soviet Union or towards Congress as circumstances required. Senator Clairborne Pell, a later chairman of the Senate Foreign Relations Committee, said on the day of Nixon's resignation, 9 August 1974, that each of the segments of the alliance against détente did not want a change of direction back to confrontation and conflict. 'Each wants only to attach a condition to détente', said Pell, 'apparently without realizing that the cumulative weight of the conditions could sink the ship'.[24] A new president, Gerald Ford, assumed command when, if not the ship of state, then at least détente, was clearly sinking.

13

THE DEMISE OF DETENTE, 1974–80

Nixon's successor, Gerald Ford, retained Kissinger as Secretary of State and sought a continuation of the policies towards the Soviet Union inherited from Nixon. The undermining of détente, however, which had begun in 1973–4, accelerated in pace during the presidencies of Ford and of Jimmy Carter, following Carter's victory in the presidential election of 1976. Why did the process of détente, which in the early 1970s appeared to hold out such promise and to command broad support within the United States, deteriorate so severely in the course of 1970s? The answer lies essentially in two sets of factors: first, Soviet actions, such as Third World interventions and a rapid build-up of its military strength, and second, domestic developments within American politics and society which shaped American attitudes towards the Soviet Union. The complex interplay between those two sets of factors requires analysis in order to assess their relative weight in bringing about the demise of détente by 1980.

On his accession to the presidency on 9 August 1974, Ford aimed above all to restore stability and confidence in the US government after the turmoil of Watergate. Ford's main interest was in domestic affairs, and his attention was focused primarily on America's economic problems, especially control of inflation. Kissinger's power in the exercise of foreign policy consequently grew in some respects, but in other respects Kissinger's power was kept in greater check, particularly with the appointments in November 1975 of Brent Scowcroft as National Security Adviser (whereas Kissinger had served both as Secretary of State and National Security adviser since September 1973) and of Donald Rumsfeld, a close associate of Ford, as Secretary of Defense. Ford sought a continuation of Nixon's policies towards the Soviet

Union, especially by means of the Helsinki Agreement in 1975 and negotiations on SALT II, but increasingly Soviet policies and US domestic considerations compelled adjustments and modifications from the approach of Nixon and Kissinger in the heyday of détente in the early 1970s.

The Helsinki Agreement, signed on 1 August 1975, seemed to indicate a continuation of détente and was in many respects one of détente's fullest flowers. The final session of the Conference on Security and Co-operation in Europe (CSCE) at Helsinki, attended by representatives of every nation in Europe (except Albania) plus the United States and Canada, brought to fruition years of negotiation on various European security issues. Ford and Brezhnev represented the United States and the Soviet Union to mark the occasion. By the Helsinki Final Act, post-war boundaries of Europe were given international recognition, rather than simply bilateral recognition, especially the boundaries between the Soviet Union and Poland, the Soviet Union and Romania and between Poland and East Germany. Agreement was reached on confidence-building measures, such as notification of military exercises close to borders in order to help to reduce fears of surprise attack. On human rights, the Soviets accepted that democratic freedoms and human rights were legitimate concerns on the diplomatic agenda, and the Soviets specifically agreed to the freer and wider dissemination of information of all kinds. Hence, as Raymond Garthoff has put it, the Helsinki Agreement 'provided a new basis for complaints by dissidents themselves, but more important it provided a basis (even if a contested one) for the expansion of foreign interest'.[1] Furthermore, machinery was established for follow-up CSCE conferences on human rights to monitor progress. In the longer term, CSCE proved to be one of the most significant fruits of détente. In the short term, however, in the mid to late 1970s, the Helsinki Agreement hindered as much as helped the process of détente. The myth arose within the United States that the Helsinki Agreement implied international acceptance of Soviet hegemony over Eastern Europe, whereas, as Strobe Talbott writes, 'nothing of the kind is contained in the documents or in the text, between the lines or otherwise'.[2] Moreover, misunderstanding arose over the provisions on human rights, which produced acrimonious exchanges between Soviet and American representatives at the follow-up conferences in Belgrade and Madrid.

Similarly, with regard to arms control negotiations, Ford pressed ahead with the negotiation of SALT II. In November 1974 Ford met Brezhnev in Vladivostok, and agreement was reached on virtually all the terms of a SALT II treaty. Equal ceilings for the strategic nuclear arsenal of both sides were accepted, namely a 2,400 overall aggregate in missiles and bombers, including 1,300 MIRVs on each side. After the Vladivostok meeting Ford confidently predicted that 'As soon as the technicians ironed out the few remaining problems, we would sign a SALT II accord'.[3] Since SALT I did not expire until 1977, progress seemed well advanced for the replacement of SALT I by SALT II in 1977, with negotiations to commence then on SALT III. Protracted discussions ensued in 1975–6, however, on the remaining SALT II issues, especially whether Soviet Backfire bombers and American Cruise missiles should be covered by the treaty limits. Meantime, murmurs of discontent over the SALT process from such figures as Henry Jackson became more voluble, with the result that SALT II was still not completed when Ford left office in January 1977.

The most visible and substantial cause of discontent with détente through the 1970s lay in Soviet exploitation of Third World disputes, such as in Angola, Ethiopia, Somalia, Vietnam, Cambodia, El Salvador, Nicaragua and Afghanistan. In Angola, in the months before independence was granted by Portugal in November 1975 the Soviets gave aid to the Marxist Popular Movement for the Liberation of Angola (MPLA) in its bid for power over its rivals, the National Union for the Total Independence of Angola (UNITA) and the National Front for the Liberation of Angola (FNLA). The CIA gave aid to UNITA and the FNLA, but in January 1976 Congress, fearing another quagmire such as Vietnam, passed the Clark amendment, prohibiting any further CIA covert aid to Angolan factions. Meantime, Soviet aid to the MPLA, who had installed themselves in the capital city of Luanda, became more substantial, with the Soviet airlift of 17,000 Cuban troops to Angola. Ford denounced this Soviet action as 'inconsistent with the aims and objectives of détente'.[4] Kissinger, in testimony before the Senate Foreign Relations Committee, stated that 'a continuation of actions like those in Angola must threaten the entire web of Soviet–US relations'.[5]

In Ethiopia, after a chaotic period following the overthrow of Emperor Haile Selassie in 1974, Lieutenant Colonel Mengistu Haile Mariam seized power in February 1977 and turned

Ethiopia's revolution towards a more radical and anti-American course. American aid missions and communication stations were closed down and in May 1977 Mengistu flew to Moscow and accepted the offer of the dispatch to Ethiopia of Soviet, Cuban and East German military advisers. In June 1977 Ethiopia invaded the Ogaden region, which was contested by Ethiopia and neighbouring Somalia. In a confusing turn of events, the invasion led Somalia, which had a Marxist government, to turn towards the United States in its political orientation and to seek American military assistance. Ethiopia held on to Ogaden but became embroiled in an endemic civil war between the Marxist government of Mengistu, which continued to receive Soviet and Cuban aid, and anti-Communist guerrillas.

In Vietnam, the Soviet government made no effort to restrain the North Vietnamese in their final drive to victory in the spring of 1975. Instead, further insult was added to the humiliation of the American eviction from Vietnam by the Soviet take-over of former American facilities such as the naval base at Cam Ranh Bay. In 1978 the Soviets signed a Treaty of Friendship and Co-operation with Vietnam, which gave encouragement to the Vietnamese to invade Cambodia in 1979. Although the Cambodian government which was overthrown was the horrific, genocidal regime of Pol Pot and the Khmer Rouge, the United States did not view the Vietnamese invasion as the liberation of Cambodia but as the expansion of a Soviet-backed aggressive Communist power.

Closer to home, the United States became increasingly concerned by Communist insurgencies in El Salvador and Nicaragua, which had support from the Soviet Union either directly or indirectly through Cuba. In El Salvador a Communist guerrilla movement threatened the military government, which was a right-wing regime guilty of human rights violations, especially the assassination of political opponents by death squads. The United States was engaged in an effort to persuade the El Salvador regime to reform and feared that Soviet and Cuban assistance to the insurgents could bring to power a Communist regime rather than a reformed pro-American regime. In Nicaragua, the Carter administration welcomed the overthrow in 1979 of the dictator Anastasio Somoza by the Sandinistas and gave aid to the new Nicaraguan government. As in Cuba in 1959–60, however, the Nicaraguan government of the Sandinistas gradually showed itself to be not the progressive democracy which the United States imagined but a left-wing government which imprisoned political opponents and turned for aid to Cuba and the Soviet Union. Moscow's willingness to supply aid, even though in not very large quantities, was one of the final nails in détente's coffin.

The last nail came with the Soviet invasion of Afghanistan in December 1979. Moscow had for centuries interfered to some extent in Afghanistan, dating back to rivalry with the British in India, and the United States had paid little attention to and acquiesced in the gradual increase in Soviet influence in Afghanistan, culminating in the coming to power of a Communist regime in 1978, which signed a Treaty of Friendship with the Soviet Union. The dispatch of 100,000 Soviet troops on 27 December 1979, however, together with the cynical removal from power and assassination of the Afghan ruler, Hafizullah Amin, who had proved an unreliable Soviet ally, and his replacement by a Soviet puppet, Babrak Karmal, was a blatant use of force which had a shattering impact on Carter. Carter stated that the invasion of Afghanistan 'made a more dramatic change in my opinion of what the Soviet ultimate goals are than anything they've done in the previous time I've been in office'.[6] Carter's remark added to the impression of his naïveté, but it strengthened the president's support for the administration hardliners who interpreted the Soviet action not as a defensive move to consolidate control over a wayward ally on the Soviet border and to ensure against the spread of Marxist fundamentalism in Soviet Central Asia, but as an aggressive move consistent with the traditional Soviet pattern of unremitting expansion and aimed in particular at expansion through Afghanistan into Iran, the Gulf states and the Middle East.

The Soviets also appeared to meddle in the internal affairs of such countries as South Yemen, Mozambique and various other countries in the area from Africa to South-West Asia which Carter's National Security Adviser Zbigniew Brzezinski termed 'the arc of crisis'.[7] Soviet interventions in the Third World throughout the 1970s appeared to support the view that Soviet proselytizing aims were unaltered and that the fundamental goal of the universal expansion of Communism remained firmly in place. Brezhnev in fact constantly reiterated that détente did not prohibit Soviet support of revolutionary national liberation movements, stating in 1976, for example, that 'détente does not and cannot in the slightest abolish or change the laws of the class struggle'.[8] To many Americans the vague formulations of the

Basic Principles Agreement of 1972 seemed to be meaningless verbiage, failing to develop a code of conduct which could produce restraints in behaviour on the Soviet side.

In addition to Third World incursions, Soviet repression in Eastern Europe, especially in Poland, soured the spirit of détente. Throughout the 1970s the United States continued its policy of quiet encouragement of nationalism and Titoism in the East European satellites. Massive loans were made by American banks, which led to unacceptable levels of indebtedness. Out of the economic malaise of Eastern Europe grew Solidarity, the Polish trade union which sought the rights of a free trade union and which grew into a broader political movement seeking greater freedom for Poland from Soviet control. The Soviets did not wish to engage in another invasion as in Czechoslovakia in 1968, but, with the Brezhnev Doctrine in place, pressure was placed by Moscow on the Polish government to keep Solidarity firmly in check. Soviet intimidation of Poland added to the increasing disenchantment of American public opinion towards the Soviet Union.

Meantime, increases in Soviet military strength, especially its nuclear arsenal, gave the impression that arms control agreements were utilized by the Soviets to press their advantage. The Soviets adhered to the terms of SALT I, but in the categories of weapons outside the SALT I limits the Soviet arsenal expanded considerably. In 1972 the United States had 1,710 missiles (1,054 land-based ICBMs and 656 SLBMs) while the Soviet Union had 2,350 missiles (1,618 land-based ICBMs and 740 SLBMs). The Soviets maintained their lead in number of missiles throughout the 1970s, but whereas the United States had held a large lead in the number of warheads, compared to missiles, by the end of the decade the Soviets deployed the SS-18 in large numbers, a very large missile with multiple warheads. Moreover, aside from intercontinental missiles with a capability to strike targets in the United States, in 1977 the Soviets deployed the SS-20, a triple-warhead missile with a 1,000-mile range capable of reaching targets in Europe, Japan and China. Furthermore, Soviet increases in conventional forces, especially in the navy, seemed to exceed by far any conceivable defensive requirements. The apparently menacing growth of Soviet military strength led American public opinion increasingly to feel that emphasis on American military strength was a wiser course to pursue than the vain hope of better relations and détente.

Yet, while Soviet policies with regard to Third World incursions, Poland and growth of military power were clearly of major importance in causing détente's demise in the 1970s, these Soviet policies assumed vastly greater significance because they interacted with trends within American politics and society which were liable to produce a souring of détente. It is significant that support for détente in Western Europe declined only slightly through the 1970s compared to the wild swing in the United States from enthusiastic embracement of détente in 1972 to its virtually total rejection by 1980.

Lacking a natural constituency, détente ran into serious political difficulty once its most powerful proponent, Richard Nixon, had fallen. The strongest attack came from Henry Jackson, who, as chairman of the Senate Armed Services Committee, relentlessly criticized SALT I, arguing, for example, that SALT I allowed the Soviets a lead in the number of missiles over the United States. Counter-arguments to Jackson had prevailed in the Senate debate on the ratification of SALT I in 1972, such as the American advantages in number of warheads as opposed to number of missiles, American superiority in accuracy and the American lead in manned bombers. But Jackson's quest for an issue on which to derail détente had borne fruit in the Jackson–Vanik amendment. Moreover, as political opposition to détente grew, Congress also passed in September 1974 the Stevenson amendment, introduced by Senator Adlai Stevenson III, which limited Export–Import Bank credit to the Soviet Union to $300 million over four years, compared to $469 million over the preceding fifteen months. Ford and Kissinger tried to persuade Congress that the Jackson amendment was provocative interference in Soviet internal affairs, while the Stevenson amendment would weaken the leverage of economic incentives in America's relations with the Soviet Union. But the Jackson and Stevenson amendments remained attached to the Trade Reform Bill when it was passed by Congress and signed with some trepidation by Ford on 3 January 1975. A week later, the Soviets responded with an official refusal to comply with the terms, so that the entire economic package of the 1972 summit, including Lend-Lease repayment and the grant of Most Favored Nation status, was rejected. Détente had been dealt a devastating blow, as Kissinger had feared and Jackson had desired.

Conservative Republicans were swift to follow the criticisms of détente raised by Jackson, who was a Democratic hawk.

Conservative Republicans had been stunned into silence when détente was introduced by Nixon, a right-of-centre Republican with a previous reputation as a fierce anti-Communist. But with Nixon's resignation the natural opposition to détente of conservative Republicans rose to the surface and received outspoken expression from Ronald Reagan. Criticism of détente suited Reagan's political ambitions as well as matching his natural inclinations. Elected governor of California in 1966 at the age of 55, Reagan had hoped to become president in 1976 following two terms of a Nixon presidency. Nixon's resignation in 1974 and Ford's succession upset Reagan's ambitions. Hence, rather than supporting Ford for renomination as Republican candidate for president in 1976 and delaying his own presidential bid until 1980, when at the age of 69 he might be considered too old, Reagan opted to challenge Ford for the Republican nomination in 1976. A justification for this challenge was that Ford, who was alleged to have become a prisoner of the Washington establishment, supported détente, which Reagan vigorously attacked as 'a one-way street'.[9] Reagan's attacks hit a responsive chord in wide segments of the American public and although he did not succeed in taking the Republican presidential nomination from Ford in 1976, Reagan won many of the primaries and came close to winning the nomination.

In response to such political challenges, Ford acknowledged that détente, which had been a major political asset to Nixon in his re-election in 1972, was a serious political liability in 1976. On 5 March 1976 Ford declared in Peoria, Illinois, in the heartland of America, that the word 'détente' was expunged from his political vocabulary, to be replaced by 'peace through strength'.[10] Ford accurately assessed that détente had taken on connotations of appeasement as well as association with disgraced former president Nixon, but Ford lacked the political finesse to cope with the rising disenchantment with détente. In 1975 Ford accepted Kissinger's advice not to invite to the White House Alexander Solzhenitsyn, the celebrated Soviet dissident who had been driven into exile in 1974. Kissinger urged that public endorsement of Soviet dissidents by the US government was counter-productive, severely alienating the Soviet government and leading it to be even more repressive, whereas quiet diplomacy through private channels could secure the release of dissidents, when the Soviet government could feel more relaxed and ease its seige mentality.

189

However valid Kissinger's general argument was on this matter, Ford's refusal to meet Solzhenitsyn was a grave political blunder, giving the impression that détente implied kowtow to Moscow, including a Soviet veto on the White House guest list. As Coral Bell has put it, 'The Solzhenitsyn episode appeared to have been the largest single public relations disaster for détente'.[11] Ford compounded the problem by an unfortunate remark regarding Eastern Europe in one of the presidential election debates with Carter in 1976. 'There is no Soviet domination of Eastern Europe', said Ford, 'and there never will be under a Ford administration'.[12] Ford was advancing the somewhat sophisticated view that the peoples of Poland and other Eastern European countries would never give up their spiritual independence and accept permanent Soviet dominance. But his remark, which was widely publicized as a major gaffe of the campaign, gave the impression that either Ford was ignorant and naïve or that détente involved a tacit acceptance of indefinite Soviet control over Eastern Europe.

Jimmy Carter embodied and exploited the new mood of American public opinion in its attitude towards foreign policy in general and towards the Soviet Union in particular. Nixon had attempted to pragmatize American foreign policy. From 1976, however, there was renewed desire for the United States to reassert itself ideologically and morally. Carter captured this mood in his emphasis on human rights. Rejecting the quiet diplomacy approach as typical of the allegedly amoral *realpolitik* of Kissinger's methods, Carter spoke out strongly in his campaign speeches and Inaugural Address in criticism of the repression of Soviet and East European dissidents. When Andrei Sakharov wrote a letter to the White House in February 1977, Carter issued his reply publicly, expressing 'our firm commitment to promote respect for human rights not only in our own country, but also abroad'.[13] Vladimir Bukovsky was received at the White House by Vice-President Walter Mondale. The State Department issued a statement of sympathy for Charter 77, a dissident group in Czechoslovakia founded in 1977, which included the playwright Vaclav Havel. Carter publicly protested over Soviet refusal to allow larger numbers of Jews to emigrate and over the imprisonment of Jewish refusniks such as Anatoly Shcharansky.

A broad consensus within the United States agreed with Carter's expression of support for dissidents and America's

commitment to human rights. Furthermore, in the longer term
the emphasis on human rights as a central plank in American
foreign policy seemed to be justified and to pay great dividends
by the end of the 1980s. This was, however, due to the ongoing
discussions as part of the Helsinki process and even more so to
the changed circumstances in the Soviet Union from the
mid-1980s onwards rather than to Carter's undiplomatic
provocations. In the short term, in the circumstances of the
1970s, Carter presided over a sharp deterioration in relations
with the Soviet Union, which regarded his human rights
initiative as unjustifiable interference in internal affairs. Carter's
Secretary of State Cyrus Vance argued that 'My preference with
human rights was to emphasize quiet diplomacy'.[14] Even
Brzezinski, Carter's Polish-American anti-Soviet National
Security Adviser, admitted that, with regard to Carter's letter to
Sakharov, 'One has to concede that this event did not help the
relationship between the new administration and the Soviet
Union'.[15] Carter's sanctimonious, born-again Christian manner
riled Brezhnev and his colleagues. Also, Carter appeared to
single out the Soviet Union in his human rights criticisms,
ignoring human rights violations in other countries such as Iran
and China. More basically, as Raymond Garthoff has written,
'The Carter administration ... created the impression in the
minds of the Soviet leaders that the United States would be
satisfied only with a fundamental change of their system'.[16]
Kissinger warned in 1974 that

> The temptation to combine détente with increasing pressure
> on the Soviet Union will grow. Such an attitude would be
> disastrous. We would not accept it from Moscow. Moscow will
> not accept it from us. We will finally wind up again with the
> Cold War and fail to achieve either peace or any humane
> goal.[17]

Carter, though in an inconsistent and vacillating manner,
changed American policy from co-existence to conversion. He
aimed to achieve a satisfactory relationship with the Soviet Union
not by mutual toleration of different systems but by bringing
about change in the Soviet system. This was the fundamental
objective of the proponents of containment also, but they aimed
to achieve this goal by a subtle process of evolution rather than
by moralistic preaching from the rooftops, which was liable to
backfire and to create tensions which would destroy détente.

US relations with China in the Carter years added further to the deterioration in relations with the Soviet Union. In the bureaucratic battles between Brzezinski and Vance, Brzezinski emerged triumphant with regard to playing the China card against the Soviet Union to the full extent. In 1978 Brzezinski made a visit to China during which he emphasized his anti-Soviet views and talked in terms of a US–Chinese strategic relationship against the Soviet Union. On 1 January 1979 the United States normalized relations with China with the establishment of diplomatic relations. In July 1979 a trade agreement was signed, and in January 1980 Most Favoured Nation status was granted. As Raymond Garthoff has put it, there had been 'movement from the triangular diplomacy of the early 1980s to American–Chinese quasi alliance by the end of the decade'.[18] Under Brzezinski's influence, Garthoff suggests, Carter had embarked on the 'development of a rapprochement with China on an anti-Soviet basis'.[19]

Carter's policy towards the Middle East further alienated the Soviets. In his campaign of 1976 Carter criticized Kissinger's shuttle diplomacy and advocated the reconvening of a general Middle Eastern conference co-chaired by the United States and the Soviet Union. In office, however, Carter developed a close relationship with Anwar Sadat of Egypt and Menachim Begin of Israel, culminating in the Camp David agreement in 1978. Carter's Middle East policies followed, therefore, in the Kissinger tradition of cutting out Soviet influence in the Middle East and pursuing unilateral American advantage rather than attempting to co-operate with the Soviet Union in a search for a comprehensive solution to the problems of the Middle East.

The deteriorating state of US–Soviet relations in the Carter years was demonstrated above all in the field of arms control. In his Inaugural Address, Carter proclaimed 'our ultimate goal – the elimination of all nuclear weapons from this earth'.[20] Instead of progressing towards this utopian objective, Carter presided over massive increases in the nuclear arsenals of the two superpowers and a poisoning of diplomatic relations between them. Carter's policy on arms control, as on human rights and on the Middle East, was to some extent shaped by domestic politics, in particular the tendency of a challenger for political office to take a differing point of view from the incumbent for its own sake. Hence, Carter differed from Ford and Kissinger on arms control, criticizing the terms of SALT II which had been negotiated at Vladivostok as failing to produce cuts in the nuclear weapons but merely setting levels to which each side could build up.

Carter's lack of experience in foreign policy thereby led him to send Vance to Moscow in March 1977 with significantly different terms for SALT II, involving deep cuts in the nuclear arsenals of both sides. Since Brezhnev had made known his view that the Vladivostok agreements should be completed first, with further reductions to be considered thereafter in SALT III, the new American proposals in March 1977 aroused Soviet suspicions. Not only were Vance's proposals rejected, but negotiations stalled on the terms which had been virtually completed by the Ford administration, with the result that SALT II, with terms very similar to the Vladivostok agreement, was not signed until June 1979. Wariness over the reception likely to face the treaty in the Senate caused Carter to proceed slowly with the ratification process and, following the Soviet invasion of Afghanistan in December 1979, to withdraw the treaty from Senate consideration. The terms of SALT II were adhered to by both sides until 1986, but lack of Senate ratification destroyed its symbolic significance, which was as important as its specific terms. Since the late 1960s arms control had been the main bellweather of East–West relations. The withdrawal of the SALT II treaty from the US Senate therefore marked not only the derailment of the arms control process but the death of détente.

Criticisms steadily grew of America's military weakness compared to the Soviet Union. Since his dismissal as Defense Secretary in 1975, James Schlesinger had criticized the levels of US defence spending, while the Pentagon's estimates of the Soviet military build-up were somewhat inflated in order to maximise the Pentagon's share of the US budget. In March 1976 a bipartisan group of experts, including Paul Nitze, Eugene Rostow, Elmo Zumwalt and Max Kappelman, formed the Committee on the Present Danger, warning that a window of vulnerability was being opened which could allow a surprise Soviet first strike to destroy America's entire land-based missile force on the ground. Such allegations of America's defensive weakness provided useful ammunition to Ronald Reagan as he prepared for a renewed bid for the presidency in 1980.

In fact, the so-called window of vulnerability envisaged a very far-fetched scenario, requiring an attack by incoming missiles of such precise co-ordination as to hit all American ICBMs at exactly the same time. Even if such a very theoretical ICBM vulnerability existed, the United States had also a retaliatory strike force of SLBMs, manned bombers and forward-based nuclear weapons in Europe. The myth developed that the United States cut back drastically on the modernization of its defences in the 1970s, enabling the Soviets to surge ahead. In fact, aside from Carter's cancellation of the B–1 bomber (a decision reversed by Reagan in 1981) and of the neutron bomb, there were no cut-backs in weapons systems in the 1970s. On the contrary, in the 1970s the United States deployed 550 Minuteman ICBMs with triple warheads, developed the multi-warhead MX missile, converted the submarine-based missile force from single warhead Polaris missiles to longer-range, more accurate, multi-warhead Poseidon missiles, continued development of Trident missiles, modernized the B-52 bomber fleet with new avionics and short-range attack missiles, developed air-launched Cruise missiles, continued research on the Stealth bomber, and developed ground-launched Cruise missiles and Pershing II missiles for deployment in Europe in accordance with a NATO decision in 1979. The number of Soviet targets which the United States could attack increased from 1,700 in 1970 to 7,000 in 1980. In 1977 the United States had a lead in nuclear warheads over the Soviet Union of 8,500 to 4,000 and in 1980 the lead was 9,200 to 6,000. All of the advanced weapons systems of the US defence expansion of the 1980s were developed in the 1970s. After Afghanistan the defence budget was increased by 5 per cent to enable larger increases in spending on conventional defence. The wide acceptance of the myth of America's vulnerability and neglect of defences in the 1970s illustrates that détente's demise resulted from perceptions, anxieties, frustrations and other intangible elements within American society as much as from the actuality of an increased security threat from the Soviet Union.

The sources of the anxieties and frustrations lay in the weakening of America's economic position, the aftermath of Vietnam and Watergate, and the ineptitude of Carter's adminis- tration, culminating in the humiliation of the Iranian hostages affair, all of which cumulatively found an outlet in a re-focus of condemnatory ire against the old scapegoat, the Soviet Union. The Soviets were only peripherally, or not at all, involved in these issues. In these matters, therfore, détente was the victim of pent-up forces within American society in the 1970s which had little direct relation to the Soviet Union but which produced an emotional outburst against Soviet perfidity as a catharsis for the complex assortment of difficulties which America experienced in the 1970s.

The oil price rise of 1973 not only caused acute short-term problems for the United States but marked the end of the era of American economic dominance and the exposure of America's vulnerability to the economic power of other countries. When OPEC doubled oil prices in 1979, following the revolution in Iran, the United States was powerless to do other than simply pay the higher prices, just as America had meekly accepted the quadrupling of oil prices in 1973 rather than taking retaliatory measures or making a show of force. Meantime, the rising economic strength of Western Europe and Japan jeopardized America's long-term economic prospects. The Soviet Union was only marginally involved in these developments, yet Soviet political backing and supply of arms to Arab countries such as Syria and Iraq led to an association in the minds of American public opinion of Soviet meddling in the Middle East as responsible for America's chronic economic problems of energy price rises, inflation, recession and trade gaps.

With regard to the traumas of Watergate and Vietnam, the Soviets were in no way involved with the former and only to a minor extent with the latter. Yet these traumas, along with the economic shocks, were the main causes of the malaise which affected the American body politic in the 1970s and which found an outlet in the swing from détente to confrontation against the Soviet Union. Détente came to be associated with a time when America curled up and licked its wounds following the humiliations of Watergate and Vietnam.

Moreover, the sense of frustration was increased by the perception of weakness created by Carter's diplomacy. However well intentioned, Carter's inexperience in foreign affairs produced an impression of incompetence and confusion which led ultimately to failure and humiliation. In addition to the constant bureaucratic battles between Vance and Brzezinski, contradictory statements by Andrew Young, US ambassador to the United Nations, added to the sense of an administration speaking with many different voices. Carter's ineptitude was frequently demonstrated, such as his pressure on Chancellor Helmut Schmidt to accept deployment of the neutron bomb in West Germany only for Carter to change his mind and cancel deployment, or Carter's discovery in August 1979 of a Soviet brigade in Cuba which had been in Cuba for years, producing a protest over the brigade followed by meek acquiescence and quiet dropping of the issue. The Iranian hostages affair in 1979–80 served as an embodiment of America's feebleness and subjection to constant indignities. Not only was America unable to prevent the overthrow of the Shah of Iran in January 1979 by Ayatollah Khoemeni, who denounced America as 'the great Satan', but the United States was powerless to rescue the fifty-three members of the American embassy staff who were taken hostage on 4 November 1979. The failed US rescue attempt in April 1980, ending when too many helicopters developed mechanical failure to allow the continuation of the mission and when one helicopter then crashed into a transport aeroplane, provided a vivid embodiment of Carter's bungling policies. The Soviet Union was not involved in the Iranian affair, but the Soviet invasion of Afghanistan in December 1979 led to fears of Soviet expansion through Afghanistan into Iran and onward into the Middle East, thereby associating the Soviet Union with Iran and America's troubles there.

While these undercurrents of frustration grew in America, the image of the Soviet Union in the United States was not ameliorated by people-to-people contacts. The range of exchange programmes established between 1972 and 1974, building on earlier programmes since the 1950s, failed to make any appreciable impact on American consciousness in the 1970s. In 1975, as a result of a programme established at the Moscow summit in 1972, a joint mission in space took place, with three American astronauts and two Soviet cosmonauts, including a space walk by an American astronaut who was pulled back into the space capsule by a Soviet cosmonaut. Yet, even such a spectacular joint venture made only a slight temporary impact and was soon forgotten. Other aspects of US–Soviet relations, such as trade and cultural and educational exchanges, produced results which disappointed the hopes of idealists that personal contacts would humanize US–Soviet relations and make possible a co-existence in which the importance of competing ideologies would diminish.

With regard to trade, the most substantial item consisted of American wheat sales. In 1975 the Soviets entered a long-term purchasing agreement to cushion the impact of massive sales as occurred in 1972. With poor Soviet harvests in many years in the 1970s, Soviet purchases of American grain were considerable, but as a protest over the invasion of Afghanistan a boycott was imposed on wheat sales in 1980. The debacle over the Jackson amendment removed much of the carrot in Soviet trade, and by 1976 Kissinger was less hopeful of utilizing trade incentives as a means of modifying Soviet behaviour in foreign policy. Soviet trade with Western Europe increased at the expense of trade with the United States, but a number of American companies continued the tradition of American business since the 1920s of engaging in economic enterprises in the Soviet Union despite the lack of a formal trade agreement. Pepsi-Cola, for example, achieved success in establishing their product in the Soviet Union and receiving payment in the form of Russian vodka sold abroad by a third party. Armand Hammer continued to develop projects for Occidental Petroleum. But most American business ventures in the Soviet Union were not very profitable, with massive difficulties in dealing with an autarchic bureacracy, while lack of credits reduced the potential of the Soviet market. The number of Americans who travelled on business to the Soviet Union grew and personal contacts with Soviet citizens were generally cordial. But the impact on the US government or on American public opinion of those contacts was slight.

Cultural and educational exchanges expanded as a result of agreements between 1972 and 1974, with, for example, a US Bicentennial Exhibition in Moscow in 1976 and a Soviet Sixtieth Anniversary of the Revolution Exhibition in Los Angeles in 1977. The numbers of students and scholars exchanged under the biennial agreements negotiated since 1958 increased, but the numbers involved remained small. On new areas such as the environment, four meetings were held throughout the 1970s, to exchange information on environmental matters such as acid rain. Direct flights from Moscow to New York by Pan American Airways made tourist travel easier, so that the number of American tourists to the Soviet Union grew to 100,000 per annum by the end of the 1970s.

Economic, cultural, educational and other social exchanges, however, did not create a significant constituency within the United States in support of détente. Instead, such exchanges became the first victims of the souring of détente, serving as easy targets for the expression of protest by the suspension of such exchanges. In 1976 the Ford administration postponed several visits of delegations on housing and energy in protest over Cuban involvement in Angola. In 1978 Carter imposed a ban on high-level contacts as a protest over the treatment of Anatoly Shcharansky. In 1980 Carter suspended virtually all exchanges in protest over Afghanistan and, most notably, imposed a boycott of the Moscow Olympics by American athletes. In 1980 Carter even allowed to lapse the 1958 Cultural Agreement when negotiations on its renewal were due. Meantime, on the Soviet side, jamming of Voice of America was resumed in August 1980, after freedom from jamming since the Helsinki Agreement in 1975, while jamming of Radio Free Europe began again in Poland, in order to prevent the Poles from receiving broadcasts about Solidarity.

By 1980, therefore, the American image of the Soviet Union had reverted to the concept of the threatening, expansionist, perfidious, nuclear sabre-rattling menace. Partly this had been brought about by Soviet actions in the Third World and in Europe and by Soviet military expansion, but in other respects détente broke down due to forces within American society which were partly rational and which were partly emotional and found an outlet in condemnation of the Soviet Union. By 1980 there was a resurgence of nationalism and nostalgia in America and a resentment against détente as a policy of weakness. It was a mood well suited for Ronald Reagan, who promised a strengthening of America's defences and a firm posture against the Soviet threat. As Nixon had warned Brezhnev in 1974, 'If détente unravels in America, the hawks will take over'.[21]

14

REAGAN AND THE NEW COLD WAR, 1981–5

Ronald Reagan's election in 1980 brought into the White House a president with no experience in foreign affairs and relatively little interest in the outside world. As Coral Bell puts it, 'Even his kindest friends did not attribute to President Reagan any profound knowledge of world affairs'.[1] Reagan's standpoint towards the Soviet Union reflected the attitudes and mindset of small town America. Reagan was, moreover, representative of the new American right. Reagan had been born and raised in humble circumstances in a small town in Illinois before he went west to find fame and fortune as a Hollywood film star and latterly as a public relations spokesman for General Electric. His politics changed with his financial circumstances, so that the registered Democrat of the 1930s who admired Franklin Roosevelt became the registered Republican of the 1960s who came to prominence politically as a Goldwater supporter in 1964. But Reagan was a gentler, more subtle representative of the right than Goldwater, whose zealousness had frightened middle America. Reagan was a superb practitioner of what Robert Dallek has termed the 'politics of symbolism' and an excellent embodiment of the image which the new right wished to project.[2] Similarly, with regard to foreign policy, Reagan projected the image of an evangelistic crusader for freedom against totalitarian Communist tyranny. But Reagan's appeal in 1980 went beyond satisfaction of the aspirations of his natural constituency on the right to satisfaction of the aspirations of the majority of Americans who were tired of the humiliations and sense of weakness which America had endured from Vietnam to the Iranian hostages crisis.

The prospects for any improvement in US–Soviet relations

were slight during Reagan's first term, with continuing crises in Poland and Afghanistan and with a decrepit Soviet leadership. Brezhnev hung on to power in his dotage until his death in 1982, to be succeeded by Yuri Andropov, who almost immediately became seriously ill and died in February 1984, succeeded by Konstantin Chernenko, who was gravely ill from the day he took office until his death a year later. 'The Kremlin was doubling as a geriatric ward and funeral parlor', as Mandelbaum and Talbott put it.[3] There was little possibility of constructing a fruitful relationship with the Soviet Union in these circumstances. But the questions which arise with regard to Reagan's policy towards the Soviet Union in his first term are: Did Reagan act in a dangerously provocative manner towards the Soviet Union which threatened peace? Was Reagan's defence build-up excessive and damaging to America's economy and world position in the longer term? Or is it the case that Reagan's firm policies laid the basis for the new détente which occurred in his second term and beyond?

From the mid-1970s Reagan had denounced détente as 'a one way street'.[4] At his first press conference as president on 29 January 1981, Reagan bluntly stated that Soviet leaders 'reserve unto themselves the right to commit any crime, to lie, to cheat. . . . When you do business with them, even at a détente, you keep that in mind'.[5] In a series of speeches over the next two years, Reagan was forthright in his condemnation of Soviet Communism. He dismissed Communism 'as a sad, bizarre chapter in human history whose last pages are now being written'.[6] In similar terms he said in a speech to the British parliament on 8 June 1982 that the West would 'leave Marxism and Leninism on the ashheap of history'.[7] In his most celebrated statement, Reagan said to Florida evangelists on 8 March 1983 that the Soviet Union was an 'evil empire'.[8]

Reagan's defenders argue that this straight talking had a salutary impact on Soviet perceptions of the United States and helped to create stability. Reagan's critics argue that his blunt words and aggressive attitude towards the Soviet Union heightened tensions for no good purpose other than to pander to the prejudices of the American right wing. The resentment of the Soviet leadership over Reagan's comments was expressed, for example, on 28 September 1983 by Andropov, who accused Reagan of 'smearing the Soviet people in what amounts to obscenities alternating with pharisaical pronouncements about morality and humanism'.[9] In terms of an exchange of rhetoric between leaders, a full-blown new Cold War had broken out.

Implicit in Reagan's ritualistic anti-Sovietism was a total rejection of the concept of military and political parity which had been central to détente in the early 1970s. Instead, as Raymond Garthoff has written, 'under the confrontational approach of the Reagan administration the very legitimacy of the Soviet system had been repeatedly challenged by the president himself'.[10] Reagan endorsed the viewpoint, for example, of James Burnham, a champion of 'liberation' in the 1950s, awarding Burnham a Medal of Freedom in 1983 and stating at the award ceremony that 'I owe him a personal debt, because throughout the years travelling on the mash-potato circuit I have quoted him widely'.[11] Carter, in an inconsistent manner, had shifted American policy towards the Soviet Union from co-existence to conversion. Reagan, with solid consistency, adhered to the view of the Soviet Union which he had always held, namely that peaceful and friendly co-existence with a Communist state was inherently impossible and that a good relationship with the Soviet Union could be attained only by the conversion of the Soviet system into a political and social structure akin to Western capitalist democracy.

On the issue of defence spending, Reagan's firm anti-Soviet attitude was equally manifest. Between 1981 and 1986, the Pentagon's budget rose from $171 billion to $376 billion, as Reagan presided over the largest peacetime expansion of America's defence in history. But increased defence expenditure was not financed by increased taxation. On the contrary, income tax was cut by 10 per cent in 1981, a further 10 per cent in 1982 and a further 5 per cent in 1983, with reductions in the top rate from 70 per cent to 50 per cent and with new tax write-offs conceded to business. The loss of government revenue by these tax cuts was offset to some extent by a rise in business taxes in 1982, while government expenditure was cut on certain domestic programmes. Moreover, the tax cuts stimulated the economy and helped to bring America out of recession, so that government income from taxation grew with economic expansion. The large increases in defence spending and deep cuts in taxation, however, were not balanced by the cuts in domestic spending and increased government income from economic growth and the 1982 business tax raises. The net result was a massive US government deficit, which grew alarmingly through the years of

Reagan's presidency. US government deficits grew from 1981 to 1984 to over $200 billion per annum, the national debt doubling between 1981 and 1986.

Among the many serious consequences of such fiscal imprudence, US interest rates and trade deficits grew, so that the United States in Reagan's presidency changed from a creditor nation to a debtor nation, rapidly becoming the world's largest debtor nation. Reagan cast aside Eisenhower's warning that a sound economy was one of the main lines of America's defence and that increases in defence spending which unbalanced the budget and weakened the economy would weaken America's defensive position in the long term. Secretary of Defense Caspar Weinberger had acquired the reputation as a budget cutter ('Cap the Knife') as Nixon's Budget Director, but at the Pentagon he pressed for increases in every area of America's defence, regardless of the fiscal consequences. Congress was willing to collaborate, given the economic benefit to almost every Congressional district from such large increases in government expenditure. Even in liberal states such as Massachusetts, high-technology industries, which led the 'economic miracle' in the administration of Governor Michael Dukakis, benefited enormously from the defence increases. Moreover, American public opinion was converted to support defence increases after, as Reagan's Budget Director David Stockman put it, 'watching the grim footage of the charred remains of the US servicemen being desecrated by the Iranian mullahs at the site known as Desert One'.[12]

In the Reagan defence build-up, the navy was scheduled to increase from 454 ships to 600 ships, including 15 aircraft carrier groups. Substantial increases were made in service pay, and large sums were appropriated for ammunition and spare parts. The B-1 bomber, cancelled by Carter, was restored. No other new nuclear weapons system aside from the B-1 was introduced, and indeed with regard to the MX missile Reagan scaled down Carter's deployment proposals, rejecting the elaborate scheme of an underground railroad system in Utah and Nevada on which 200 MX missiles and decoys would be moved around, and instead simply basing MX missiles in hardened concrete silos, with the number reduced from 200 to 50. Nevertheless, although the great bulk of the defence increase was in non-nuclear defence, the three parts of the US nuclear triad received additions in the number of warheads, and a clear image was projected of a vast increase in every aspect of America's defence.

The comprehensive scale of America's defence increases were intended to give pause to the Soviets in their plans for adventurism. Their impact on American and European public opinion, however, combined with some careless comments by Reagan and by other officials regarding the possibility of nuclear war, aroused fears of American aggressiveness which rose to paranoia. Secretary of State Alexander Haig, for example, somewhat casually stated in Congressional testimony that NATO had contingency plans to fire a nuclear shot across the bows, while Reagan mused at a press conference that he could conceive of circumstances in which a nuclear war might be fought but be limited to Europe. Moreover, the Pentagon's 1982 Defense Guidance Plan accepted the premise that a protracted nuclear war with the Soviet Union could be fought and recommended improved civil defence measures. These statements and plans were not in themselves unreasonable, being for the most part restatements of long-formulated contingency measures, but combined with Reagan's anti-Soviet rhetoric they created widespread public alarm. The Nuclear Freeze movement gained wider support, with half a million demonstrators in New York's Central Park in June 1982 to denounce the nuclear arms race, just as in Britain the Campaign for Nuclear Disarmament (CND), which had almost disappeared since its heyday in the 1950s, swelled in membership. In 1983 the television film *The Day After*, on the aftermath of nuclear war, was a sign of the mood of the times, as in Britain the television film *Threads* in 1982, an even more realistic portrayal of the consequences of nuclear war, made a disturbing impact.

Partly as a means to defuse the mounting public anxiety, Reagan introduced new arms control proposals. The evidence is clear, however, that Reagan had little interest in arms control and that his major objective was to build up America's strength in order to face down the Soviets. This standpoint was shared by the leading figures in the administration, such as Weinberger, Haig and especially Assistant Secretary of Defense for International Affairs Richard Perle. The head of the Arms Control and Disarmament Agency, Eugene Rostow, and his assistant, Paul Nitze, had been leading lights in the Committee on the Present Danger. At his confirmation hearings on 18 June 1981 Rostow admitted that the administration had not agreed on an arms control policy. 'It may be that a brilliant light will strike our officials', he testified. 'But I don't know anyone who knows what it is yet that we want to negotiate about'.[13] Perle believed that arms control had a lulling effect on public opinion in the West and should be avoided in favour of unfettered military and political competition.

Reagan believed that the Soviets had taken advantage of the United States in the past with regard to disarmament agreements and that the Soviets should therefore make deeper cuts. Moreover, Reagan, for all of his occasional loose talk about nuclear weapons, had a deep horror of the possibility of nuclear war. On 12 June 1982 he spoke of 'the unimaginable horror of nuclear war. . . . To those who protest against nuclear war, I can only say, "I'm with you" '.[14] Reagan therefore advanced proposals on arms control for deep cuts in nuclear arsenals. His critics argued that these were not serious proposals but were bound to be rejected by the Soviets and were put forward merely to appease public opinion. His defenders argue that these forthright proposals were designed to serve American interests by deeper cuts on the Soviet side than the American side and to rid the world of large numbers of nuclear weapons by significant reductions on both sides.

In November 1981 Reagan proposed a zero option with regard to intermediate range nuclear forces (INF), that is, that the Soviets should remove all their SS-20s as well as the older SS4s and SS5s, while the United States would not deploy Cruise or Pershing II missiles. In July 1982 Paul Nitze, chief American INF negotiator, and his Soviet counterpart, Yuri Kvitsinsky, went for a 'walk in the woods' near Geneva and reached an informal compromise agreement of seventy-five SS-20s on the Soviet side and seventy-five Cruise missiles on the NATO side. The rejection of the walk in the woods agreement by Washington was interpreted by Reagan's critics as evidence that the administration was not seriously interested in an agreement but sought deployment of the intimidating Pershing II missiles as well as Cruise missiles in large numbers. Reagan's defenders argue that the president stubbornly insisted on the zero option.

In May 1982 Reagan unveiled proposals regarding strategic nuclear weapons. Reagan criticized SALT as merely limiting the growth of nuclear weapons. The new negotiations were therefore entitled Strategic Arms Reduction Talks (START). With the very conservative Edward Rowny as chief negotiator the prospects for a break-through seemed slight, especially with American proposals that no more than 50 per cent of warheads should be land based, which clearly disadvantaged the Soviet side which had 72 per cent of its nuclear weapons land based compared to 25 per cent land based on the American side, with the greater American strength in SLBMs and bombers, which were not affected by the treaty. Meantime, the Mutual Balanced Force Reduction (MBFR) talks on conventional arms reductions continued in Vienna with no prospect of an agreement.

In December 1983, with the deployment of the first Cruise missiles in Britain, the Soviets walked out of the INF and START talks, and no further negotiations on nuclear arms control took place for the rest of Reagan's first term. Reagan's critics argue that this was the intended purpose from the beginning, with no serious intention of engaging the Soviets in any constructive manner but with the aim of building up an American military advantage and asserting superiority. Reagan's defenders argue that the affirmation of American strength and unwillingness to flinch before Soviet bullying helped to stabilize international relations and to bring about successful arms control agreements in the longer run.

The atmosphere in arms control negotiations was further poisoned by American charges of Soviet breaches of previous agreements. Until the Reagan administration, the US government took the view that negotiation of an arms control agreement with the Soviets was an exasperating process but that, when an agreement was reached, the Soviets, although they would take advantage of loopholes, would not engage in outright violations. The Reagan administration, however, charged the Soviets with wholesale violations of agreements. The most conspicuous charge related to the Soviet deployment of a large radar facility in Kransnoyarsk in central Siberia in violation of the ABM treaty, which did not permit such radar facilities in inland locations. Other charges related, for example, to violations of SALT I by the use of codes in the testing of ICBMs. In January 1984 the administration reported to Congress that the Soviet Union had violated virtually all of the arms agreements to which it was a party.

Reagan's greatest interest in defence matters, however, lay in the Strategic Defense Initiative (SDI), which he outlined in a speech on 23 March 1983. 'Let me share with you a vision of the future which offers hope', he said in his speech:

It is that we embark on a program to counter the awesome

Soviet missile threat with measures that are defensive. . . .
What if free people could live secure in the knowledge that
their security did not rest upon the threat of instant
retaliation to deter a Soviet attack, that we could intercept
and destroy strategic ballistic missiles before they reached
our soil or that of our allies?[15]

This was, in fact, not at all a new idea. From the 1950s, with
systems of interceptor aeroplanes, to the ABM in the early 1970s,
strategic thinkers had worked on the possibility of shielding the
United States against an attack by Soviet nuclear weapons. The
conclusion reached, however, especially in the ABM debate, was
that if one side attempted to build such a defensive shield, the
other side would construct new offensive measures to overwhelm
it. The result would be that a major escalation in the arms race
would take place which would leave neither side with any greater
security. Thus a preferable alternative was thought to be the
approach taken in the ABM treaty, namely agreement by both
sides not to develop a defensive shield, so that neither side
required increased offensive counter-measures.

Reagan, however, with little interest in the details and
subtleties of defence matters, with his faith in a technological
quick fix as a solution to complex problems and with his horror
of the effects of nuclear war, saw SDI ('Star Wars', as it was
popularly named) as the panacea to save America. Encouraged
by scientists such as Edward Teller, a Senior Fellow at the
conservative Hoover Institution, Reagan pressed for an initiative
to develop new technology, such as laser beams and giant mirrors
in space, which could create a defensive shield to protect America
against a nuclear attack. This simplistic concept had a superficial,
childish appeal, which Reagan carried to its extreme with the
proposal that the United States develop SDI and then make it
available also to the Soviets, so that both sides could feel safe from
nuclear attack. Such an idea clearly belonged to a world of
fantasy. The sophisticated technology of SDI could, with only a
little adaptation, be switched from defensive to offensive
purposes, so that to make this available to the Soviet Union was
a preposterous suggestion. Moreover, the means of delivery of
nuclear weapons were potentially so numerous that the
technological problems of constructing a comprehensive
defensive system were almost certainly insurmountable. Above
all, as long appreciated, an American attempt to develop a

defensive shield would lead the Soviets to deploy offensive counter-measures, producing an escalated arms race with greater uncertainty and no greater security for the United States.

Reagan was virtually alone in his utopian hope of constructing a comprehensive defensive shield. But others saw limited value in SDI, either in protecting some American missile silos or in using SDI as a bargaining chip in arms control negotiations. Moreover, Congress was, as always, susceptible to giving support to a programme which would have extensive economic spin-offs, especially in high technology. Support for SDI from these various interests, combined with Reagan's formidable political skills, led SDI to become a central part of the administration's defence policy. Reagan's critics argue that SDI illustrated the unrealistic and provocative nature of his policy towards the Soviet Union. His defenders suggest that SDI, more than any other single matter, concentrated Soviet minds, creating such fear of a new round of technological competition with the United States that the Soviets turned towards the path of conciliation.

Among Reagan's advisers, some, such as Richard Pipes, the hardline senior NSC Kremlinologist in 1981–2, advocated economic and defence policies specifically designed to overstretch the Soviet economy and thereby to bring about dissent and ultimately the downfall of the Soviet regime. Reagan did not, however, consistently pursue such policies. On 24 April 1981 he lifted the grain embargo imposed by Carter as a protest over Afghanistan, thereby bowing to a domestic constituency – American farmers – rather than continuing the single most important instrument of US economic leverage against the Soviet Union. Reagan attempted to use economic measures in retaliation against the imposition of martial law in Poland in December 1981. These measures created difficulties with America's allies, however, when the United States put pressure on Western European countries to renege on agreements to sell gas pipe to the Soviet Union for the Siberian gas pipeline. When the European countries refused, the United States forbade subsidiaries of American companies in Europe to supply parts for the pipeline. In November 1982 George Shultz, who replaced Haig as Secretary of State in June 1982, worked out a settlement of the dispute. The incident illustrated the very limited effect of economic sanctions on the Soviet Union. US trade with the Soviet Union was of such a relatively small volume that economic measures made little impact. In 1983, for example, US exports to the Soviet Union amounted to $2 billion, of which $1.5 billion was agricultural products, while imports from the Soviet Union amounted to $550 million, mainly oil and raw materials. A report by the Congressional Office of Technology Assessment in May 1983 concluded that American embargoes designed to punish the Soviet Union over Afghanistan and Poland had no major effect on the Soviet economy. Likewise, although the Reagan administration advocated a strict interpretation of controls for export of high technology to the Soviet Union, the administration also wished to expand America's high technology presence in global markets, with the result that American high technology often found its way to the Soviet bloc via third countries.

With regard to Eastern Europe, the Reagan administration sought to bring pressure on the Soviet Union for liberalization. Eastern European nations such as Hungary were in fact quietly changing, easing themselves from Soviet control not by direct challenge but through a deeper social evolution and by the reassertion of their national personalities. In 1983 Peter Vrarkoryi made the first ever visit by a Hungarian Foreign Minister to the United States. The United States sought to encourage this process of evolution in Eastern Europe. Vice-President George Bush stated in Vienna on 23 September 1983 that the United States would extend greater political and economic support to Eastern European countries which exerted a more independent line from the Soviet Union, while the United States would not reward countries with 'closed societies and belligerent foreign policies'.[16] But Hungary did not welcome such pressure, issuing a statement that 'the United States must accept Hungary as it is, with its different alliances and its different social systems'.[17] With regard to Poland, the United States imposed economic sanctions against Poland and the Soviet Union in protest against the imposition of martial law under General Wojciek Jaruzelski in December 1981 and the imprisonment of Solidarity leaders. Western European nations felt that such sanctions were self-defeating and that, since martial law was preferable to a Soviet invasion, economic contacts with Poland should be maintained and quiet diplomacy pursued. But the Reagan administration was more forthright in its con-demnation of repression in Poland, as the United States was more outspoken in support of dissident groups such as Charter 77 in Czechoslovakia. The Reagan administration did not anticipate immediate change in Eastern Europe, but it felt that to proclaim open support for liberalization was morally right and would bring about change in the long run. As George Shultz said in August 1984, 'We will never accept the idea of a divided Europe. Time is not on the side of imperial domination. We may not see freedom in Eastern Europe in our lifetime. Our children may not see it in theirs. But someday it will happen'.[18]

The Reagan administration was similarly outspoken in its support of dissidents within the Soviet Union. Reagan said in his address to the British parliament on 8 June 1982 that 'In the Communist world . . . man's instinctive desire for freedom and self-determination surfaces again and again. . . . We know that there are those who strive and suffer for freedom within the confines of the Soviet Union itself'.[19] Reagan spoke out for the refusniks, Soviet Jews who were refused permission to emigrate from the Soviet Union. Reagan's critics argued that such policies were provocative and self-defeating. Soviet leaders, it was argued, were very sensitive to apparent interferences in Soviet internal affairs, so that criticism of human rights within the Soviet Union was bound to worsen US–Soviet relations. Moreover, Soviet leaders would retaliate against public criticisms, thereby bringing further harm to dissidents rather than help. The number of Jews allowed to emigrate, for example, fell from 51,000 in 1979 to 9,500 in 1981 to 1,000 in 1984. Reagan's critics suggest that public condemnation of the Soviet human rights record satisfied American conservatives' desire for self-righteousness but seriously damaged US–Soviet relations and increased the difficulties of dissidents. Reagan's defenders argue that outspoken criticism would bring results in the long term, whereas the alternative policy of quiet diplomacy was moral cowardice and an abandonment of courageous individuals who were struggling to assert their right to freedom.

The Reagan administration's crusading zeal in support of freedom and against Communism was even more vociferously pronounced with regard to Third World conflicts. With Jeanne Kirkpatrick, US ambassador to the United Nations, as the most prominent exponent of the American commitment to go on to the ideological offensive, the administration declared open support for opponents of Communism in Angola, Ethiopia, Cambodia, Afghanistan, Nicaragua and El Salvador. This crusade against Communism world-wide aligned the United States with unsavoury, undemocratic allies, but Kirkpatrick justified support for right-wing regimes on the grounds that they were open to reform in the course of time, whereas Communist regimes were not. Hence, arms shipments were increased to UNITA in Angola, which had also support from South Africa. Above all, the CIA supplied arms to the mujahadin rebels in their war against the Soviet-backed regime in Afghanistan. In China, Reagan was initially inclined to follow his right-wing instincts and give support to Taiwan, but he was persuaded by Haig that the China card against the Soviet Union was more important than support for Taiwan. Reagan's soft-pedalling towards China (which, despite the economic reforms of Deng Xiao-Ping, was an even more repressive society than the Soviet Union) further alienated Moscow.

The area in which Reagan himself was most involved in the world-wide anti-Communist crusade was Central America. Reagan ignored the view that the political instability of the region was indigenous, the consequences of low commodity prices, unjust land distribution and extremes of wealth and poverty. A token effort was made early in Reagan's administration with the Caribbean Basin Initiative to use American aid as an incentive to bring about economic reform in the region as a means to combat Communism, but the aid offered, through private enterprise channels, was so small as to make almost no impact, and interest in the Initiative was soon lost. Instead, Reagan fixed the blame for Central America's problems on the external virus of Communism which came from Moscow via Cuba. In March 1982 Reagan pointed to 'the expansion of Soviet-backed, Cuban-managed support for violent revolution in Latin America'.[20] Reagan had no qualms in extending aid to the government of El Salvador which, even after the election of the moderate José Napoleon Duarte in 1983, engaged in serious human rights violations in its war against Marxist guerrillas. Reagan used the excuse of a potential hostage crisis in Grenada to send in US marines in 1983 to rescue American medical students and at the same time to overthrow the Marxist government, an action which even Margaret Thatcher criticized.

Reagan's deepest desire, however, which became almost an obsession, was to bring down the Sandinista government led by Daniel Ortega in Nicaragua. In 1981 Reagan began to send aid to the Contras (diminutive of *contrarevolutionarios*), a coalition of anti-Sandinista forces ranging from disillusioned former Sandinistas who felt that Ortega had betrayed the Nicaraguan revolution, to right-wing former supporters of the deposed dictator Somoza. Reagan declared his unqualified support for the 'freedom fighters', the Contras, but Congress and public opinion were more ambivalent. Congress gave hesitant support for CIA aid to the Contras, but by 1984 indiscrete CIA operations, such as the mining of harbours in Nicaragua, and human rights violations by the Contras, especially indiscriminate killing of civilians, led Congress to pass the Boland amendment, ending aid to the Contras. Reagan was determined to reverse this action by Congress, but meantime plans were formulated by zealots such as Colonel Oliver North to seek sources of aid for the Contras other than official government support.

In virtually every respect, then, from direct relations with the Soviet Union to regional conflicts such as Nicaragua, Reagan's policies were a return to Cold War fundamentalism, confrontational in approach with a self-righteous reassertion of the superiority of American values. The Reagan administration had, therefore, little interest in developing non-political contacts, such as cultural, scientific and educational exchanges, as a means to humanize the relationship and to soften the mutual demonic image. In the last year of Carter's presidency a number of exchanges had been allowed to lapse as a protest over Afghanistan and Poland, and in Reagan's first term this process gathered pace, with the termination not only of programmes from the Nixon–Kissinger era but even long-established programmes dating back to the 1950s. The cultural agreement negotiated biennially since 1958 was not renewed in 1980 and not renegotiated until 1984. The number of American tourists to the Soviet Union declined from the level of the 1970s. The Soviets boycotted the 1984 Los Angeles Olympic Games – as a tit-for-tat for the American boycott of the Moscow Olympics in 1980. The study of the Soviet Union and of the Russian language declined in American schools and colleges, as Averell Harriman noted in donating $11 million to the Institute for the Advanced Study of the Soviet Union at Columbia University. 'Americans who complain that the Soviet Union is a closed society', Harriman noted, 'need to acknowledge that we have done pitifully little to open our minds'.[21]

In 1983 a childish appeal for greater US–Soviet human contact was made by a 10-year-old girl in Maine, Samantha Smith. She woke up one morning and 'wondered if this was going to be the last day of the Earth'. On thinking about the arms race, she thought that 'It all seemed so dumb to me'. She therefore sent a letter to Yuri Andropov, writing that 'If we could only be friends by just getting to know each other better, then what are our countries arguing about? Nothing could be more important than not having a war if war could kill everything'.[22] Andropov wrote back and invited her to the Soviet Union, where she was feted as a symbol of US–Soviet friendship. Although Andropov was manifestly securing propaganda points, Samantha Smith's basic message hit a responsive chord in American public opinion. Many Americans agreed with the view of Svetlana Alliluyeva, Stalin's daughter who sought exile in the United States and subsequently returned to the Soviet Union, that the United States and the Soviet Union are

> two nuclear powers whose ideas about each other are based on totally obsolete propaganda. . . . There are no two nations in the world so similar as Americans and Russians. . . . They could just come to each other and fall on each other's necks and perfectly understand each other. There is the same openness and healthy cheerfulness in each case.[23]

A more sceptical view, however, was put forward, for example, by Donald Greenberg, editor of *Science and Government Report* who wrote in May 1984 that 'Proponents cling to the potentially romantic notion that personal contacts with the West will have softening effects on the nastier aspects of Soviet behaviour. . . . The evidence of this hopeful proposition is scanty'.[24] This sceptical viewpoint predominated through most of Reagan's first term.

Following a relentlessly hostile attitude in Reagan's first two years, by mid-1983 there were signs of an amelioration of Reagan's attitude towards the Soviet Union. No longer did Reagan make 'evil empire' speeches. As Reagan looked towards the election of 1984, the issue on which he was vulnerable was that he was aggressive and potentially trigger-happy in his policy towards the Soviet Union. Moves towards an improvement in relations took place over the summer of 1983, but they were brought to an abrupt halt on 1 September 1983 when the Soviets shot down South Korean airliner 007 over the Sakhalin Islands, with sixty-one Americans aboard, including a Congressman, Larry MacDonald. Reagan denounced the shooting down of 007 as 'a heinous act' and asked, 'What can be the scope of legitimate discourse with a state whose values permit such atrocities?'[25] In

December 1983 the deterioration in relations sunk to a new low when the Soviets walked out of nuclear arms control talks.

Soon, however, Reagan took steps to engage in dialogue. Walter Mondale, in his campaign for the Democratic nomination in 1984, charged that Reagan had been too confrontational. Reagan deflected this charge with a conciliatory speech on 16 January 1984, stating that 'Neither we nor the Soviet Union can wish away the differences between our two societies and philosophies. But we should always remember we do have common interests. . . . There is no credible alternative but to steer a course which I would call deterrence and peaceful competition'.[26] Reagan effectively defused the charge that he was a warmonger in the course of the 1984 election campaign, especially in the debates with Mondale. In November 1984 Reagan won a landslide re-election victory, taking every state except Mondale's home state of Minnesota. After the election it became clear that Reagan's change to a more conciliatory and constructive attitude towards the Soviet Union was not only for reasons of electoral advantage. In January 1985 Shultz agreed with Gromyko on the resumption of nuclear arms control talks in March 1985.

Reagan's policies towards the Soviet Union in his first term have justifiably been heavily criticized on many counts. Reagan had scant knowledge of foreign policy and his ignorance of basic details was at times alarming. His harshly anti-Soviet speeches were needlessly provocative and helped to create the unhealthy mood of panic and fear in the early 1980s. The excessive build-up of defence, paid for by borrowing rather than by taxes, was fiscal irresponsibility of a high order which seriously weakened America's economy and her political and defensive capability for the long term. Reagan's overall attitude was ritualistic anti-Sovietism, uncritically proclaiming the righteousness of America's universal democratic mission and grossly exaggerating the extent to which many of the world's problems arose from conspiracy in Moscow.

Yet, for all of his prejudices and his ignorance of detail, Reagan's defenders advance a plausible argument that he pursued commonsense, old-fashioned policies which produced shock in the short term but greater stability and better prospects for peace in the longer term. Reagan felt that the Soviets respected strength and plain speaking, and he demonstrated both. His defensive build-up, especially SDI, aroused fear on the

Soviet side of on upward spiral of the arms race which would be difficult to match and induced them to seek negotiations and better relations rather than arms competition and confrontation. Reagan's displays of force, such as support for the Contras and the invasion of Grenada, made plain that Soviet aggression in the Third World would meet with firm retribution. Above all, Reagan, whose intuitive political skills were masterly, provided a catharsis for the underlying frustrations which had built up in American life in the 1970s, especially, but by no means exclusively, on the right. The restoration of self-confidence which Reagan brought about, even if in an illusory manner in his practice of the politics of symbolism, was an essential prerequisite for the renewal of détente. The other vital prerequisite was a more receptive leadership in the Soviet Union. By good fortune, at the very time that Reagan brought about restored faith in America a dynamic new leader was about to come to power in the Soviet Union. The scene was thereby set for a US–Soviet relationship in Reagan's second term which would differ quite extraordinarily from the relationship in his first term.

15

REAGAN AND GORBACHEV, 1985–9

The slight thaw in US–Soviet relations in 1984 was followed by a spectacular change in the relationship in Reagan's second term as president, following the succession of Mikhail Gorbachev as Soviet leader in March 1985. How far was the change in Soviet policy in the Gorbachev era the result of American policy, especially the policy of firmness and strength in Reagan's first term, or how far did Soviet policy change as a result of internal developments within the Soviet Union which were influenced by American policy only to a slight degree? This is perhaps the key question in examining the remarkable developments in US–Soviet relations in the second term of Reagan's presidency.

Following the agreement between Shultz and Gromyko in January 1985, nuclear arms control talks resumed in March 1985. The Nuclear and Space Talks, as they were now called, consisted of three separate sets of talks on INF, START and SDI, but issues at each of the talks were to be discussed 'in their relationship'.[1] The issues were fraught with difficulty in themselves, let alone in their relationship with one another. But since arms control was the main bellweather of the overall US–Soviet relationship, the resumption of talks in March 1985, after the break since the Soviet walk-out in December 1983, was an indication of a thaw in the new Cold War of the early 1980s.

In the same month, March 1985, Chernenko's death and his succession by Gorbachev opened one of the most remarkable chapters in America's relationship with the Soviet Union. Reagan's close ally, Margaret Thatcher, had given a glowing report on Gorbachev after his visit to Britain in December 1984, saying that he was a man whom she 'could do business with'.[2] Similarly, the Canadians gave a very favourable report on Gorbachev after a visit by him to Canada. Although Gorbachev had risen through the ranks of the Communist Party and had come to prominence as a protégé of Andropov, he seemed to be of a different mould to the older generation of leaders and, at the relatively youthful age of 54, he seemed willing to take a fresh look at issues and to initiate reforms.

Reagan hardliners claimed that the succession of a reformer was the direct result of America's tough policies of the early 1980s. 'Had it not been for Reagan', argued conservative columnist John McLaughlin, 'the Soviets probably would have kept in power somebody like Yegor Ligachev, believing that the Brezhnev hardline would ultimately pay off and that Reagan would be unable to sustain popular support for Euromissiles and defense spending'.[3] Reagan's critics suggest that it was simply his good fortune that due to internal developments within the Soviet Union a new leader had emerged who was bent on modernizing the Soviet economy and Soviet society, which necessitated better relations with the West. As Alexander Dallin and Gail Lapidus put it, Reagan's policies perhaps gave support to

> those within the Soviet policy-making community who see the 'American threat' in the most extreme and alarmist terms, who are most sceptical of the prospects for co-operative relationships between the two superpowers, and who prefer greater reliance on Soviet military and economic power to increased interdependence with the United States.[4]

Despite widespread attraction to Gorbachev and to his wife Raisa in the American media and public opinion, there was suspicion in many quarters within the United States that Gorbachev differed from previous Soviet leaders only in superficialities of style and appearance and that in fundamental objectives he did not differ at all from his predecessors. As Andrei Gromyko said of Gorbachev, 'This man smiles a lot, but he has iron teeth'.[5] Many American policy-makers feared that Gorbachev's smiles would lull Western public opinion into a false sense of security, after which Gorbachev's iron teeth would appear and the Russian bear would pounce. Since the 1950s there had been a constant suspicion of Soviet peace offensives designed to deceive gullible Western public opinion, and many leading figures in American government and the press continued until the late 1980s to suspect that Gorbachev was simply conducting a very persuasive peace offensive which would serve traditional Soviet goals. In 1987 the *International Herald Tribune* editorialized that by means of *glasnost* and *perestroika* the Soviet system

> must be made more efficient so that it can get on with achieving its hegemonic goals. . . . We have long experience with the Soviet policy of trying to maintain good relations with governments while undermining the political and social systems that sustain them. For many years, the undermining encompassed attempts at actual subversion and the promotion of unrest through Communist parties with mass membership. Mr Gorbachev represents the Soviet conclusion that it is more cost effective to charm NATO to death.[6]

Reagan shared such suspicions, but on the other hand he was attracted to the prospect of personal diplomacy as a means to achieve dramatic break-throughs, and his wife Nancy encouraged him to seek his place in history as a peacemaker. The tone of Reagan's public comments regarding the Soviet Union continued to be temperate. In a BBC interview on 30 October 1985, for example, he said that 'We don't like their system. They don't like ours. But we're not out to change theirs'.[7] On the Soviet side a more forthcoming approach was manifested following the replacement in May 1985 of Andrei Gromyko, the long-serving, stoney-faced, nay-saying Foreign Minister, by Eduard Shevardnadze, who was pleasant in personality and forward-looking in attitude. Signals were sent by the United States of a desire for a summit meeting with Gorbachev, which took place at Geneva in November 1985. Little of substance was achieved, but in symbolic terms the meeting made a profound impact. After a formal negotiating session, Reagan and Gorbachev walked together with only their interpreters to a hunting lodge in the grounds where, beside a roaring log fire, they engaged in an informal exchange of views. The television pictures of Reagan and Gorbachev together by the fireside made a deep and lasting impression on the image of the Soviet Union in the United States.

Reagan was determined, however, to negotiate from a position of strength, so that the defence build-up continued apace. In response to criticism that defence increases were beyond the capacity of the American economy, Robert MacFarlane, National Security Adviser in 1985, pointed out that the proportion of GNP spent on defence in the 1950s amounted to 10 per cent, in the 1960s to 8.5 per cent, whereas, after a decline to 5 per cent in the late 1970s, the figure in 1985 was 7 per cent. But critics continued to argue that defence increases were indiscriminate and wasteful and added to the alarming Federal deficit. Cuts in domestic spending after 1981–2 proved to be slight, and although the economy steadily grew, the combination of tax cuts and defence increases resulted in an increase in the national debt in Reagan's presidency from $1 trillion in 1980 to $2.5 trillion by 1988. Paul Kennedy, in a best-selling book, *The Rise and Fall of the Great Powers* (1987) suggested that the United States fitted a historical pattern of nations which declined when they engaged in 'imperial overstretch', namely when their military expenditure on overseas commitments overstretched the capacity of the domestic economy.[8]

The aspect of defence which Reagan was most determined to develop was SDI. An impediment, however, was the ABM treaty of 1972, which stated that 'Each party undertakes not to develop, test or deploy ABM systems or components which are sea-based, air-based, space-based or mobile land-based'.[9] Moreover, the ABM treaty was of unlimited duration. Reagan aides therefore sought loopholes and engaged in extraordinary legal casuistry. Abraham Sofaer, the State Department counsellor, argued that from the entire negotiating record of the treaty rather than from simply the terms of the treaty itself, a broad interpretation could be advanced which permitted experiments (rather than tests) on sub-components (rather than components). As Governor Mario Cuomo said of Sofaer, 'Abe Sofaer is a great New York lawyer. If they tell him, "Make it legal, Abe", he'll make it legal'.[10] Joan Hoff-Wilson suggests that blatant evasion of the ABM treaty constituted illegalities 'comparable to those involved in the Iran–Contra scandal'.[11] It stood in stark contrast to Reagan's harsh condemnation of Soviet violations of arms control treaties. But Reagan was single-minded regarding SDI and insisted upon the broad interpretation of the ABM treaty, which permitted testing and virtually all but actual deployment, rather than the strict interpretation which allowed no more than fundamental laboratory research.

When little progress was made at the Nuclear and Space Talks in 1985–6, Reagan was willing to respond to Gorbachev's impatience and agreed to a meeting in Reykjavik in Iceland. The meeting was scheduled for October 1986, a few weeks before the Congressional elections in November 1986, and given the immensely favourable publicity attached to the Geneva summit,

Reagan hoped that the Reykjavik meeting would have beneficial effects on Republican fortunes in the November elections. The meeting was declared to be a preparatory meeting for a full-scale summit which could take place later, but Gorbachev arrived with detailed proposals, so that Reykjavik was in itself a full-scale summit. Gorbachev made sweeping proposals of a zero option in Europe regarding INF, a 50 per cent mutual reduction in strategic nuclear weapons regarding START and a ten-year compliance with the strict interpretation of the ABM treaty with regard to SDI. Reagan responded with even more sweeping proposals, namely the abolition of all ballistic missiles within ten years. Gorbachev raised his offer to utopian heights, proposing the abolition of all nuclear weapons within ten years. Reagan responded positively, but he insisted on the retention of SDI. Gorbachev refused to accept, arguing that with no nuclear weapons on either side there was no need for a defensive shield against nuclear weapons. Disagreement on SDI led to the breakdown of the talks, and television pictures of a grim-faced Reagan and Gorbachev departing from one another in disagreement at Reykjavik were a distinct contrast to the pictures from Geneva in 1985.

The Reykjavik summit was, as Strobe Talbott has written, 'one of the strangest episodes in the annals of nuclear diplomacy'.[12] Proposals with far-reaching implications were hastily prepared at late-night sessions with inadequate staff support or proper facilities and without due consultation with allies. There was relief in many quarters that no ill-considered agreements had been signed. The breakdown at Reykjavik, however, left arms control negotiations at an impasse. Moreover, although SALT I had expired and SALT II had never been ratified and was declared to be fatally flawed by Reagan, the Reagan administration abided by SALT I and SALT II until 1986, even retiring a Poseidon submarine in early 1986 when a Trident submarine was deployed in order to keep within SALT II limits. But in late 1986 the administration decided to deploy air-launched Cruise missiles on B-52s, even though this put the United States over SALT II limits.

Shultz attempted to salvage the deteriorating situation and found negotiations fruitful with Shevardnadze, who wished to develop 'new thinking' in Soviet foreign policy and with whom Shultz struck up a very good personal relationship. The issue on which Shultz found that the Soviets were willing to reach agreement was INF. Although the Nuclear and Space Talks were to cover INF, START and SDI 'in their relationship', the Soviets were willing to consider INF on its own. The United States was concerned, however, with regard to INF, that even if the Soviets removed all SS-20s deployed in the western parts of the Soviet Union which were targeted against Western Europe, SS-20s would remain in the Soviet Union east of the Ural Mountains targeted against China, which would cause serious verification problems, with fears that SS-20s could swiftly be moved west of the Urals in a crisis. Moreover, the United States agreed with West German anxieties over SS-12s and SS-23s, which although less formidable with a shorter range than SS-20s, were technically intermediate-range rather than short-range missiles and were threatening to Western Europe. The Soviet side met these anxieties with a bold counter-proposal of a double zero, the removal of Pershing Is as well as Pershing IIs and Cruise missiles on the NATO side, while the Soviets would remove all SS-20s from east as well as west of the Urals and also remove all SS-12s and SS-23s. This break-through made possible the completion of the INF treaty, which was signed at a further summit meeting in Washington in December 1987. Gorbachev exercised his public relations skills brilliantly, with a walk-about on the streets of Washington adding to the 'Gorbymania' which had affected American public opinion. At the INF signing ceremony, the arrival together of the president of the United States and the General Secretary of the Communist Party of the Soviet Union, in obvious harmony and with much pomp, to the tune of the Star-Spangled Banner and the Internationale, was high drama which made a deep impression on the American public, raising for the first time the prospect that the Cold War was coming to an end.

Progress on START, however, proved to be disappointing. In pursuit of the target of a 50 per cent reduction in strategic nuclear weapons, the United States proposed a ceiling of 6,000 weapons on each side, with a subceiling of 4,900 on ICBMs and the remainder on SLBMs and bombers. Technical problems, especially on verification, proved to be much more difficult than with regard to INF. The zero agreement on INF simplified verification considerably, so that destruction of SS-20s and of ground-launched Cruise missiles began immediately, with a goal of total elimination of INF weapons on each side within three years. A START settlement, with a reduced but still very high figure for strategic nuclear weapons, involved much more complicated problems. Similarly, talks on conventional force reductions proved difficult, with the same problems in the newly named Conventional Forces in Europe (CFE) talks which had beset MBFR talks since 1973, with no agreement even on the numbers of forces which were currently on each side, let alone the numbers to which each side could be reduced. On chemical weapons, progress was made, though not by bilateral agreement but as a result of a unilateral Soviet concession in 1987 that the Soviet Union would cease to manufacture chemical weapons and begin to destroy its stockpile.

Reagan was therefore unable to cap the end of his presidency with a START treaty to match the INF treaty. Reagan's fourth summit meeting, in Moscow in May 1988, did not include substantial agreements on arms control. The symbolism was very evident, however, in Reagan walking through Red Square holding hands with Nancy and engaging in amiable conversation with Gorbachev and his wife Raisa. Reagan had come to the heart of the 'evil empire' and its reality seemed far removed from its image in the early 1980s. When asked in Moscow if he still regarded the Soviet Union as an 'evil empire', Reagan replied that such a description was of 'another time, another era'.[13] Moreover, in December 1988 the threat from the Soviet Union as a military power receded significantly with Gorbachev's unilateral concessions announced in a speech at the United Nations of the withdrawal of 1,000 tanks from Europe and the gradual realignment of Soviet forces in Europe from an offensive to a defensive configuration.

Although the US–Soviet relationship was being transformed at the symbolic level and in personal relations between leaders, however, this was not reflected in co-operation over regional conflicts. In the Middle East, the United States continued to exclude the Soviet Union from involvement in Arab–Israeli negotiations. With regard to China, the continuing US–Chinese détente proceeded steadily, with the United States increasing trade and arms sales to China while turning a diplomatic blind eye to Chinese human rights abuses. Throughout the Third World, the Reagan administration pressed ahead with its ideological commitment to the defeat of Communism globally, with the declaration of the Reagan Doctrine in 1985 specifying that the United States was committed not only to the containment of the spread of Communism but also to the support of anti-Communist forces which were engaged in struggles to bring down Marxist regimes. In Angola, for example, Congress repealed the 1976 prohibition on aid to anti-Communist forces, and aid began to be sent to the UNITA forces led by Jonas Savimbi in their continuing struggle with the MPLA Marxist government, which was supported by Cuban troops. Above all, aid was stepped up to the mujahedin in their war against the Marxist government in Afghanistan and the Soviet troops supporting the government. In February 1986 the United States began to supply the mujahedin with Stinger missiles, a shoulder-fired rocket with a guidance system which homed in on the heat of an aircraft or helicopter, which greatly strengthened the mujahedin against Soviet air power and added significantly to the pressure on the Soviets to come to a settlement and to withdraw from Afghanistan. In April 1988 an agreement was signed for Soviet withdrawal within nine months, and in January 1989 the last Soviet troops left Afghanistan.

Reagan's greatest obsession in Third World conflicts continued to be Nicaragua. The Boland amendment in June 1984, imposing a Congressional ban on aid to the Contras, had reduced American pressure on the Sandinista government. Moreover, the World Court in the Hague ruled in June 1986 that American aid to the Contras was in violation of international law and Nicaragua's sovereignty. Reagan, however, ignored international opinion and dismissed the World Court ruling as typical Third World, anti-Western bias. As for the Congressional ban, this was circumvented by raising aid for the Contras from other sources, such as Texas oil companies and foreign govern-ments such as Saudi Arabia and Brunei. The legality of raising money from these sources for this purpose was questionable. Undoubtedly illegal, however, although there is no clear-cut evidence that Reagan himself gave approval, was the extraordinary Iran–Contra plan, whereby arms were sold to Iran in exchange for Iranian assistance in freeing American hostages, with the profits from the arms sales being diverted to the Contras. Before the Iran–Contra scandal became public in November 1986, Reagan persuaded Congress to lift the ban on US aid to the Contras, pointing out that Daniel Ortega had flown to Moscow four days after Congress renewed the ban in 1985 and obtained large sums in aid from the Soviet Union. In August 1986 Congress agreed to a grant of $100 million aid to the Contras. The exposure of the Iran–Contra scandal in autumn 1986, however, weakened Reagan's position, with the disclosure of extraordinary details such as a trip to Tehran by National Security Adviser Robert MacFarlane in disguise, the shredding of documents by Colonel Oliver North and his secretary Fawn Hall, and false testimony to Congressional committees by Admiral John Poindexter, MacFarlane's successor as NSC adviser. Nevertheless, Congress agreed to $10 million in 1987 and $43 million in 1988 in non-military aid to the Contras, while Sanchez Oscar Arias, president of Costa Rica, proposed a plan providing for free elections in Nicaragua and the disbandment of the Contras.

Reagan's policy towards Nicaragua illustrated the most extreme aspects of right-wing zealotry in his foreign policy, with the issues viewed in ideological rather than human terms, in simplistic terms of Communist conspiracy with its roots in Moscow rather than the outcome of indigenous social injustice, with blindness to the undemocratic position of many of the 'freedom fighters' and with a ready resort to the use of force, applied with brutality and with scant respect for the rule of law. Yet, while Daniel Ortega and the Sandinistas were viewed in demonic, ideological terms, the Soviet leader and the Soviet people came to be viewed increasingly in human terms. During Reagan's second term as president the range of exchanges and interpersonal contacts between the United States and the Soviet Union swelled to a flood, profoundly altering the image of the Soviet Union in the United States. At the Geneva summit in 1985 a number of exchange agreements which had lapsed in the early 1980s were re-established and other agreements added. In 1986 the US Surgeon-General went to the Soviet Union for the first joint meeting on medicine and public health since 1978. In April 1986 the National Academy of Science renewed its two-year agreement with the Soviet Academy of Science. Various American universities introduced exchange programmes with Soviet universities, such as Stanford University and the University of Novosibirsk. Trade increased, in spite of the continuing impediment of the Jackson amendment, which barred Most Favored Nation status until emigration restrictions on Soviet Jews were eased. The Voice of America ceased to be jammed in 1985, while television programmes in America such as *Comrades* showed the Soviet people with a human face.

Meantime, Americans watched Gorbachev's internal reforms within the Soviet Union with bemusement but essentially with satisfaction. *Glasnost* and *perestroika* were seen by Americans as moves towards political democracy and a free-market economy. The easing of Soviet restrictions on press censorship were welcomed in the United States. Reform of the Soviet political system was not widely understood in the United States, but Americans were pleased to see moves away from dictatorship by the Communist Party to rule of law under a president and an elected legislature, with a gradual delegation of power to the fifteen republics in a more federal and less centralized system. By the end of Reagan's presidency, the Soviet reforms had still not gone far. Gorbachev continued to insist on the primacy of the role of the Communist Party, as stipulated in Article VI of the Soviet constitution, and Gorbachev insisted vehemently that he was still a Communist. Leading American politicians continued to express scepticism with regard to Gorbachev. Senator Robert Dole, for example, seeking the Republican nomination for president in 1988, said 'What alarms me about Mr Gorbachev, for all that he brings that is new, is that he also brings something that is very, very old: the convictions of a committed, tough as nails Communist'.[14]

Despite such remaining reservations with regard to Gorbachev, however, the relationship with the Soviet Union as Reagan left office in January 1989 had been transformed out of all recognition from 1985, let alone from 1981. The transformation was undoubtedly largely due to changes within the Soviet Union which were the outcome of developments within Soviet society rather than changes brought about by American policies or American pressure. Above all, the Soviet economy had sunk into such a state of stagnation that a radically new approach was demanded, though there was no agreement on the particular approach. Moreover, the succession of decrepit old leaders in the early 1980s created a desire for vigorous change. Into this situation came the dynamic, charismatic figure of Mikhail Gorbachev, the Soviet Union's John F. Kennedy, determined to 'get the country moving again' and, although a committed Communist, willing to ride the waves in whichever direction they took him in reforming Communism and Soviet society. Along with his key associate, Foreign Minister Shevardnadze, Gorbachev concluded that 'new thinking' in foreign policy was an essential concomitant of internal domestic reform.

Nevertheless, even if it is accepted that the principal causes of the extraordinary change in the US–Soviet relationship in Reagan's second term lay in the internal dynamics of Soviet politics and society, Reagan's supporters argue that it was Reagan's policies of firmness and strength which to an important extent convinced the Soviets of the need to turn away from confrontation and adventurism and to seek accommodation with the United States. Vice-President George Bush, for example, said in January 1988 that Gorbachev's policies were the result of 'our strength . . . our steadiness . . . our resolve'.[15] Even a reasonably dispassionate commentator, Coral Bell, in assessing the 'paradox' of Reagan's profound ignorance of foreign affairs and yet the successful outcome of his policies, writes of SDI, for example, that Reagan's critics 'argued that the "Star Wars" idea would be the kiss of death for arms control, but probably it proved the most effective negotiating lever that the West ever invented in that field, even if it was rather a strategic confidence trick'.[16] Reagan's critics, however, have a stronger case in arguing that Reagan's policies hampered rather than helped the process of reform within the Soviet Union which brought about the new US–Soviet relationship. Gerald Segal, for example, argues that the major impetus to reform in the Soviet Union was the reality of successful competing systems in Western Europe, Japan and even Hungary. Segal concludes that

> The more people in the West, most notably President Reagan, tried to rub the Soviet Union's nose in this reality, the less likely it was that reform could be contemplated in the Kremlin. It was only in the second Reagan administration, when . . . détente was offered, that Soviet reformers felt freer to think more radical thoughts. The leadership in Moscow was far too proud to bend to overt pressure and it might even be argued that the ending of the Cold War might have come earlier in the Gorbachev era if the United States had been less confrontational.[17]

Moreover, in his last two years in office (1987–8) Reagan was no longer negotiating from a position of secure strength but from a weakened political position following the Republican loss of the Senate in the 1986 Congressional elections, the waning of public support for further large-scale defence increases and, above all, the Iran–Contra affair, which threatened to destroy Reagan's presidency. In some respects, therefore, as much as Gorbachev needed a new relationship with the United States in order to pursue his domestic policies, Reagan needed Gorbachev in 1987–8 in order to save his presidency from disaster and to focus public attention on the drama of summit meetings and the new relationship with the Soviet Union and away from internal political difficulties.

The incoming Bush administration in January 1989, however, was not so immediately concerned with the question of how far Reagan's policies were responsible for the changes in the Soviet Union but with the question of how the United States should respond to those changes as they swept into full flood in 1989.

16

THE BUSH ERA

Following George Bush's inauguration as president in January 1989 there ensued a kaleidoscope of events which made 1989 an extraordinary year, leading on to equally spectacular developments in 1991. Communist rule collapsed through Eastern Europe, while within the Soviet Union fundamental changes took place. Bush's response to these events was quiet caution. Did Bush show lack of imagination in an overly cautious approach, leaving the United States as merely a spectator to these great events instead of playing a more creative role in trying to shape their course? Or did Bush demonstrate prudent statesmanship, pursuing quiet, low-key diplomacy and accepting the limits of America's ability to influence events, while exercising power sensibly to the extent which was possible?

With his succession from vice-president to president, Bush felt the need to establish himself as his own man and to distance himself somewhat from his predecessor. Moreover, Bush felt that Reagan had become too enamoured with Gorbachev. Bush set out to make his mark as a professionally competent president with a sound grasp of detail, in contrast to Reagan. He chose very professional advisers on foreign policy. As Secretary of State Bush appointed James Baker, a close friend who as Reagan's Chief of Staff from 1981 to 1984 and Secretary of the Treasury from 1985 to 1988 had shown great skill in working with Congress. As National Security Adviser, Bush appointed Brent Scowcroft, a former general and an intellectual who had served with distinction as National Security Adviser in Ford's administration. As Secretary of Defense, after the rejection by Congress of Bush's first choice, John Tower, on account of alleged drinking problems, Bush selected Richard Cheney, a well-respected Congressman from Wyoming. Significantly, all three of these figures had played important roles in Ford's administration – Baker as campaign manager in 1976, Scowcroft as National Security Adviser and Cheney as White House Chief of Staff. They had experienced, therefore, the crumbling of détente in the 1970s and the political problems as well as the national security concerns which ensued. Consequently, these advisers were inclined to reinforce Bush's own tendency towards wariness.

Bush ordered a policy review, to be conducted over four months in early 1989, covering every aspect of US–Soviet relations. This was criticized in some quarters as slowing the momentum of the progress in Reagan's last two years. Moreover, the results of the policy review, when proclaimed in a series of four speeches by Bush in May 1989, seemed disappointing, lacking depth or originality. The policy review advocated a standpoint of 'status quo plus', a phrase which illustrated not only Bush's caution but also his penchant for garbled prose and uninspiring use of language.[1] Bush conceded that 'the vision thing' was not his strong point.[2] The analysis of US–Soviet relations advanced in Bush's speeches was quite reasonable, but the proposals for an appropriate American response seemed weak. Bush suggested that the current situation demonstrated the success of containment as pursued since the late 1940s. Truman, Kennan and such figures, said Bush, 'believed that the Soviet Union, denied the easy course of expansion, would turn inward and address the contradictions of its inefficient, repressive and inhumane system. And they were right. The Soviet Union is now publicly facing this hard reality. Containment worked'.[3] With regard to America's next step, however, Bush's suggestions were rather vague. 'We seek the integration of the Soviet Union into the community of nations', he said. 'Ultimately our objective is to welcome the Soviet Union back into the world order.'[4] Moreover, Bush, as ever, urged caution. He pointed out that the Soviet Union had 'promised a more co-operative relationship before, only to reverse course and return to militarism'.[5] Hence, he warned that 'in an era of extraordinary change, we have an obligation to temper optimism – and I am optimistic – with prudence'.[6]

Bush's speeches met with some heavy criticism. 'President George Bush has delivered his fourth, final, flat and flimsy speech on East–West relations', editorialized the *New York Times*.[7]

The *International Herald Tribune* described the speeches as 'grudgingly defensive. . . . Meant to redefine US foreign policy, they actually displayed a disturbing poverty of thought'.[8] Some of Bush's advisers frankly expressed the view that the United States should do nothing in response to events in Eastern Europe. Robert Gates, Deputy National Security Adviser, warned of the cycles in Soviet revisionism and advocated a do-nothing policy apart from accepting Soviet concessions. Richard Cheney advocated a defence policy based on the assumption that Gorbachev 'would ultimately fall. And when that happens, he's likely to be replaced by somebody who will be far more hostile'.[9] Bush reprimanded Cheney for those remarks, but Bush's critics argued that Bush was not addressing himself to the issue of whether Gorbachev's survival was in America's interests and, if so, how the United States could help Gorbachev to succeed in a manner suitable to America's interests.

Meantime, events within the Soviet Union and Eastern Europe gathered momentum. In March 1989 elections took place in the Soviet Union for a Congress of People's Deputies. Television coverage of the sessions of the Congress showed the extent of *glasnost*, with, for example, severe criticisms of Gorbachev by Andrei Sakharov, the dissident whom Gorbachev had freed from internal exile in Gorki. In May 1989, Boris Yeltsin, whom Gorbachev had appointed leader of the Moscow Communist Party in 1985 but who subsequently became a critic of Gorbachev as too hesitant a reformer and who was consequently dismissed from the Politburo in 1988, was, despite Gorbachev's efforts to prevent it, elected chairman of the Russian Supreme Soviet. Meantime, in Hungary parliament passed legislation in January 1989 permitting opposition parties in elections scheduled for spring 1990. Even more astonishingly, on 2 May 1989 Hungary dismantled the barbed wire fence along the border with Austria – the Iron Curtain was literally torn down. The following month, in June 1989, the body of Imre Nagy, the hero of the Hungarian Revolution in 1956, was exhumed and buried with ceremony. In Poland, President Jaruzelski, who had sought to crush Solidarity in the early 1980s, accepted its status as a free trade union and its right to run candidates in elections to be held in June 1989. In the elections, Solidarity won 99 of the 100 Senate seats and all 161 seats which it was allowed to contest in the lower house, the Sejm. Jaruzelski sought ways to avoid the installation of a non-Communist government, but, following a telephone conversation with Gorbachev, he accepted Tadeusz Mazowiecki, former editor of Solidarity's newspaper, as prime minister of Poland.

Gorbachev's attitude towards Poland and Hungary was made clear in his renunciation of the Brezhnev Doctrine and Soviet assurance that interventions as in Czechoslovakia in 1968 would not be repeated. Foreign Ministry spokesman Gennadi Gerasonov stated that 'The Brezhnev Doctrine is dead. . . . You know the Frank Sinatra song "My way". Hungary and Poland are doing it their way. We now have the Sinatra Doctrine'.[10] Bush was typically cautious in his approach to Hungary and Poland, visiting the two countries in July 1989 and offering aid of such a modest sum, $300 million, that Congress raised the figure to $1 billion.

Within the US administration, those who were sceptical that deep changes were taking place continued to be vociferous. Vice-President Dan Quayle stressed 'the darker side of Soviet foreign policy'.[11] Under-Secretary Lawrence Eagleburger said that 'For all its risks and uncertainties, the Cold War was characterized by a remarkably stable and predictable set of relations among the great powers'.[12] Other figures urged a more positive outlook. 'It may be time to abandon incrementalism for a leapfrog approach', former Assistant Secretary of State Richard Holbrooke stated, 'to see if we can really make a basic change in the relationship'.[13] Newspaper columnist Ellen Goodman wrote that 'As for the Cold War model? This is not some well-tarnished antique to be preserved. It is an obsolete monster and we are well rid of it. What we need now, and quickly, are new models for the post-war world'.[14] But Bush did not suggest any new models. His bland, laconic approach was severely criticized by Senate Majority Leader George Mitchell. 'President Bush must reach beyond the status quo thinking that appears to dominate administration thinking', said Mitchell. 'He must cast aside the ambivalence, the hesitation and the timidity and adopt a more energetic and engaged policy'.[15] Bush replied that 'These changes we're seeing in Eastern Europe are absolutely extraordinary, but I'm not going to be stampeded into overreacting to any of this. The Democrats on Capitol Hill have been calling me timid. I have other, better words, like "cautious", "diplomatic", "prudent" '.[16]

Bush's leading confidant, James Baker, however, was gradually moving towards advocacy of a more positive approach. Meetings with Shevardnadze in Moscow in May and in Wyoming in September convinced Baker that great opportunities presented themselves and should be seized. 'We want *perestroika* to succeed', Baker said in a speech in October:

> We have reached this conclusion not because it is our business to reform Soviet society or to keep a particular Soviet leader in power – we can really do neither – but because *perestroika* promises Soviet actions more advantageous to our interests. Our task is to search more creatively for those points of mutual US–Soviet advantage that may be possible'.[17]

Baker therefore proposed US aid to the Soviet Union, not of a grandiose nature, but, for example, technical accountancy assistance. Bush responded to the extent of agreeing to a summit meeting with Gorbachev in Malta in early December 1989, saying that he did not 'want to have two gigantic ships pass in the night because of failed communication'.[18]

Meantime, the momentum of change in Eastern Europe reached even more dramatic levels with developments in November 1989 in East Germany, Bulgaria and Czechoslovakia. The dismantling of the barbed wire fence between Hungary and Austria produced a fatal haemorrhaging of East Germany, as refugees streamed through Hungary to Austria and on to West Germany. At the same time demands for reform within East Germany produced massive rallies in Dresden, Leipzig and other East German cities. On 7 October Gorbachev visited East Germany and told the East German leader Erich Honoecker that a leadership which isolated itself from its people no longer had the right to rule. Honoecker was inclined towards the traditional approach of repression, and on 9 October he ordered the use of force in Leipzig. But he was persuaded to rescind the order by the head of security, Egon Krenz, and on 18 October Honoecker resigned, to be replaced by Krenz. In early November Krenz flew to Moscow, where Gorbachev told him that the East Germans must take their own initiatives to resolve their problems. On 9 November the Berlin Wall was opened. To scenes of wild jubilation in Berlin and deep contentment in Washington, the ugliest and most visible symbol of the East–West divide was breached. On 3 December the East German party leadership resigned, with a caretaker government left to prepare East German elections in March 1990, which resulted in the victory of the Christian Democrats, who were committed to German reunification.

The day after the Berlin Wall was opened, the old-guard leader in Bulgaria, Todor Zhikov, was removed from office and replaced by a younger reform Communist, Peter Mladenov. In Czechoslovakia, the overthrow of the regime had deeper popular roots. Mass demonstrations became daily events, but the regime knew that no support for suppression was forthcoming from Moscow. Consequently, on 24 November the Czechoslovak politburo resigned, and incredibly, Vaclav Havel, a leading dissident who had been in prison in early 1989, became president of Czechoslovakia, with Alexander Dubcek, the hero of the 1968 Prague Spring, chairman of parliament.

Bush scarcely had time to absorb the implications of these extraordinary developments when he met Gorbachev at the Malta summit on 2–3 December. Bad weather curtailed the meetings somewhat, since it was impossible on occasion for the leaders to make the journey between the US and Soviet ships in Valetta harbour. Nevertheless, the Malta summit moved Bush further to Baker's position that it was in America's interests that *perestroika* should succeed and that Gorbachev should survive. Bush became aware of the political recriminations at home if Gorbachev were to fall and to be replaced by a reactionary. Bush, therefore, in briefing NATO allies in Brussels on 4 December on the Malta summit, stated that 'What we've got to do is to be sure that we conduct ourselves in such a way that the changes, the political reforms, can keep going forward', and he advised that the West should not gloat triumphantly and 'dance on the Berlin Wall'.[19]

While Bush took hesitant steps in his relations with the Soviet Union in its process of reform, he was decisive in his policy towards China in its policy of brutal repression. Bush regarded himself as an expert on China, following his service as head of the liaison office in Beijing in 1974–5. He felt that quiet diplomacy and behind-the-scenes encouragement of reform was the correct approach towards the Chinese rather than public criticism of human rights violations. Through the 1970s and 1980s Americans paid little attention to China's undemocratic, repressive policies and hoped that economic liberalization would gradually lead to political freedom. Demonstrations in Beijing in the spring of 1989 raised hope that events were moving in this direction. The massacre of protestors in Tiananmen Square on 4 June 1989, however, profoundly altered American attitudes towards China. Yet Bush confined himself to diplomatic protests, maintaining economic agreements and arms sales with only very minor sanctions. In July he sent Under-Secretary Lawrence Eagleburger and National Security Adviser Brent Scowcroft on a secret mission to China, and they were sent again publicly in December. Bush was severely criticized for alleged willingness to kowtow to Beijing. Aside from the motive of a desire to maintain channels of communication with the Chinese government in order to encourage progressive change in the long term, it seemed that old Cold Warriors in the Bush administration wished to preserve the China card to play against Moscow.

In December 1989 the final chapter of the East European revolutions took a bloody form in Romania. On 17 December President Nicolai Ceaucescu ordered the secret police, the Securitate, to fire on demonstrators in the city of Timasoara, resulting in over seventy deaths. Ceaucescu denounced foreign agents and fascist thugs as the source of the trouble, but at a rally on 21 December Ceaucescu was jeered and booed. As demonstrations continued, army leaders told Ceaucescu that the army would not fire on the people. Fighting broke out between the Securitate and demonstrators, who were supported by the army. Ceaucescu and his wife Elena attempted to escape in a helicopter but were captured, tried by a military tribunal and summarily executed on 25 December. The dramatic revolutions in Eastern Europe had come to their climactic end. Ceaucescu's fate demonstrated the wisdom of old-guard leaders elsewhere in Europe in not attempting resistance. Crucial to their decision to yield without a fight was the knowledge that no support for repression was forthcoming from Moscow.

Within the Soviet Union reform proceeded apace. Economic reforms were drawn up to introduce elements of a market system into the Soviet economy. Gorbachev insisted that his aim was to reform Communism rather than to replace it. Yet, while he initially insisted on the preservation of Article VI of the Soviet constitution which assigned to the Communist Party the guiding role in Soviet society, on 7 February 1990 the Central Committee accepted the elimination of Article VI and the acceptance of the principle of multi-party democracy. This led swiftly to the election of non-Communists in many of the fifteen republics, whose claims for greater autonomy steadily grew.

On two matters, however, Gorbachev was not willing to yield, namely the unilateral secession of Soviet republics and the admission of a united Germany into NATO. In Lithuania elections brought to power Sajudis, a non-Communist nationalist party led by Vytautas Landsbergis, and on 11 March 1990 the Lithuanian parliament declared that Lithuania's incorporation into the Soviet Union in 1940 was illegal and that Lithuania was therefore an independent state. The United States had never recognized the incorporation into the Soviet Union of the three Baltic states of Estonia, Latvia and Lithuania, but when Bush met leaders of the Baltic republics in exile, he told them that his sympathies required reconciliation with 'his feeling that there must be a way to support Gorbachev's overall efforts for democratic reforms'.[20] Bush ignored the non-binding resolution passed by 416 votes to 3 by the House of Representatives calling for the recognition of Lithuania. The Bush administration hoped that a compromise settlement could be reached within the terms of a new Soviet law which permitted secessions of republics provided that certain conditions were met. Bush made occasional gestures to protect himself politically, such as a statement on a mid-West political tour in June 1990 that he wanted 'to see Lithuania have its freedom. We are committed to self-determination for the Baltic states'.[21] But Bush was not prepared to take any major steps on Lithuania's behalf which would increase Gorbachev's difficulties with conservatives and which would damage US–Soviet relations.

On Germany, however, the United States stood firmly with West German Chancellor Helmut Kohl in the insistence that a united Germany should be a member of NATO. The Soviets were initially opposed to German unification, but by January 1990 Gorbachev accepted this as inevitable but resisted German membership in NATO. The Soviets made a variety of counter-proposals, such as that Germany should be neutral or should have a status like France of NATO membership without integration of its armed forces or should belong to both NATO and to the Warsaw Pact. In May 1990 representatives of East and West Germany, the United States, the Soviet Union, Britain and France, held talks in which the United States sought to satisfy legitimate Soviet concerns while winning Soviet acceptance of German membership in NATO. The United States exercised pressure on Kohl, for example, to accept the prohibition of the stationing of NATO troops in the former East German territory. By the end of 1990 Germany was reunited and accepted into NATO, with Soviet acquiescence. Agreement was attained partly by generous terms of German financial aid for the resettlement by 1994 of Soviet troops based in East Germany and partly by American persuasion that a united Germany was less of a threat to the Soviet Union when integrated within Europe in NATO than a Germany which was isolated or given an inferior status of less than full NATO membership.

The changes in Eastern Europe and the consequent diminution in the military threat to the West were not reflected in significant arms reductions by the Bush administration. The Pentagon accepted that agreements with the new governments of Hungary and Czechoslovakia to withdraw Soviet forces, in addition to withdrawal from East Germany, immensely diminished the Soviet offensive capability. Moreover, the Warsaw Pact had disintegrated as a military alliance. Cheney, however, advocated that, from a prudent defence position based on a worst-case analysis, American defence reductions should be very modest. Cheney proposed cuts of 2 per cent per annum between 1990 and 1994, involving the withdrawal of some American troops from Europe but leaving significant numbers in order to maintain Europe's confidence. Bush agreed, stating that he would rather be 'cautious' than 'reckless' in the transition from the military balance of the Cold War to a new international order.[22]

Within Congress and public opinion criticisms were raised that Bush was making a much too timid response to the profound diminution in the military threat to the West. Les Aspin, Chairman of the House of Representatives Armed Services Committee, stated that 'We cannot assume that peace has broken out and begin dismantling our military. But neither can we ignore the enormous changes taking place in the world today'.[23] Public opinion hoped for a 'peace dividend' as swords were turned into ploughshares. There was, however, a myriad of vested economic interests opposed to reductions in defence spending. In some instances defence cuts proposed by the Pentagon were rejected by Congress because of the effect on employment in Congressional districts. In June 1990 when William Gray, the Democratic Whip in the House of Representatives, asked Cheney why greater defence cuts were not possible, Cheney jokingly but pointedly replied to Gray, a Representative from a district in Philadelphia, that consideration could perhaps be given to closure of the Philadelphia Naval Yard.

Moreover, progress in arms control negotiations was extremely slow. Baker said in October 1989 that

Over the last forty years, arms control played only a limited role in shaping the US–Soviet relationship because our political differences were simply too wide to allow enduring and substantial progress.... Now, *perestroika* in Soviet domestic and foreign policy could in part lift that shadow. The political prerequisite for enduring and strategically significant arms control may finally be materializing'.[24]

Yet negotiations on cuts in strategic nuclear weapons and in conventional forces seemed to become bogged down in detail. In the START talks, verification issues proved tortuous, and it seemed that the goal of a 50 per cent reduction was unlikely to be achieved. In the CFE talks, NATO advanced proposals for non-provocative defence, that is, force levels which were unsuitable for offence but unambiguously sufficient for a credible defence. To translate such worthy principles into agreements on numbers of troops and weapons, however, proved to be extremely difficult, even in the improved international climate. With regard to SDI, waning public support, rather than agreements in negotiations, led to reductions in its funding.

With regard to regional conflicts, Soviet 'new thinking' did not lead to an end to support of clients in Africa, Central America and Afghanistan. The United States continued to give aid to the Afghan rebels, but divisions among the rebels led to lack of success in bringing about the downfall of the Soviet-backed regime of General Najibullah. In Africa, the United States continued to aid anti-Communist insurgents while the Soviets aided Marxist regimes in Angola and Ethiopia. Nevertheless, progress was made in negotiations on Angola, and an agreement was reached in 1989 on the withdrawal of Soviet-backed Vietnamese forces from Cambodia.

In the regional conflict of greatest importance to the United States, Nicaragua, the Bush administration achieved a spectacular success. Aside from security considerations, Central America was important to Bush politically, given the strength of refugee communities, especially in Florida, and the priority attached to Central America by American conservatives who were unconvinced of Bush's conservative credentials. Baker worked to achieve a consensus within Congress and among central American allies for continuing aid to the Contras, though on a reduced level, while the Sandinistas accepted a ceasefire in exchange for the promise of free elections in April 1990. The unexpected defeat of Daniel Ortega and the Sandinistas in the election by a coalition led by Violetta Chamorro gave Bush a success for the Reagan Doctrine greater than Reagan ever achieved. A similar outcome in El Salvador was not attainable, but although Baker assigned to Moscow 'special responsibility' for a new rebel offensive in November 1989, which led to hundreds of deaths in the interminable civil war, it was in fact clear that Salvadoran insurgents benefited from Kremlin largesse only modestly and at second or third remove through Cuba and Nicaragua, and it was inconceivable that El Salvador would become a Soviet base in Central America capable of installing Soviet missiles and exporting Marxist revolution throughout the region. Soviet aid to Cuba, including economic subsidies amounting to $5 billion per annum, continued to be a major source of grievance to the United States. Baker went so far as to state that 'Soviet behaviour toward Cuba and Central America remains the biggest obstacle to a full, across-the-board improvement in relations between the United States and the Soviet Union'.[25] Castro's advocacy of old-style Communism and denunciation of *perestroika*, however, left him isolated, a discredited old figure from the past rather than the *enfant terrible* who threatened, with Moscow's backing, to spread Communism throughout Central America and beyond.

With regard to economic relations, Bush made typically cautious moves. He continued to withhold Most Favored Nation (MFN) status, since the Soviet Union did not meet the strict requirement of the Jackson amendment with regard to emigration of Soviet Jews, though by 1990 over 100,000 Jews were allowed to emigrate and MFN status was extended to China and not withdrawn after the Tienanmen Square massacre. Some liberalization of trade took place, such as the removal in June 1990 of many controls over the export of high technology to third countries which might re-export items to the Soviet Union. A number of American companies expanded business with the Soviet Union. In April 1990, for example, in the largest ever deal between an American company and the Soviet Union, Pepsico signed an agreement to barter Soviet ships and vodka in exchange for Pepsi-Cola. In the most highly publicized business venture in the Soviet Union, MacDonald's opened a branch in Moscow. The prospects for successful profitable business ventures in the Soviet Union, however, were not good, and the volume of American trade remained small and was greatly exceeded by Soviet trade with Western Europe, especially Germany.

While slow progress characterized economic relations, a flood of developments took place in exchanges of almost every other kind, especially educational, cultural, scientific and interpersonal. An increasing number of American universities formed exchange links with Soviet universities. A joint student magazine, *Montage*, was produced quarterly by Stanford and Moscow State University. Environmental co-operation developed greatly, with Soviet oil-skimming ships assisting in clean-up operations in Alaska after the *Exxon Valdez* spill, while a joint US–Soviet national park on both sides of the Bering Straits was planned. With greater accessibility to Western newspapers and television programmes, the flow of cultural ideas as well as political information flooded into the Soviet Union. Voice of America and even Radio Liberty were unjammed in 1989, but the need for such clandestine means of communication had diminished and their future came to be questioned. The number of American tourists exceeded 100,000 per annum, and only increased prices and shortages of hotel accommodation held back further increases in numbers. Marriages between Soviet and American citizens became less rare, notably the wedding in 1990 of Roald Sagdayev, a former leader of the Soviet space programme and a member of the Congress of People's Deputies, and Susan Eisenhower, granddaughter of President Eisenhower. The image of the Soviet Union in the United States was transformed, and while at the level of public opinion this change was superficial and susceptible to a volatile swing backward, an increasingly large number of exchanges of professional groups and their counterparts deepened links and increased support for the view that human contacts removed many of the sources of hostility.

Such an impression was embodied above all in Gorbachev himself, who demonstrated his unrivalled public relations again at the next summit meeting in the United States in June 1990. The meetings with Bush at the White House and Camp David did not produce substantial agreements. But in their travels to Minnesota and California, Gorbachev and Raisa charmed the American public and demonstrated the depth of 'Gorbymania' in the American heartland. San Francisco was so wonderful, said Gorbachev, that citizens should pay a special tax for the privilege of living there. With more natural ability than an American politician wooing the voters, Gorbachev won the hearts of the American public. In a major speech at Stanford University, Gorbachev declared that the Cold War was over. With friendly personal relations between political leaders at the top and between larger numbers of Americans and Soviet counterparts at lower levels, the American public was willing to hope that the Cold War was indeed over.

The doubt remained, however, whether good relations would continue if Gorbachev were to fall. While Gorbachev's prestige and popularity were enormously high abroad, with *Time* magazine, for example, naming him Man of the Decade, his difficulties at home rose to critical proportions. Above all, *perestroika* had failed to produce any visible improvement in the Soviet economy, especially with regard to consumer goods. At the same time, conservatives feared the diminution of authority which resulted in a growing crime rate, ethnic violence and separatist demands. On the left, Yeltsin continued to criticize the slow pace of Gorbachev's reforms. Yeltsin, however, had acquired the image in the United States of a troublesome, opportunistic maverick, and his image was further besmirched by reports of drunken and bizarre behaviour on his part, especially on a visit to the United States in September 1989, during which he was conspicuously not invited to the White House. Yeltsin was not seen as a viable liberal alternative to Gorbachev by the Bush administration, which felt that the most likely successor to Gorbachev, if he fell from power, would be an old-guard authoritarian dictator.

A crucial question which faced American policy-makers, therefore, was whether the United States should attempt to assist Gorbachev to sustain his position. A heated debate took place on this issue in American academic, journalistic and governmental circles. Some argued that Gorbachev's domestic problems were so enormous that his fall was inevitable, so that there was no sense in any American rescue attempt. 'The system cannot be reconstructed and refined. . . . Gorbachev is beyond our help', as it was put in an article anonymously authored by Z, later revealed as Martin Malia, a Berkeley Soviet specialist.[26] Richard Cheney argued that US economic assistance to the Soviet Union was ill-advised so long as Moscow spent 'enormous amounts of its national wealth on military hardware'.[27] William Safire, a conservative columnist, argued that aid to Gorbachev could halt the reform process rather than encourage its further development. Safire wrote that if *perestroika* 'means making the Soviet Union safe for cosmetized communism – if it means delaying and denying the world-wide surge of freedom that has so surprised the men who set it in train – we want *perestroika* to fail'.[28] Francis Fukuyama, a former official in the State Department Policy Planning Staff, argued in a celebrated article entitled 'The End of History?' that American assistance was unnecessary since the inevitable trends of history were moving the world to the universal triumph of democracy. 'What we may be witnessing', wrote Fukuyama, 'is not just the end of the Cold War . . . but the end of history as such: that is, the end point of mankind's ideological evolution and universalization of Western liberal democracy as the final form of human government'.[29]

Other critics, however, warned that the United States was indulging to a dangerous degree in taking pleasure in watching Communists writhe. Columnist Stephen Rosenfeld, for example, warned that, without an appropriate American response to Gorbachev's policies, reactionaries in the Soviet Union would overthrow him. Rosenfeld wrote that

> there is the nagging question of what the Kremlin traffic will bear, of just how 'unequal' a dialogue the Soviet Union is prepared to maintain. A current of introspection and renewal is running strong in Moscow, but everything else we know tells us that a streak of patriotism, pride and xenophobia lurks near the surface'.[30]

Bush himself took the position which had evolved since late 1989 that Gorbachev's survival was in America's interests. 'As I've said many times before', Bush said in June 1990, 'we want to see *perestroika* succeed'.[31] If this was the administration's conclusion, the further question arose as to what action the United States might take to help the consolidation and continuation of reform in Eastern Europe and the Soviet Union. Some figures such as Senator Bill Bradley favoured an extensive programme of economic aid to Eastern Europe similar to the Marshall Plan. 'The $300 million Mr Bush proposed to bolster economic growth and democracy', said Bradley, 'is barely enough to bail out a failed savings and loan institution, much less to jump start national economies that have been dead for decades'.[32] Bradley proposed that 1 per cent of the US military budget be set aside for East European reconstruction. Little support was forthcoming in Congress, however, for such a plan. As for economic aid to the Soviet Union, even Bradley conceded that 'The Soviet Union is a different circumstance'.[33] Baker stated that economic aid should be restricted to such limited matters as sharing business expertise. Western European nations were much more enthusiastic proponents of economic aid to the Soviet Union. In June 1990 Chancellor Kohl proposed at the meeting of the Group of Seven, the seven leading industrial democracies, $15 billion in aid to the Soviet Union over three years. In West Germany's case this was partly to win Soviet acceptance of German membership in NATO, but President Mitterand of France and the leaders of most other European countries, except Margaret Thatcher of Britain, strongly favoured economic aid as a sound investment in order to continue good relations with the Soviet government and to tie the Soviet economy increasingly to the West. Bush dismissed this pressure for greater economic aid and focused more attention on the conventional arms control agreement, the CFE treaty, which was finally signed in the summer of 1990.

In August 1990 a severe test of the new US–Soviet relationship was presented by the Iraqi invasion of Kuwait. Baker was fortuitously travelling in the Soviet Union with Shevardnadze at the time, and on 3 August a joint statement was issued condemning the invasion. The new US–Soviet relationship was clearly illustrated when, in contrast to many earlier Middle East conflagrations, the Soviets voted with the United States in the United Nations and denounced Iraq's action. The Soviets cut off arms supplies to Iraq, and although some Soviet advisers remained in Iraq, the Soviets also supplied 'valuable intelligence information' to the United States regarding Iraqi forces.[34]

Over the autumn and winter of 1990–1, however, developments within the Soviet Union took a more ominous turn, threatening the continuation of a warm US–Soviet relationship and complicating co-operation on the Gulf crisis. Gorbachev's popularity, always lower at home than abroad, plummeted as the Soviet economy steadily declined. Moreover, Gorbachev was unwilling to make drastic reforms from a command economy to a market system. In October 1990 Gorbachev rejected the radical plan drawn up by Grigori Shatalin to transform the Soviet economy to a market system in 500 days. Ideologically, Gorbachev adhered to his aim to reform Communism rather than to replace it, while politically Gorbachev was increasingly dependent on conservative elements, particularly the KGB, the army and the Communist Party, as he lost the support of public opinion and of liberal reformers. Growing conservative power was made evident with the dramatic resignation in December 1990 of Shevadnadze, who warned of a move towards dictatorship.

Although Shevardnadze was replaced by Alexander Bessertmyth, former ambassador in Washington, which suggested no change in foreign policy, conservative influence made itself felt on such matters as arms control, Lithuania and the Gulf War. Evasions of provisions of the CFE treaty came to light, such as the transfer of three army divisions to naval forces in order to avoid the treaty's provisions. In Lithuania, on 13 January 1991 Soviet troops stormed a television antenna surrounded by demonstrators, killing fifteen, and while Gorbachev claimed that local commanders were responsible, there were fears of a general crack-down on the Baltic republics. With regard to the Gulf War, while Soviet co-operation continued on key issues, the dissatisfaction of Soviet conservatives was evident, leading Gorbachev to seek a settlement on terms which were unacceptable to the United States, sending three times, for example, a Soviet mediator to Iraq, Yevgenyi Primakov, who had close contact with Saddam Hussein.

The spectacular, rapid Allied victory in the Gulf War removed difficulties with regard to Soviet policy during the crisis. Indeed, Baker was eager to draw the Soviet Union into post-war Middle East negotiations as co-chair of a Middle East peace conference rather than to exclude the Soviets from the Middle East as previously. Moreover, in April 1991 Gorbachev reached agreement on a Union Treaty to be signed in August which would delegate wide powers to the republics. Agreement on the Union Treaty seemed to symbolize Gorbachev's redirection towards a reform path. Nevertheless, as Robert Gates, Deputy NSC Adviser, put it in May 1991, 'This is a historic time of decision for the Soviet Union. Will it succeed in advancing into a different better future – as we hope – or will it retreat into a more familiar but unhappy past? For now, and likely for years to come, we must be prepared for either eventuality'.[35]

In this situation Bush's critics advocated bolder US policies to protect Gorbachev's position and to encourage further Soviet reform. In particular, it was argued that massive economic assistance should be offered in exchange for Soviet reform. Graham Allison, director of the John F. Kennedy School of

Government at Harvard, suggested a 'grand bargain'. Allison pointed out that Gorbachev's fall and the consequent reaction or chaos in the Soviet Union was such a dire potential peril to the United States that, to try to prevent this, expenditure of a sum equivalent to a fraction of the defence budget was a prudent investment. Allison proposed 'a bargain of Marshall Plan proportions: substantial financial assistance to Soviet reforms *conditional* upon continuing political pluralization and a coherent economic program for moving rapidly to a market economy'.[36] Critics of the grand bargain, however, argued that the grant of large sums of aid would encourage Gorbachev to use aid as a substitute for reform instead of an inducement to the required economic reconstruction.

Richard Nixon, for example, advised against 'counter-productive Western painkillers'.[37] Moreover, the imposition of conditions, Henry Kissinger argued, would be resented and was liable 'to become controversial and the focal point of internal Soviet opposition'.[38] Kissinger's argument appeared to be supported by Gorbachev's statement in his speech accepting the Nobel Peace Prize in June 1991 that it was 'futile and dangerous to set conditions and to say, "We'll understand you and believe you as soon as you, the Soviet Union, come completely to resemble us." '[39] European leaders were more strongly in favour of greater economic aid, but at the London meeting of the Group of Seven in July 1991 Bush resisted pressure, especially from Germany, to embark upon large-scale economic aid. Critics chided that Bush, as the *San Francisco Examiner-Chronicle* put it, was a 'visionless president' whose 'tight-fisted, blinkered performance in London' failed to take, like the Marshall Plan, 'the same bold leap of self-interest to realize that what's good for the post-Communist Soviet Union is good for us'.[40] Bush's response was that 'The reforms have got to be detailed a bit more before blank cheques are written, and even then it would be difficult. We're not rolling in cash'.[41]

The Bush administration felt that its steady course towards the Soviet Union reaped rewards in such issues as Third World conflicts and arms control. The Soviet Union was in steady retreat regarding Third World incursions, with the downfall of the Marxist regime of Colonel Mengistu in Ethiopia and a settlement of the Angolan civil war in May 1991. In August 1991 the START treaty was finally signed, with limits set at 6,000 nuclear weapons on each side, a reduction of approximately 30 per cent. Although the numbers remained grotesquely high, the completion of the treaty put in place important verification procedures for possible future reductions, while the Soviets made major concessions in reducing considerably the number of their very heavy ICBMs, the SS-18. The summit meeting in Moscow in early August 1991 at which the START treaty was signed appeared to indicate that US–Soviet relations were back on course after the difficulties of the preceding winter. Bush showed his support for Gorbachev, travelling from Moscow to the Ukraine and speaking out in Kiev, where the Ukranian parliament had voted in June for independence from the Soviet Union, against the dangers of nationalism and separatism.

On 18 August 1991 news was received from Moscow which Washington had always dreaded, namely a TASS announcement that 'for reasons of health' President Gorbachev had given up his duties – an obvious cover story for a coup by reactionaries.[42] The eight-man Committee of National Emergency which had seized power, headed by Vice-President Gennadi Yanayev, Prime Minister Valentin Pavlov, Defence Minister Dmitri Yazov, KGB chief Vladimir Kryuchkov and Interior Minister Boris Pugo, claimed that they wished a continuation of current foreign policy. But their immediate repression of the press and their rejection of the Union Treaty due to be signed the next day, made obvious their determination to clamp down and to return the Soviet Union to the old regime, as in Brezhnev's days or worse. As fears arose of a return to the Cold War, there were recriminations in some quarters that Bush's inactivity had allowed this to happen. 'We have been pushed to the sidelines, reduced to the status of observers', said Charles William Maynes, editor of *Foreign Policy*, for example, 'because we didn't help Gorbachev and the reformers as we should have done'.[43] The course of events which swiftly ensued, however, was not shaped by the policies of Bush or other Western nations but by the dramatic actions of the opponents of the coup. The key role was played by Boris Yeltsin, whose authority had grown since his walk-out from the Communist Party in July 1990 and his election as president of Russia in May 1991 and who on 19 August climbed up on to a tank, denounced the coup plotters and won the support of the crowd which gathered round and of many segments of the army and KGB. Faced with demonstrations against the coup leaders in Leningrad and other cities as well as in Moscow and with significant sections of the armed forces refusing to obey orders,

the coup quickly collapsed, and on 21 August ᴄ
restored to power and the coup leaders arrested,
Pugo, who committed suicide.

Even in comparison to the whole series of extrᴀ
dramatic events of the preceding few years, the failed ᴄ
an event of momentous significance. It doomed any prosᵧ ᴇof
a return to power of conservative hardliners. The particular
future shape of the Soviet Union remained to be determined, but
as statues of Lenin were taken down in Vilnius, Kiev and
elsewhere, as Gorbachev resigned as General Secretary of the
Communist Party and the activities of the Communist Party in
Russia were banned and its property nationalized, the path of the
Soviet Union away from Communism was unquestioned. The
implications for East–West relations were clear: whereas
hesitancy to declare an end to the Cold War had been in order
up to this point, the failed coup of 18–21 August 1991 marked
the end of the Cold War.

As the Soviet Union began to disintegrate, with declarations of
independence by one republic after another, Bush was willing to
take some bolder steps. The United States recognized the
independence of Latvia, Lithuania and Estonia, though not until
recognition had been offered by other nations and assurance
received of Gorbachev's acceptance of the independence of the
Baltic states. Regarding nuclear disarmament, on 27 September
1991 Bush announced wide-scale unilateral reductions, with the
return to the United States of nuclear artillery shells from
Europe, the removal of tactical nuclear weapons from American
ships and the abandonment of plans to deploy mobile MX and
Midgetman missiles. Moreover, the round-the-clock alert status
of B-52s, which had existed since the 1950s, was brought to an
end. As the *New York Times* put it, 'These nuclear bombers, poised
on never-ending "strip-alert", have long given relentless, roaring
evidence of the potential for nuclear annihilation'.[44] In response,
Gorbachev announced similar reductions. The Soviet decision to
begin to dismantle tactical nuclear weapons was particularly
welcome to the United States, since, despite reassurances
regarding security of control over nuclear weapons, the United
States was deeply worried that tactical nuclear weapons could fall
into the hands of a rogue general, unstable republican leader or
terrorist group. Indeed, one of Bush's main interests in
continuing to prop up Gorbachev as Soviet leader was to ensure
that Soviet nuclear weapons would be under secure control.

,onically, Bush became the first American president endangered by a weak Soviet Union rather than by a strong Soviet Union.

Gorbachev, although restored to power, found that his authority was inexorably diminished in the autumn of 1991 and that separatist moves within the Soviet republics grew stronger. In these circumstances American support of Gorbachev was of little avail. Gorbachev's hapless efforts to revive the Union Treaty came to nothing. In November, his former right-hand man, Shevardnadze, returned as Foreign Minister, but developments had gone too far for any individual to reverse or to control them. On 1 December a referendum on independence in Ukraine, following the parliamentary vote for independence in June, produced an outcome of over 80 per cent in favour. Gorbachev's prospects of holding together the Soviet Union grew dim. On 8 December Yeltsin held a secret meeting with the leaders of the Ukraine and Byelorussia, at which they agreed to form a Commonwealth of Independent States to replace the Soviet Union. Extraordinarily, Yeltsin telephoned Bush to inform him of this development even before he informed Gorbachev. The other republics, except Georgia, decided to join the Commonwealth of Independent States, which had such weak powers, however, that effectively the republics had decided to dissolve the Soviet Union and to become independent nations.

Gorbachev accepted the failure of his attempts to hold together the Soviet Union. The major concern of the United States was to ensure a peaceful transfer of power and orderly control over the Soviet nuclear arsenal. American leaders were strongly sympathetic to Gorbachev and Shevardnadze and uneasy over the succession in Russia of Yeltsin, despite the latter's commitment to market reforms and to democracy. 'American officials do not like Mr Yeltsin', it was reported. 'In part it is because he is less predictable than Mr Gorbachev and in part because he did in their friends'.[45] One American official described Yeltsin as 'gruff, feisty and rude. "Even though we like his politics more", he said, "we still find the man off-putting" '.[46] On a visit by Baker to Moscow in December, however, clear assurances were given of an orderly transfer of control over nuclear weapons from Gorbachev to Yeltsin and the peaceful transfer of power from the Soviet government to the successor states. Despite lingering unease over Yeltsin and reluctance to accept the demise of the regime of Gorbachev and Shevardnadze, with which the American leadership felt comfortable, the United States rejoiced with incredulity when on 25 December the red flag was taken down from above the Kremlin and replaced by the Russian national flag. At midnight on 31 December the Soviet Union was officially dissolved.

With his quiet caution, then, George Bush emerged as the triumphant victor in whose administration the *coup de grâce* was delivered to the ideology and the power centre which had terrified and mortally threatened the United States for decades. The American victory had clearly come about largely as a result of developments within the Soviet Union rather than as the direct consequence of American policies. How far, however, can Bush's policies be judged to have helped to the extent possible to move events towards the favourable outcome? Strobe Talbott concludes that 'Bush has been the perfect US president for this phase of East–West relations. He is a gracious winner, skilful at assuring Gorbachev that he won't be sorry for all the concessions he has made'.[47] Sidney Blumenthal, however, describes Bush's role scathingly, writing that 'not being boastful' was a limited contribution and that otherwise Bush's policies were vacuous.[48]

In fact, the skills in personal diplomacy by Bush and Secretary of State Baker made a significant contribution on such issues as reassuring the Soviets that a reunited Germany within NATO was not a serious threat to their security, or in proceeding slowly and delicately on such an issue as the independence of the Baltic states. On issues of economic aid, Bush seems more open to the criticism that his policies were negative, parsimonious and unimaginative. Bush was, however, responding to political and economic realities in the United States. Even at the height of Gorbymania, there was little support for sending American tax dollars to the Soviet Union. Facing a budget deficit rising to gargantuan heights, Bush took a major political gamble in June 1990 when he broke his 1988 campaign pledge and agreed to tax increases. With budgetary constraints made even more serious with the disastrous Savings and Loans collapse, the American taxpayer was in no mood to extend massive largesse to the Soviet Union, while Bush became vulnerable to the charge that he was a foreign-policy president who paid more attention to the plight of people abroad than to people at home. In 1947 Truman needed to present the Soviet threat in dire terms in order to win Congressional support for the Marshall Plan, at a time when the United States had easily the strongest economy in the world. By

1990–1 the Communist bogey was disappearing and with it went the main incentive for the extension of large-scale foreign aid. Bush's lack of practical measures to assist Gorbachev arose not only from failures in imaginative powers with regard to the new realities of the international scene but also from a sound grasp of the realities of domestic American politics and the state of the American economy.

17

THE LESSONS OF HISTORY

In 1917 Woodrow Wilson led the United States into a great crusade for the triumph of democracy. To Wilson's horror, not only did his quest for the expansion of democracy meet with failure but also the United States found itself confronted with the competing ideology of Communism, which was proclaimed as the true path to peace, prosperity and social justice. Even more frightening, the proponents of Communism appeared to be ruthless fanatics who had seized power in a large and potentially very powerful country (i.e. Russia), and they vociferously proclaimed that the laws of history predetermined the inevitable collapse of capitalism and the triumph of Communism. Furthermore, the new leaders of Russia declared their dedication to hasten this historical process by undermining foreign governments in order to bring closer the day of the allegedly inevitable downfall of capitalist governments everywhere. From Woodrow Wilson's presidency onwards, therefore, every American administration faced the challenge of trying to demonstrate the superiority of the American ideology of democracy and free-enterprise capitalism and holding back the forward march of Communism. By 1991, the contest appeared to be over, with a massive ideological loss of confidence on the Soviet side, while an increasing number of countries embraced democracy and a market economy. What lessons, then, does history offer with regard to the conduct of American policy towards the Soviet Union since 1917? Some commentators suggest that throughout most of the period since 1917 the United States exaggerated the threat from Soviet Communism. Robert V. Daniels, for instance, concludes that Americans 'misread the meanings of Marxism on World Revolutions and they failed to appreciate the changes in the relations between theory and practice under the Soviet regime'.[1] Charles Bohlen, although broadly a hardliner towards the Soviet Union, wrote that 'The main Bolshevik aim is to protect the Soviet system, above all in Russia and secondarily in the satellite countries. The extension of Communism to other areas is a theoretical and secondary goal'.[2] To an even greater extent revisionist historians argue that the US government misinterpreted Soviet policy. Stalin's triumph over Trotsky in the 1920s, it is argued, resulted in a Soviet government dedicated to the goal of Socialism in One Country rather than the promotion of world revolution, while the expansion into Eastern Europe after the Second World War is explained in terms of the defensive objective of protecting Soviet security rather than the offensive aim of expanding Communism as far as possible. As for Communist revolutions in Third World countries, most commentators agree that Vietnam was a misreading on America's part of what was in its origins an anti-colonial struggle as a step in the unending expansion of Communism directed by the Kremlin. In other Third World countries, such as in Central America, as McGeorge Bundy, National Security Adviser in the 1960s, has written, 'Much of US concern about turmoil in those small countries is absurdly exaggerated. Central America is not the soft underbelly of American security'.[3]

Yet, on the basis of the evidence available to successive American administrations the threat of expansion by the Soviet Union was quite reasonably viewed as very real and very grave. The Soviet Union persistently advanced the claim to represent a new form of political and social organization which had universal significance, the true cause of all mankind, a system which would create not only higher economic productivity but a 'new man', the 'new Soviet man'. The Soviet Union regarded itself as the *avant-garde* of world revolution, and the special political, economic and ideological appeal of the Soviet Union throughout the world posed a serious threat to the United States, especially in the Depression years of the 1930s, in the time of turmoil following the Second World War and in Third World countries throughout the post-war era. Communist parties in industrialized countries stirred up social unrest, which was the forerunner to a Soviet take-over in Czechoslovakia in 1948, for example, and which threatened to occur in Western European countries in a similar manner. In the Third World the Soviet Union endeavoured to exploit the demise of colonial empires to promote its interests in such countries as Egypt, Indonesia, Ghana and the Congo. Khrushchev proclaimed that 'wars of national liberation' were the wave of the future, and such struggles by Communist guerrilla forces were assured of the support of the Soviet Union, which, Khrushchev boasted, would bury the West. Brezhnev took the opportunity to take advantage of conflicts in Ethiopia, Somalia and Angola and to expand influence in such Middle East countries as Syria and Iraq. In Latin America, Castro's triumph in Cuba not only brought a Soviet-backed Communist regime within a hundred miles of America's shores but threatened to lead to Communist expansion into other Central and Latin American countries.

In the inter-war years the Soviets placed emphasis on ideological warfare, when the Soviet Union was weak and when capitalism was harsh and appeared more liable to collapse. The amelioration of capitalism since the New Deal made such a collapse seem less likely, while a post-Second World War depression, which was widely predicted in the Soviet Union and deeply dreaded in the West, did not occur. Hence, from the late 1940s the Soviet Union became as much a military adversary as an ideological opponent. The extraordinary strength of the Red Army, which was demonstrated against Germany in the Second World War, and the imposition of Communist regimes in Eastern Europe in the Red Army's wake, left the United States in fear of expansion of Communism by means of the massive conventional armed force of the Soviet Union. In 1949 there was added the shock of the development of a Soviet atomic bomb, which, combined with the advanced state of Soviet technology in rocketry, gave the Soviet Union the capability by the end of the 1950s to strike targets in the United States with nuclear missiles against which the United States had no defence, and in succeeding decades the Soviet nuclear arsenal grew to gargantuan proportions.

In the light of all of these Soviet proclamations and actions, only the most imprudent American government could have optimistically operated on the basis that the Soviets were indulging in ideological hot air and had only defensive intentions. The very reasonable consensus within American government and public opinion was that the Soviet Union had expansionist ambitions which posed a grave ideological and military threat to the United States. The main issues in the debate regarding America's policy towards the Soviet Union do not concern, therefore, whether there was a Soviet threat but how the United States dealt with the Soviet threat.

In response to the perceived Soviet threat the United States considered three possible policy options: isolationism; the overthrow of Communism by force; the containment of Soviet expansion. An examination of America's policy regarding these options provides the most significant of the lessons of history which can be derived from the study of American policy towards the Soviet Union.

Isolationism was a not unreasonable policy for the United States in the 1920s. Communism had not extended beyond the Soviet Union (except to Outer Mongolia) and the Soviet Union was weak and backward, so that the threat to the United States from Soviet Communism was remote. American emergence from isolationism was, of course, not related to the policies of the Soviet Union but to the aggression of the Axis powers and Japan. Drawn to the centre of the world stage in the Second World War, any American inclination to withdraw to the sidelines into isolationism after the war was offset by the new threat from the Soviet Union. American's rejection of isolationism and American embracement of internationalism was embodied in Senator Arthur Vandenberg, a leading isolationist in the 1930s who became one of the main architects of America's policy of international commitment in the late 1940s.

Nevertheless, not far below the surface in many quarters in American society there was lingering support for isolationism. Senator Robert Taft officially proclaimed his rejection of the isolationist position to which he fervently adhered in the 1930s, but Taft's views on such matters as the withdrawal of American troops from Europe and reliance on the nuclear deterrent were not dissimilar from the Fortress America concept which had wide support in America in the 1930s. Indeed, throughout the Cold War period proposals to withdraw American troops from Europe by Taft in the 1950s, by Senator Mike Mansfield in the 1960s and 1970s, and by Senator Sam Nunn in the 1980s hit a responsive chord throughout parts of America which caused serious worries to various administrations in defeating such proposals in Congress. The British were always afraid that isolationism had deep underlying appeal in the United States and that a long-term confrontation with the Soviet Union would test American patience too far, producing a reversion to isolationism. Yet, although isolationism was far from dead in the post-war period, the solid consensus within every administration from Truman to Bush, supported by a clear majority in public opinion, was that the lessons of the 1930s demonstrated the folly of isolationism and that in the confrontation with Soviet Communism the United States must not repeat the mistakes of the 1930s but must be fully engaged internationally in the contest against Communism.

The second policy option, the overthrow of Communism by force, was rarely employed and, when attempted, met with disastrous failure on a number of occasions and with only limited success on others. Intervention in Russia in 1918–20 provided the most conspicuous illustration of disastrous failure as a result of resort to force. Even at a time when the Bolshevik grip on power seemed weak and it appeared possible, as Winston Churchill put it, to crush the snake in its nest, the size of Russia and the xenophobia of its people produced the outcome that not only did Allied armed intervention fail militarily but the interference of foreigners on the White side enabled the Reds to rally the sentiments of Russian patriotism behind them and assisted them in the consolidation of their power. Similarly in North Korea in 1950 Douglas MacArthur's troops were regarded by the North Korean people as foreign conquerors rather than liberators from Communism, thereby assisting Kim Il Sung to consolidate his power in North Korea. Even more so, the landing of American-backed Cuban exiles at the Bay of Pigs in 1961 did not trigger off an anti-Communist uprising in Cuba but enabled Castro to gain the support of the mass of Cubans who resented yet another armed intervention by the Yankees.

The use of force had more success in CIA covert operations in the Eisenhower era and in the application of the Reagan Doctrine in the 1980s. The regimes which the CIA played a role in bringing down, in Iran in 1953 and in Guatemala in 1954, were left-wing nationalistic governments rather than Soviet satellites, and they were replaced by rather reprehensible governments which, especially in the case of Iran, did not serve America's interests in the long term. Nevertheless, an argument can be advanced that to some extent the crude use of American force by means of CIA covert operations played a part in keeping these nations out of the Soviet orbit. American support in the 1980s to rebels against Communist governments in Afghanistan, Angola and Nicaragua had some measure of success. In Afghanistan, American aid to the mujahedin insurgents hastened the withdrawal of Soviet troops, serving, as Bruce Jentleson puts it, as 'the best example of coercive diplomacy for foreign policy restraint' in the Reagan era.[4] In Angola, American aid to anti-Communist rebels brought negotiations a little closer. In Nicaragua, aid to the Contras was an important element in bringing pressure on the Sandinista government to agree to a settlement which included free elections, resulting in the fall of the Sandinistas from power in the elections in 1990. Hence, to a limited extent, at the margins of the US-Soviet conflict, the use of force to bring down Communist regimes had a measure of success. At the centre of the confrontation in Europe, however, and in US policy towards China, the violent overthrow of Communism was manifestly not a feasible option. American impotence in the face of the Soviet crushing of the East German revolt in 1953, the Hungarian revolution in 1956 and the Prague Spring in 1968 plainly illustrated that any attempt to overthrow Communist regimes in the satellite countries, let alone in the Soviet Union itself, carried a grave risk of initiating a Third World War, a risk which the United States was not prepared to take. The one American attempt at forcible roll-back of Communism, in North Korea in 1950, made clear the potentially disastrous consequences of the use of American force to overthrow a Communist regime whose survival was deemed vital to the security of either of the two major Communist powers, China and the Soviet Union.

Between the extremes of isolationism on the one side and violent overthrow of Communism on the other the United States steered a middle course – containment. The policy was given its intellectual underpinnings by George Kennan in his advocacy of 'a long-term, patient but firm and vigilant containment of Russian expansionist tendencies', in the belief that 'Soviet power, like the capitalist world of its conception, bears within it the seeds of its own decay'.[5] In 1989 George Bush stated that

The grand strategy of the West during the post-war period has been based on the concept of containment: checking the Soviet Union's expansionist aims, in the hope that the Soviet Union would one day be forced to confront its internal contradictions. The ferment in the Soviet Union today affirms the wisdom of this strategy.[6]

Does the history of American policy towards the Soviet Union teach the lesson that Bush was correct in claiming the success of containment?

The greatest difficulty for Americans in pursuing containment was the exercise of patience, which has never been an American virtue. America's historical experience in foreign policy has been to remain aloof from foreign entanglements and, when reluctantly drawn in, as in the Spanish–American War in 1898, the First World War in 1917 and the Second World War in 1941, to use massive force to achieve as rapid and total a victory as possible and to seek then to withdraw. Containment involved a long-term international commitment with restraint in the use of force and with little prospect of a dynamic, complete victory in the short term. In his 'X' article in *Foreign Affairs* in 1947 Kennan suggested that a period of ten to fifteen years of patient, firm containment might be necessary. In fact, more than forty years of containment were required before it seemed to produce results in the late 1980s. The exercise of firm patience over such a long period was a new experience for Americans, and, not surprisingly, expressions of impatience burst out, such as the demand for 'liberation' and 'roll-back of Communism' in the Republican platform in 1952. James Burnham complained that 'Containment has no goal. . . . Its inner law is: let history do it'.[7] Kennan, however, as John Lewis Gaddis has pointed out, argued that 'the most effective means of modifying Soviet behaviour lay in a combination of deterrents and inducements'.[8] Kennan argued in his 'X' article that

> The possibilities for American policy are by no means limited to holding the line and hoping for the best. It is entirely possible for the United States to influence by its actions the internal developments, both within Russia and throughout the entire Communist movement, by which Russian policy is largely determined.

Yet Kennan's prescription for action in this regard was very limited. He suggested a 'modest measure of informational activity which this government can conduct in the Soviet Union and elsewhere' and (much more important in Kennan's view) the power of America's example,

> the degree to which the United States can create among the peoples of the world generally the impression of a country which knows what it wants, which is coping successfully with the problems of its internal life and with the responsibilities of a World Power, and which has the spiritual vitality capable

of holding its own among the major ideological currents of the time'.[9]

This was not a formula to satisfy the desire of impatient Americans who wished to smash the Reds and to do so quickly. Within the pursuit of containment, therefore, there evolved the search for methods to hasten the historical process of bringing about evolution within Communist countries. Kennan had used the analogy of building a dam which would contain Soviet expansion and force the water pressing against it to back up into rivers, streams and rivulets deep within Soviet society. Americans found it unsatisfactory simply to let the water on the other side of the dam take its own course. They wished, as it were, to stir up the water on the Soviet side of the dam and to direct its flow as it flooded through Soviet society. In other words, successive American administrations sought to devise means to bring about change within the Soviet bloc rather than simply to build a barrier of containment and, as Burnham had objected, leave the rest to history.

In the quest for such means, differing views emerged on whether the most effective means were methods of amelioration such as the development of personal contacts through summit meetings, cultural agreements, educational exchanges, trade and so on, or methods of coercion such as economic warfare, radio propaganda and military pressure. Hawks were inclined towards the latter approach, while doves were inclined towards the former. The United States swithered between one approach and the other in its relations with the Soviet Union.

With regard to summit meetings, Franklin Roosevelt's wartime conferences, especially Yalta, added to American prejudice against summit meetings, which had existed since Woodrow Wilson's experience at Versailles. Hence, for the first decade of the Cold War, from Potsdam in 1945 to Geneva in 1955, no meetings took place between American and Soviet leaders, despite the urgent pleas of Winston Churchill, for example, to Truman and Eisenhower to engage in talks with Stalin or, even more so, with Stalin's successors after 1953. As Roger Makins, British ambassador to the United States from 1953 to 1956, noted:

Generally speaking, Americans are afraid of international conferences. The belief that simple-minded Americans are no match for the subtle and unscrupulous foreigners and that their representatives are bound to be outsmarted dies hard. They are afraid of being trapped by the Russians, or of being led down the garden path by their allies, or both.[10]

Summit meetings acquired an association with appeasement and betrayal, as at Munich and Yalta, causing American presidents such as Eisenhower to be very careful before agreeing to a summit. Eisenhower's meetings with Khrushchev in 1955 and 1959 produced a sense of better personal relations between the leaders – the 'spirit of Geneva' in 1955 and the 'spirit of Camp David' in 1959 – but this proved to be ephemeral. Eisenhower's final summit at Paris in 1960 and Kennedy's meeting with Khrushchev in Vienna in 1961 appeared to be counter-productive. The conclusion was reached, therefore, especially in professional diplomatic circles, that summit meetings had serious disadvantages and few advantages. It was argued that it was a dangerous illusion to imagine that personal meetings with Soviet leaders ameliorated their policies or attitudes. On the other hand, it was felt that Soviet leaders cynically used such meetings to their advantage. The result, it was suggested, was that public expectations were raised by the drama of a summit meeting, only to be deflated, with the final outcome worsened rather than improved relations.

With Johnson's meeting with Kosygin in 1967, however, and especially with Nixon's three summits with Brezhnev between 1972 and 1974, it came to be felt, particularly by American public opinion, that meetings between leaders helped to humanize the US–Soviet relationship and to enable Soviet leaders to gain a better understanding of the American viewpoint and thereby to reduce the risk of war. Ford's meeting with Brezhnev at Vladivostok in 1974 and Carter's meeting with Brezhnev at Vienna in 1979, however, made little impact when détente was breaking down. But summit meetings made a great impact when the new détente developed in the mid-1980s, especially Reagan's four summit meetings with Gorbachev between 1985 and 1988 and to some extent Bush's meetings with Gorbachev in 1989, 1990 and 1991.

In addition to meetings of leaders, Americans hoped to influence Soviet policy by meetings of government officials and legislators at lower levels. The visits of a steady stream of American Congressmen to the Soviet Union from the 1960s onwards and increasingly frequent visits by officials from such departments as Commerce, Labor, State and Defense undoubtedly had an effect in helping to personalise relationships and to put matters into better perspective. It might be suggested, however, that the importance of the impact of such personal contacts was in ratio to the degree of receptiveness on the other side. This was illustrated, for example, in meetings of foreign ministers. During the long tenure of Soviet Foreign Minister Andrei Gromyko (1957–85) meetings with US Secretaries of State from Dulles to Shultz appeared to make little impression on the stoney-faced Gromyko, whereas the close personal relations which were developed with Eduard Shevardnadze by Shultz and by James Baker clearly had considerable influence on Soviet thinking.

Aside from meetings of political figures, it was hoped that non-political communication through cultural agreements, educational exchanges, sports meetings, tourist visits and a wide range of people-to-people contacts could bring down barriers and help to defuse the ideological conflict. Such hopes were viewed with scepticism by most US administrations, who repeatedly employed the instrument of cutting off such exchanges as a very ineffective mark of protest against Soviet foreign policy, such as the boycott of the 1980 Moscow Olympic Games as a protest over Soviet intervention in Afghanistan. Among large numbers of ordinary American people, however, the concept of citizen diplomacy aroused great enthusiasm as the panacea to solve the conflict between the United States and the Soviet Union. If only people from both sides could come together instead of politicians, such enthusiasts felt, common humanity would overwhelm national and ideological differences. Meetings of ordinary American and Soviet people which took place suggested that there was truth in such an idea. In the 1920s Americans who were engaged in famine relief in the Soviet Union or who travelled as tourists found that the Russian people were naturally friendly and generally well-disposed to Americans, so that such encounters no doubt made some impact on the closed society of the Soviet Union. From the 1930s to the 1950s, however, the Soviet Union was a firmly closed society which allowed very few opportunities for travel or other contacts by Americans, except for selected left-wing delegations or malleable and somewhat naïve groups who were shepherded on carefully conducted tours and manipulated for Soviet propaganda purposes. The Cultural Agreement of 1958 made possible cultural, scientific and educational exchanges which brought a degree of exposure of American culture and American values to the Soviet Union. But the Cultural Agreement, with its biennial renewal negotiations, was bureaucratic in its mechanisms and limited in its extent.

On the Soviet side, fear of defection added another element to the already rigorous process of screening Soviet citizens who were permitted to travel to the United States under such programmes. Soviet students who came to the United States, for example, were much older than American students, more commonly in science and technology rather than in humanities or social science and faithful Communist Party members who were ideologically sound. Apart from exchanges under the Cultural Agreement, American cities, universities, labour unions and other such institutions succeeded in arranging visits and exchanges with Soviet counterparts. Yet, as the sister cities programme illustrated, for example, American visitors to the Soviet cities enjoyed the friendly contacts with Soviet civic counterparts, but Soviet delegations to the United States were carefully selected safe party members who offered a stonewall defence of Soviet policies and were less likely to be seduced by the attractions of the American way of life.

In the late 1980s the range of contacts became a flood, and in the age of *glasnost* the impact on Soviet society was manifestly deep. In the process of bringing about an amelioration of Soviet society in the years since the Bolshevik Revolution, however, the role of people-to-people contacts has, despite the great goodwill and enthusiasm of many eager American participants, been very limited. The numbers permitted to engage in exchanges were so small and Soviet control so tight that truly meaningful people-to-people exchanges could only follow a change in the overall US–Soviet relationship rather than act as an agent of such change to any significant degree.

A matter of more substance than personal contacts was the issue of trade. American policy with regard to trade and economic relations with the Soviet Union provides good illustrations of the differing approaches of amelioration and coercion as the more effective means of influencing the Soviet Union. Supporters of the former approach argued that a growth in Soviet prosperity was in the West's interest and should be assisted, since increasing prosperity would modify and liberalize the Soviet Union in its economic structure, ideology and foreign policy. The British on various occasions put forward this view to the Americans. At Bermuda in 1953, for example, Churchill urged Eisenhower that 'Time and patience must play their part. "Encourage, encourage", Sir Winston repeated, "the world by stimulating prosperity and getting people in a more agreeable state of mind. That will see us through to a period of time when a much better scene will come" '.[11] Sir David Eccles, the President of the British Board of Trade, put it even more explicitly in 1958, stating that 'The free world should not hesitate to increase its trade with the Communists, for it is through trading and growing rich that we have the best chance of making them prefer a quiet life'.[12] Armand Hammer, in his endless travels to the Soviet Union and frequent meetings with Soviet leaders, emphasized the potential for better understanding between the two countries which wider economic contacts would bring. Stalin's daughter, Svetlana Alliluyeva, who defected from the Soviet Union and married an American before returning later to the Soviet Union, similarly emphasized the mutual economic and political advantages in the development of US–Soviet trade. 'Throughout history trade has opened doors', she wrote in 1984:

> What the world needs now is for economists and bankers to get together and map out the best way to increase economic co-operation. . . . The market in Russia is enormous and could save western countries from inflation, from unem-ployment, from poverty. But you will never get that from military advisers meeting in Geneva talking about warheads and missiles'.[13]

Against this liberal approach, several counter-arguments were advanced. A stronger Soviet economy, it was argued, would not make the Soviets more peace-loving but would add to potential Soviet military strength and make the Soviets more dangerous. As for economic benefits, the Soviets had little interest in the development of extensive long-term trade, it was suggested, but planned to create an autarkic economy, importing single items of Western models to copy and to manufacture in the Soviet Union rather than to develop an ongoing trading relationship which would benefit Western economies. Instead of assisting the Soviet economy, it was argued, the United States should pursue a policy of denial to the Soviets in order to weaken their potential military strength and their consequent ability to engage in foreign adventurism. Trade should be engaged in, it was suggested, only on a conditional basis, namely on the condition of Soviet concessions with respect to their political behaviour.

THE LESSONS OF HISTORY

The lesson from the history of trade as a factor in US–Soviet relations appears to be that, whether pursued in an ameliorative or in a coercive manner, trade made only a marginal impact on the overall relationship. The volume of trade was extremely small. In 1979, for example, US exports to the Soviet Union amounted to $3.6 billion and imports from the Soviet Union $1.5 billion, but in 1980 this figure fell to $873 million in exports and $430 million in imports. On the Soviet side, foreign trade was a tiny part of GNP – 1 per cent in 1982, for example. Any economic benefits to the United States from trade with the Soviet Union were inconsequential, with the possible exception of the value of grain sales. On the Soviet side, imports from the United States were of small importance, with the significant exception of grain and certain items of high technology. The hopes of increased trade following US diplomatic recognition in 1933 never materialized, and the dreams of the vast, untapped market in such a huge, undeveloped country remained as illusory as the myth of the China market in an earlier time.

As for an extension of personal contacts through trade, it was indeed the case that more extensive and in many ways more meaningful personal contacts were made through trade than any other means. While most foreign factories were confiscated in 1918–19, some American companies were exempted, such as Singer Sewing Machine and International Harvester, and both through business contacts and training programmes many American firms, from Ford in the 1920s to Pepsi-Cola in the 1970s and MacDonald's in the 1980s, were involved in extensive dealings in the Soviet Union. Such contacts undoubtedly were of some value in humanizing the US–Soviet relationship. Yet the idea that trade is conducive to goodwill and peace was by no means fully proved. An enthusiast such as Armand Hammer was the exception rather than the rule. For large numbers of American companies, the experience of dealing with the Soviet governmental trade monopoly proved to be exasperating, frustrating and unprofitable.

The record suggests that growing prosperity in the Soviet Union – and the desire for even greater growth – did indeed have an ameliorative effect. In 1920 the American vice-consul in Vladivostok, Otto Glaman, surveying what he regarded as a very bleak situation after the defeat of Admiral Kolchak and the Whites, concluded that

There only remains the possibility of waiting for a slow evolution of the Soviet government, with perhaps many vicissitudes, from its present Communism, or inimical character, to a form which must resolve itself out of better economic conditions ... when the laws of nature will re-adjust themselves and the individual will claim property rights in direct proportion to the wealth created by his own endeavors and for the benefit of his own fire-side. And this, in my estimation, will be a long process of evolution.[14]

By the 1980s this process of evolution had reached the stage where rising expectations within Soviet society created an irrepressible demand for reform of the economic system. Moreover, Gorbachev concluded that political liberalization was an essential concomitant of successful economic liberalization, so that *perestroika* could not succeed without *glasnost* and democratization. The argument that economic development in the Soviet Union had in the long run a liberalizing effect seems, therefore, to be supported by the evidence of the historical record. The evidence does not sustain, however, the view that trade or any other economic link with the United States, or with Western countries, played a role of great significance in this evolution of the Soviet economy and society.

Similarly, US efforts to employ trade as a coercive instrument in relations were largely ineffective. In its mildest form, trade was used as an important part of the web of interconnecting links in the grand design of détente as envisaged by Henry Kissinger. Nixon and Kissinger hoped that the Soviets would develop a degree of dependency on such economic exchanges and would therefore desist from behaviour in foreign policy which would endanger their loss. Soviet foreign policy in the 1970s, however, with interference in Third World Countries and a continuing strategic arms build-up, suggested that trade incentives did not provide the United States with sufficient leverage on Soviet policy to act as an effective tool of restraint.

To an even lesser extent was trade an effective instrument as a means of trying to alter Soviet domestic policies. Its effect tended, if anything, to be counter-productive. As has been said, the Jackson amendment, for example, far from bringing about an increase in the number of Soviet Jews who were allowed to emigrate by the threat of withholding Congressional endorsement of the trade agreement which had been negotiated in 1972,

THE LESSONS OF HISTORY

led to a sharp reduction in the number of Jews who were allowed
to emigrate and to Soviet rejection of the entire trade package. It
was clear that the Soviets were not willing to bow to such blatant
coercion as the Jackson amendment implied.

Moreover, US policies which were geared to deny the Soviets
access to certain goods, either from the United States or from
other countries, largely ended in failure and perhaps did as
much damage to America's relations with her allies as to the
Soviet economy. The bitter disputes with allies, especially Britain,
over the Battle Act and COCOM controls in the 1950s and over
the Siberian gas pipeline in the early 1980s provided
considerably more benefit to the Soviet Union in the form of
divisions within NATO than any harm to the Soviets by denial of
required materials. With the lack of agreement among the allies
on the goods which should not be exported to the Soviet bloc, the
Soviets were in most instances able to obtain from other countries
any goods which the United States refused to export, so that
American trade restrictions simply provided advantages to
business competitors in other countries. Moreover, even with
regard to strategic items which all the allies agreed should be
withheld, the Soviets gained by military and industrial espionage
a great deal of what was denied by trade. Decades of denial in the
post-Second World War period did not appear to retard Soviet
military capability significantly. The efforts made by the United
States in its policies on export control proved to be an exercise in
futility, making little dent on the Soviet economy or military
potential and providing the Soviet government with a scapegoat
for the slow pace of post-war Soviet economic recovery. The
lesson of history regarding US attempts to squeeze the Soviet
economy as a means to influence behaviour is clear: the Soviets
repulsed the stick as much as the carrot as a mechanism to
determine their conduct at home or abroad, and Soviet ability to
do so was greatly enhanced by the lack of multilateral
co-operation in support of US efforts.

One of the most direct means employed by the United States
to bring about change in the Soviet Union was radio
broadcasting. From 1947 the Voice of America (VOA) beamed
out broadcasts in Russian and in later years added Ukrainian,
Latvian, Lithuanian, Estonian, Georgian, Armenian and
Azerbeijani to the parts of the Soviet Union where these
languages were spoken. While VOA aired news and other
programmes about America, news and programmes about the

Soviet Union were provided by Radio Liberation, which began broadcasting in 1953, changing its name in 1959 to Radio Liberty. Radio Liberty expanded its range of languages from Russian to other languages of the Soviet Union and in addition to its transmitter in Spain for broadcasts to the western parts of the Soviet Union, Radio Liberty broadcast to Siberia and eastern Central Asia from a transmitter in Taiwan until 1971. The impact of all of these hours of broadcasting on Soviet opinion is difficult to judge. Radio Liberty was jammed until 1989 and VOA was jammed from 1948 to 1963, from 1968 to 1973 and from 1980 to 1985. Hence, listeners in the Soviet Union to Radio Liberty and for many years to VOA needed to strain their ears and to maintain their patience in listening to broadcasts accompanied by howling and screeching noises from interference from jamming. Nevertheless, there were periods when VOA was free from jamming – from 1963 to 1968, from 1973 to 1980 and since 1985. Moreover, jamming covered towns and cities but not rural areas, so that VOA and Radio Liberty were clearly audible in the *dachas* of city dwellers and on their car radios in journeys in the country as well as always in the homes of country dwellers. Also, for a few hours at twilight each day, for technical reasons, jamming could not operate. Hence, the possibility existed for Soviet listeners to hear VOA and Radio Liberty. How many took the opportunity and how far they believed what they heard, however, are matters which are very difficult to judge.

VOA and Radio Liberty assessed that between 10 and 15 per cent of the population of the Soviet Union listened to their broadcasts, but assessments are based on information from visitors and emigrés who were by definition untypical and not very reliable sources. With regard to the credibility of these radio stations to Soviet listeners, VOA in the early Cold War years and Radio Liberation in its years before it changed its name to Radio Liberty tended to be stridently anti-Communistic, which may have given a propagandistic tone which reduced their credibility. VOA was suspect as the official voice of the US government, while Radio Liberty had the hallmark of a radio station operated by Soviet emigres of a very conservative mindset. Moreover, Radio Liberty's credibility suffered the severe blow of the exposure in 1971 of its source of funding – it had claimed to be funded by patriotic Americans, but, as *Ramparts* magazine revealed in 1971, it was in fact financed by the CIA through dummy foundations. Some critics, such as Senator J. William Fulbright, questioned the value of these radio transmissions, especially Radio Liberty, suggesting that they were relics of the early Cold War and needless irritations to the Soviet Union. The Soviets, however, unquestionably regarded them as more than irritants, spending very large sums on jamming and protesting vigorously through diplomatic channels against this alleged interference in Soviet internal affairs. Radio Liberty provided to Soviet citizens who listened much fuller and more accurate information on events within their homeland than they could possibly obtain from Soviet sources and, passed along the grapevine, this information percolated through wide segments of Soviet public opinion. Radio Liberty, for example, obtained through the CIA one of the earliest copies of Khrushchev's secret speech denouncing Stalin in 1956 and broadcast it to the Soviet Union. The more factual tone adopted by VOA from 1953 and by Radio Liberty from 1959 enhanced their credibility, and VOA even showed willingness to give unfavourable reports about the United States, such as broadcasts on Watergate in 1973–4. Hence, while sweeping claims for the influence of radio broadcasting cannot be made, its impact, which is impossible to measure accurately, must certainly not be discounted.

The issues of trade and radio broadcasting also related to another direct means employed by the United States to influence events in the Soviet Union, namely through the East European satellites. American policy-makers were much more optimistic regarding the possibilities of bringing about change in such countries as Poland and Czechoslovakia than within the Soviet Union, but the far-reaching, long-term American goal was not only to detach the satellites from the Soviet Union but also thereby to bring about change ultimately within the Soviet Union itself. Hence, the United States tried to encourage centrifugal forces within the Soviet bloc. In trade policies, the Eisenhower, Kennedy and Johnson administrations were eager to distinguish between trade with the Soviet Union and trade with East European countries, strongly encouraging the latter in order to pull the economic interest of Eastern Europe away from the tight control of Moscow. But these efforts were frustrated by objections in Congress to trade with Communist countries, and especially due to concerns that goods with potential military value might be transferred to the Soviet Union if exported to Eastern Europe. In the 1970s, when trade with Eastern Europe did expand, the political goals of encouraging polycentrism were overshadowed by the economic difficulties of the massive debts which such countries as Poland ran up. Hence, trade and economic policy, which had seemed the most promising means of detaching the satellites from the Soviet Union and influencing their development, proved to be a disappointment in this regard.

Radio broadcasting was more successful in making a much clearer impact in Eastern Europe than in the Soviet Union. Radio Free Europe (RFE), which put on news and programmes about Eastern Europe – in the same way that Radio Liberty served the Soviet Union, and which like Radio Liberty was a CIA-financed station run largely by emigrés – broadcast from Munich to the countries of Eastern Europe from 1950 onwards. The claims of RFE and VOA regarding the number of listeners in Eastern European countries are much higher than the estimated number of listeners to VOA and Radio Liberty in the Soviet Union, up to 40 per cent in Poland, 30 per cent in Czechoslovakia and 20 per cent in Hungary, Bulgaria and Romania. In some countries, such as Hungary and Romania, there was no jamming, while in Poland, despite jamming, RFE claimed that during the martial law crisis in 1981 the percentage of listeners was as high as 70 per cent. Moreover, the United States was able to issue literature in Eastern Europe through the United States Information Agency to a much greater extent than in the Soviet Union. The first efforts at distribution of literature, from balloons which dropped 300 million leaflets over Eastern Europe between 1953 and 1956, was discontinued when radio broadcasting became firmly established. Perhaps more influential was the dissemination of literature in an official manner through United States Information Agency (USIA) offices in American embassies. Moreover, USIA grants to groups and to individuals to enable them to attend conferences and, where possible, to travel to the United States, exercised influence. Among prominent leaders in the Hungarian reforms in 1989–90, for example, Imre Pozgay, Gyula Ham, Arpad Goncz and Janos Kis were recipients of USIA grants to travel to America.

The realistic objective of American policy in Eastern Europe was to encourage the assertion of nationalism and a relative degree of independence among East European countries. In the 1940s, the United States accepted its inability to save Eastern Europe from the Red Army, and proposals to force Soviet withdrawal from Eastern Europe by the threat of atomic attack in the period of American atomic monopoly from 1945 to 1949 were never seriously considered. The East German revolt in 1953 and especially the Hungarian revolution in 1956 made plain the hopelessness of attempts to overthrow Soviet rule by force. American policy was therefore not directed to stirring up revolt in Eastern Europe but to working quietly to preserve the national identity of the satellite states. The model which was encouraged was Yugoslavia. Competent American diplomats in Belgrade in 1948 appreciated the significance of Tito's break with Stalin, so that American aid to Yugoslavia began with Export–Import Bank loans in 1948–9 and Marshall Plan surpluses in 1950, while Truman in 1951 declared Yugoslavia vital to American security and eligible for American military assistance. American policy in Eastern Europe aimed to encourage Titoism in Poland, Czechoslovakia and other such countries in the hope that nationalistic Communism would be a first step to even greater freedom. As John F. Kennedy put it, 'Without having a nuclear war we want to permit what Thomas Jefferson called "the disease of liberty" to be caught in areas which are now held by the Communists'.[15]

Alexander Dubcek's movement for Communism with a human face raised the hopes of reform Communism spreading throughout Europe and ultimately liberalizing the Soviet Union itself. The brutal crushing of the Prague Spring, however, and American impotence in the face of the unqualified declaration of the Brezhnev Doctrine made it seem that American power to bring about change in Eastern Europe was almost completely lacking. When Solidarity was suppressed in the early 1980s, with Polish martial law as a substitute for Soviet tanks, the United States could do little more than protest from the sidelines, with little hope or expectation of bringing about significant change in Eastern Europe.

George Shultz pinpointed the key element in the East European situation in testimony to the Senate Foreign Relations Committee in January 1985, stating that 'We hope to see the day when the Soviet Union learns to think anew of its own security in terms compatible with the freedom, security and independence of its neighbors'.[16] Within a much shorter space of time than Shultz anticipated such was precisely the conclusion reached in the 'new political thinking' of Soviet foreign policy. By 1989, as political scientist Bennet Korvig put it, 'in the Kremlin's "new political thinking" the East European empire was increasingly seen as economically burdensome, politically intractable and strategically superfluous'.[17] The crucial Soviet reassessment of its policy in Eastern Europe in the late 1980s was brought about by a wide variety of internal and external factors, but American protests and pressure over the years had clearly played their part in convincing the Soviet government that its security was better served by freeing the satellites rather than by retaining unreliable vassals in Eastern Europe which brought hostility, suspicion and opprobrium from the West.

American pressure on the Soviet Union was also applied by US policy towards China. Just as the United States tacitly encouraged Titoism in Eastern Europe, so the United States from the early 1970s encouraged nationalistic Communism in China and used the China card against the Soviet Union. The United States quite reasonably viewed the Communist victory in China in 1949 and the Sino-Soviet treaty of 1950 as the most ominous development in the expansion of Communism since the Bolshevik Revolution in 1917. As evidence surfaced of the Sino-Soviet split in the 1950s and 1960s, however, American policy towards China remained rigidly dogmatic, until the Nixon administration in the early 1970s changed policy and exploited China's hostility towards the Soviet Union to America's advantage. Significantly, while US–Soviet relations in the 1970s and 1980s were characterized by wild gyrations from détente to hostility, US–Chinese relations in the same period remained very steady, as the United States and China developed a quasi-alliance against the Soviet Union. Even after the Tiananmen Square massacre in 1989, Bush kept channels open to the Chinese. The lesson of history of US relations with China as an instrument in dealing with the Soviet Union seems very clear: American policy towards China in the 1950s and 1960s seems extremely foolish, helping to prolong the last vestiges of Sino-Soviet co-operation, while American policy since the early 1970s demonstrated pragmatic, statesmanlike implementation of a shrewd policy of utilizing China as a very important barrier to Soviet expansion.

The final, and most significant, way in which the United States tried to bring about change within the Soviet Union was through military deterrence. Primarily, American military power constituted the military barrier of containment. Secondarily, however, it was suggested by some US policy-makers, such as Richard Pipes, NSC adviser on Soviet affairs in 1981–2, that the competition of the arms race would overstrain the Soviet economy and build up internal tensions which might even culminate in revolt and in the overthrow of the Soviet regime. To some extent the arms competition did indeed build up such tensions within the Soviet Union, especially in the mid-1980s when fear of the economic strain of an escalating round of arms increases was an important motive for the Soviet change to Gorbachev's policies of reform. On the other hand, even in the Gorbachev years up to 1988 the Soviet Union continued to modernize its strategic nuclear forces and to increase its defence spending. Moreover, over the longer span of history the lesson seems clear that the Soviet Union was prepared to endure almost any hardship which the regime imposed in the diversion of resources from civilian to military development.

Furthermore, the economic strain on the American side became difficult to sustain. The folly of extremely large defence increases combined with tax cuts in the Reagan years upset the balance in America between the short-term security afforded by large defence forces and the longer-term security afforded by rising economic productivity and income, exacerbating America's growing fundamental weakness in economic competition with nations with low military budgets, particularly Japan and West Germany. The strain on the Soviet economy from the competition of the arms race, then, was unquestionably a factor of significance in the exercise of American pressure to induce change within the Soviet Union, but the evidence would not support the simplistic conclusion that the Soviets were squeezed by this competition until they could go on no longer and consequently changed course.

America's military strength, however, was designed primarily to serve as a deterrent against Soviet expansion and thereby to act as the substantial barrier of containment. Since this deterrent, above all the nuclear deterrent, kept the peace and, for the most part, prevented Soviet expansion for more than forty years, the argument can be advanced that the nuclear deterrent, for all its risks, succeeded in its task. Throughout history two nations with such fundamental disagreements between them have virtually always resorted to warfare. As William Hyland put it, 'Never before has such a broad and deep struggle lasted so long without a major war'.[18] The claim can therefore be advanced that the existence of nuclear weapons kept the peace.

The peace which was preserved, however, with a nuclear sword of Damocles hanging over the superpowers and the world, was so precarious that it would be an unwise lesson to learn from the history of US–Soviet relations that nuclear deterrence guarantees the maintenance of peace. Such episodes as the Cuban missile crisis brought a catastrophic war perilously close. Furthermore, since the United States was unwilling to build up a defensive capability to match the Soviets in conventional strength, on the grounds that such a defence effort would destroy the economies of the United States and Western Europe, reliance was placed on the nuclear deterrent to prevent a Soviet conventional attack, with the United States reserving the option to engage in the first use of nuclear weapons.

It can be argued that this strategy was successful, preserving peace and defending Western interests at an affordable cost and allowing the United States and Western Europe to build up prosperous economies behind a secure defensive shield. On the other hand, it was morally dubious for the West to refuse to expand the necessary resources to build up a sufficiently strong conventional defence and instead to rely on the threat of the first use of nuclear weapons. Moreover, the credibility of such a strategy, which was fundamentally based on a bluff or a mutual suicide pact, was open to question. There was always doubt whether a president of the United States would in fact order a nuclear strike against the Soviet Union in the event of a Soviet conventional attack in Europe, with the certain knowledge that such an American strike would bring a retaliatory Soviet nuclear strike against the United States.

The United States sought to lower the risk of war and the cost of defence through the process of arms control. The history of US–Soviet relations teaches a discouraging lesson on the prospects for the attainment of significant arms control agreements between hostile powers. With its deep distrust of the Soviet Union, a basic US policy was the maintenance of sufficient military strength. This raised, however, the issue of what constituted sufficiency and whether the attainment of what the United States regarded as sufficiency constituted a level of armed force which the Soviets regarded as threatening. Harry Truman wrote that 'In our dealings with the Russians we had learned that we had to lead from strength and that any show of weakness was fatal'.[19] But American policies to assure US security inevitably increased Soviet insecurity, producing the inexorable upward spiral of the arms race, with US technological advances rapidly matched by the Soviet Union. The attainment of absolute security, such as by SDI, was shown to be a mirage. Yet the alternative approach of arms control, attempting to gain mutual agreement on equal levels of armaments at as low a level as possible, proved to be theoretically possible but in practice unworkable.

The SALT treaties came as close as the United States and the Soviet Union could achieve in managing the arms race, but the inadequacies of the SALT process were obvious. From the United Nations disarmament talks in the 1950s to the bilateral US–Soviet meetings in the 1970s and 1980s, arms control proved to be a hopeless task. Its complexities were so vast, the fear of cheating so great and the opportunities for propaganda so tempting that the years of talks involving mountains of paper in endless proposals and discussions accomplished virtually nothing by way of substantial results. Talks helped to a minor extent in reducing tensions, but the United States placed too much emphasis on arms control talks and arms control agreements as indicators of the overall state of US–Soviet relations. As Richard Nixon put it, 'If we are to reduce the risks and dangers of war, we must leapfrog the sterile arms control debate and go to the heart of the problem: the political differences between the United States and the Soviet Union'.[20] Significant arms control agreements, such as the INF treaty in 1987 and CFE in 1990, occurred only after a change had taken place in the overall US–Soviet relationship. Certainly, as the INF treaty illustrated, attainment of a meaningful arms reduction agreement added substantially to the continuation of the process of improved overall relations. For the most part, however, the history of US–Soviet relations teaches that disarmament follows from rather than leads to more cordial political relations.

Throughout the Cold War, then, the United States placed little faith in disarmament or negotiation but relied on military force, especially nuclear weapons, to deter Soviet aggression. The American deterrent was powerless to prevent Communist expansion in such countries as Cuba, Vietnam, Angola and Afghanistan. For the most part, however, especially in the key central area in Europe, deterrence was successful. As Winston Churchill had suggested, 'It may be that we shall, by a process of sublime irony, have reached a stage where safety will be the steady shield of terror, and survival the twin brother of annihilation'.[21] But US–Soviet relations offers a very dangerous model for the preservation of peace between two hostile powers, which would not be recommended for universal application.

In the pursuit of containment, then, the United States relatively effectively deterred Soviet expansion, but efforts to bring about change within the Soviet Union by such means as economic measures and radio propaganda tended to illustrate the limits of American power with respect to internal developments within the Soviet Union. Yet, while American policy towards the Soviet Union was in many respects determined by rational considerations of calculated efforts to contain the Soviet Union and to exercise whatever means were available to the United States to shape the course of Soviet policy, in other respects, as an important theme of this book has brought out, American policy was determined by much less rational considerations, which arose from within American domestic life, such as psychological attitudes, political calculations and economic interests. Hence, the conduct of American policy towards the Soviet Union was in practice much more confused and complex than a tidy analysis of the elements involved in the policies of containment might suggest.

American policy towards the Soviet Union has been characterized by volatility, with frequent swings in the mood of a mercurial public opinion from euphoria to hostility. These capricious and impetuous tendencies have risen partly from impatience and frustration but even more so from sensitivity to an assault on America's ideology. American adherence to the ideals of freedom are deeper and more complex than a straightforward rational belief in the virtues of political democracy and free-enterprise capitalism. The less tangible element is the emotional belief in such ideals, which are linked to American nationalism, patriotism and a civic religion which binds together a very diverse people throughout a vast land. Thus there has been a deep-seated, explosive emotionalism in American attitudes to Communism and towards the Soviet Union. The ideological struggle has been viewed in Manichean terms of righteousness against evil, with the United States the new Jerusalem and the Soviet Union the enemy at the gate. However, as Lord Inverchapel, British ambassador to the Soviet Union in 1947, for example, noted, 'Americans are congenitally incapable of appreciating that others may not share their unshakeable belief in their own righteousness'.[22] As a result there has been a strong tendency in America to interpret events in conspiratorial terms. From the time of the Pilgrim Fathers America has had a strong sense of mission, and since the days of the Salem witch trials there has been an accompanying tendency to search for the enemy within who is conspiring with the devil against the goals of America's holy mission. These attitudes were expressed in secular terms in Woodrow Wilson's crusade to make the world safe for democracy and in America's encounter with the Bolshevik conspiracy to spread Communism world-wide. These emotional attitudes rendered impossible the pursuit of a wholly rational policy on the part of the United States. Hence, for example, the United States did not distinguish between social revolutions and radical nationalism on the one hand and Soviet expansion on the other hand. Henry Wallace warned in 1947 that 'every reactionary government and every strutting dictator will be able to hoist the anti-Communist skull and bones and demand that the American people rush to his aid'.[23] The truth of Wallace's prediction was amply illustrated by American support for a host of unsavoury regimes from Diem in Vietnam to Somoza in Nicaragua and Pinochet in Chile. There was perhaps some logic in the view, as Jeanne Kirkpatrick argued, that a right-wing totalitarian government was susceptible to eventual change and should therefore be supported against a potentially totalitarian Communist regime which was much less likely to be removed from power. Such an argument, however, was largely an attempt to rationalize a policy which arose from prejudice, fear and ignorance. A pragmatic policy of accommodation with left-wing reformers, such as the regime in Guatemala in 1954 or with nationalistic Communists such as in Vietnam in the 1960s, was ruled out by the assumption that such movements were part of the Communist conspiracy directed from Moscow and which would ultimately undermine and destroy the American way of life.

The distortion of American adherence to freedom into chauvinistic self-idealization was aggravated by the strain on civil liberties imposed by the long ideological conflict. Throughout history wars have inevitably brought restrictions on civil liberties, and the ideological conflict with Communism, especially the Cold War since 1945, proved to be no exception. In 1917 Woodrow Wilson had agonized over the dangers to civil liberties which entry into the First World War would bring. In the 1920s and 1930s isolationists such as Hiram Johnson warned that in fighting for democracy abroad America might lose democracy at home. Although such extremes as the loss of democracy in war did not materialize, the isolationists had a strong case in warning of the jeopardy to civil liberties at home in the event of a long conflict abroad. For example, the very long conflict with Communism increased the pressure to conform within American society. Paradoxically, as America engaged in global evangelism in the cause of freedom, freedom became more restricted at home, sometimes grotesquely, as in the McCarthy era, sometimes more subtly, as, for example, in the manner in which secrecy became more prevalent in the national security state which developed after the Second World War. As frequently occurred in war, super-patriotism was able to usurp liberty, as freedom became associated with the flag and with anti-Communism as much as with the basic rights of the individual.

In such an atmosphere foreign policy was not conducted by a process of cold, dispassionate calculation of American interests. With regard to policy towards China, for example, the United States in the 1950s and 1960s acted against its national interests and failed to exploit the Sino-Soviet split largely because emotions over China went so deep, with McCarthyist accusations of disloyalty on the part of State Department officials. In foreign economic policy, attempts to use trade as an instrument of influence on Soviet policy came to grief as American policy-makers found it impossible to win support in Congress for relatively subtle policies such as trade with Eastern Europe in order to detach satellites from Moscow when this confronted simplistic, emotional counter-arguments that trade with Communists was, as Eisenhower's Defense Secretary Charles Wilson put it, like 'selling firearms to the Indians'.[24] Indeed, Philip Funigiello concludes that with regard to America's trade policy towards the Soviet Union the United States

> imposed and has persisted in trade controls and economic sanctions more for domestic political purposes and to give a visible, if meaningless, demonstration to the rest of the world that the United States disapproves of Moscow's aggressive international behaviour, than either to bring down the Soviet Union or cause it to modify its actions.[25]

Yet, along with deep emotional anti-Communism, Americans are psychologically attuned to optimism. Consequently, American foreign policy towards the Soviet Union has experienced swings of mood to naïve euphoria as well as to aggressive hostility. The image of the Soviet Union in the United States has been primarily negative, represented in spy novels and comic strips as well as in newspapers in terms of brutality, amorality and blood-thirsty fanaticism, embodied in the cold cruelty of Stalin or the aggressive, threatening bullying of Khrushchev. But at times a more positive image has been projected of the Soviet people as friendly, such as Soviet soldiers laughing and dancing when they met American troops at the Elbe in 1945, or in wartime images of Stalin as a benign Uncle Joe, while Khrushchev on his visit to the United States in 1959 was projected on American television as a cuddly, jovial teddy bear figure rather than the awesome Russian grizzly bear whom Americans feared. American public opinion was wont, as a result, to engage in mood swings in the direction of hope of friendly relations such as at the time of diplomatic recognition in 1933 or as a result of the Second World War co-operation with 'our great Soviet ally' or when Nixon and Brezhnev achieved accord in 1972. Yet, since such episodes of cordiality proved to be short-lived, the American temperament was inclined to a swing to the other extreme, with bitter feelings of deception and betrayal being added to the fundamental distrust of the Soviets. A figure such as William Bullitt, with his optimistic enthusiasm in 1919 and in 1933 to bring about US–Soviet harmony and with his later extreme vituperation in his condemnation of the Soviet Union, embodied American attitudes in this regard. Hence, the psychological temperament of the American people has contributed to wilder gyrations in American policy towards the Soviet Union than was the case, for example, in British or West German relations with the Soviet Union.

The vicissitudes of domestic politics was a further factor of great significance in shaping American policy towards the Soviet Union. The hallowed principle that 'politics stops at the water's edge' was more honoured in the breach than in the observance. The commonly cited golden age of bipartisanship in 1947–8, with Senator Arthur Vandenberg as its patron saint, was unusual and short-lived. Bipartisanship in those years arose not simply from the triumph of disinterested, patriotic concern for the national welfare over concern for party advantage but also because the Republicans fully expected to win the elections of 1948 and to continue the policies which they had helped to frame in 1947–8 when they controlled Congress but not the presidency. Once the Republicans suffered the surprising defeat in the presidential and Congressional elections of 1948, bipartisanship in foreign policy soon evaporated, to be replaced by a desire to exploit any issue, in foreign or domestic policy, for party advantage.

The natural tendency in a democracy is for the party in opposition to advocate the opposite policy to the party in power for the sake of differentiation from the party in office as much as on account of the merits of the policy involved. Such a tendency has had a significant impact on the development of America's policy towards the Soviet Union. In 1952 Eisenhower essentially agreed with the Truman policy of containment, but in the 1952 campaign he was willing to utilize the criticisms of containment and advocacy of liberation by Dulles and others in order to help the Republican cause in the election. In 1960 Kennedy attacked the missile gap which he alleged that Republican defence policy had allowed, and although once elected Kennedy discovered that no such missile gap existed, he nevertheless engaged in a major build-up of America's missile forces, partly to maintain the credibility of his 1960 campaign accusations. In 1976 Carter, seeking to differentiate himself from Kissinger's foreign policy, emphasized the issue of human rights, which he implemented in his presidency in a manner which seriously affected relations with the Soviet Union. In 1980 Reagan, realizing that his strongest political card lay in the perception of Carter as weak, campaigned for huge increases in defence expenditure which, when implemented by Reagan in office, seriously disturbed the Soviets. In 1984 the warning to Reagan by his pollsters that his aggressive anti-Soviet stance was his most serious political liability in his bid for re-election was one reason for Reagan's change in attitude towards the Soviet Union. In 1988 Bush's desire to distance himself from Reagan and to establish himself as his own man was one reason for his initial caution and relative coolness towards Gorbachev in the first months of his presidency.

Alexis De Tocqueville wrote in his classic study, *Democracy in America*, that 'it is especially in the conduct of their foreign relations that democracies appear to me decidedly inferior to other governments'.[26] The merits of democratic control over foreign policy weighed against the drawbacks of potential manipulation of national security issues in demagogic fashion for partisan gain can be debated as a theoretical issue. The historical reality is very clear, however, that in the pursuit of America's foreign policy towards the Soviet Union, domestic political considerations have, for better or for worse, been determining influences of very considerable importance.

A final source of domestic influence on foreign policy lay in economic interests. It was not a Marxist but a Republican former general, Dwight D. Eisenhower, who warned of the role of the military-industrial complex. The importance of lobbyists for arms manufacturers, aircraft corporations and other such defence-related industries is difficult to measure and by its nature almost impossible to document. Of clearer historical significance has been the relationship between policies of defence expenditure and the health of the American economy through the Cold War years. The traumatic effect of the Depression in the 1930s created a broad political consensus in favour of whatever policies would save America from a repetition of such economic woes. The paradox of economic recovery brought about by the Second World War led to the acceptance of military expenditure as the pump-priming boost which would sustain the health of the American economy. The dispersal of defence industries throughout virtually every Congressional district in the country and the large amount of Federal money which was brought, for example, to universities by research contracts, together with the economic benefits to local communities, developed, as Eisenhower pointed out, a vast web of interconnected interests in support of a continuation of high levels of defence expenditure.

By the 1980s America's economic difficulties of huge budget and trade deficits, to which high levels of defence spending were an important contributory factor, made evident the imprudence of American neglect of the economic underpinnings of its security. Nevertheless, the economics of military Keynesianism which sustained America's economy since the end of the Depression pulled America out of the recession of the early 1980s, so that whatever doubts were raised on the wisdom of a matter such as SDI, its economic impact in high-tech industries was so great that this played a significant role in quietening opposition to SDI. Thus, while the activities of individual lobbyists should not be exaggerated, the pervasive influence of economic interests in helping to determine American policy is clear. A wide community had been created which had a stake in perceiving the other superpower as a mortal threat or at least in prejudicing American policy towards a worst-case analysis in its assessment of the Soviet Union.

Even with dispassionate calculation, America's ability to influence policy within the Soviet Union was quite limited. Since America's policy was shaped not only by careful calculations of American interest but also by the disruptive impact of domestic factors, America's ability to influence the Soviet Union was even more limited. Hence, to a much greater extent than American interference from the Western side of the barrier of containment, change came about in the Soviet Union as a result of the inner dynamics of Soviet society, combined in the 1980s with the extraordinary personality of Mikhail Gorbachev. By the mid-1980s Gorbachev realized that the Soviet economy had stagnated, with negligible growth rates since the late 1970s and poorer prospects with falling oil prices, so that without economic reform and greater access to Western technology and capital the Soviet Union would fall hopelessly behind the United States, Western Europe, Japan and even China. Also, Gorbachev knew that the revolution in mass communications, rather than simply the impact of the Voice of America and Radio Liberty, rendered futile the Stalinist strategy of isolation and ideological indoctrination. Moreover, Gorbachev sensed the seething unrest growing in the Soviet Union in an age of rising expectations, but his safety valve of *glasnost* did not simply defuse pent-up frustrations but also created demands for even greater change. At the same time, Gorbachev accepted that the old thinking in foreign policy had united the world's major powers against Moscow and saddled the Soviet Union with unsustainable burdens in subsidies to foreign clients. Finally, Gorbachev appreciated that Communism had lost its appeal world-wide and was perceived as the road to stagnation and repression. Initially, Gorbachev's goal was to reform Communism and to attain *perestroika* and *glasnost* in Eastern Europe as well as in the Soviet Union and to give Communism with a human face a renewed universal appeal. But as the pace of change ran much deeper than Gorbachev could control, he was prepared in the late 1980s to ride the waves to wherever they took him in the direction of Soviet federalism, democratization and economic liberalization.

One element which Kennan emphasized in 1947 as a crucial factor in leading the Soviet Union towards the direction which it eventually took under Gorbachev in the late 1980s was America's example. How far can it be argued that the United States succeeded in offering the example of a successful society which pursued effective foreign and domestic policies and maintained its spiritual vitality and thereby influenced the Soviet Union to change direction? In certain respects such a claim may legitimately be advanced. American democracy manifestly held deeper popular acceptance and offered greater prospects for freedom and prosperity than Soviet Communism. In foreign policy the United States demonstrated statesmanlike leadership in defending and fostering democracy in Western Europe, and the successful development of democracy, unity and economic growth in Western Europe made a profound impact on Eastern Europe. As James Baker put it in a speech in Berlin in December 1989, 'The success of this great European experiment, perhaps more than any other factor, has caused Eastern Europe to recognize that people as well as nations cooperate more productively when they are free to choose'.[27] In domestic policy a steadily growing American economy in the post-Second World War era provided abundance for the great majority of the American people, while the worst abuses of racialism were reformed by civil rights legislation.

In other respects, however, the American record was so tarnished that it reduced the extent to which American example led to ultimate American triumph in the ideological conflict of the twentieth century. In foreign policy, compromise of American principle was rampant not only in support of vicious, undemocratic regimes in the name of anti-Communism, culminating in the catastrophe of Vietnam, but also in flagrant violation of international law such as in CIA covert operations or in support for the Contras in Nicaragua, which, however useful as a source of pressure to induce the Sandinistas to come to terms, brought death to thousands of innocent Nicaraguans in action which was condemned by the World Court as unlawful. In domestic policy, the minority who did not enjoy the general prosperity were neglected as America declared surrender in the War on Poverty and pursued taxation polices in the 1980s which widened the gap between the rich and poor. Affordable health care and an adequate public school education were unavailable to an increasingly large number of the population, while politics became trivialized and corrupted by the excessive costs of political campaigns which involved vast sums of money for debasing television commercials and ended with elections in which, even at the presidential level, scarcely half the electorate voted.

The collapse of Soviet Communism was due more to its own inner failings than to the influence of the American example. The Bolshevik model established by Lenin and made hideous by Stalin was not susceptible to transformation into a more benign form of Communism. The result of the ideological conflict of the twentieth century does not necessarily prove the superiority of

American-style democracy and capitalism over Communism. As Robert Litell, an American novelist who frequently visited the Soviet Union, wrote in 1990:

> Capitalism has outlasted Communism and is now standing over its open grave.... We should shed a tear.... For behind the original Communist idea was a vision for the human race that was essentially optimistic and idealistic: the notion that men and women could function by giving to society the best of their abilities and in return receive from that society what they needed to live decently. So we should shed a tear for ourselves: for burying that notion; for coming to the conclusion that the human race does not have this potential; for deciding that a society functions more efficiently when it appeals to the profit motive, to greed, to the instinct that transforms ordinary people into consumers, then pushes them to accumulate for the sake of accumulation.[28]

Yet history must deal with the past that was, not with the past that might have been. The US competition was not with a civilized brand of democratic Communism but with Soviet totalitarian Communism with aggressive expansionist tendencies. What lessons does history teach regarding American policy in its contest with Soviet Communism?

For the most part America's policy towards the Soviet Union teaches a lesson of successful implementation of a sensible policy. In the face of a threatening ideology and aggressive military power the United States held its ground resolutely until the other side yielded. On the whole, containment was successful. The United States was shown to have relatively limited ability to alter the course of events within the Soviet Union but was for the most part able to hold back Soviet expansion and to induce the Soviet Union ultimately to turn inward and to reform. Nuclear deterrence involved horrifying risks, but in a world in which nuclear weapons could not be disinvented, it preserved the peace and defended Western interests at an affordable cost. The domestic influences on American policy and the shabbiness of many aspects of internal policy significantly tarnished the American model of democratic statesmanship, but, given the inherent imperfections of any system of government, American democracy showed itself to possess the basic spiritual strength to sustain it through the long contest with the Soviet Union.

Yet, while the lessons of success may be learned, they should not be misapplied. Throughout the history of the United States, the American record in learning from history is poor. The United States has tended to misapply the lessons from one historical experience to a later historical experience. In the 1960s, for example, the United States pursued policies of the rejection of appeasement which were applicable to the 1930s but which were inappropriate in the very different situation of Vietnam. In the later stages of the Cold War, the United States pursued policies of a vast military build-up which were applicable to the late 1940s and early 1950s but which were less appropriate to the situation of the early 1980s when economic competition with Japan and Western Europe had emerged as a major new challenge to the United States. If America is to learn from history, the United States needs to learn not to misapply policies appropriate to the containment of Soviet Communism in a later conflict to which such policies may be quite inappropriate.

Moreover, the United States should learn the lesson that the successful application of containment towards the Soviet Union involved a patient acceptance of the limits of American power. The United States should therefore resist the temptation to go beyond containment and to embark upon a quest for universal conversion to American-style democracy and free-enterprise capitalism. While American encouragement of democracy is desirable, it is neither vital to America's interests nor within the reaches of American power to bring about the downfall of non-democratic systems of government world-wide in the manner in which American policy helped to bring down Soviet Communism. Rather than aspiring to achieve universal conversion to American-style democracy and free-enterprise capitalism, the United States should seek, first, a world safe for pluralism, with co-existence between differing political, religious, social and economic systems, and second, concentration on reform of democracy at home, striving to remedy the flaws which mar the American model of democracy and detract from America's ability to present as fully as possible an example of a nation in which social justice and political freedom flourish and which other nations would seek to emulate.

NOTES

PREFACE

1 *San Francisco Chronicle*, 5 June 1990.
2 John L. Gaddis, *The Long Peace: Inquiries into the History of the Cold War*, New York, Oxford University Press, 1987, p. 8.
3 Geir Lundestad, 'Moralism, Presentism, Exceptionalism, Provincialism and Other Extravagances in American Writing on the Early Cold War Years, *Diplomatic History*, 1989, vol. 13, no. 4, p. 545.
4 Peter G. Boyle, 'The British Foreign Office View of Soviet–American Relations, 1945–46', *Diplomatic History*, 1979, vol. 13, no. 3, pp. 307–20; idem., 'The British Foreign Office and American Foreign Policy, 1947–48', *Journal of American Studies*, 1982, vol. 16, no. 3, pp. 373–89; idem., 'Britain, America and the Transition from Economic to Military Assistance 1948–51', *Journal of Contemporary History*, 1987, vol. 22, no. 3, pp. 521–38; idem. (ed.) *The Churchill-Eisenhower Correspondence, 1953–55*, Chapel Hill, University of North Carolina Press, 1990.

1 THE RUSSIAN REVOLUTION AND AMERICAN INTERVENTION, 1917–20

1 Arthur S. Link (ed.) *The Papers of Woodrow Wilson*, Princeton, Princeton University Press, 1966– (continuing), vol. 41, p. 525.
2 *Foreign Relations of the United States, 1918, Russia*, Washington, US Government Printing Office, 1931, vol. 1, p. 6.
3 Link (ed.) *The Papers of Woodrow Wilson*, vol. 41, p. 524.
4 George F. Kennan, *Russia and the West under Lenin and Stalin*, Boston, Little, Brown, 1960, p. 28.
5 Link (ed.) *The Papers of Woodrow Wilson*, vol. 45, p. 537.
6 Petrograd to Foreign Office, 18 February 1918, FO371/3284/30368, Public Record Office, Kew, Surrey.
7 Washington to Foreign Office, 22 December 1917, FO371/3020/242611, PRO.
8 *FRUS, 1918, Russia*, vol. 1, p. 235.
9 Link (ed.) *The Papers of Woodrow Wilson*, vol. 48, pp. 641–2.

10 *Congressional Record*, 65 Congress, 3 Session, 1919, p. 1167.
11 Ibid., p. 2263.
12 Beatrice Farnsworth, *William C. Bullitt and the Soviet Union*, Bloomington, Indiana University Press, 1967, pp. 53–4.
13 Robert K. Murray, *Red Scare*, Minneapolis, University of Minnesota Press, 1955, p. 23.
14 Michael J. Heale, *American Anti-Communism: Combating the Enemy Within*, Baltimore, Johns Hopkins University Press, 1990, p. 51.
15 William Preston, *Aliens and Dissenters: Federal Repression of Dissenters, 1903–33*, Cambridge, Mass., Harvard University Press, 1963, p. 89.
16 *Congressional Record*, 65 Congress, 3 Session, 1919, p. 2266.

2 THE ERA OF NON-RECOGNITION, 1921–33

1 Julius H. Barnes, 'The Facts that Answer Trotsky', *Nation's Business*, November 1925, vol. XIII, p. 20.
2 George W. Baer (ed.) *A Question of Trust: The Origins of Soviet–American Relations: The Memoirs of Loy W. Henderson*, Stanford, Hoover Institution Press, 1986, p. 149.
3 John L. Gaddis, *Russia, the Soviet Union and the United States*, 2nd. edn, New York, McGraw-Hill, 1990, p. 113.
4 Baer (ed.) *A Question of Trust*, pp. 165–6.
5 *Business Week*, 14 May 1930, p. 12. Quoted, Joan Hoff-Wilson, *Ideology and Economics: US Relations with the Soviet Union, 1918–33*, Columbia, University of Missouri Press, 1976, p. 83.
6 *New York Times*, 24 April 1932.
7 Minute by Laurence Collier, 1 May 1933, FO371/17263/N3231, Public Record Office, Kew, Surrey.
8 Maurice Isserman, 'Three Generations: Historians View American Communism', *Labor History*, 1985, vol. 26, no. 4, p. 540.
9 George F. Kennan, *Russia and the West under Lenin and Stalin*, Boston, Little, Brown, 1960, p. 185.
10 Arthur M. Schlesinger, Jr, *The Crisis of the Old Order, 1919–1933*, Boston, Houghton, Mifflin, 1957, p. 222.
11 *FRUS, Russia, 1933–39*, p. 14.

3 FROM RECOGNITION TO WORLD WAR, 1933–41

1 Noel Charles to Laurence Collier, 23 April 1934, FO371/18324/N 2592, Public Record Office, Kew, Surrey.
2 George W. Baer (ed.) *A Question of Trust: The Origins of Soviet–American Relations: The Memoirs of Loy W. Henderson*, Stanford, Hoover Institution Press, 1986, p. 294.
3 Edward M. Bennett, *Franklin D. Roosevelt and the Search for Security: Soviet–American Relations, 1933–39*, Wilmington, Scholarly Resources, p. 39.
4 Eugene Lyons, 'To Tell or Not to Tell', *Harper's*, June 1935, vol. CLXXI, p. 110.

5 *The New Republic*, 14 June 1943, pp. 800–1. Quoted, William L. O'Neill, *A Better World: The Great Schism: Stalinism and the American Intellectuals*, New York, Simon & Schuster, 1982, p. 20.
6 *New York Herald Tribune*, 22 April 1939. Quoted, Thomas R. Maddux, *Years of Estrangement: American Relations with the Soviet Union, 1933–41*, Tallahasee, University Presses of Florida, 1980, p. 100.
7 *Omaha Morning World Herald*, 25 August, 1939. Quoted, Maddux, *Years of Estrangement*, pp. 103–4.
8 A.F.H. Wiggan to Laurence Collier, 15 December 1934, FO371/18324/N 6955, PRO.
9 Robert Dallek, *Franklin D. Roosevelt and American Foreign Policy, 1932–45*, New York, Oxford University Press, 1979, p. 208.
10 *New York Times*, 24 July 1941.
11 John Wheeler-Bennett (ed.) *Action This Day: Working with Churchill*, London, Macmillan, 1968, p. 89.
12 Hamilton Fish Radio Broadcast, 30 June 1941. Quoted, Maddux, *Years of Estrangement*, p. 148.

4 WARTIME ALLIANCE, 1941–5

1 Linda R. Killen, *The Soviet Union and the United States*, Boston, Twayne, 1989, p. 39.
2 Charles E. Bohlen, *Witness to History, 1929–69*, New York, W.W. Norton, p. 123.
3 H.W. Brands, *Inside the Cold War: Loy Henderson and the Rise of an American Empire*, New York, Oxford University Press, 1991, p. 111.
4 Martin Gilbert, *Road to Victory, 1941–45*, vol. 7 of *Winston S. Churchill*, London, Heinemann, 1986, p. 181.
5 *Life*, 29 March 1943, vol. 14, no. 13, p. 23.
6 Milovan Djilas, *Conversations with Stalin*, New York, Harcourt, Brace & World, 1962, p. 114.
7 Warren Kimball (ed.) *Churchill and Roosevelt: The Complete Correspondence*, Princeton, Princeton University Press, 1984, vol. 3, p. 501.
8 *Foreign Relations of the United States: The Conferences at Malta and Yalta, 1945*, Washington, US Government Printing Office, 1955, p. 973.
9 Diane S. Clemens, *Yalta*, New York, Oxford University Press, 1970, p. 198.
10 Adam Ulam, *The Rivals: America and Russia since the Second World War*, New York, Viking, 1971, p. 18.
11 Denna F. Fleming, *The Cold War and Its Origins, 1917–60*, Garden City, Doubleday, 1961, p. 215.
12 Harry S. Truman, *Year of Decisions, 1945*, vol. 1 of *The Memoirs of Harry S. Truman*, Garden City, New York, Doubleday, 1955, p. 85.
13 Walter Isaacson and Evan Thomas, *The Wise Men: Six Friends and the World They Made: Acheson, Bohlen, Harriman, Kennan, Lovett, McCloy*, New York, Simon & Schuster, 1986, p. 267.
14 *Foreign Relations of the United States: The Conference of Berlin (The*

Potsdam Conference), 1945, Washington, US Government Printing Office, 1960, I, 218–19.
15 Isaacson and Thomas, *The Wise Men*, p. 283.
16 Kimball (ed.) *Churchill and Roosevelt*, vol. 3, p. 605.
17 *FRUS, Potsdam*, I, 92.
18 'Yanks meet Reds', Yorkshire Television, 7 May 1985.
19 Martin J. Sherwin, *A World Destroyed: The Atomic Bomb and the Grand Alliance*, New York, Alfred A. Knopf, 1975, p. 112.
20 Barton J. Bernstein, 'Marshall, Truman and the Decision to Drop the Bomb', *International Security*, 1991–2, vol. 16, no. 3, p. 219.
21 J. Samuel Walker, 'The Decision to Drop the Bomb: A Historiographical Update', *Diplomatic History*, 1990, vol. 14, no. 1, p. 111.

5 THE ORIGINS OF THE COLD WAR, 1945–50

1 Arthur M. Schlesinger, Jr, 'The Origins of the Cold War', *Foreign Affairs*, 1967, vol. 46, no. 1, p. 23.
2 Herbert Feis, *From Trust to Terror, 1945–50*, New York, W.W. Norton, 1970, p. 36.
3 Dean Acheson, *Present at the Creation: My Years in the State Department*, New York, W.W. Norton, 1969, p. 197.
4 James F. Byrnes, *All in One Lifetime*, New York, Harper & Row, 1958, p. 326.
5 Harry S. Truman, *Year of Decisions, 1945*, vol. 1 of *The Memoirs of Harry S. Truman*, Garden City, Doubleday, 1955, p. 493.
6 X, 'The Sources of Soviet Conduct', *Foreign Affairs*, 1947, vol. 25, no. 4, p. 575.
7 *Public Papers of the Presidents of the United States, Harry S. Truman, 1947*, Washington, US Government Printing Office, 1963, pp. 178–9.
8 Gar Alperovitz, *Cold War Essays*, Garden City, New York, Doubleday, 1966, p. 44.
9 *New York Times*, 13 September 1946. Quoted J. Samuel Walker, *Henry A. Wallace and American Foreign Policy*, Westport, Conn., Greenwood, 1976.
10 Acheson, *Present at the Creation*, p. 195.
11 Leo Sziland, 'Shall We Face the Facts?', *Bulletin of the Atomic Scientists*, 1949, vol. V, p. 273.
12 Denna F. Fleming, *The Cold War and Its Origins 1917–60*, Garden City, Doubleday, 1961, p. 327.
13 Feis, *From Trust to Terror*, p. 142.
14 Henry Stimson and McGeorge Bundy, *On Active Service in Peace and War*, New York, Harper & Bros., 1947, p. 644.
15 John L. Gaddis, 'The Emerging Post-Revisionist Synthesis on the Origins of the Cold War', *Diplomatic History*, 1983, vol. 7, no. 3, p. 189.
16 James V. Compton (ed.) *America and the Origins of the Cold War*, Boston, Houghton Mifflin, 1972, p.xiv.

17 Geir Lundestad, *The American 'Empire'*, Oslo, Norwegian University Press, 1990, p. 24.

18 Walter Isaacson and Evan Thomas, *The Wise Men: Six Friends and the World They Made: Acheson, Bohlen, Harriman, Kennan, Lovett, McCloy*, New York, Simon & Schuster, 1988, p. 19.

19 Martin Gilbert, *Never Despair, 1945–65*, vol. 8 of *Winston S. Churchill*, London, Heinemann, 1988, p. 205.

20 Halifax to Foreign Office, 4 November 1945, FO371/44539/ AN3373, Public Record Office, Kew, Surrey.

21 Minute by Bernard Gage, 15 November 1945, FO371/44539/ AN3447, PRO.

22 Geoffrey Harrison to C.F.A. Warner, 25 March 1947, FO371/66426/ N13771, PRO.

23 Clark Clifford, *Counsel to the President*, New York, Random House, 1991, p. 200.

24 Minute by Peter Pares, 18 January 1949, FO371/74174/AN135, PRO.

24 Paul Boyer, *By the Bomb's Early Light: American Thought and Culture at the Dawn of the Atomic Age*, New York, Pantheon, 1985, p.xix.

6 THE UNITED STATES, THE SOVIET UNION AND CHINA

1 *United States Relations with China*, Washington, US Government Printing Office, 1949, p.xvi.

2 *New York Times*, 22 August 1949.

3 Herbert Feis, *Churchill, Roosevelt, Stalin: The War They Waged and the Peace They Sought*, Princeton, Princeton University Press, 1957, p. 407.

4 Herbert Feis, *From Trust to Terror, 1945–50*, New York, W.W. Norton, 1970, p. 203.

5 Earl Latham, *The Communist Controversy in Washington: From the New Deal to McCarthy*, Cambridge, Mass., Harvard University Press, 1966, p. 233.

6 Inverchapel to Foreign Office, 20 December 1947, FO371/61057/ AN4252, Public Record Office, Kew, Surrey.

7 Inverchapel to Foreign Office, 2 March 1948, FO371/68108/AN849, PRO.

8 *Congressional Record*, 81 Congress, 1 Session, 1950, pp. 4407–8.

9 *A Decade of American Foreign Policy: Basic Documents, 1941–49*, Washington, US Government Printing Office, 1950, p. 264.

10 *New York Times*, 18 April 1950.

11 *Public Papers of the Presidents of the United States, Harry S. Truman, 1950*, Washington, US Government Printing Office, 1965, p. 11.

12 *New York Times*, 1 November 1944.

13 Tang Tsou, *America's Failure in China, 1941–50*, Chicago, University of Chicago Press, 1964, p. 202.

14 Ibid., p. 208.

15 Dean Acheson, *Present at the Creation: My Years in the State Department*, New York, W.W. Norton, 1969, p. 202.
16 Jock Balfour to C.F.A. Warner, 28 March 1947, FO371/66295/4045, PRO.
17 Minutes of an Extraordinary Meeting of the Russia Committee, 11 March 1949, FO371/77601/N2581/1023/28, PRO.
18 *Department of State Bulletin*, vol. XVIII, no. 554, 23 January 1950, p. 115.
19 Ibid.
20 William W. Stueck, *The Road to Confrontation: American Policy Towards China and Korea, 1947–50*, Chapel Hill, University of North Carolina Press, 1981, p. 118.
21 Harry S. Truman, *Years of Trial and Hope, 1946–53*, vol. 2 of *The Memoirs of Harry S. Truman*, Garden City, New York, Doubleday, 1956, pp. 95–6.
22 Stueck, *Road to Confrontation*, p. 124.

7 THE KOREAN WAR, 1950–3

1 *Department of State Bulletin*, vol. ix, no. 232, 11 December 1943, p. 393.
2 Harry S. Truman, *Years of Trial and Hope, 1946–63*, vol. 2 of *The Memoirs of Harry S. Truman*, Garden City, Doubleday, 1955, p. 351.
3 Memo prepared for Minister of State, 26 June 1950, FO371/84058/FK1015/62, Public Record Office, Kew, Surrey.
4 *Foreign Relations of the United States, 1950, vol. VII, Korea*, Washington, US Government Printing Office, 1976, p. 351.
5 Bruce Cumings, *The Roaring of the Cataract, 1947–50*, vol. 2 of *The Origins of the Korean War*, Princeton, Princeton University Press, 1990, p. 667.
6 Dean Acheson, *Present at the Creation: My Years in the State Department*, New York, Norton, 1969, p. 405.
7 *People's Daily*, Beijing, 29 June 1950. Quoted, Glenn D. Paige, *The Korean Decision*, New York, Free Press, 1968, pp. 210–11.
8 Tang Tsou, *America's Failure in China, 1941–50*, Chicago, University of Chicago Press, 1964, p. 562.
9 Gordon H. Chang, *Friends and Enemies: The United States, China and the Soviet Union, 1948–72*, Stanford, Stanford University Press, 1990, p. 76.
10 Acheson, *Present at the Creation*, p. 446.
11 *FRUS, 1950, Korea*, p. 459.
12 *Department of State Bulletin*, vol. xxiii, no. 582, 28 August 1950, p. 331.
13 Burton I. Kaufman, *The Korean War: Challenge in Crisis, Credibility and Command*, Philadelphia, Temple University Press, 1986, p. 85.
14 *FRUS, 1950, Korea*, p. 904.
15 Tsou, *America's Failure in China*, p. 572.
16 *New York Times*, 1 October 1950.
17 Peter Lowe, *The Origins of the Korean War*, London, Longman, 1986, p. 188.

18 Truman, *Years of Trial and Hope*, p. 423.
19 *Department of State Bulletin*, vol. xxiv, no. 621, 28 May 1951, p. 847.
20 Charles E. Bohlen, *Witness to History, 1929–69*, New York, W.W. Norton, 1973, p. 303.
21 Ibid.
22 Kaufman, *The Korean War*, p. 39.
23 George F. Kennan, *Memoirs, 1950–1963*, Boston, Little, Brown, 1972, p. 159.
24 Roger Dingman, 'Atomic Diplomacy during the Korean War', *International Security*, 1988–9, vol. 13, no. 3, p. 91.

8 THE RED SCARE AND McCARTHYISM

1 Fred J. Cook, *The Nightmare Decade: The Life and Times of Senator Joe McCarthy*, New York, Random House, 1971, p. 149.
2 Earl Latham, *The Communist Controversy in Washington: From the New Deal to McCarthy*, Cambridge, Mass., Harvard University Press, 1966, p. 15.
3 Allen J. Matusow (ed.) *Joseph R. McCarthy*, Englewood Cliffs, Prentice-Hall, 1970, pp. 2–3.
4 Richard H. Rovere, *Senator Joe McCarthy*, New York, Harcourt, Brace, 1959.
5 *Chicago Sun-Times*, 12 March 1950.
6 David Caute, *The Great Fear: The Anti-Communist Purge under Truman and Eisenhower*, New York, Simon & Schuster, 1978, p. 194.
7 Washington to Foreign Office, 14 November 1953, FO371/103496/AU1013/48, Public Record Office, Kew, Surrey.
8 Lately Thomas, *When Even Angels Wept: The Senator Joseph McCarthy Affair*, New York, William Morrow, 1973, p. 87.
9 Ibid.
10 *Congressional Record*, 81 Congress, 2 Session, 15 September 1950, p. 14914.
11 Washington to Foreign Office, 14 November 1953, FO371/103496/AU1013/48, PRO.
12 Stephen J. Whitefield, *The Culture of the Cold War*, Baltimore, Johns Hopkins University, 1991, pp. 115–16.
13 Eric Goldman, *The Crucial Decade*, New York, Alfred A. Knopf, 1959, pp. 257–8.
14 Cook, *Nightmare Decade*, p. 98.
15 Ibid., p. 102.
16 Rovere, *McCarthy*, p. 103.
17 Cook, *Nightmare Decade*, pp. 364–5.
18 Thomas C. Reeves, *The Life and Times of Joe McCarthy*, New York, Stein & Day, 1982, p. 307.
19 Cook, *Nightmare Decade*, p. 349.
20 *Congressional Record*, 83 Congress, 2 Session, 1954, pp. 2886–7.
21 Dean Acheson, *Present at the Creation: My Years in the State Department*, W.W. Norton, 1969, p. 468.

22 Cook, *Nightmare Decade*, p. 143.
23 Ibid., pp. 69–70.
24 Richard M. Fried, *Nightmare in Red: The McCarthy Era in Perspective*, New York, Oxford University Press, 1990, pp. 125–6.
25 J. William Fulbright, *The Crippled Giant*, New York, Random House, 1972, p. 25.
26 George F. Kennan, *Memoirs, 1950–1963*, Boston, Little, Brown, 1972, p. 228.

9 THE EISENHOWER ERA, 1953–61

1 Richard M. Nixon, *Six Crises*, Garden City, Doubleday, 1962, p. 161.
2 C.L. Sulzberger, *A Long Row of Candles*, New York, Macmillan, 1970, pp. 991–2.
3 Eisenhower to Dulles, 18 March 1953, John Foster Dulles Papers, White House Memo Services, Box 1, Dwight D. Eisenhower Library, Abilene, Kansas.
4 Richard H. Rovere, *Senator Joe McCarthy*, New York, Harcourt, Brace, 1959, p. 18.
5 H.W. Brands, *Cold Warriors: Eisenhower's Generation and American Foreign Policy*, New York, Columbia University Press, 1988, p. 12.
6 Townsend Hoopes, *The Devil and John Foster Dulles*, Boston, Little, Brown, 1973, p. 130.
7 James Burnham, *Containment and Liberation*, New York, John Day, 1953, pp. 42–3.
8 Walter Lippmann, *The Cold War*, New York, Harper, 1947, p. 9.
9 John Foster Dulles, 'A Policy of Boldness', *Life*, vol. 32, no. 20, 19 May 1952, p. 146.
10 John W. Spanier, *American Foreign Policy since the Second World War*, 7th edn, New York, Praeger, 1977, p. 101.
11 *New York Times*, 26 August, 1952.
12 United States, Congress, Senate, Committee on Foreign Relations, *Nomination of John Foster Dulles*, 83 Cong., 1 sess., 1953, p. 6.
13 Bennett Kovrig, *The Myth of Liberation: East-Central Europe in US Diplomacy since 1941*, Baltimore, Johns Hopkins University Press, 1973, p. 122.
14 Denise Folliott (ed.) *Documents on International Affairs, 1953*, London, Oxford University of Press, 1956, p. 13.
15 Winston S. Churchill to Dwight D. Eisenhower, 11 March 1953, Peter G. Boyle (ed.) *The Churchill–Eisenhower Correspondence, 1953–55*, Chapel Hill, University of North Carolina Press, 1990, p. 31.
16 Eisenhower to Churchill, 11 March 1953, ibid., p. 32.
17 *Public Papers of the Presidents of the United States, Dwight D. Eisenhower, 1953*, Washington, US Government Printing Office, 1960, p. 182.
18 Churchill to Eisenhower, 21 April 1953, Boyle (ed.) *The Churchill–Eisenhower Correspondence*, p. 46.
19 Eisenhower to Churchill, 25 April 1953, ibid., p. 47.

20 Evelyn Shuckburgh, *Descent to Suez: Diaries, 1951–56*, London, Weidenfeld & Nicolson, 1986, p. 81.
21 William Hayter to Anthony Eden, 26 October 1954, FO371/111706/1073/22, Public Record Office, Kew, Surrey.
22 John Colville, *Fringes of Power: Downing Street Diaries, 1939–55*, London, Hodder & Stoughton, 1955, p. 683.
23 Charles M.W. Moran, *Churchill: The Struggle for Survival, 1940–65*, Boston, Houghton Mifflin, 1966, p. 440.
24 Churchill to Eisenhower, 8 August 1954, Boyle (ed.) *The Churchill–Eisenhower Correspondence*, p. 167.
25 Oral History Interview, 16 March 1965, John Foster Dulles Papers, Princeton University. Quoted, Lloyd C. Gardner, *Approaching Vietnam: From the Second World War to Dienbienphu, 1941–56*, New York, W.W. Norton, 1988, p. 202.
26 Dwight D. Eisenhower, *Mandate for Change, 1953–56*, vol. 1 of *White House Years*, 2 vols, Garden City, Doubleday, 1963, p. 373.
27 Gordon H. Chang, 'To the Nuclear Brink: Eisenhower, Dulles and the Quemoy-Matsu Crisis', *International Security*, 1988, vol. 12, no. 4, p. 97.
28 Kovrig, *The Myth of Liberation*, p. 185.
29 Ibid., p. 191.
30 Adam Ulam, *The Rivals: America and Russia since the Second World War*, New York, Viking, 1971, pp. 311–12.
31 *FRUS 1952–54, V: Western European Security*, p. 1759.

10 KENNEDY AND KHRUSHCHEV, 1961–3

1 John F. Kennedy, *Why England Slept*, New York, W. Funk, 1940.
2 *Public Papers of the Presidents of the United States, John F. Kennedy, 1961*, Washington, US Government Printing Office, 1962, p. 1.
3 William E. Leuchtenburg, *A Troubled Feast: American Society since 1945*, Boston, Little, Brown, 1973, p. 132.
4 Frank Costigliola, 'The Pursuit of Atlantic Community: Nuclear Arms, Dollars and Berlin', Chapter 2 of Thomas G. Paterson (ed.) *Kennedy's Quest for Victory: American Foreign Policy, 1961–1963*, New York, Oxford University Press, 1989, p. 32.
5 Arthur M. Schlesinger, *A Thousand Days: John F. Kennedy in the White House*, Boston, Houghton Miffin, 1965, p. 251.
6 Trumbull Higgins, *The Perfect Failure: Kennedy, Eisenhower, and the CIA at the Bay of Pigs*, New York, W.W. Norton, 1987, p. 107.
7 Walter Isaacson and Evan Thomas, *The Wise Men: Six Friends and the World They Made: Acheson, Bohlen, Harriman, Kennan, Lovett, McCloy*, New York, Simon & Schuster, 1986, p. 608.
8 Michael R. Beschloss, *The Crisis Years: Kennedy and Khrushchev, 1960–63*, New York, Edward Burlingane Books, 1991, p. 278.
9 Ibid., p. 67.
10 James G. Blight, *On the Brink: Americans and Soviets Re-examine the Cuban Missile Crisis*, 2nd edn, New York, Farrar, Strauss & Giraux,

1990; Raymond L. Garthoff, 'The Havana Conference on the Cuban Missile Crisis', *Cold War International History Project Bulletin*, 1992, Issue 1, pp. 2–3.

11 Garthoff, 'Havana Conference', p. 2.

12 Ibid., p. 3.

13 Raymond L. Garthoff, *Reflections on the Cuban Missile Crisis*, rev. edn, Washington, Brookings Institution, 1989, p. 30.

14 Roger Hilsman, *To Move a Nation: The Politics of Foreign Policy in the Administration of John F. Kennedy*, Garden City, Doubleday, 1967, p. 166.

15 Garthoff, *Reflections on the Cuban Missile Crisis*, p. 47.

16 Ibid., p. 24.

17 Ibid.

18 *Public Papers of the Presidents of the United States, John F. Kennedy, 1962*, Washington, US Government Printing Office, 1963, p. 807.

19 Schlesinger, *A Thousand Days*, p. 841.

20 Ibid., p. 547.

21 Ibid.

22 Kenneth P. O'Donnell and David F. Powers, *Johnny, We Hardly Knew Ye: Memories of John Fitzgerald Kennedy*, Boston, Little, Brown, 1972, p. 16.

23 George C. Herring, *America's Longest War: The United States and Vietnam, 1950–75*, 2nd edn, New York, Alfred A. Knopf, 1986, p. 106.

24 *Public Papers of the Presidents of the United States, John F. Kennedy, 1963*, Washington, US Government Printing Office, 1964, p. 569.

25 Ibid., p. 659.

26 Schlesinger, *A Thousand Days*, p. 860.

27 *Public Papers, Kennedy, 1962*, p. 525.

11 JOHNSON, VIETNAM AND CZECHOSLOVAKIA, 1963–9

1 Walter Isaacson and Evan Thomas, *The Wise Men: Six Friends and the World They Made: Acheson, Bohlen, Harriman, Kennan, Lovett, McCloy*, New York, Simon & Schuster, 1986, p. 642.

2 Lyndon B. Johnson, *The Vantage Point: Perspective of the Presidency, 1963–69*, New York, Holt, Rinehart & Winston, 1971, p. 24.

3 Ibid., p. 471.

4 *Public Papers of the Presidents of the United States, Lyndon B. Johnson, 1963–64, II, July 1 – December 31, 1964*, Washington, US Government Printing Office, 1965, p. 1164.

5 *Public Papers of the Presidents of the United States, Lyndon B. Johnson, 1965, I, January 1 – May 31, 1965*, Washington, US Government Printing Office, 1966, p. 471.

6 Johnson, *The Vantage Point*, p. 472.

7 Ibid., p. 474.

8 Ibid., p. 472.

9 Ibid., p. 473.
10 William G. Hyland, *Mortal Rivals: Superpower Relations from Nixon to Reagan*, New York, Random House, 1987, p. 14.
11 Zdenek Mlynar, *Nightfrost in Prague: The End of Humane Socialism*, New York, Karz, 1980, p. 240.

12 NIXON, KISSINGER AND DETENTE, 1969–74

1 Roger Morris, *Richard Milhous Nixon: The Rise of an American Politician*, New York, Henry Holt, 1990, p. 580.
2 Henry A. Kissinger, *Nuclear Weapons and Foreign Policy*, New York, Harper Bros., 1957; Richard M. Nixon, *RN: The Memoirs of Richard Nixon*, New York, Grosset & Dunlap, 1978, p. 340.
3 *New York Times*, 11 April 1988.
4 William G. Hyland, *Mortal Rivals: Superpower Relations from Nixon to Reagan*, New York, Random House, 1987, p. 340.
5 Ibid.
6 Nixon, *RN*, p. 390.
7 Frank Snepp, *Decent Interval: The American Debacle in Vietnam and the Fall of Saigon*, New York, Random House, 1977.
8 Henry A. Kissinger, *White House Years*, Boston, Little, Brown, 1979, p. 161.
9 *Department of State Bulletin*, vol. 62, 26 January 1970, p. 83.
10 Hyland, *Mortal Rivals*, p. 82.
11 Strobe Talbott, *Master of the Game: Paul Nitze and the Nuclear Peace*, New York, Alfred A. Knopf, 1988, p. 111.
12 Nixon, *RN*, p. 618.
13 *Public Papers of the Presidents of the United States, Richard Nixon, 1972*, Washington, US Government Printing Office, 1974, p. 662.
14 *New York Times*, 27 October 1972.
15 Kissinger, *White House Years*, p. 1270.
16 Nixon, *RN*, p. 880.
17 Richard Pipes, *US–Soviet Relations in the Era of Détente*, Boulder, Colorado, Westview Press, 1981, p.xiii.
18 Raymond L. Garthoff, *Détente and Confrontation: American–Soviet Relations from Nixon to Reagan*, Washington, The Brookings Institution, 1985, p. 386.
19 Henry A. Kissinger, *Years of Upheaval*, Boston, Little, Brown, 1982, p. 985.
20 Ibid., p. 594.
21 Joan Hoff-Wilson, '"Nixingerism", NATO and Détente', *Diplomatic History*, 1989, vol. 13, no. 4, p. 520.
22 *Los Angeles Times*, 14 August 1989.
23 *Public Papers of the Presidents of the United States, Richard Nixon, 1974*, Washington, US Government Printing Office, 1975, p. 472.
24 *New York Times*, 9 August 1974.

13 THE DEMISE OF DETENTE, 1974–80

1 Raymond L. Garthoff, *Détente and Confrontation: American–Soviet Relations from Nixon to Reagan*, Washington, The Brookings Institution, 1985, p. 493.
2 Strobe Talbott, *The Russians and Reagan*, New York, Vintage Books, 1984, pp. 28–9.
3 Gerald R. Ford, *A Time To Heal*, New York, Harper & Row, 1979, p. 156.
4 *Department of State Bulletin*, vol. 74, no. 1909, 26 January 1976, p. 100.
5 *Department of State Bulletin*, vol. 74, no. 1912, 16 February 1976, p. 180.
6 *New York Times*, 1 January 1980.
7 Zbigniew Brzezinski, *Power and Principle: The Memoirs of the National Security Adviser, 1977–81*, New York, Farrar, Strauss & Giroux, 1983, p. 120.
8 Garthoff, *Détente and Confrontation*, p. 532.
9 Lou Cannon, *President Reagan: The Role of a Lifetime*, New York, Simon & Schuster, 1991, pp. 220, 281.
10 Garthoff, *Détente and Confrontation*, p. 548.
11 Coral Bell, *The Diplomacy of Détente: The Kissinger Era*, New York, St Martin's Press, 1977, p. 213.
12 William G. Hyland, *Mortal Rivals: Superpower Relations from Nixon to Reagan*, New York, Random House, 1987, p. 178.
13 Gaddis Smith, *Morality, Reason and Power: American Diplomacy in the Carter Years*, New York, Hill & Wang, 1986, p. 67.
14 Cyrus Vance, *Hard Choices: Critical Years in America's Foreign Policy*, New York, Simon & Schuster, 1983, p. 46.
15 Brzezinski, *Power and Principle*, p. 156.
16 Garthoff, *Détente and Confrontation*, p. 573.
17 *Department of State Bulletin*, vol. 71, no. 1842, 14 October 1974, p. 516.
18 Garthoff, *Détente and Confrontation*, p. 713.
19 Ibid., p. 702.
20 *Public Papers of the Presidents of the United States, Jimmy Carter, I, January 20 to June 24, 1977*, Washington, US Government Printing Office, 1977, p. 3.
21 Richard M. Nixon, *RN: The Memoirs of Richard Nixon*, New York, Grosset & Dunlap, 1978, p. 1031.

14 REAGAN AND THE NEW COLD WAR, 1981–5

1 Coral Bell, *The Reagan Paradox: American Foreign Policy in the 1980s*, Aldershot, Edward Elgar, 1989, p. 3.
2 Robert Dallek, *Ronald Reagan and the Politics of Symbolism*, Cambridge, Mass., Harvard University Press, 1982.

3 Michael Mandelbaum and Strobe Talbott, *Reagan and Gorbachev*, New York, Vintage Books, 1987, p. 27.

4 Lou Cannon, *President Reagan: The Role of a Lifetime*, New York, Simon & Schuster, 1991, pp. 220, 281.

5 *Public Papers of the Presidents of the United States, Ronald Reagan, 1981*, Washington, US Government Printing Office, 1982, p. 57.

6 *Public Papers of the Presidents of the United States, Ronald Reagan, 1983*, vol. 1, January 1 to July 31, 1983, Washington, US Government Printing Office, 1984, p. 364.

7 *Public Papers of the Presidents of the United Staes, Ronald Reagan, 1982*, vol. 1, January 1 to July 2, 1982, Washington, US Government Printing Office, 1983, p. 747.

8 *Public Papers, Reagan, 1983*, vol. 1, p. 364.

9 Mandelbaum and Talbott, *Reagan and Gorbachev*, p. 121.

10 Raymond L. Garthoff, *Détente and Confrontation: American–Soviet Relations from Nixon to Reagan*, Washington, Brookings Institution, 1985, p. 1080.

11 Sidney Blumenthal, *Pledging Allegiance: The Last Campaign of the Cold War*, New York, Harper Collins, 1990, p. 8.

12 David Stockman, *The Triumph of Politics: The Inside Story of the Reagan Revolution*, New York, Harper & Row, 1986, p. 107.

13 *Time*, 6 July 1981, p. 8.

14 *Los Angeles Times*, 12 June 1983.

15 *Public Papers, Reagan, 1983*, vol. 1, p. 442.

16 *Washington Post*, 27 September 1983.

17 Ibid.

18 George Schultz, 'Power and Diplomacy: An Address by Secretary Shultz to the Veterans of Foreign Wars, Chicago, August 20, 1984', US Department of State Bureau of Public Affairs, Current Policy no. 606, p. 3.

19 *Public Papers, Reagan*, 1982, vol. 1, p. 745.

20 *Time*, 3 March 1982, p. 16.

21 *Times Higher Education Supplement*, 1 October 1982.

22 *International Herald Tribune*, 29 August 1985.

23 *The Observer*, 25 March 1984.

24 *International Herald Tribune*, 27 April 1984.

25 *Public Papers of the Presidents of the United States, Ronald Reagan, 1983*, vol. 2, July 2 to December 31, 1983, Washington, US Government Printing Office, 1985, p. 1224.

26 *Public Papers of the Presidents of the United States, Ronald Reagan, 1984*, vol. 1, January 1 to June 29, 1984, Washington, US Government Printing Office, 1986, p. 41.

15 REAGAN AND GORBACHEV, 1985–9

1 Strobe Talbott, *Master of the Game: Paul Nitze and the Nuclear Peace*, New York, Alfred A. Knopf, p. 255.

2 *The Times*, 12 March 1985.

3 *Washington Post National Weekly Edition*, 22–8 August 1988. Quoted, Lloyd C. Gardner, 'Lost Empires', *Diplomatic History*, 1989, vol. 13, no. 4, p. 13.

4 Alexander Dallin and Gail Lapidus, 'Reagan and the Russians', Chapter 7 in Kenneth A. Oye *et al.* (eds) *Eagle Defiant: United States Foreign Policy in the 1980s*, Boston, Little, Brown, 1983, p. 192.

5 *New York Times*, 19 March 1985.

6 *International Herald Tribune*, 29 November 1987.

7 Michael Mandelbaum and Strobe Talbott, *Reagan and Gorbachev*, New York, Vintage Books, 1987, p. 54.

8 Paul M. Kennedy, *The Rise and Fall of the Great Powers*, New York, Random House, 1987, p. 515.

9 Raymond, L. Garthoff, *Policy versus the Law: The Reinterpretation of the ABM Treaty*, Washington, The Brookings Institution, 1987, p. 22.

10 Talbott, *Master of the Game*, p. 243.

11 Joan Hoff-Wilson, '"Nixingerism", NATO and Détente', *Diplomatic History*, 1989, vol. 13, no. 4, p. 520.

12 Talbott, *Master of the Game*, p. 325.

13 Robert Dallek, 'American Reactions to Changes in the USSR', Chapter 3 in Robert Jervis and Seweryn Bailer, *Soviet–American Relations After the Cold War*, Durham, NC, Duke University Press, 1991, p. 56.

14 Sidney Blumenthal, *Pledging Allegiance: The Last Campaign of the Cold War*, New York, Harper Collins, 1990, p. 86.

15 Ibid., p. 74.

16 Coral Bell, *The Reagan Paradox: American Foreign Policy in the 1980s*, Aldershot, Edward Elgar, 1989, pp. 76–7.

17 Gerald Segal, 'Ending the Cold War', *Diplomacy and Statecraft*, 1990, vol. 1, no. 3, p. 42.

16 THE BUSH ERA

1 Sidney Blumenthal, *Pledging Allegiance: The Last Campaign of the Cold War*, New York, Harper Collins, 1990, p. 330.

2 Ibid., p. 52.

3 *Public Papers of the Presidents of the United States, George Bush, 1989, I, January 20 to June 30, 1989*, Washington, US Government Printing Office, 1990, p. 541.

4 Ibid.

5 Ibid.

6 Ibid., p. 584.

7 *New York Times*, 26 May 1989.

8 *International Herald Tribune*, 27–8 May 1989.

9 Blumenthal, *Pledging Allegiance*, p. 328.

10 *Time*, 6 November 1989.

11 Ibid.

12 *International Herald Tribune*, 17 November 1989.

13 *Time*, 6 November 1989.

14 *International Herald Tribune*, 17 November 1989.
15 Ibid., 30 October 1989.
16 Ibid., 26 October 1989.
17 Ibid., 18 October 1989.
18 Ibid., 1 November 1989.
19 Ibid., 5 December 1989.
20 Ibid., 12 April 1990.
21 *Los Angeles Times*, 14 June 1990.
22 *International Herald Tribune*, 12 February 1990.
23 Ibid., 18 October 1989.
24 Ibid., 24 October 1989.
25 Ibid., 16 November 1989.
26 Z, 'To the Stalin Mausoleum', *Daedalus*, 1990, vol. 119, no. 1, p. 338.
27 *New York Times*, 28 June 1990.
28 *International Herald Tribune*, 15 December 1989.
29 Francis Fukuyama, 'The End of History?', *The National Interest*, 1989, no. 16, p. 4.
30 *International Herald Tribune*, 25 May 1989.
31 Ibid., 1 June 1990.
32 Ibid., 30 March 1990.
33 Ibid.
34 Graham E Fuller, 'Moscow and the Gulf War', *Foreign Affairs*, 1991, vol. 70, no. 3, p. 61.
35 *International Herald Tribune*, 7 May 1991.
36 Graham Allison and Robert Blackwill, 'America's Stake in the Soviet Future', *Foreign Affairs*, 1991, vol. 70, no. 3, p. 93.
37 *International Herald Tribune*, 3 June 1991.
38 *Los Angeles Times*, 7 July 1991.
39 *International History Tribune*, 6 June 1991.
40 *San Francisco Examiner-Chronicle*, 21 July 1991.
41 *International Herald Tribune*, 17 June 1991.
42 *New York Times*, 19 August 1991.
43 Ibid., 20 August 1991.
44 Ibid., 30 September 1991.
45 *International Herald Tribune*, 23 December 1991.
46 Ibid.
47 *Time*, 5 August 1991.
48 Blumenthal, *Pledging Allegiance*, p. 212.

17 THE LESSONS OF HISTORY

1 Robert V. Daniels, *Russia: The Roots of Confrontation*, Cambridge, Mass., Harvard University Press, 1985, p. 105.
2 Charles E. Bohlen, *Witness to History, 1929–69*, New York, W.W. Norton, 1973, p. 270.
3 McGeorge Bundy, 'From Cold War toward Trusting Peace', *Foreign Affairs*, 1989–90, vol. 69, no. 1, p. 211.

4 Bruce W. Jentelson, 'The Reagan Administration and Coercive Diplomacy', *Political Science Quarterly*, 1991, vol. 106, no. 1, p. 59.

5 X, 'The Sources of Soviet Conduct', *Foreign Affairs*, 1947, vol. 25, no. 4, pp. 575, 580.

6 *Public Papers of the Presidents of the United States, George Bush, 1989, I, January 20 to June 30, 1989*, Washington, US Government Printing Officer, 1990, p. 602.

7 James H. Burnham, *Containment or Liberation*, New York, J. Day, 1953, pp. 42–3.

8 John L. Gaddis, *Strategies of Containment*, New York, Oxford University Press, 1982, p. 49.

9 X, 'The Sources of Soviet Conduct', p. 581.

10 Roger Makins to Harold Macmillan, 17 March 1955, FO371/114364 AU 1022/16, Public Record Office, Kew, Surrey.

11 *Foreign Relations of the United States, 1952–54*, Volume V, *Western European Security*, Washington, D.C., US Government Printing Office, 1983, p. 1760.

12 Philip J. Funigiello, *American–Soviet Trade in the Cold War*, Chapel Hill, University of North Carolina Press, 1988, p. 111.

13 *The Observer*, 25 March 1984.

14 Vice-Consul Otto Glaman to Consul-General Ernest L. Harris, 20 March 1920, Ernest L. Harris Papers, Box 2, Hoover Archives, Stanford, California.

15 Stephen E. Ambrose, *Rise to Globalism*, New York, Harper & Row, 1975, p. 275.

16 US Senate, Hearings before the Committee on Foreign Relations, 31 January 1985.

17 Bennett Korvig, 'Eastern Europe out of the Cold: Finlandization and Beyond', *Diplomacy and Statecraft*, 1990, vol. 1, no. 3, p. 112.

18 William Hyland, *Mortal Rivals: Superpower Relations from Nixon to Reagan*, New York, Random House, 1987, p. 246.

19 Harry S. Truman, *Years of Trial and Hope 1946–53*, vol. 2 of *The Memoirs of Harry S. Truman*, Garden City, Doubleday, 1956, p. 228.

20 Richard M. Nixon, *Real Peace*, Boston, Little, Brown, 1984, p. 78.

21 *Parliamentary Debates*, (Hansard), House of Commons, 1954–55, Fifth Series, vol. 537, col. 1899, 1 March 1955.

22 Inverchapel to Foreign Office, 21 March 1947, FO371/61054/AN 1100, PRO.

23 Henry Wallace, 'The Way to Fight Greece', *New Republic*, 17 March 1947, p. 13.

24 Funigiello, *American–Soviet Trade*, p. 76.

25 Ibid., p. 217.

26 Alexis De Tocqueville, *Democracy in America*, New York, 2 vols, New York, Vintage Books, 1954, vol. I, p. 243.

27 James Baker, 'A New Europe, a New Atlanticism: Architecture for a New Era', 12 December 1989, *Current Policy*, no. 1233, US Department of State Bureau of Public Affairs, Washington, D.C.

28 *International Herald Tribune*, 24 April 1990.

BIBLIOGRAPHICAL ESSAY

This bibliographical essay is intended to provide a brief indication of the most important primary sources on US–Soviet relations and a brief guide to the most useful further reading. It is not intended to be an exhaustive listing of the vast collection of primary and secondary courses on the subject.

PRIMARY SOURCES

The most important manuscript sources are the US State Department papers in the National Archives in Washington. State Department papers on US–Soviet relations are open up to 1959. Second in importance are the collections of papers in presidential libraries, which consist of not only the papers of the presidents but also the papers of many figures in the president's administration. The relevant presidential libraries are the Herbert Hoover Library, West Branch, Iowa; the Franklin D. Roosevelt Library, Hyde Park, New York; the Harry S. Truman Library, Independence, Missouri; the Dwight D. Eisenhower Library, Abilene, Kansas; the John F. Kennedy Library, Cambridge, Massachusetts; the Lyndon B. Johnson Library, Austin, Texas; the Gerald R. Ford Library, Grand Rapids, Michigan; the Jimmy Carter Library, Atlanta, Georgia. The presidential libraries of Richard Nixon in Yorba Linda, California, and Ronald Reagan in Simi Valley, California, are not yet open for research, but many important Nixon papers are available at the Nixon Presidential Materials Project of the National Archives in Alexandria, Virginia. British Foreign Office papers, Cabinet papers and prime minister's papers, which are located in the Public Record Office, Kew, Surrey, and which are opened thirty years after events, are very useful manuscript sources which give a perspective from abroad on US policy towards the Soviet Union.

Of published primary sources, the most important by far is *Foreign Relations of the United States*, which consists of volumes of documents on US foreign policy – approximately ten volumes for each year – compiled by the State Department Office of the Historian. Volumes of *FRUS* have been published on the years up to the late 1950s. The *Department of State*

Bulletin, which has been published since 1939 to the present, is a useful source for speeches by the Secretary of State and other officials. *Public Papers of the Presidents of the United States*, which consist of annual volumes of presidential statements since Truman's presidency, is a useful source for official statements by presidents. On the Congressional side, hearings before Congressional committees, especially the Senate Committee on Foreign Relations, are an important source, especially since the question and answer format of such hearings leads at times to a probing into subjects in a critical manner. Some examples of the vast number of Congressional hearings relevant to US–Soviet relations are *Russian Propaganda: Hearings before a Sub-committee of the Committee on Foreign Relations*, US Senate, 66 Congress, 2 Session, 1920; *European Recovery Program: Hearings before the Committee on Foreign Relations*, US Senate, 80 Congress, 2 Session, 1948; *Nomination of John Foster Dulles: Hearings before the Committee on Foreign Relations*, US Senate, 83 Congress, 1 Session, 1953; *United States Relations with Communist Countries: Hearings before the Committee on Foreign Relations*, US Senate, 93 Congress, 2 Session, 1974; *United States–Soviet Scientific Enchanges: Hearings before a Sub-committee of the Committee on Foreign Affairs*, US House of Representatives, 99 Congress, 2 Session, 1986; *The INF Treaty: Hearings before the Committee on Foreign Relations*, US Senate, 100 Congress, 2 Session, 1988.

Memoirs constitute one of the most important sources on US–Soviet relations. By their nature memoirs need to be used with caution, since the authors are inevitably defensive of their own roles. Moreover, while some memoirs are analytical and revealing, others are superficial and misleading. Among the vast number of memoirs by US State Department experts, ambassadors, Secretaries of State, presidents, Secretaries of Defense and National Security Advisers, some are extremely important, such as the memoirs of George Kennan, Dean Acheson and Henry Kissinger, while others are thin and superficial. The memoirs of three American experts on the Soviet Union are particularly valuable, namely George F. Kennan, *Memoirs, 1925–50*, Boston, Little, Brown, 1967; George F. Kennan, *Memoirs, 1950–63*, Boston, Little, Brown, 1972; Charles E. Bohlen, *Witness to History, 1929–69*, New York, W.W. Norton, 1973; and George W. Baer (ed.) *A Question of Trust: The Origins of US–Soviet Diplomatic Relations: The Memoirs of Loy W. Henderson*, Stanford, Hoover Institution Press, 1986. Other useful accounts by US diplomatic and military officials involved in Soviet policy include Edgar S. Sisson, *One Hundred Red Days*, New Haven, Yale University Press, 1931; William S. Graves, *America's Siberian Adventure, 1918–20*, New York, Cape & Smith, 1931; Joseph E. Davies, *Mission to Moscow*, New York, Simon & Schuster, 1941; W. Averell Harriman, *Special Envoy to Churchill and Stalin, 1941–46*, New York, Random House, 1975; William H. Standley and Arthur A. Artegon, *Admiral Ambassador to Russia*, Chicago, Henry Regenery, 1955; John R. Deane, *The Strange Alliance: The Story of Our Efforts at Wartime Co-operation with Russia*, New York, Viking, 1947; William D. Leahy, *I Was There*, New York, Whittlesey House, 1950; Walter Bedell Smith, *My Three Years in Moscow*, New York,

J.P. Linpincott, 1950; Paul H. Nitze, *From Hiroshima to Glasnost*, New York, Grove, Wiedenfeld, 1989.

On Communism in the United States, interesting memoirs are Louis F. Post, *The Deportations Delirium of Nineteen-Twenty*, Chicago, Charles Kerr, 1923, Alger Hiss, *Recollections of a Life*, New York, Henry Holt, 1988; Whittaker Chambers, *Witness*, New York, Random House, 1952; Howard Fast, *Being Red*, Boston, Houghton Mifflin, 1990.

Two very important memoirs by National Security Council Advisers are Henry Kissinger, *White House Years*, Boston, Little, Brown, 1979, and Zbigniew Brzezinski, *Power and Principle: Memoirs of the National Security Adviser, 1977–81*, New York, Farrar, Strauss & Giroux, 1983. Two useful memoirs by a War Secretary and a Defense Secretary (the War Department was renamed the Defense Department in 1947) are Henry L. Stimson and McGeorge Bundy, *On Active Service in Peace and War*, New York, Harper, 1947, and Caspar Weinberger, *Fighting for Peace: Seven Critical Years in the Pentagon*, New York, Warner Bros., 1990. An interesting memoir by a Secretary of Defense who held many earlier advisory posts is Clark Clifford, *Counsel to the President*, New York, Random House, 1991.

Among memoirs by Secretaries of State the two most significant are Dean Acheson, *Present at the Creation: My Years in the State Department*, New York, W.W. Norton, 1969, and Henry Kissinger, *Years of Upheaval*, Boston, Little, Brown, 1982. Other memoirs by Secretaries of State which are of value include Cordell Hull, *The Memoirs of Cordell Hull*, 2 vols, New York, Macmillan, 1948; Edward R. Stettinius, Jr, *Roosevelt and the Russians: The Yalta Conference*, Garden City, Doubleday, 1949; James F. Byrnes, *All in One Lifetime*, New York, Harper & Bros., 1958; Dean Rusk, *As I Saw It*, New York, W.W. Norton, 1990; Cyrus Vance, *Hard Choices: Critical Years in American Foreign Policy*, New York, Simon & Schuster, 1983; Alexander M. Haig, *Caveat: Realism, Reagan and Foreign Policy*, New York, Macmillan, 1984.

Among presidential memoirs, the most important for US–Soviet relations is Richard M. Nixon, *RN: The Memoirs of Richard Nixon*, New York, Grosset & Dunlap, 1978. Other presidential memoirs of value are Herbert Hoover, *Memoirs*, 3 vols, New York, Macmillan, 1951–52; Harry S. Truman, *The Memoirs of Harry S. Truman*, 2 vols, Garden City, Doubleday, 1955–56; Dwight D. Eisenhower, *White House Years*, 2 vols, Garden City, Doubleday, 1963–65; Lyndon B. Johnson, *The Vantage Point: Perspectives of the Presidency, 1963–69*, New York, Holt, Rinehart & Winston, 1971, Gerald R. Ford, *A Time To Heal*, New York, Harper & Row, 1979; Jimmy Carter, *Keeping Faith*, New York, Bantam, 1982; Ronald Reagan, *An American Life*, New York, Simon & Schuster, 1990. Also useful are Arthur S. Link (ed.) *The Papers of Woodrow Wilson*, Princeton, Princeton University Press, 1966– (continuing), and editions of presidential correspondence, particularly Warren F. Kimball (ed.) *Churchill and Roosevelt: The Complete Correspondence*, 3 vols, Princeton, Princeton University Press, 1985, and Peter G. Boyle (ed.) *The Churchill–Eisenhower Correspondence, 1953–55*, Chapel Hill, University of North Carolina Press, 1990.

BIBLIOGRAPHICAL ESSAY

SECONDARY SOURCES

The most useful general surveys of US–Soviet relations since 1917 are John L. Gaddis, *Russia, the Soviet Union and the United States: An Interpretative History*, 2nd edn, New York, McGraw-Hill, 1990, and Linda R. Killen, *The Soviet Union and the United States*, Boston, G.K. Hall, 1988. An account from the Soviet perspective is Nikolai Sivachev and Nikolai Yakolev, *Russia and the United States*, Chicago, University of Chicago Press, 1979. Accounts written from an International Relations rather than a historical viewpoint include George Liska, *Re-Thinking US–Soviet Relations*, Oxford, Basil Blackwell, 1987; Ralph K. White, *Fearful Warriors: A Psychological Profile of US–Soviet Relations*, New York, Collier Macmillan, 1984; Thomas B. Larson, *Soviet–American Rivalry*, New York, W.W. Norton, 1978; Richard J. Barnet, *The Giants: Russia and America*, New York, Simon & Schuster, 1977; Anatol Rapoport, *The Big Two: Soviet–American Perceptions of Foreign Policy*, New York, Bobbs-Merrill, 1971; Joseph S. Nye (ed.) *The Making of America's Soviet Policy*, New Haven, Yale University Press, 1984.

There are several biographies of significant figures in US–Soviet relations, especially Beatrice Farnsworth, *William C. Bullitt and the Soviet Union*, Bloomington, Indiana University Press, 1967; T. Michael Ruddy, *The Cautious Diplomat:Charles E. Bohlen and the Soviet Union, 1929–69*, Kent, Kent State University Press, 1986; H.W. Brands, *Inside the Cold War: Loy Henderson and the Rise of the American Empire*, New York, Oxford, University Press, 1991; William L. Hixson, *George F. Kennan: Cold War Iconoclast*, New York, Columbia University Press, 1989; David A. Mayers, *George Kennan and the Dilemmas of US Foreign Policy*, New York, Oxford University Press, 1988; Anders Stephanson, *Kennan and the Art of Foreign Policy*, Cambridge, Mass., Harvard University Press, 1989. An excellent multibiography of several figures is Walter Isaacson and Evan Thomas, *The Wise Men: Six Friends and the World They Made: Acheson, Bohlen, Harriman, Kennan, Lovett, McCloy*, New York, Simon & Schuster, 1986.

On American intervention in Russia 1918–20 the most useful accounts are George F. Kennan, *Soviet–American Relations, 1917–20*, 2 vols, Princeton, Princeton University Press, 1956–8, Benjamin D. Rhodes, *The Anglo-American Winter War with Russia, 1918–19*, Westport, Greenwood, 1988; Richard Goldhurst, *The Midnight War: American Intervention in Russia, 1918–20*; New York, McGraw-Hill, 1978; John Silverlight, *The Victors' Dilemma: American Intervention in the Russian Civil War*, New York, Waybright & Talley, 1978; Betty M. Unterberger, *The United States, Revolutionary Russia and the Rise of Czechoslovakia*, Chapel Hill, University of North Carolina Press, 1989; Robert J. Maddox, *The Unknown War with Russia: Wilson's Siberian Intervention*, San Rafael, Presidio Press, 1977; Leonid I. Strakhovsky, *American Opinion about Russia, 1917–20*, Toronto, University of Toronto Press, 1961; Christopher Lasch, *The American Liberals and the Russian Revolution*, New York, Columbia University Press, 1962.

On the Red Scare 1919–20 the best accounts are Michael J. Heale, *American Anti-Communism: Combating the Enemy Within, 1830–1970*,

301

Baltimore, Johns Hopkins University Press, 1990; Robert K. Murray, *Red Scare*, Minneapolis, University of Minnesota Press, 1955; William Preston, *Aliens and Dissenters: Federal Suppression of Radicals, 1903–33*, Cambridge, Mass., Harvard University Press, 1963; Stanley Coben, *A. Mitchell Palmer: Politician*, New York, Columbia University Press, 1963; Richard G. Powers, *Secrecy and Power: The Life of J. Edgar Hoover*, New York, Free Press, 1988.

On the era of non-recognition, 1921–33, the most useful works are Joan Hoff-Wilson, *Ideology and Economics: US Relations with the Soviet Union, 1918–33*, Columbia, University of Missouri Press, 1974; Peter G. Filene, *Americans and the Soviet Experiment, 1917–33*, Cambridge, Mass., Harvard University Press, 1967; Benjamin M. Weissman, *Herbert Hoover and Famine Relief to Soviet Russia, 1921–23*, Stanford, Hoover Institution Press, 1974; James K. Libbey, *Alexander Gumberg and Soviet–American Relations, 1917–33*, Lexington, University Press of Kentucky, 1977. On US diplomatic recognition of the Soviet Union in 1933, see Robert P. Browder, *The Origins of Soviet–American Diplomacy*, Princeton, Princeton University Press, 1953, and Edward M. Bennett, *Recognition of Russia*, Waltham, Blaisdell, 1971.

On the years from diplomatic recognition to the Second World War, the most useful accounts are Thomas R. Maddux, *Years of Estrangement: American Relations with the Soviet Union, 1933–1941*, Tallahassee, University Presses of Florida, 1980; Edward M. Bennett, *Franklin D. Roosevelt and the Search for Security: Soviet–American Relations, 1933–1939*, Wilmington, Scholarly Resources, 1985; William L. O'Neill, *A Better World: The Great Schism: Stalinism and the American Intellectuals*, New York, Simon & Schuster, 1982; Frank A. Warren, *Liberals and Communism: The 'Red Decade' Revisited*, Bloomington, Indiana University Press, 1966; Hugh De Santis, *The Diplomacy of Silence: The American Foreign Service, the Soviet Union and the Cold War, 1933–47*, Chicago, University of Chicago Press, 1980; Robert Dallek, *Franklin Roosevelt and American Foreign Policy, 1932–1945*, New York, Oxford University Press, 1979; Raymond H. Dawson, *The Decision to Aid Russia, 1941: Foreign Policy and Domestic Politics*, Chapel Hill, University of North Carolina Press, 1959.

On the Second World War alliance, the most significant works are Robin Edmonds, *The Big Three: Churchill, Roosevelt and Stalin in Peace and War*, New York, W.W. Norton, 1991; Edward M. Bennett, *Franklin D. Roosevelt and the Search for Victory: American–Soviet Relations, 1939–45*, Wilmington, Scholarly Resources, 1990; Herbert Feis, *Churchill, Roosevelt, Stalin: The War They Waged and the Peace They Sought*, Princeton, Princeton University Press, 1957; William H. McNeill, *America, Britain and Russia: Their Co-operation and Conflict, 1941–46*, New York, Oxford University Press, 1953; Robert Beitzell, *America, Britain and Russia, 1941–43*, New York, Alfred A. Knopf, 1968; Ralph B. Levering, *American Opinion and the Russian Alliance, 1939–45*, Chapel Hill, University of North Carolina Press, 1976; Warren F. Kimball, *The Juggler: Franklin Roosevelt as Wartime Statesman*, Princeton, Princeton University Press, 1991; Dwight D. Tuttle, *Harry L. Hopkins and Anglo-American–Soviet Relations, 1941–45*, New York, Garland, 1983;

Mark A. Stoler, *The Politics of the Second Front*, Westport, Greenwood, 1977; George C. Herring, *Aid to Russia, 1941–46*, New York, Columbia University Press, 1973; Robert H. Jones, *The Roads to Russia: United States Lend-Lease to the Soviet Union*, Norman, University of Oklahoma Press, 1969; Russell D. Buhite, *Decisions at Yalta*, Wilmington, Scholarly Resources, 1986; Diane S. Clemens, *Yalta*, New York, Oxford University Press, 1970; Gar Alperovitz, *Atomic Diplomacy: Hiroshima and Potsdam*, London, Secker & Warburg, 1966; Martin J. Sherwin, *A World Destroyed: The Atomic Bomb and the Grand Alliance*, New York, Alfred A. Knopf, 1975; Barton J. Bernstein (ed.) *The Atomic Bomb*, Little, Brown, 1976; Lisle A. Rose, *Dubious Victory: The United States and the End of World War II*, Kent, Kent State University Press, 1973.

Whereas the number of books on US–Soviet relations pre-Second World War is not particularly large, there is a vast literature on the period since 1945 in general and on aspects of the origins of the Cold War in particular. The most useful surveys of US–Soviet relations since 1945 are Walter LaFeber, *America, Russia and the Cold War, 1945–90*, 6th edn, New York, McGraw-Hill, 1991; Thomas G. Paterson, *Meeting the Communist Threat: Truman to Reagan*, New York, Oxford University Press, 1989; Adam B. Ulam, *The Rivals: America and Russia since World War II*, New York, Viking, 1971; John W. Spanier, *American Foreign Policy since World War II*, 7th edn, New York, Praeger, 1977; John L. Gaddis, *Strategies of Containment*, New York, Oxford University Press, 1982; John L. Gaddis, *The Long Peace: Inquiries into the History of the Cold War*, New York, Oxford University Press, 1987; Geir Lundestad, *The American 'Empire'*, Oslo, Norwegian University Press, 1990; George F. Kennan, *The Nuclear Decision: Soviet–American Relations in the Atomic Age*, New York, Pantheon Books, 1982; Richard W. Stevenson, *The Rise and Fall of Détente: Relaxation of Tensions in US–Soviet Relations, 1953–84*, London, Macmillan, 1985; Mark Garrison and Abbot Gleason (eds) *Shared Destiny: Fifty Years of Soviet–American Relations*, Boston, Beacon Press, 1985; William G. Hyland, *The Cold War Is Over*, New York, Oxford University Press, 1991.

On the debate on the origins of the Cold War, the most useful traditionalist account is Herbert Feis, *From Trust to Terror, 1945–50*, New York, W.W. Norton, 1970. Revisionist accounts include Gabriel and Joyce Kolko, *The Limits of Power: The World and United States Foreign Policy, 1945–54*, New York, Harper & Row, 1972; Lloyd C. Gardner, *Architects of Illusion: Men and Ideas in American Foreign Policy, 1941–49*, Chicago, Quadrangle Books, 1970; Gar Alperovitz, *Cold War Essays*, Garden City, Doubleday, 1966; Denna F. Fleming, *The Cold War and Its Origins, 1917–60*, 2 vols, Garden City, Doubleday, 1961. The post-revisionist interpretation was established by the very important book by John L. Gaddis, *The United States and the Origins of the Cold War, 1941–47*, New York, Columbia University Press, 1972. Another important post-revisionist account is Daniel Yergin, *Shattered Peace: The Origins of the Cold War and the National Security State*, Boston, Houghton Mifflin, 1977. Discussion of the different interpretations of the origins of the Cold War can be found in James V. Compton (ed.) *America and the Origins of the Cold*

War, Boston, Houghton Mifflin, 1972; Robert J. Maddox, *The New Left and the Origins of the Cold War*, Princeton, Princeton University Press, 1973; Thomas G. Paterson (ed.) *Cold War Critics: Alternatives to American Foreign Policy in the Truman Years*, Chicago, Quadrangle Books, 1971. A useful recent analysis is Randall B. Woods and Howard Jones, *Dawning of the Cold War: The United States' Quest for Order*, Athens, University of Georgia Press, 1991.

Of the vast number of monographs on particular aspects of the origins of the Cold War 1945-50 the most useful include Deborah W. Larson, *Origins of Containment: A Psychological Explanation*, Princeton, Princeton University Press, 1985; James L. Gormly, *The Collapse of the Grand Alliance, 1945-48*, Baton Rouge, Louisiana State University Press, 1987; Robert L. Messer, *The End of an Alliance: James F. Byrnes, Roosevelt, Truman and the Origins of the Cold War*, Chapel Hill, University of North Carolina Press, 1982; Lynn E. Davis, *The Cold War Begins: Soviet–American Confrontation over Eastern Europe*, Princeton, Princeton University Press, 1974; Bruce R. Kuniholm, *The Origins of the Cold War in the Near East: Great Power Conflict and Diplomacy in Iran, Turkey and Greece*, Princeton, Princeton University Press, 1980; Geir Lundstad, *America, Scandinavia and the Cold War*, New York, Columbia University Press, 1980; Lawrence S. Kaplan, *The United States and NATO: The Formative Years*, Lexington, University Press of Kentucky, 1984; Gregg Herken, *The Winning Weapon: The Atomic Bomb in the Cold War, 1945-50*, New York, Alfred A. Knopf, 1980; Thomas G. Paterson, *Soviet–American Confrontation: Postwar Reconstruction and the Origins of the Cold War*, Baltimore, Johns Hopkins University Press, 1973; Justus D. Doenecke, *Not to the Swift: The Old Isolationists in the Cold War Era*, Lewisburg, Bucknell University Press, 1979; J. Samuel Walker, *Henry A. Wallace and American Foreign Policy*, Westport, Greenwood, 1976.

On relations between China, the Soviet Union and the United Staes, the most significant books are Gordon Chang, *Friends and Enemies: The United States, China and the Soviet Union, 1948-72*, Stanford, Stanford University Press, 1990; Russell D. Buhite, *Soviet–American Relations in Asia, 1945-54*, Norman, University of Oklahoma Press, 1981; Akira Iriye (ed.) *The Origins of the Cold War in Asia*, New York, Columbia University Press, 1977; William W. Stueck, *The Road to Confrontation: American Policy Toward China and Korea, 1947-50*, Chapel Hill, University of North Carolina Press, 1981; David A. Mayers, *Cracking the Monolith: US Policy Against the Sino-Soviet Alliance, 1945-49*, Baton Rouge, Louisiana State University Press, 1986; Lisle A. Rose, *Roots of Tragedy: The United States and the Struggle for Asia, 1945-53*, Westport, Greenwood, 1976; Tang Tsou, *America's Failure in China, 1941-50*, Chicago, University of Chicago Press, 1964; Dorothy Borg and Waldo Heinrichs (eds) *Uncertain Years: Chinese-American Relations, 1947-50*, New York, Columbia University Press, 1980; Edwin W. Martin, *Divided Counsel: The Anglo-American Response to Communist Victory in China*, Lexington, University Press of Kentucky, 1986.

On the Korean War, the most useful works are James I. Matray, *The Reluctant Crusade: American Foreign Policy in Korea, 1941-50*, Honolulu,

University of Hawaii Press, 1985; Peter Lowe, *The Origins of the Korean War*, London, Longman, 1986; Burton I. Kaufman, *The Korean War: Challenges in Crisis, Credibility and Command*, Philadelphia, Temple University Press, 1986; Bruce Cumings (ed.) *Child of Conflict: The Korean-American Relationship, 1943–53*, Seattle, University of Washington Press, 1983; Callum A. MacDonald, *Korea: The War before Vietnam*, New York, Free Press, 1987; Rosemary Foot, *The Wrong War: American Policy and the Dimensions of the Korean Conflict, 1950–53*, Ithaca, Cornell University Press, 1985.

On the Red Scare and McCarthyism there is a very extensive literature, which includes, however, many superficial, sensationalist books of low quality. On the other hand, there are many valuable works on the subject, including Richard M. Fried, *Nightmare in Red: The McCarthy Era in Perspective*, New York, Oxford University Press, 1990; Earl Latham, *The Communist Controversy in Washington: From the New Deal to McCarthy*, Cambridge, Mass., Harvard University Press, 1966; David Caute, *The Great Fear: The Anti-Communist Purge under Truman and Eisenhower*, New York, Simon & Schuster, 1978; Fred J. Cook, *The Nightmare Decade: The Life and Times of Senator Joe McCarthy*, New York, Random House, 1971; Robert M. Griffith, *The Politics of Fear: Joseph R. McCarthy and the Senate*, 2nd edn, Amherst, University of Massachussetts Press, 1987; Richard H. Rovere, *Senator Joe McCarthy*, New York, Harcourt, Brace & Co., 1959; Thomas C. Reeves, *The Life and Times of Joe McCarthy*, New York, Stein & Day, 1982; Richard M. Freeland, *The Truman Doctrine and the Origins of McCarthyism*, New York, Alfred A. Knopf, 1972; Stanley I. Kutler, *The American Inquisition: Justice and Injustice in the Cold War*, New York, Hill & Wang, 1982; Ronald Radosh and Joyce Milton, *The Rosenberg File*, New York, Holt, Rinehart & Winston, 1983; Allen Weinstein, *Perjury: The Hiss–Chambers Case*, New York, Alfred A. Knopf, 1978; Larry Ceplair and Steven Englund, *The Inquisition in Hollywood*, New York, Anchor Press, 1980; Verne W. Newton, *The Cambridge Spies: The Untold Story of MacLean, Burgess and Philby in America*, Lanham, Madison Books, 1991.

On the Eisenhower era, the most useful books include Chester J. Pach and Elmo Richardson, *The Presidency of Dwight D. Eisenhower*, Lawrence, University Press of Kansas, 1991; Stephen E. Ambrose, *Eisenhower*, 2 vols, New York, Simon & Schuster, 1983–4; Robert Divine, *Eisenhower and the Cold War*, New York, Oxford University Press, 1981; Charles C. Alexander, *Holding the Line: The Eisenhower Administration, 1952–61*, Bloomington, Indiana University Press, 1975; Richard A. Melanson and David Mayers (eds) *Re-evaluating Eisenhower*, Urbana, University of Illinois Press, 1987; Townsend Hoopes, *The Devil and John Foster Dulles*, Boston, Little, Brown, 1972; Richard Immermann (ed.) *John Foster Dulles and the Diplomacy of the Cold War*, Princeton, Princeton University Press, 1990; H.W. Brands, *Eisenhower's Generation and American Foreign Policy*, New York, Columbia University Press, 1988; Bennett Kovrig, *The Myth of Liberation: East-Central Europe in US Diplomacy and Politics since 1941*, Baltimore, Johns Hopkins University Press, 1973; Iwan W. Morgan, *Eisenhower versus 'The Spenders': The*

Eisenhower Administration, the Democrats and the Budget, 1953–60, London, Pinter, 1990; Barbara B. Clowse, *Brainpower for the Cold War: The Sputnik Crisis and the National Defense Education Act of 1958*, Westport, Greenwood, 1981; Michael R. Beschloss, *Mayday: Eisenhower, Khrushchev and the U-2 Affair*, New York, Harper & Row, 1986.

On the Kennedy years, the most important works are Michael R. Beschloss, *The Crisis Years: Kennedy and Khrushchev, 1960–63*, New York, Edward Burlingame Books, 1991; Arthur M. Schlesinger, Jr, *A Thousand Days: John F. Kennedy in the White House*, Boston, Houghton Mifflin, 1965; Theodore Sorensen, *Kennedy*, New York, Harper & Row, 1965; Lord Longford, *Kennedy*, London, Weidenfeld & Nicolson, 1976; Roger Hilsman, *To Move a Nation: The Politics of Foreign Policy in the Administration of John F. Kennedy*, Garden City, Doubleday, 1967; Herbert S. Parmet, *JFK: The Presidency of John F. Kennedy*, New York, Dial Press, 1983; Thomas G. Paterson (ed.) *Kennedy's Quest for Victory: American Foreign Policy, 1961–63*, New York, Oxford University Press, 1989; Richard J. Walton, *Cold War and Counter-revolution: The Foreign Policy of John F. Kennedy*, New York, Viking Press, 1972; Henry Fairlie, *The Kennedy Promise: The Politics of Expectation*, Garden City, Doubleday, 1973; David Burner, *John F. Kennedy and a New Generation*, Boston, Little, Brown, 1988; Paul Harper and Joan Krieg (eds) *John F. Kennedy: The Promise Re-visited*, New York, Greenwood, 1988; Trumbull Higgins, *The Perfect Failure: Kennedy, Eisenhower and the CIA at the Bay of Pigs*, New York, W.W. Norton, 1987; Robert A. Divine (ed.) *The Cuban Missile Crisis*, 2nd edn, New York, Markus Weiner, 1988; Raymond L. Garthoff, *Reflections on the Cuban Missile Crisis*, rev. edn, Washington, The Brookings Institution, 1989; James G. Blight, *On the Brink: Americans and Soviets Re-examine the Cuban Missile Crisis*, 2nd edn, New York, Farrar, Strauss & Giraux, 1990; Glenn T. Seaborg, *Kennedy, Khrushchev and the Test Ban*, Berkeley, University of California Press, 1981.

On Lyndon Johnson, the formation of his attitudes to foreign policy issues can be found in Robert Dallek, *Lone Star Rising: Lyndon Johnson and His Times, 1908–1960*, New York, Oxford University Press, 1991. On Vietnam there is an extremely extensive literature, the most useful of which for US–Soviet relations include George C. Herring, *America's Longest War: The United States and Vietnam, 1950–75*, 2nd edn, New York, Alfred A. Knopf, 1986; Neil Sheehan (ed.) *The Pentagon Papers*, New York, Bantam Books, 1971; Brian Van De Merk, *Into the Quagmire: Lyndon Johnson and the Escalation of the Vietnam War*, New York, Oxford University Press, 1991; Larry Berman, *Lyndon Johnson's War: The Road to Stalemate*, New York, W.W. Norton, 1989; David L. Dileo, *George Ball, Vietnam and the Rethinking of Containment*, Chapel Hill, University of North Carolina Press, 1991; Patrick L. Hatcher, *The Suicide of an Elite: American Interventionists and Vietnam*, Stanford, Stanford University Press, 1990.

On the 1970s and 1980s two extremely useful books are Raymond L. Garthoff, *Détente and Confrontation: American–Soviet Relations from Nixon to Reagan*, Washington, The Brookings Institution, 1985; and William G. Hyland, *Mortal Rivals: Superpower Relations from Nixon to Reagan*. Both authors served in government, so that their books are a combination of memoir, historical analysis and political interpretation. Garthoff's *Détente and Confrontation* is perhaps the single, most important book on an aspect of US–Soviet relations.

On Nixon and Kissinger, the most significant works are Coral Bell, *The Diplomacy of Détente: The Kissinger Era*, New York, St Martin's Press, 1977; Robert S. Litwak, *Détente and the Nixon Doctrine: American Foreign Policy and the Pursuit of Stability, 1969–76*, Cambridge, Cambridge University Press, 1984; Stephen E. Ambrose, *Nixon*, 3 vols, New York, Simon & Schuster, 1987–91; Herbert S. Parmet, *Richard Nixon and His America*, Boston, Little, Brown, 1990; Robert D. Schulzinger, *Henry Kissinger: Doctor of Diplomacy*, New York, Columbia University Press, 1989.

On the decline of détente in the 1970s, the most useful books are Mike Bowker and Phil Williams, *Superpower Détente: A Reappraisal*, London, Sage, 1988; Donald S. Spencer, *The Carter Implosion: Jimmy Carter and the Amateur Style of Diplomacy*, New York, Praeger, 1988; David S. McLellan, *Cyrus Vance*, Totowa, Rowman & Allanheld, 1985; Fred W. Neal (ed.) *Détente or Debacle: Common Sense in US–Soviet Relations*, New York, W.W. Norton, 1979.

On Reagan and the New Cold War, 1981–85, the most important books are Strobe Talbott, *The Russians and Reagan*, New York, Vintage Books, 1984; Robert Dallek, *Ronald Reagan: The Politics of Symbolism*, Cambridge, Mass., Harvard University Press, 1984; Coral Bell, *The Reagan Paradox: American Foreign Policy in the 1980s*, Aldershot, Edward Elgar, 1989; Fred Halliday, *From Kabul to Managua: Soviet–American Relations in the 1980s*, New York, Pantheon Books, 1989; Jeff McMahon, *Reagan and the World: Imperial Policy in the New Cold War*, New York, Monthly Review Press, 1985; Kenneth A. Oye *et al.* (eds) *Eagle Defiant: United States Foreign Policy in the 1980s*, Boston, Little, Brown, 1983; Morris H. Manley (ed.) *Crisis and Confrontation: Ronald Reagan's Foreign Policy*, Totowa, Rowman and Littlefield, 1988; Alexander Dallin, *Black Box: KAL 007 and the Superpowers*, Berkeley, University of California Press, 1985; Roy Gutman, *Banana Diplomacy: The Making of American Policy in Nicaragua, 1981–87*, New York, Simon & Schuster, 1988.

On Reagan and Gorbachev, 1981–5, the most useful accounts are Michael Mandelbaum and Strobe Talbott, *Reagan and Gorbachev*, New York, Vintage Books, 1987; Seweryn Bailer and Michael Mandelbaum (eds) *Gorbachev's Russia and American Foreign Policy*, Boulder, Westview Press, 1987; Arnold Horelick (ed.) *US–Soviet Relations: The Next Phase*, Ithaca, Cornell University Press, 1986; Thomas W. Simons, Jr, *The End of the Cold War?*, New York, Macmillan, 1990; Raymond L. Garthoff, *Policy versus the Law: The Reinterpretation of the ABM Treaty*, Washington, The Brookings Institution, 1987; E. Bradford Burns, *At War in Nicaragua: The Reagan Doctrine and the Politics of Nostalgia*, New York, Harper & Row, 1987.

On the Bush era, the most useful books are Sidney Blumenthal, *Pledging Allegiance: The Last Campaign of the Cold War*, New York, Harper Collins, 1990; Robert Jarvis and Seweryn Bailer (eds) *Soviet–American*

Relations After the Cold War, Durham, NC, Duke University Press, 1991; Michael Pugh and Phil Williams (eds) *Superpower Politics: Change in the United States and the Soviet Union*, Manchester, Manchester University Press, 1990.

On the issues of the arms race and arms control there is an immense literature. Among the most useful books on defence and the arms race are McGeorge Bundy, *Danger and Survival: Choices About the Bomb in the First Fifty Years*, New York, Random House, 1988; John Newhouse, *War and Peace in the Nuclear Age*, New York, Alfred A. Knopf, 1989; Ronald Powaski, *March to Armageddon: The United States and the Nuclear Arms Race*, New York, Oxford University Press, 1987; Charles R. Morris, *Iron Destinies, Lost Opportunities: The Arms Race between the USA and the USSR, 1945–1987*, New York, Harper & Row, 1988; Erik Beukel, *American Perceptions of the Soviet Union as a Nuclear Adversary*, London, Pinter, 1989; Gregg Herken, *Counsels of War*, New York, Alfred A. Knopf, 1985. On arms control, significant books include Coit D. Blacker, *Reluctant Warriors: The United States, the Soviet Union and Arms Control*, New York, W.H. Freeman & Co., 1987; John H. Barton, *The Politics of Peace: An Evaluation of Arms Control*, Stanford, Stanford University Press, 1981; Alva Myrdal, *The Game of Disarmament: How the United States and Russia Run the Arms Race*, rev. edn, New York, Pantheon, 1982; Alexander L. George, Philip J. Farley and Alexander Dallin (eds) *US–Soviet Security Co-operation: Achievements, Failures, Lessons*, New York, Oxford University Press, 1988. Interesting insights into arms control negotiations can be learned from a series of three books by Strobe Talbott, *Endgame: The Inside Study of SALT II*, New York, Harper & Row, 1979; *Deadly Gambits: The Reagan Administration and the Stalemate in Nuclear Arms Control*, New York, Alfred A. Knopf, 1984; and *The Master of the Game: Paul Nitze and the Nuclear Peace*, New York, Alfred A. Knopf, 1988. On the important and controversial subject of intelligence, two well-balanced accounts are John Ranelagh, *The Agency: The Rise and Decline of the CIA*, New York, Simon & Schuster, 1986; and Rhodri Jeffreys-Jones, *The CIA and American Democracy*, New Haven, Yale University Press, 1989.

The military-industrial complex and the economic impact of the Cold War have been extensively covered. Among the most useful books on the subject are Hugh G. Mosley, *The Arms Race: Economic and Social Consequences*, Lexington, D.C. Heath & Co., 1985; James L. Clayton (ed.) *The Economic Impact of the Cold War*, New York, Harcourt, Brace & World, 1970; Steven Rosen (ed.) *Testing the Theory of the Military-Industrial Complex*, Lexington, D.C. Heath & Co., 1973. On trade and economic relations with the Soviet Union, the most important accounts are Philip Funigiello, *American–Soviet Trade in the Cold War*, Chapel Hill, University of North Carolina Press, 1988; James K. Libbey, *American–Soviet Economic Relations, 1770s–1990s*, Claremont, Regina Books, 1989; Marshall I. Goldman, *Détente and Dollars: Doing Business with the Soviets*, New York, Basic Books, 1975; Bruce W. Jentleson, *Pipeline Politics: The Complex Economy of East–West Trade*, Ithaca, Cornell University Press, 1986.

On cultural and educational exchanges, the most useful books are

J.D. Parks, *Culture, Conflict and Co-existence: American–Soviet Cultural Relations, 1917–58*, Jefferson, McFarland, 1983; Yale Richmond, *US–Soviet Cultural Exchanges, 1958–86*, Boulder, Westview Press, 1987; Nish Jamgotch, Jr, *US–Soviet Co-operation: A New Future*, New York, Praeger, 1989. On interpersonal relations a good account is Gale Warner and Michael Schuman, *Citizen Diplomats: Pathfinders in Soviet–American Relations*, New York, Continuum, 1987.

On radio propaganda the literature is relatively limited. The most useful accounts are Sig Mickelson, *America's Other Voice: the Story of Radio Free Europe and Radio Liberty*, New York, Praeger, 1983; Kenneth R.M. Short (ed.) *Western Broadcasting over the Iron Curtain*, London, Croom, Helm, 1986; Donald R. Browne, *International Radio Broadcasting: The Limits of the Limitless Medium*, New York, Praeger, 1982; Robert W. Piersin, *The Voice of America: A History of the International Broadcasting Activities of the US Government, 1940–62*, New York, Arno Press, 1979; Ludmilla Alexeyeva, *US Broadcasting to the Soviet Union*, Washington, Helsinki Watch, 1986.

Finally, on the image of the Soviet Union in the United States, important works include Benson L. Grayson (ed.) *The American Image of Russia*, New York, Frederick Ungar, 1978; Peter G. Filene (ed.) *American Views of Soviet Russia, 1917–65*, Homewood, Dorsey Press, 1968; William Welch, *American Images of Soviet Foreign Policy*, New Haven, Yale University Press, 1970; Stephen F. Cohen, *Sovieticus: American Perceptions and Soviet Realities*, New York, W.W. Norton, 1985.

Aside from books, of very great importance, especially for the more recent period, are journals. Among the most significant are *Diplomacy and Statecraft, Diplomatic History, Foreign Affairs, International Affairs, International History Review, International Security, Political Science Quarterly, World Politics*. The most useful weekly, monthly or quarterly magazines are *Time, Newsweek, The New Republic, US News and World Report*, and *The National Interest*. The most useful newspapers are the *New York Times, Washington Post, Los Angeles Times*, and *International Herald Tribune*.

INDEX

ABM (anti-ballistic missiles) 158, 170–1
ABM Treaty: defensive shield 206; Moscow summit 169, 170–1; and SDI 218, 219
Acheson, Dean: China 73, 77, 80, 81, 92–3; Communism 58, 106; containment 106; Cuba 137; on Korea 91; McCarthy 106–7, 115; New Deal 113; *Present at the Creation* 67; reputation 113; as traditionalist 54; US defence perimeter 86; West Germany 97
Afghanistan 186, 196, 210, 222, 236, 253–4
Albania 159
Algeria, US troops 41
Alliance for Progress 138
Allied Control Commission agreements 56
Alliluyeva, Svetlana 212, 260
Allison, Graham 242–3
Allison, John 90
America *see* US
American Communist Party 26–7, 31, 43
American Federation of Labor 14
American Relief Administration (ARA) 19–20
Americans for Democratic Action 103
Andropov, Yuri 130, 200–1, 212
Angola 184, 210, 222, 236, 243, 254

anti-ballistic missiles *see* ABM system
appeasement 34, 39, 135, 257, 281
ARA (American Relief Administration) 19–20
Arab oil boycott 177
Architects of Illusion (Gardner) 67
arms control negotiations: difficulties 235–6, 270; Geneva summit 125; Glassboro summit 158; Reagan 203–4; START 204–5, 215, 219, 243; verification 59, 170, 220, 236, 244; *see also* SALT talks
arms race 54, 269, 270
atomic bomb 50–3, 58–9, 65
atomic testing 126, 131
Attlee, Clement 94, 95
Austin, Warren 90–1
Austrian peace treaty 125
Azerbaijan 58

B–1 bomber 170, 202
B–52 bombers 245
Baker, James 227, 230–1, 235–6, 241, 279
Baltic states 5, 17, 35, 234, 245
Baruch Plan 58–9, 65
Basic Principles Agreement 172, 177, 187
Battle Act, US 98, 263
Bay of Pigs invasion 137–8, 151, 253
Begin, Menachim 192

Bell, Coral 190, 225
Beria, Lavrenti 121
Berlin 61, 131–2, 139
Berlin Wall 139, 231
Bevin, Ernest 87
bipartisanship 275–6
Blunt, Anthony 105
Bohlen, Charles: Bolsheviks 250; Korean War 96; Nazi-Soviet relations 34; Soviets in World War II 41; Stalin 51–2; Truman 48; US/Soviet reconciliation 44
Bohr, Niels 51
Boland amendment 222
Bolshevik Revolution 3, 4
Bolsheviks: Allies against 7, 9, 10; armistice agreement 11; Baltic states 17; Bohlen 250; Britain 5, 10; as German agents 7; vs Provisional Government 2–3, 18–19; US recognition 3, 4, 5–7, 28
bombers 131, 170, 194, 202, 245
bombing incidents, US 15
Borah, William E. 10, 21
boycotts 177, 198, 211, 258
Brest-Litovsk, Treaty of 3, 5, 6
Brezhnev, Leonid 153, 155, 172, 175, 176, 251
Brezhnev Doctrine 161, 186–7, 230
brinkmanship 126
Britain: appeasement 34, 39; Bolsheviks 5; China 81, 94; Communist infiltration 105; Cruise missiles 205; Formosa 89; Iran 126; NATO 69; rearmament 97; trade with Soviet Union 259–60; US relations 263
Brzezinski, Zbigniew 186, 191, 195
budget deficit 247
Bukharin, Nikolai 18, 33
Bukovsky, Vladimir 190
Bulganin, Nikolai 121
Bulgaria 232
Bullitt, William 11, 25, 29–31, 32, 275

Burgess, Guy 105
Bush, George: budget deficit 247; Communism 227; containment 228; criticised 230, 243; Eastern Europe 208; Gorbachev 276; human rights 232–3; policy review US/Soviet relations 228
Byrnes, James 59, 64

Cairo conference 84–5
Cambodia 166, 177, 185, 236
Camp David: (1973) Nixon/Brezhnev 175–6; (1978) agreement 192
Campaign for Nuclear Disarmament 203
capitalism 3, 4, 112–13, 249, 278–80
Captive People's Resolution 121
Caribbean Basin Initiative 210
Carter Jimmy, US President 190–1, 192, 195, 276
Castro, Fidel 132–3, 137–8, 141–2, 237; see also Cuba
Catholic Church 21, 25
Ceaucescu, Nicolai 233
Central America 210–11, 250
CFE (Conventional Forces in Europe) talks 221, 236, 241, 242, 271
Cheney, Richard 227–8, 229, 235, 239
Chernenko, Konstantin 200
Chiang Kai-shek: Cairo conference 84–5; Formosa 78–9, 127; Nationalists 71, 72, 73; Roosevelt 47; US aid 74–6
Chicherin, George 18, 20
Chile 179
China: Britain 81, 94; Communist expansion 71–3, 75, 76–7; human rights 232–3; Japan 72; Kennedy 139–40; Korea 84, 92–5; Mao Zedong 71, 74–5, 80–3, 89, 167; MFN status 237; Nationalists 71–3, 75, 76, 128–9; Nixon 167–8; Open Door policy 24, 72; People's

Republic 71, 77; Reagan 210; Roosevelt 47; Soviet Union 80; Stalin 74; Tienanmen Square 232–3, 268; United Nations membership 167; Yalta 73–5

China–Soviet Union–US triangle 83, 179

Churchill, Winston: Bolsheviks 10; Cairo conference 84–5; deterrence 271; Eisenhower 122–4; Iron Curtain 67–8; military occupation 49; Nazis 37–8; and Roosevelt 40–1, 42; Soviet leadership 122; and Stalin 42, 46, 48; trade with Soviets 259–60; and Truman 49; and UNO 47

CIA operations: Afghanistan 210; Angola 184, 254; Chile 179; Cuba 133, 141–2; Eisenhower 125, 136–7; funding for radio 264–5, 266; Guatemala 253–4; Iran 126–7; Italy 63; Nicaragua 254, 279

citizen diplomacy 258

civil liberties 105, 106, 108, 273, 279

Clark amendment (1976) 184

CND 203

coalition governments 62–3

COCOM (Co-ordinating Committee of the Paris Consultative Group of Nations) 98, 263

Cold War: ended 245; fundamentalism 211; revisionist interpretation 62–6; thawing 116; traditional interpretation 54–62

Cominform 56

Comintern 12, 25, 26–7, 31, 43

Committee on the Present Danger 193

Commonwealth of Independent States 246

Communism: Bush 227; and capitalism 112–13, 249, 278–80; Caribbean and

Central America 156–7; Catholic Church 21, 25; collapse 227; and democracy 249, 278–80; education 108; Eisenhower 118–19; elections 55–6; Mao Zedong 74–5, 80; nationalistic 150, 267, 268; Nixon 119; propaganda 12, 31; Reagan 209–10, 221, 276; reforms 278; US attitudes 13–14, 16, 32, 102, 106, 253–4

Communist expansion 58–61; China 71–3, 75, 76–7; Cold War 54–5; Far East 127–9, 153; Third World 153, 186

Communist infiltration 101–3, 105, 106

Communist International 12

Communist Labor Party 12, 13, 26–7

Communist Party 12, 13–14

Conference on Security and Co-operation in Europe (CSCE) 183

containment: Acheson 106; Bush 228; Kennan 60, 97, 254–6; liberation 120–1; military 96; success 280, 281; Vietnam 153

Contras 222–3, 236–7, 254, 279; see also Nicaragua

Conventional Forces in Europe: see CFE

Coolidge, Calvin 20–1

Cooper Amendment 177

Cowley, Malcolm 32

CREEP (Campaign to Re-elect the President) 174

Cruise missiles 194, 204, 205, 220

CSCE (Conference on Security and Co-operation in Europe) 183

Cuba: Bay of Pigs 137–8, 151, 253; CIA 133, 141–2; missile crisis 141–8, 151, 270; nuclear weapons 142, 143–4; quarantined 145–6; Revolution 132–3; Soviet Union 142, 237, 251; see also Castro

Cuban troops, to Angola 184

INDEX

Cultural Agreement (1958) 157, 198, 258–9
Czech legion 8
Czechoslovakia: Communism 56–7; dissidents 208; Dubcek 159, 160–1; Havel 232; Prague Spring 267; radio broadcasts 265

Daniels, Robert V. 249
Davies, John Patton 80
Davies, Joseph 36, 43, 49
Dawes Plan 17
Day After, The (film) 203
Debs, Eugene 14
debt settlement 17, 25, 26, 27–8, 30–1
Declaration on Liberated Europe 47
defection 259
defence expenditure 68, 70, 126, 201–3, 217–18
Defense Guidance Plan (1982) 203
democracy: vs Communism 3–5, 249, 278–80; reforms needed 281
Democracy in America (De Tocqueville) 276
Department of the Army 110, 111
détente: Brezhnev 186; commercial benefits 171–2; criticized 179–81; demise 182; in difficulties 188; Helsinki Agreement 183; Kissinger 163, 179, 262; Nixon 163; Reagan 189, 200; Truman 68; U-2 shot down 132; Yom Kippur War 176–7
deterrence, nuclear 268–71, 280
Diem, Ngo Ding 127–8, 140, 149, 150
Dien Bien Phu 127
diplomatic relations, US/USSR 18–19, 24–6, 28, 29–30
dissidents 189, 208, 209, 229
Dole, Robert 224
Dominican Republic 156–7
Dubcek, Alexander 159, 160–1, 232, 267

Dulles, Allen 133, 137
Dulles, John Foster 78, 118, 120, 121, 126, 276

Eagleburger, Lawrence 230, 233
East Germany 121, 231, 267; see also Germany
Eastern Europe: economic aid 240–1; indebtedness 187; revisionist view 62–3; satellites 265; Soviet policy 55, 66; Stalin 45; US 46, 208
economic aid, to Soviet Union 65
economic interests 276–7
EDC (European Defence Community) 97, 125
Egypt 192
Eisenhower, Dwight D. 41, 42–3, 116; Churchill 122–4; CIA 125, 136–7; Communism 118–19; containment 276; Farewell Address 133, 134; Korea 99; and McCarthy 110, 117, 118–20; military/economic link 277; in NATO 96; Nixon 118; and Zhukov 50
El Salvador 185, 210, 237
elections, under Communism 55–6
espionage 14, 263
Estonia 5, 17, 35, 234, 245
Ethiopa 184–5, 243
European Defence Community (EDC) 97, 125
exchange programmes 196, 197, 223, 238
EXCOM (Executive Committee of the National Security Council) 144, 145, 146
Export–Import Bank loans 267

Finland 35–6, 63
First World War: see World War I
Fish, Hamilton 32, 38
FNLA, Angola 184
Foch, Ferdinand 11
Ford, Gerald 20, 33, 182, 184, 189
Foreign Assistance Act 76
Formosa 78–9, 89, 127, 128; see also Taiwan

313

France 34, 127, 141
Francis, David 1–2, 5, 7, 10
Franks, Oliver 87
free-enterprise capitalism vs
    Communism 112–13, 249
Fuchs, Klaus 52, 104
Fukuyama, Francis 240
Fulbright, William 114, 137, 165

Gardner, Lloyd 67
Garthoff, Raymond 142, 143,
    183, 191, 192, 201
Gaulle, Charles de 141
General Electric 20
General Intelligence Division 13
Geneva agreement (1954) 127–8
Geneva summit: (1955) 125;
    (1985) 217
Gerasonov, Gennadi 230
Germany 5, 57, 63–4, 168,
    233–5; see also East Germany;
    West Germany
glasnost 217, 223–4, 229, 259,
    262, 278
Glassboro 158
Goldwater, Barry 136, 154
Gorbachev, Mikhail 215–16;
    Bush 276; public relations
    220, 238–9; resigned 244;
    restored 245, 246–7; Soviet
    economy 241–2; Soviet
    reforms 229–30, 233–4, 278
Government Operations
    Committee 110–11
grain sales 207, 261; see also
    wheat sales
Greece 60, 63
Green Berets 137
Grenada 210
Gromyko, Andrei 143, 178, 216,
    217
Guatemala 126, 253–4

Haig, Alexander 203
Haiphong, bombing 169
Hammer, Armand 20, 197, 260
Harding, Warren 15, 18, 19
Harriman, Averell 20, 38, 48, 67,
    211
Harris, E.L. 8

Havel, Vaclav 190, 232
Hayter, William 124
Heale, Michael 14
Helsinki Agreement 183
Henderson, Loy 18, 22, 30,
    41–2, 92
Hiss, Alger 31, 104, 106
Hitler, Adolph 24, 34, 35, 37, 38
Ho Chi Minh 140, 141, 153
Hollywood, and Communism
    107–8
Holmes, Oliver Wendell 13
Honduras, CIA 126
Hoover, Herbert 19, 21–3
Hoover, J. Edgar 13, 32
Hopkins, Harry 38, 49
House Unamerican Activities
    Committee 107
Huang Hua 82
Hughes, Charles Evans 18
human rights 183, 190–1, 232–3,
    276
Hungarian Revolution 121,
    129–30
Hungary 55, 159, 208, 229, 230,
    267
hydrogen bomb 96
Hyland, William 164–5, 269

ICBMs (intercontinental ballistic
    missiles): SALT I 170, 187;
    Soviet 130, 244; START 220;
    US 130–1, 136; vulnerability
    194
Immigration Act (1924), US 24
Indo-China, and France 127
Industrial Workers of the World
    (IWW) 14
INF (intermediate range nuclear
    forces) 215, 219, 220, 271
inflation 174–5, 182
intercontinental ballistic missile
    see ICBMs
intermarriages 238
International Information
    Agency 110–11
Iran 57–8, 64, 126–7, 253
Iran–Contra plan 222–3, 225
Iranian hostages 194, 196
Iraq, invading Kuwait 241

Iron Curtain 49, 67–8, 229, 231
isolationism, US 34, 38–9, 69,
    252–3, 273–4
Israel 130, 176, 192
Italy 63

Jackson, Henry 176, 178, 184, 188
Jackson–Vanik amendment
    (1973) 178, 188, 197, 223,
    237, 262–3
Japan: atomic bomb 52; China
    72; expansionism 23–4; Soviet
    Union 47, 52–3; US 29, 40–1;
    Wilson 8
Jaruzelski, Wojciek 208, 229–30
Jewish emigration: Carter 190;
    Jackson–Vanik amendment
    178, 223, 237, 262–3; Reagan
    209; see also Soviet Jews
Johnson, Hiram 10, 15, 23, 273–4
Johnson, Lyndon 150, 152,
    156–7, 197
Johnson Act (1934), US 33

Kamenev, Lev 18, 33
Katyn Forest massacre 45
Kennan, George: Bolsheviks 3;
    China/Soviet relationship 80;
    containment 60, 97, 120,
    254–6; Korea 90; Malik 98;
    McCarthy 115; in Moscow 98;
    Soviet expansion 45–6, 60;
    US/Soviet reconciliation 44,
    45–6; Vietnam 157–8; in
    Yugoslavia 141
Kennedy, John F. 135–6, 151;
    China 139–40; Cuban missile
    crisis 147–8; Khrushchev
    138–9, 146–7; missile gap
    276; Vietnam 140–1, 149–50
Kennedy, Robert 147
Kerensky, Alexander 2–3
Khrushchev, Nikita 121;
    Kennedy 138–9, 146–7;
    Nixon 132; Stalin 129
Kim Il Sung, North Korea 85, 88
Kirkpatrick, Jeanne 209–10, 273
Kirov, Sergei 33
Kissinger, Henry 164; détente
    163, 179, 262; Ford 182; Le

Duc Tho 166, 169; *Nuclear
Weapons and Foreign Policy*
164; shuttle diplomacy 176–7,
192; Soviet dissidents 189;
Soviet reform 243; Vietnam
173
Kohl, Helmut 234, 241
Korea: armistice negotiations
    98–9; China 84, 92–5;
    Eisenhower 99; elections
    85–6; Nixon 99; prisoners of
    war 99; significance to US
    88–9, 90; 38th Parallel 84, 85,
    91–2; Truman 87, 92, 94; see
    also North Korea; South Korea
Korean War 70, 79, 84, 88–9,
    90–8
Kornilov revolt 3
Kosygin, Alexei 155, 158
Kuwait, invaded 241

Laird, Melvin 170
Lansing, Robert 4, 6
Laos 140, 166, 177
Latvia 5, 17, 22, 35, 234, 245
League of Nations 5
Le Duc Tho 166, 169
Lend-Lease, to Soviet Union 41,
    44, 65, 171–2, 188
Lend-Lease Act (1941), US 37,
    38, 65, 171–2, 188
Lenin, Vladimir Ilyich 2–4,
    17–18, 43
liberation vs containment 120–1
Liberty League 113
Lithuania 5, 17, 35, 234, 242, 245
Litvinov, Maxim 25–6, 28, 30,
    38, 41–2
Los Angeles Olympics, boycotted
    211
loyalty boards 103, 105, 108, 119
Lvov, Prince 2

MacArthur, Douglas: Chinese
    intervention 93–4;
    homecoming 112; Inchon
    89–90; North Korea 91–2; US
    defence perimeter 86
MacFarlane, Robert 217, 223
MacLean, Donald 105

Macmillan, Harold 131–2
MAD (mutual assured
    destruction) 158
Malenkov, Georgi 121–2
Malik, Jacob 98
Malta summit (1989) 231, 232
Manchuria, Japanese invasion 24
Manhattan Project 50–2
Mao Zedong: Communism 74–5,
    80; 'On People's Democratic
    Dictatorship' 83; People's
    Republic of China 71; Soviet
    Union 80, 82; Taiwan 89; US
    81, 167
Marshall, George 41, 72, 75, 93,
    106–7
Marshall Plan 61, 65–6, 68–9,
    96–7, 267
Matsu 128
McCarran Act (1950), US 103,
    105
McCarthy, Joseph 108–12;
    Acheson 106–7, 115; China
    77; Eisenhower 110, 117,
    118–20; Kennan 115; Red
    Scare 101–2
McCarthyism 79, 112, 114–15, 274
McNamara, Robert: Cuba 145;
    defence costs 136; Johnson
    152; nuclear arms 158, 171;
    Vietnam 150
MFN: see Most Favoured Nation
    status
Military Assistance Program 96–7
military expenditure,
    pump-priming 277
military occupation zones 49, 50,
    57
Miliukov, Paul 2
MIRVs (multiple independently
    targeted re-entry vehicles)
    169–70, 184
missile gap 136, 276
missiles, nuclear: ABM 158,
    170–1; Cruise 194, 204, 205,
    220; ICBM 130–1, 136, 170,
    187, 194, 220, 244; MX 202;
    Pershing I 220; Pershing II
    194, 204, 220; Poseidon 194;
    SLBM 136, 187, 194, 205,

220; SS series 142, 187, 204,
    220; Trident 194
Mission to Moscow (film) 43, 107
Molotov, V.I. 34, 41, 48, 59, 74,
    121
Mondale, Walter 190, 213
Moscow Olympics boycott 198
Moscow summit: (1972) 169;
    (1988) 221
Most Favoured Nation status
    32–3, 171, 188, 237–8
MPLA, Angola 184, 222
multiple independently targeted
    re-entry vehicles: see MIRVs
Murmansk 7
Murrow, Ed 111
mutual assured destruction 158
Mutual Balanced Force
    Reduction (MBFR) 205
MX missiles 202

nationalistic Communism 150,
    187, 267, 268
NATO (North Atlantic Treaty
    Organization) 61; CFE talks
    236; Eisenhower 96; Korean
    War 96; nuclear capability
    220; and rearmament 117;
    united Germany 233–5; US
    joining 69; West Germany 125
Nazi-Soviet Pact 35, 37
Nazis 32, 34, 37–8
New Deal 112, 113, 114, 119
New Economic Policy 17–18
Nicaragua: aid to Contras 236–7,
    254, 279; CIA 254, 279;
    Iran–Contra scandal 222–3,
    225; Reagan 210–11, 222–3;
    Sandinistas 185–6, 222, 223,
    236, 237
Nicolas II, Tsar of Russia 1
Nixon, Richard 163–4; Brezhnev
    172, 175; in China 167–8;
    Communism 119; criticized
    180–1; détente 163; on
    Eisenhower 118; impeached
    174, 176; and Khrushchev
    132; Korea 99; US/Soviet
    relations 172–3, 179; Vietnam
    164–5

North, Oliver, Colonel 223
North Atlantic Treaty
    Organization: *see* NATO
North Korea 84, 86–7, 88, 253,
    254; *see also* Korea
North Star (film) 107
North Vietnam 141, 168–9, 177;
    see also Vietnam
nuclear alert 176, 245
nuclear arms cuts 204, 213
nuclear capabilities 155–6, 187,
    194, 220, 251
nuclear co-operation 124
nuclear deterrence 268–71, 280
nuclear disarmament 245
Nuclear Freeze Movement 203
Nuclear Non-proliferation
    Treaty 158
Nuclear and Space Talks 215, 218
nuclear test limitations 148, 179
*Nuclear Weapons and Foreign
    Policy* (Kissinger) 164

occupation zones 49, 50, 57
oil price rise 195
oil refineries 64
Olympic Games boycotted 198,
    211, 258
OPEC (Organization of
    Petroleum Exporting
    Countries) 177
Open Door, China 24, 72
Oppenheimer, Robert 51
Overman Committee 12

Palmer, A. Mitchell 12–13, 15
Pearl Harbour 38
'People's Democratic Dictatorship,
    On' (Mao Zedong) 83
People's Republic of China: see
    China
perestroika: arms control 236;
    economics 262; effectiveness
    239–40; US attitudes 216–17,
    223–4, 231
Perle, Richard 178, 203–4
Pershing I 220
Pershing II 194, 204, 220
Pescadores 128
Philby, Kim 105

Philippines 24
Pipes, Richard 176, 207, 268
pluralism 281
Poindexter, John, Admiral 223
Poland: boundaries 45, 183;
    Germany 5, 168; government
    45, 49, 55; Hitler 35;
    Jaruzelski 208, 229–30;
    Solidarity 187, 229–30, 267;
    Soviet Union 45–7, 129
Polaris submarines 131, 194
Poole, Frederick C., General 9–10
Poseidon missiles 194
post-revisionism 66–7
post-war boundaries 183
Potsdam conference 50, 52
Prague Spring 267
Present at the Creation (Acheson) 67
press censorship, Soviet 224
Prevention of Nuclear War 175
prisoners of war 7
Provisional Government 2–3,
    18–19
purges 18, 33–4

Quayle, Dan 230
Quemoy 128

Radek, Karl 33
radicals imprisoned 13
radio broadcasting 130, 198,
    263–5, 266; *see also* Voice of
    America
Radio Free Europe 130, 198, 266
Radio Liberation 264
Radio Liberty 238, 264
Rapallo, Treaty of 21
Reagan, Ronald 199–200; arms
    control 203–4; China 210;
    Communism 209–10, 221,
    276; détente 189, 200;
    Gorbachev 217; in Moscow
    221; Nicaragua 210–11,
    222–3; Soviet Union 200–1
Reagan Doctrine 221–2
rearmament 97, 117, 125
Red Army 41, 42, 43, 251
red peril 69–70
Red Scare 12–14, 34, 101–2, 112
religious freedom 25, 26

Republican Party 113–14, 116–17, 120–1
revisionist historians 62–3, 250
Reykjavik meeting 218–19
Rhee, Syngman, South Korea 85, 88, 99
Rise and Fall of Great Powers, The (Paul Kennedy) 218
Robins, Raymond 6
Roosevelt, Franklin: Cairo conference 84–5; China 47; Churchill 40–1, 42; debt settlement 31; Eastern Europe 46; Soviet Union 19, 24–6, 28; Stalin 37–8, 40–1, 42; UNO 43
Roosevelt administration 37
Roosevelt–Litvinov Agreements 26, 27, 30–1
Rosenbergs, Julius and Ethel 52, 104
Rosenfield, Stephen 240
round-the-clock alert 245
Romania 55, 159, 168, 183, 233
Rumsfield, Donald 182
Rusk, Dean 95, 139–40, 150, 152
Russia: Bolsheviks 2–3, 4, 7, 10, 11, 17; Provisional Government 2–3, 18–19; US troops 9–10, 11–12; Whites 11, 12; *see also* Soviet Union
Russian Revolution 1–2

Sadat, Anwar 192
Safire, William 239–40
Sakharov, Andrei 190, 191, 229
SALT I talks 158, 168, 169–70, 178, 187, 188, 219
SALT II talks 178, 183, 184, 193, 219
SAMs (surface-to-air missiles) 143
Sandinistas 185–6, 222, 223, 236, 237
Savings and Loans collapse 247
Schlesinger, Arthur, Jr 27, 55, 103, 147, 149, 150
Scowcroft, Brent 182, 227–8, 233
SDI: arms control 215, 270–1; economic impact 277; legality of 218; Reagan 205–7, 225; Reykjavik 219

secret police 30, 43
See It Now (Murrow) 111
Segal, Gerald 225
Service, John Stewart 80, 104
Shatalin, Grigori 241
Shcharansky, Anatoly 190, 198
Shevardnadze, Eduard 217, 219, 241, 242
show trials 33
Shultz, George 207, 208, 219, 267
shuttle diplomacy 176–7, 192
Siberia 7–8
Sino-Soviet relations 127, 156, 166
Sino-Soviet Treaty (1950) 71, 268
Sisson, Edgar 7
SLBMs (submarine-launched ballistic missiles) 136, 187, 194, 205, 220
Smith Act (1940), US 103
'Socialism in One Country' (Stalin) 18
Sofaer, Abraham 218
Solidarity 187, 229–30, 267
Solzhenitsyn, Alexander 189, 190
South Korea, invaded 84, 86
South Vietnam: defections from 155; established 128; troop withdrawal 165; *see also* Vietnam
Soviet dissidents 189, 208, 209, 229
Soviet Jews 178, 190, 209, 223, 237, 262–3
Soviet Union (USSR) 17, 32; in Afghanistan 186; aid to 65; airliner shot down 212; atomic testing 61; Britain 122, 259–60; China 79–80, 127, 156, 166; coup 244–5; credit-worthiness 21, 33; Cuba 142, 184, 237, 251; cultural nationalism 69; Eastern Europe 55, 66; economy 277–8; expansionism 45–6, 60, 250–1; Five-Year Plan 18, 23; and Hitler 34; ICBM 130–1; Iraq 241, 242; Japan 47, 52–3; liberalization 262; North Vietnam 156; Poland

45–7, 129; reform 233; Roosevelt 19, 24–6, 28; secret police 30, 43; as superpower 112; technological capabilities 131; Third World conflicts 184–6; Turkey 57, 58, 64; US view 18–19, 43, 200–1
Sputnik 130
SS–4 missiles 142, 204
SS–5 missiles 142, 204
SS–12 missiles 220
SS–18 missiles 187
SS–20 missiles 187, 204, 220
SS–23 missiles 220
Stalin, Joseph: atomic bomb 51–3; China 74; Churchill 42, 46, 48; death of 99; Eastern Europe 45; foreign policy 34; and Germany 57; Khrushchev 129; Mao 74–5; Poland 45–7; Roosevelt 37–8, 40–1, 42; 'Socialism in One Country' 18; Yalta Agreement 46–7, 48
Star Wars: see SDI
START talks 204–5, 215, 219, 220, 243
Stealth bomber 194
Steinhardt, Laurence 36–7
Stevenson, Adlai 145, 188
Stevenson amendment 188
Stinger missiles 222
Stone, I.F. 88
Strategic Arms Limitation Talks: see SALT
Strategic Arms Reduction Talks: see START
Strategic Defense Initiative: see SDI
strikes, in US 15
submarine-launched ballistic missiles: see SLBMs
summit meetings 256–7; Camp David 158; Geneva 125, 217; Glassboro 158; Malta 231, 232; Moscow 169, 170–1, 221; Reykjavik 218–19
surface-to-air anti-aircraft missiles 143
Suslov, Mikhail 155
Syria 177

Taft, Robert 252
Taiwan 89, 167, 210; see also Formosa
Talbott, Strobe 247
tax increases 247
Tehran, Conference 42
Thatcher, Margaret 215, 241
Thieu, Nguyan Van 165
38th Parallel, US crossing 89–92, 93
Threads (film) 203
Tiananmen Square massacre 232–3, 268
Tito 56, 81, 129, 267
Titoism 81, 82, 129, 141, 150, 187
Tocqueville, Alexis De 276
Tonkin Gulf Resolution 154
tourism, to Soviet Union 197, 238
trade, East Europe/US 265–6, 274
trade, US/Soviet: extent 237–8, 259–61; Jackson amendment 197; Johnson 197; MFN 32–3, 237–8; (1920s) 20–1; restrictions 12, 207–8; see also wheat sales
Trade Reform Bill 178, 188
Trident missiles 194
Trident submarines 170
Trotsky, Leon 5, 6, 18
Truman, Harry: atomic bomb 53; and Attlee 95; and China 75–6; Churchill 49; and Cold War 66; and détente 68; Korea 87, 92, 94; re-elected 114; Soviet policies 48–9; Temporary Committee on Employment Loyalty 103; as traditionalist 54; use of force 99–100; World War II 37
Truman Doctrine 60
Tudeh Party, Iran 58
Turkey: containment 60; and Soviet Union 57, 58, 64; US missiles 145, 147
Tydings committee, on McCarthyism 109–10

U–2 spy plane 131, 132, 143
Ukraine 244

un-American Activities
   committees 104
underground nuclear testing 179
Union of Russian Workers 13
Union of Soviet Socialist
   Republics: see Soviet Union
Union Treaty 242, 244
UNITA, Angola 184, 222
United Nations Organization
   43–4, 47, 78, 167
United Nations Relief and
   Rehabilitation Agency 60
United Nations Subcommittee
   on Disarmament 125
United Nations Temporary
   Commission in Korea 85
United States Information
   Agency 266
US: aid to Russia 3, 12;
   Bolsheviks 4, 5–7, 28; Britain
   263; China 72, 74–6, 77–8,
   81–2, 94, 166–8, 221, 268;
   Communism 13–14, 16, 32,
   102, 106, 253–4; Eastern
   Europe 208; famine relief
   19–20; foreign policy 278–9;
   ideology 272–3, 274–5;
   invading Cuba 138; invading
   North Korea 90; isolationism
   34, 38–9, 69, 252–3, 273–4;
   Japan 29, 40–1; Korea 88–9,
   90; military expenditure 96,
   117, 123; NATO 69; Nazi
   Germany 29; repression of
   radicals 13; Soviet reform 98,
   242–4, 252–6; Third World
   intervention 273; violence
   160; World War II 38, 40–1
US troops: to Russia 9–10; in
   South Korea 84, 87;
   withdrawn from Russia 11–12
US–Soviet relationship:
   diplomatic 18–19, 24–6, 28,
   29–30, 44, 45–6; Eisenhower
   116; Nixon 172–3, 179;
   personalized 211–12, 257–8,
   259; World War II 38, 40; see
   also Cold War
US–Soviet–China 83, 179
USSR: see Soviet Union

Vance, Cyrus 191, 195
Vanik, Charles 178
verification 59, 170, 220, 236, 244
Versailles, Treaty of 15
Versailles Conference 11
Vietnam: containment 153;
   Diem 127–8, 140, 149, 150;
   escalation 153–4, 155; Ho Chi
   Minh 140, 141, 153; Kennan
   157–8; Kennedy 140–1,
   149–50; misreading 195, 250;
   Nixon 164–5; settlement 173;
   Soviet Union 185; Tet
   offensive 160; Viet Cong 140;
   Westmoreland 159–60; see also
   North Vietnam; South
   Vietnam
Vladivostok 7–8
Voice of America 69, 110, 198,
   223, 238, 263–5

Wall Street Crash 17
Wallace, Henry 54, 273
War Powers Act, US (1973) 177
Warsaw Pact 235
Washington Conference 17
Watergate scandal 173–4, 176,
   195
Weinberger, Caspar 202
West Germany 97, 125, 168
Westmoreland, William 159–60
wheat sales 150, 171, 174, 175,
   196–7; see also grain sales
Why England Slept (Kennedy) 135
Wilkie, Wendell 43
Wilson, Woodrow 2; civil
   liberties 273; democracy 3–5,
   249; Fourteen Points address
   4–5, 15; Japan 8; non-
   interference in Russia 8–9;
   Russian self-determination
   6–7, 11; World War I 1
Winter War (1939–40) 35
World Court 279
World War I 1
World War II 37–8, 40–1

Yagoda, Genrikh 33
Yalta Agreement 46, 48, 73–5, 85
Yeltsin, Boris 229, 239, 244, 246

Yom Kippur War 176–7
Young, Andrew 195
Young Plan 17
Yugoslavia 56, 141, 267

zero option 204, 219
Zhou Enlai 81, 82, 89, 92
Zhukov, Georgi 50
Zinoviev, Grigori 18, 33